ENTERPRISE ANDROID™

Enterprise Android™

Enterprise Android™

PROGRAMMING ANDROID DATABASE
APPLICATIONS FOR THE ENTERPRISE

Zigurd Mednieks
G. Blake Meike
Laird Dornin
Zane Pan

wrox™

A Wiley Brand

Enterprise Android™: Programming Android Database Applications for the Enterprise

Published by
John Wiley & Sons, Inc.
10475 Crosspoint Boulevard
Indianapolis, IN 46256
www.wiley.com

Copyright © 2014 by John Wiley & Sons, Inc., Indianapolis, Indiana

Published simultaneously in Canada

ISBN: 978-1-118-18349-6
ISBN: 978-1-118-22747-3 (ebk)
ISBN: 978-1-118-24046-5 (ebk)

Manufactured in the United States of America

10 9 8 7 6 5 4 3 2 1

For general information on our other products and services please contact our Customer Care Department within the United States at (877) 762-2974, outside the United States at (317) 572-3993 or fax (317) 572-4002.

Wiley publishes in a variety of print and electronic formats and by print-on-demand. Some material included with standard print versions of this book may not be included in e-books or in print-on-demand. If this book refers to media such as a CD or DVD that is not included in the version you purchased, you may download this material at http://booksupport.wiley.com. For more information about Wiley products, visit www.wiley.com.

Library of Congress Control Number: 2013936843

ABOUT THE AUTHORS

ZIGURD MEDNIEKS is a consultant to leading OEMs, enterprises, investors, and entrepreneurial ventures creating Android-based systems and software. Previously, he was Chief Architect at D2 Technologies, a voice-over-IP (VoIP) technology provider. There he led engineering and product-definition work for products that blend communication and social media in purpose-built embedded systems and on the Android platform.

Zigurd is a 25-year veteran of user interface, telephony, and social media product creation in the computing and telecommunications industries. He has authored and co-authored books about Android software development, and written book chapters on telephony and inter-process communication. His first book, *C Programming Techniques for the Macintosh*, co-authored with Terry Mednieks, was published in 1986. Information about Zigurd can be found at `zigurd.com`.

G. BLAKE MEIKE is a passionate engineer and code poet with more than 20 years of experience. He has spent much of his time working with Java, building systems as large as Amazon's massively scalable Auto Scaling service and as small as a pre-Android OSS/Linux- and Java-based platform for cell phones. He is co-author of the bestselling *Programming Android* and has taught nearly a thousand people the art of writing Android apps that aren't toys.

LAIRD DORNIN graduated from Williams College in 1997 with a Bachelor of Arts degree in Computer Science. Laird began his career at Sun Microsystems working on the Java JDK (RMI) and the forward-looking Jini Technology out of Sun Labs. From there he moved to SavaJe Technologies and helped to build a full-featured Java SE mobile operating system that shipped in 2006 and provided the platform for "Device of the Show" at JavaOne. Again at Sun Microsystems, Laird continued working on SavaJe OS to integrate the WebKit browser library to provide a full-featured mobile browser. Laird is an author of two books on Android programming and now works as an architect for a major wireless carrier.

ZANE PAN began building large, scalable distributed systems at Sun Microsystems Labs working on Jini Technology in the late '90s. He has been actively designing and architecting solutions for distributed computing performance and scalability problems since then. Zane has held architect level roles at many large companies including Lotus Development Corporation, Digital Equipment Corporation, Intuit, and EMC. Most recently, Zane architected and built a large-scale mobile service backend system using Big Data and NoSQL at Nokia.

ABOUT THE TECHNICAL EDITOR

MAIJA MEDNIEKS is a senior at the Carnegie Mellon University School of Computer Science and a former buggy driver. Among her interests are knitting, Norse epics, science fiction, interactive user experience design, creating and solving puzzles for puzzle hunts, and functional programming.

ABOUT THE TECHNICAL PROOFREADER

JIM FITZGERALD has worked in many facets of the technology industry. His humble beginnings in Silicon Valley as a software engineer for Hewlett-Packard eventually led him to positions in marketing and sales before graduate school brought him back to software development and project management. He has programmed in many different languages and operating systems, from old mainframes to Windows desktops, and currently spends his time in Android and Windows mobile environments. While he considers himself more of a frontend guy, he will admit to dabbling with PHP and writing a lot of PL/SQL in the past when pressed.

When not investigating how technical things work, Jim spends his time as a bibliophile, avid artist and photographer, collecting far more books, paint brushes, and lenses than he can hope to use. Jim has a undergraduate BS degree from California Polytechnic, and a MS degree from Yale University.

CREDITS

ACKNOWLEDGMENTS

I WANT TO THANK the editors at Wiley who have the vision to publish books about Android in the enterprise; our agent, Carole Jelen, for bringing this project to us; and my co-authors who brought the concept of a book about data-oriented apps to life. I also thank Maija Mednieks and Jim Fitzgerald, the technical editor and technical proofreader, for their exacting attention to making sure our examples work.

—Zigurd Mednieks

I WOULD LIKE TO THANK my co-authors, Zigurd, Laird, and Zane, for making this book way bigger than the sum of its parts. Bob Elliott and Kevin Kent were incredibly patient with us; and the rest of the editors, Maija Mednieks, Christine Mugnolo, Kezia Endsley, and Jim Fitzgerald, kept us honest and intelligible. Marakana Inc., my employer, gave me time to work on it. A special shout out to L. Carl Pedersen for taking the time to explain SQL. As always, a project like this would be impossible without the support of my wife, Catherine. You and me, babe, 'til the wheels fall off.

—G. Blake Meike

I NEED TO THANK my sweetie, Norah, for being so patient with all the long weekends and late nights working on this ambitious project. You've been amazing for this, and for carrying another far more important project—our new son.

Thanks to my parents—we've missed trips to NH!

I'd like to thank Kevin and Robert for all their excellent support on this project. I'm excited that we managed to cover so many popular topics to create a comprehensive picture of end-to-end enterprise Android development. Thanks to Jim and Maija, our reviewers; this book contained a lot of material to cover. Thanks to my brother, Chris, and to Nathan Babb for reviewing parts of the manuscript.

Finally, thanks to my co-authors for collaborating to bring this project to completion.

—Laird Dornin

I'D LIKE TO THANK Kevin and Robert for their support on this project.

—Zane Pan

CONTENTS

INTRODUCTION

MANY ENTERPRISE-ORIENTED APPLICATIONS fit a broad template: They access data using one or more RESTful APIs. They present the data to the user. They may enable the user to modify the data, and update the data on servers. *Enterprise Android* is a book about those applications.

WHO THIS BOOK IS FOR

If you are an experienced Java or JavaScript coder, you may have some ideas about how RESTful apps should work. You can correctly think of Android as a Java OS: You write apps in Java and deploy them to an environment that, in some ways, very closely resembles a Java VM. These apps communicate with RESTful APIs to fetch data to present to the user.

But, as with many aspects of Android software development, it pays to look at how Android is designed before wading in. This book was created to give you a substantial head start at applying your experience with RESTful applications and APIs to creating Android apps that are efficient, versatile, and responsive. You will avoid the pitfalls of assuming Android programming is like web programming or client Java programming using Oracle's class libraries, and be able to do it using Android APIs effectively on the first try.

If you are a beginning Android programmer, and do not have significant experience with iOS or Java, or if you are unsure that RESTful applications are what you need to learn about, you should start with a general introduction to Android. Beginners will appreciate a book like Reto Meier's excellent *Professional Android 4 Application Development* (John Wiley & Sons, 2012) or the online tutorials at developer.android.com, which are much improved compared to the early days of Android.

If you are interested in expanding your development horizon beyond device programming by pushing into service-side development, this book builds competence handling application data on both sides of the network.

WHAT THIS BOOK COVERS

This book starts with the basics of creating an Enterprise-oriented Android app that can run on handsets and tablets. But it's not a beginner's book. You should, at least, read the online tutorials at Google's Android Developer's site before reading this book.

Android uses SQLite, and this book covers SQL and SQLite in enough depth that you will understand how data is stored in SQLite databases in Android systems.

Android wraps SQLite in database classes, and this book covers those classes in depth, as well.

When apps make use of data in the Android environment, they often use a specialized service component called a ContentProvider. This class, and the related ContentResolver class, provide a REST-like interface to data within an Android device. Using these classes has other advantages in building apps that use the *observer pattern*.

Enabling you to implement an end-to-end observer pattern is a key element of this book. Your data resides in a database behind a RESTful API on your servers. Locally, it is likely to be stored in a SQLite database inside a `ContentProvider` component. This book shows you how to make sure the data you present to the user is consistent and up to date.

Simplicity is important, too. JSON is a simple way to represent data with simplicity and flexibility where, otherwise, a complex database design might be required. This book shows you how to use JSON with SQLite to maintain simplicity in your implementation. It also shows you a complex Android database and `ContentProvider` interface, implemented with a conventional approach to database design.

You will create and deploy a server for your front end as you use the examples in this book. In particular, Chapters 5 and 6 come together at the end of Chapter 6 to form an end-to-end example of the techniques covered in this book. You'll deploy this service on Amazon and Google cloud resources in Chapter 7.

One thing you won't spend much time on is *loading indicators*. A networked app should be as responsive as a "local" app. Create, update, and delete (CRUD) should not be interposed between the user and the data the user wants. A very important part of this book explains how to keep CRUD off the network and out of the user's way, using a lightweight but powerful synchronization protocol. The book completes this approach by introducing an open source framework that encapsulates this approach.

The book concludes with an in-depth tour of Android security.

HOW THIS BOOK IS STRUCTURED

This book is called *Enterprise Android* because it is about acquiring, presenting, and updating data on devices and using cloud resources, which is the core of most enterprise applications.

This book starts with a brisk-paced introduction to Android programming that puts you on track to make an application for displaying data. This is about as fast an introduction as can be, so don't be surprised if you need to go to the online tutorials in the Android documentation to go deeper on some basics.

Following this introduction, you will be immersed in the core subject matter of this book: data. The book progresses from the bottom up: how to store data locally, how to make queries, how to get it and serve it from REST APIs, how the observer pattern is implemented in Android idioms, how to update it, and how to make this all happen with or without connectivity and with the best apparent performance. Later in the book, more UI programming oriented toward presenting data is covered. The book closes with a chapter on security.

WHAT YOU NEED TO USE THIS BOOK

This book is about Android software development, and the examples in it require the use of the Android software development kit (SDK), which is available from `developer.android.com`. The SDK is compatible with the three most widely used desktop operating systems: Windows, Mac OS X, and Linux. You may prefer to use an Android device to run the example code, but you can use an emulator, included in the SDK, running on your desktop computer.

> **NOTE** *Database code in Android has been very stable for several versions of the Android OS. Mostly due to the way we cover user interface for database apps, this book assumes you will run your programs on Android 4 or later versions. You can expect most of this book to remain current for future version of Android.*

To run the service examples in the book, you'll need to download the packages in each chapter, including the following: Apache Tomcat, ant, MySQL, and the cygwin toolkit. You'll also need an Amazon AWS account with manager privileges and a Google account.

CONVENTIONS

To help you get the most from the text and keep track of what's happening, you'll see a number of conventions throughout the book.

> **WARNING** *Warnings like this one hold important, not-to-be forgotten information that is directly relevant to the surrounding text.*

> **NOTE** *Notes offer tips, hints, tricks, and asides to the current discussion.*

As for styles in the text:

➤ New terms and important words are highlighted when they are introduced.

➤ Keyboard strokes appear like this: Ctrl+A.

➤ Filenames, URLs, and code within the text appear like so: `persistence.properties`.

➤ Code appears in two different ways:

```
We use a monofont type with no highlighting for most code examples.

We use bold to emphasize code that's particularly important in the present context.
```

SOURCE CODE

As you read the chapters in this book, you will want to run, inspect, and perhaps modify the source code files that accompany the book. Please note that all the code examples in this chapter are available at `https://github.com/wileyenterpriseandroid/Examples.git` and as a part of the book's code download at `www.wrox.com` on the Download Code tab.

To find the source code via the Wrox site, locate the book's title (either by using the Search box or by using one of the title lists) and click the Download Code link on the book's detail page to obtain all the source code for the book.

> **NOTE** *Because many books have similar titles, you may find it easiest to search by ISBN; this book's ISBN is 978-1-118-18349-6*

Alternately, you can go to the main Wrox code download page at `http://www.wrox.com/dynamic/books/download.aspx` to see the code available for this book and all other Wrox books.

ERRATA

We make every effort to ensure that there are no errors in the text or in the code. However, no one is perfect, and mistakes do occur. If you find an error in one of our books, like a spelling mistake or faulty piece of code, we would be very grateful for your feedback. By sending in errata you may save another reader hours of frustration and at the same time you will be helping us provide even higher quality information.

To find the errata page for this book, go to `http://www.wrox.com` and locate the title using the Search box or one of the title lists. Then, on the book details page, click the Book Errata link. On this page you can view all errata that has been submitted for this book and posted by Wrox editors.

> **NOTE** *A complete book list including links to each book's errata is also available at* `www.wrox.com/misc-pages/booklist.shtml`.

If you don't spot "your" error on the Book Errata page, go to `www.wrox.com/contact/techsupport.shtml` and complete the form there to send us the error you have found. We'll check the information and, if appropriate, post a message to the book's errata page and fix the problem in subsequent editions of the book.

P2P.WROX.COM

For author and peer discussion, join the P2P forums at `p2p.wrox.com`. The forums are a web-based system for you to post messages relating to Wrox books and related technologies and interact with other readers and technology users. The forums offer a subscription feature to e-mail you topics of interest of your choosing when new posts are made to the forums. Wrox authors, editors, other industry experts, and your fellow readers are present on these forums.

At `http://p2p.wrox.com` you will find a number of forums that will help you not only as you read this book, but also as you develop your own applications. To join the forums, just follow these steps:

1. Go to `p2p.wrox.com` and click the Register link.

2. Read the terms of use and click Agree.

3. Complete the required information to join as well as any optional information you wish to provide and click Submit.

4. You will receive an e-mail with information describing how to verify your account and complete the joining process.

> **NOTE** *You can read messages in the forums without joining P2P, but in order to post your own messages, you must join.*

Once you join, you can post new messages and respond to messages other users post. You can read messages at any time on the web. If you would like to have new messages from a particular forum e-mailed to you, click the Subscribe to this Forum icon by the forum name in the forum listing.

For more information about how to use the Wrox P2P, be sure to read the P2P FAQs for answers to questions about how the forum software works as well as many common questions specific to P2P and Wrox books. To read the FAQs, click the FAQ link on any P2P page.

1

Developing for Android Tablets and Smartphones

WHAT'S IN THIS CHAPTER?

➤ Getting your tools set up

➤ Testing your tools setup

➤ What a modern Android application looks like

➤ Introducing a concise application framework that works on all sizes of Android devices

➤ Exploring Android component lifecycles and the Android task model

WROX.COM CODE DOWNLOADS FOR THIS CHAPTER

Please note that all the code examples in this chapter are available at `https://github.com/wileyenterpriseandroid/Examples.git` and as a part of the book's code download at `www.wrox.com` on the Download Code tab. At various points throughout the book, the authors refer to the "Examples" directory using a pseudo-variable called, "CODE". Readers can either explicity set this value as a shell variable or can just keep in mind that the variable refers to the book example code directory.

This book is about best practices in handling data for enterprise application across the client and RESTful backend services, and this chapter gets you through the basics at a brisk pace while providing a framework, which is the starting point for the example code in this book. The advice in this chapter, especially the advice to pay attention to Android component lifecycles, will enable you to complete an Android coding project efficiently, without having to know everything about Android, and with a minimum of grief.

Many Android books were written before there were Android tablet devices, and before the APIs central to creating good UIs for those devices were a mainstream concern for Android developers. This chapter starts by assuming your apps will run on both tablets and handsets and provides a framework that embodies the best practices for doing so.

This chapter also covers tools — and knowledge resources for the tools — that you need to follow the code examples in this book.

This isn't a beginner's book. If this is your first time programming Android applications, use the information resources listed here for filling in the gaps in your knowledge of and experience with Java and Android programming.

ANDROID IS A JAVA OPERATING SYSTEM

Almost all applications and all system services in Android are coded in Java (and other JVM languages). Code is compiled to Java bytecode before being translated into Dalvik bytecode, which, in turn, runs in the Android managed runtime environment. These characteristics make Android at once familiar and strange: If you have used Java or a similar managed language before, you will find Android code fairly easy to read. You will find the tools for Android programming familiar. Many aspects of Android's managed language run time are identical to Java. Android relies on Java base classes, and wouldn't work if the semantics of the Android runtime environment were not very similar to those of a standard Java runtime environment.

If you come to this book not having written Android-specific code, you have probably never written code for an operating system like Android. Android uses managed language runtime concepts in ways you may find unfamiliar, especially in the ways Android implements modularity and memory management. In many ways, Android is the most sophisticated environment for interactive Java programs ever created.

> **WARNING** *Pay close attention to the basics of Android application program-ming and follow the key practices described in this chapter. If you try to impose your coding practices from server Java or MIDlets, or attempt to thwart the way the Android system works with applications, bugs and frustration will result.*

YOUR TOOLS AND YOUR FIRST ANDROID APP

This section covers setting up your programming tools. You will run your first example application, which is a user interface framework.

Prerequisites and Getting Ready

You can use any of the three major operating systems for PCs to develop Android software: Linux, Mac OS, or Windows. You will need three independent pieces to assemble your toolchain for creating Android applications: The Java JDK, Eclipse, and the Android SDK. All three of these pieces work on all three operating systems.

The place to find reference information on developing Android is `http://developer.android .com` and the place to get started with instructions on installing your tool set is `http://developer .android.com/guide/developing/index.html`.

Follow the instructions at the URL to install the tools you need. If you follow the instructions correctly, you will install a toolchain consisting of the three pieces listed previously.

Java and Java Knowledge

The first piece of the tool set you need is the Java Development Kit, or JDK. The JDK provides both a Java runtime environment, which is needed by Eclipse, and some tools for creating Android applications.

Java is a cross-platform runtime environment and is the key to developing Android software on any of the top three personal computer operating systems.

You will write your Android programs in Java, even though the runtime environment in the Android operating system is internally substantially different from Java runtime environments. Although you don't need to know the details of the way your programming tools are implemented using Java, you have to know Java to write Android programs. There are numerous tutorials on the web and books to help you learn Java. One free resource for learning Java is Oracle's Java Tutorials site:

```
http://docs.oracle.com/javase/tutorial/java/index.html
```

Eclipse and Eclipse Knowledge

Eclipse is the integrated development environment (IDE) you will be using. An IDE is an all-in-one software development tool that enables you to create source code with correct syntax and style, run that code, and examine and debug it if you need to find out why it isn't working correctly. As you create Android software, you will spend most of your time using the Eclipse IDE.

Eclipse is a Java program and it uses the Java run time in the JDK you installed to run on your personal computer. Eclipse is widely used for many kinds of programming, including creating Java-based server software for the kinds of applications described in this book.

The use of Eclipse is one of the reasons Android was born with a mature toolchain. You write Android programs using the Java language, and most of the toolchain for writing "normal" Java programs can be applied to Android.

Eclipse enables you to edit your code while providing quick access to documentation. It enhances productivity through automatic completion of symbols and automatic formatting. It helps you find syntax errors, and it performs static analysis that finds potential runtime errors. It also enables you to inspect running applications, stop them, single-step across code that corresponds to lines of source code, inspect variables, examine unhandled exceptions, and perform dozens of other operations that will improve your productivity in creating Android applications.

Knowing your IDE's features is key to productivity and to avoiding frustration when programs don't work. This is especially true for Eclipse, which is very powerful and has many more useful tools available for it than listed here, but it isn't as simple as some other IDEs, such as Apple's IDE for iOS development. So it is likely you will need to become more familiar with Eclipse if you are a first-time user. Tutorials on Eclipse can be found at `http://www.eclipse.org/ resources/?category=Tutorial`. To run all the examples in this book, you will need to download and install Eclipse IDE for Java EE Developers.

The Android SDK and Resources for Android Tools Knowledge

The third part of your toolchain is the Android Software Development Kit (SDK). The SDK is documented in Google's online documentation for Android developers at `http://developer`
`.android.com/index.html`.

The SDK turns the Eclipse IDE into an IDE that can create Android programs. The SDK provides plugins for Eclipse and many external components that are used to create Android applications and diagnose problems in Android software. Eclipse can be adapted to many purposes with plugins. In fact, Eclipse is made almost entirely of plugins. The set of plugins you started with when you installed Eclipse make Eclipse suitable for creating Java programs. For the purposes of this book, you will mostly work in the Eclipse IDE, and all you need to do at this point is to configure Eclipse to use the Android plugins and to be able to locate other programs installed with the SDK. You will be prompted to do so when you start Eclipse after the Android SDK is installed.

Now you have all the tools for general Android programming, and for this chapter. Later in this book, other tools specific to topics introduced in those chapters will be added to your toolchain.

Toolchain Test Drive

You can test that your toolchain is installed correctly by creating a new Android project, and selecting an example from the SDK as the basis of your project. You should be able to run your project in an Android Virtual Device (AVD).

Directions for creating a project are here:

    http://developer.android.com/training/basics/firstapp/creating-project.html

Directions for running a project are here:

    http://developer.android.com/training/basics/firstapp/running-app.html

By doing this, you have created an Android project in Eclipse, and created and run an Android application, even though you have not written any code yet. If you are successful in doing this, you can be confident your toolchain and the software it depends on have been correctly installed. The next section describes how to download and use the example code in this chapter to create another Android project. But you might want to explore your toolchain at this point.

> **NOTE** *One thing you might want to do is create more Android projects based on the example code using the option in the New Project wizard to select example applications.*

ONE CODE-BASE FOR ALL TYPES OF DEVICES

This section introduces the first code that is specific to this book. This framework is used to illustrate some important points about Android application fundamentals, to get you used to the tools you just installed, and to provide a quick way to start writing application-specific code rather than use boilerplate. There are two related approaches we adhere to in the examples in this book because we assume that enterprise deployments will be for a controlled set of mobile devices:

➤ Develop a single code-base for tablets and handsets.

➤ Develop for the latest APIs, as of this writing, and encourage the use of the back-compatibility support classes provided with the Android SDK to enable compatibility for a range of earlier versions of Android, if needed.

You will use a design pattern in which you allow the Android system to select different layouts based on screen size and pixel density and write code that is largely independent of the choice the system made. This technique makes your apps more robust by not duplicating the mechanisms Android uses to make decisions about display geometry.

Following this pattern simplifies your tasks in publishing software, makes the example code as concise as possible, and enables you to publish a single version for many kinds of devices.

Getting Started with the Code Framework Example

Here you will perform a further check that you have installed your toolchain correctly and import the example code for this chapter. Later, you will examine the code in this example, and run it in order to see what it does.

You can obtain the example code as an archive at `www.wrox.com` and `https://github.com/wileyenterpriseandroid/Examples.git`. The first thing you do to use example code is to extract the project folder from the archive into your workspace folder. Then, import the project from the archive file. You will use the File ➪ Import... command to display the Import dialog box as in Figure 1-1.

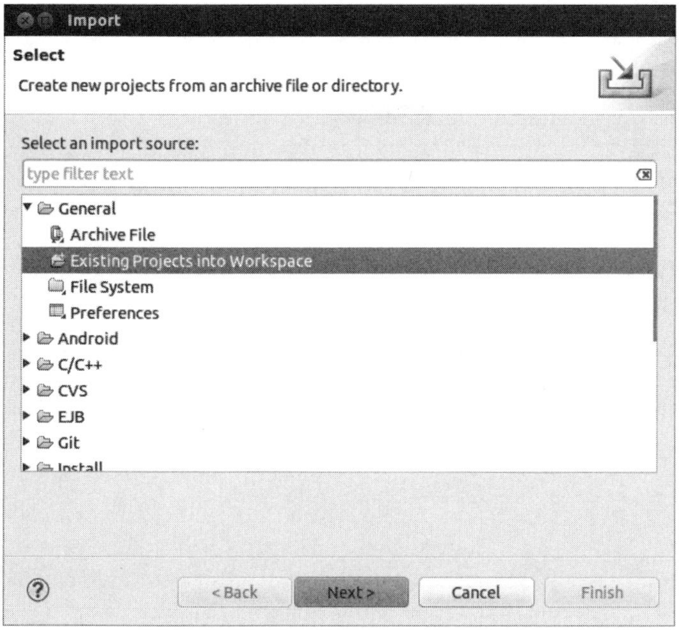

FIGURE 1-1

Select General and Existing Projects into Workspace. Pressing Next will display the Import dialog box shown in Figure 1-2. Select the folder you extracted, and press Finish. Depending on the platform you are using, the project name may differ from what you see in the screen shot in Figures 1-2 and 1-3.

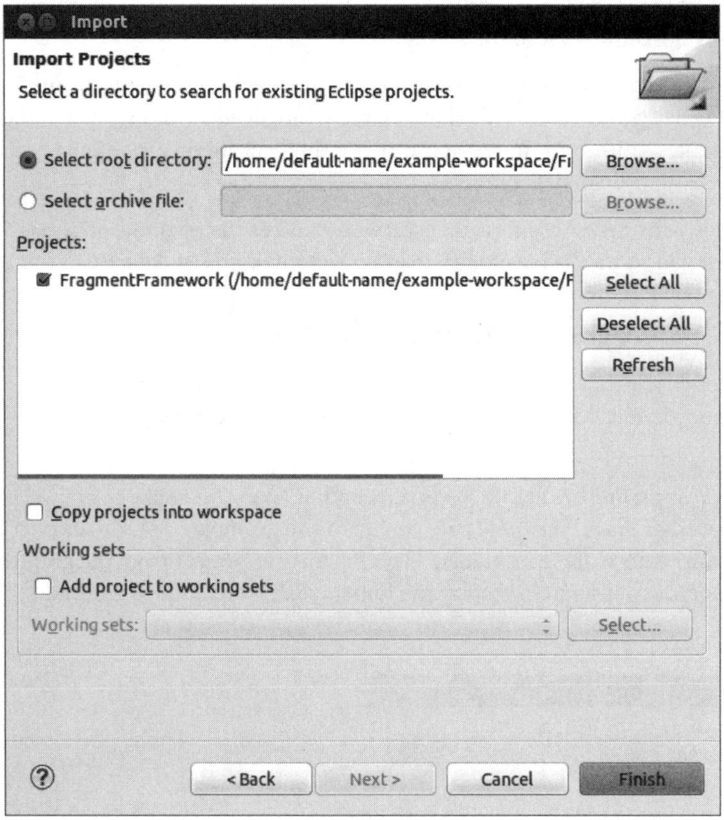

FIGURE 1-2

You should now see the example project in your Eclipse Project Explorer window, as shown in Figure 1-3.

Now right-click on the name of the project and select Run as ➪ Android Application. If you have not connected your Android device to a USB cable connected to your PC, and you have not created an emulator configuration for running examples, you will see a dialog box like the one in the Figure 1-4. If you do, press Yes.

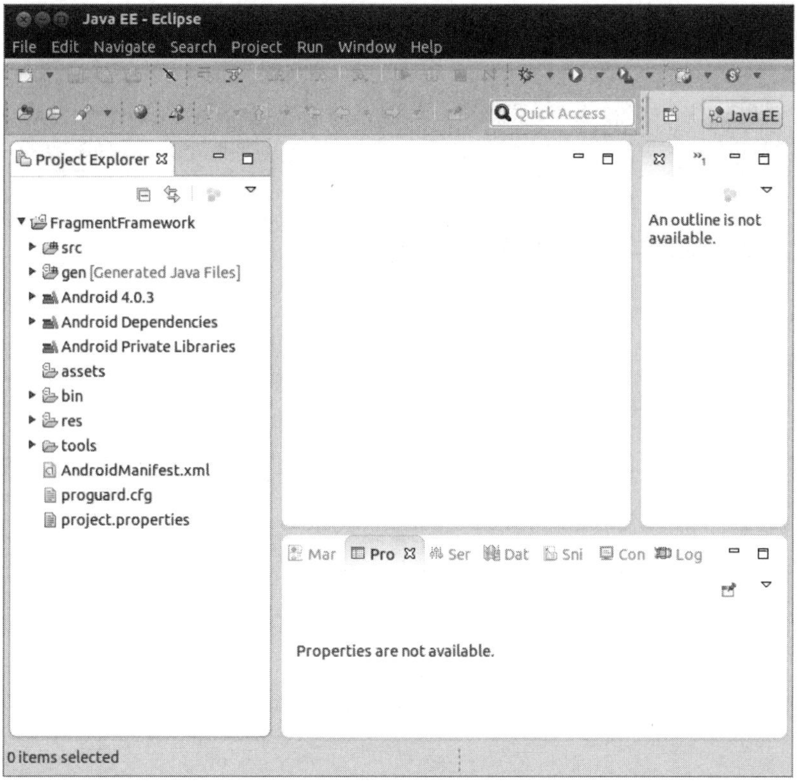

FIGURE 1-3

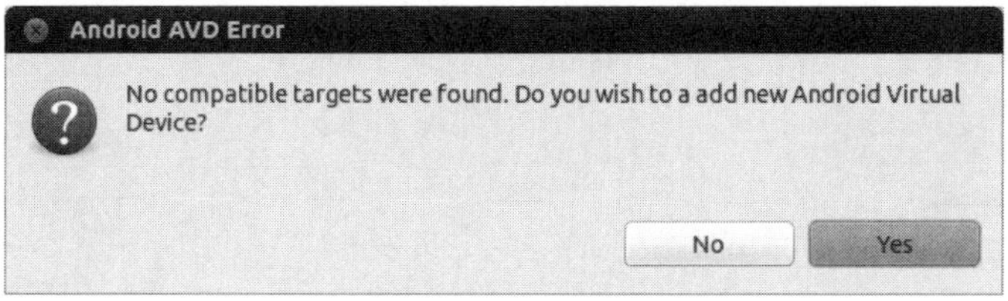

FIGURE 1-4

Pressing Yes displays the Android Virtual Device (AVD) Manager. If you got here from the error dialog box indicating no AVDs have yet been created, you will see an empty list of AVDs, as in the Figure 1-5. Press the button labeled New....

Now you see a dialog box for creating a new Android AVD. Pick Nexus 7 from the list of available AVD configurations, and name it something sensible like **nexus7**. This conveniently selects all the right parameters for emulating hardware that resembles a Nexus 7 tablet, including the correct API level for the example, as seen in the Figure 1-6.

WARNING *If you are using a Windows system for compiling and running the examples from this book, and depending on the version of the Android SDK you are using, you may need to pick a different device to emulate due to limitations on memory size of emulators on Windows.*

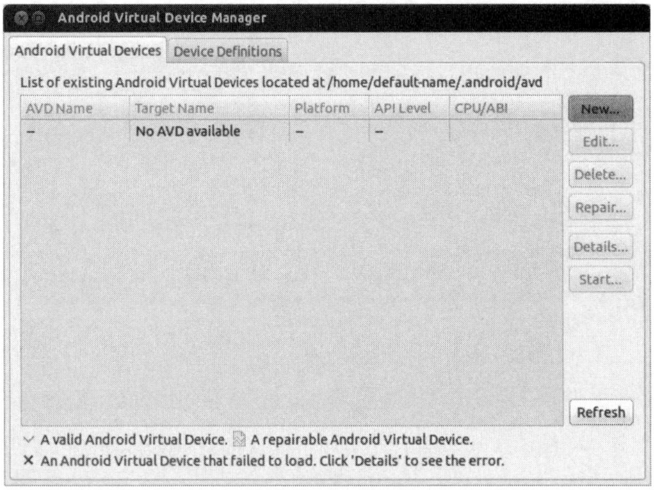

FIGURE 1-5

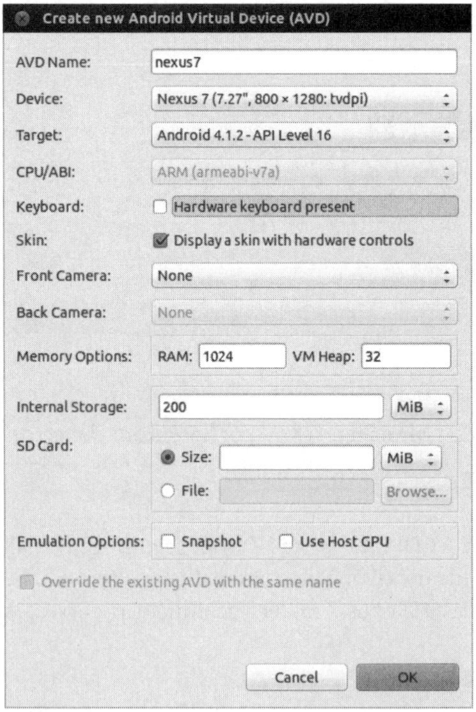

FIGURE 1-6

When you press OK, you will return to the AVD Manager and see that an AVD named nexus7 now exists in the previously empty list, as shown in the Figure 1-7. Press the button labeled Start....

FIGURE 1-7

Pressing the Start button launches the AVD. First, it may want some more information from you about how it should be rendered. The Launch Options dialog box shown in Figure 1-8 can be used to scale the display of an AVD. We won't do that, so press the Launch button.

And now...still no emulator. If you are using a fresh installation of the SDK, you may encounter the dialog box in Figure 1-9. This dialog box lets you enable the logcat view, provided by the Android SDK plugins in the Eclipse IDE. Select the Yes option here. You will need logcat a bit later in this chapter to see what your application is doing.

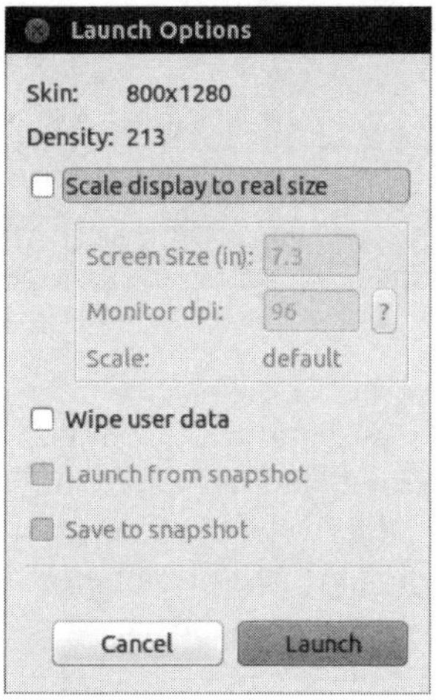

FIGURE 1-8

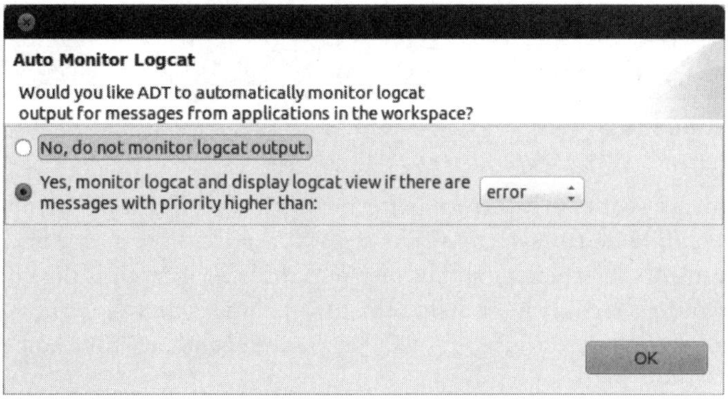

FIGURE 1-9

Now you have done it! The emulator will launch. Android will start up on the emulator, and the example application will start up in Android, as shown in Figure 1-10.

If you encountered a problem at any step here, you may need to reinstall your toolchain. If you previously validated the installation of your toolchain through to the steps where you launch an Android application, you will not encounter some of the steps here, which happen only once upon a first use after a new installation.

You now have running an example application that configures itself to different screen sizes.

Automatically Adapting to Screen Size

You can see the results of the design pattern example in this chapter by creating an AVD for a small Android device and a larger tablet style Android device (see Figure 1-10).

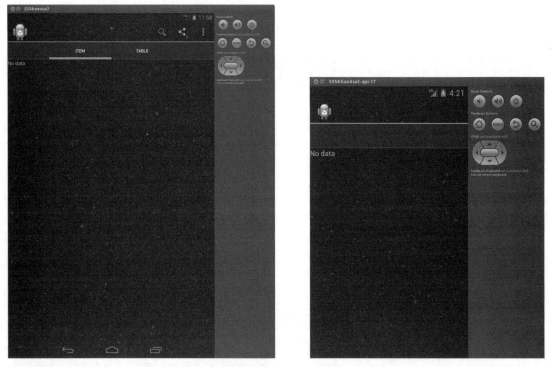

FIGURE 1-10

You can see that the design pattern used in this framework application automatically adapts, depending on the system displaying it. Users will see a single screen with a list on the left and fragments selected using tabs on the right if the screen is big enough. Otherwise, users see two separate screens, one showing the list of choices and the other containing tabs and fragments corresponding to those tabs. The content depends on the choice users make from the list.

This is a typical UI design pattern. This framework will speed your way past the obligatory parts of Android application development so you can get to the parts most useful to the enterprise application developer.

But, before you adapt this framework to the kinds of applications that use local and networked data resources, you'll first take a look at this code in greater detail and see how it embodies many of the Android features that users expect and that conform to Android best-practices for a broad class of Android applications.

COMPONENTS, VIEWS, AND LIFECYCLE

The example code in this chapter contains all the objects needed for a minimal, but typical, Android application. Since this book is about enterprise Android applications, this minimal framework application includes a field for entering search terms, a list for the results of the search/ query, and places where search results and information about those results are displayed.

Most of the classes used in this minimal application framework are components or Android widgets from the `View` class hierarchy.

Components are the large-scale building blocks of Android applications:

➤   You create a subclass of `Activity` for every major grouping of interactive functionality that is distinctive enough for the user to notice that something different is displayed on the screen.

➤   Fragments are used to organize interactive code within an activity. On big screens, multiple fragments might be visible at the same time, while on smaller screens, a single fragment is usually contained in each activity.

➤   You will subclass `Service` for code that performs long-running processing and that has no interactive elements. Service components are an important part of the code in subsequent chapters.

Components have lifecycles. You may be familiar with the concepts of components with lifecycles from the J2ME MIDlet lifecycle, where apps that are paused should release resources. But the Android component and lifecycle is far richer and more powerful. The Android lifecycle enables large, complex apps to fit in small heap sizes.

Destroying and Re-creating Components

Every instance of every component in an Android application can be destroyed, releasing the memory it used. The lifecycle methods in components enable them to save their state before they are destroyed, as well as to initialize themselves when first created, and to restore their state when they are re-created.

For components that have state, lifecycle methods indicate that a component is a candidate for being destroyed, and you have to provide code that saves the state of your component. This isn't optional. Functionally, this is a bit like "swapping." Instead of swapping all instance data, the lifecycle methods enable you to save only the data needed to restore state, in the form most convenient for doing so.

There are no workarounds. If you attempt to subvert component destruction by keeping a reference to a component, all you have done is create a memory leak.

The MainActivity Class

The code in this subclass of `Activity` (Listing 1-1) shows how to implement lifecycle handling for Android. Each lifecycle method is logged, which means you are aware of what happens when this `Activity` instance is no longer on the display, and you know when the Android system decides to destroy an instance of this `Activity`.

In your Eclipse IDE, you can use the logcat view to display this logging information. Normally, this view appears at the bottom of your screen.

Activity: The Basic Unit of User Interaction

Even though there is no code in Listing 1-1 for interacting with the users, you can call an activity the basic unit of user interaction because it represents a screen-full of user interaction.

In a subsequent section, you will see how user interaction is handled by the `Fragment` subclasses in this application.

The `Activity` class is the basis of the card-stack metaphor of user interaction in Android, and navigating between activities is an important part of user interaction. This `Activity` subclass is the main activity of this application. This is where the application starts when users touch the application's icon, and this is the bottom of the application's back-stack.

LISTING 1-1: MainActivity.java

```
package com.enterpriseandroidbook.fragmentframework;

import android.app.ActionBar;
import android.content.res.Configuration;
import android.os.Bundle;
import android.util.Log;

/**
 * @author zigurd
 *
 */
public class MainActivity extends TabbedActivity {

// String for logging the class name
private final String CLASSNAME = getClass().getSimpleName();

// Turn logging on or off
private final boolean L = true;
```

The code shown in this example for the lifecycle methods is here to help you visualize the application lifecycle. Visualizing the application lifecycle is important because it is easy to ignore. You will want to see what the Android OS is doing to your application by way of the component lifecycle in order to plan your application implementation to most readily adapt to the component lifecycle.

The code for the onCreate method that follows shows that the parent class's method should first be called, and then code specific to the subclass added. In this case, that code logs the method call, and it logs whether the method was called to create this Activity instance the first time, or whether a previous instance existed and the state of that instance should be restored. (More about that after you see some of the other lifecycle methods.) The bulk of the work performed during the onCreate call is factored out into the doCreate method. It loads the layout, sets up the action bar, and initializes the tabs in the action bar.

```java
@Override
protected void onCreate(Bundle savedState) {
super.onCreate(savedState);
// To keep this method simple
doCreate(savedState);

// If we had state to restore, we note that in the log message
if (L) Log.i(CLASSNAME, "onCreate" +
(null == savedState ? " Restored state" : ""));
}

@Override
protected void onRestart() {
super.onRestart();
// Notification that the activity will be started
if (L) Log.i(CLASSNAME, "onRestart");
}

@Override
protected void onStart() {
super.onStart();
// Notification that the activity is starting
if (L) Log.i(CLASSNAME, "onStart");
}

@Override
protected void onResume() {
super.onResume();
// Notification that the activity will interact with the user
if (L) Log.i(CLASSNAME, "onResume");
}

protected void onPause() {
super.onPause();
// Notification that the activity will stop interacting with the user
if (L) Log.i(CLASSNAME, "onPause" + (isFinishing() ? " Finishing" : ""));
```

continues

LISTING 1-1 *(continued)*

```
}

@Override
protected void onStop() {
super.onStop();
// Notification that the activity is no longer visible
if (L) Log.i(CLASSNAME, "onStop");
}
```

The code for the onDestroy method that follows next logs when this method is called. The method name onDestroy causes some confusion. What is being destroyed? In fact what happens at this point is that the Android system "destroys," or sets to null, its reference to this instance of this subclass of Activity, so it can be garbage-collected. You may think that thwarting this destruction is possible by simply holding a reference to this Activity instance. That won't work: The Android system will create a new instance of this Activity after it has "destroyed" this one, whether a reference to it is being held or not. You could prevent this now-useless instance from being garbage-collected, but it is a zombie, wreaking havoc in the heap. Note that the onDestroy method tests and logs whether the activity is "finishing" — meaning that this instance of Activity won't be re-created because it is done, not because it was destroyed to recover memory space.

```
@Override
protected void onDestroy() {
super.onDestroy();
// Notification the activity will be destroyed
if (L) Log.i(CLASSNAME, "onDestroy"
// Are we finishing?
+ (isFinishing() ? " Finishing" : ""));
}
```

The code for the onSaveInstanceState method that follows next logs when it is called. Note that a Bundle object is passed to this method. This Bundle object enables you to attach serializable objects implementing the Parcelable interface. The Bundle object itself implements the Parcelable interface, so it and all the objects it holds references to can be serialized and stored — or "persisted" in Java parlance.

This is where the Bundle object that's passed to the onCreate method comes from. If you added objects to it, they will be there when the onCreate and onRestoreInstanceState are called.

```
@Override
protected void onSaveInstanceState(Bundle outState) {
super.onSaveInstanceState(outState);
saveState(outState);

// Called when state should be saved
if (L) Log.i(CLASSNAME, "onSaveInstanceState");

}

@Override
```

```java
protected void onRestoreInstanceState(Bundle savedState) {
super.onRestoreInstanceState(savedState);
if (null != savedState) restoreState(savedState);

// If we had state to restore, we note that in the log message
if (L) Log.i(CLASSNAME, "onRestoreInstanceState" +
(null == savedState ? " Restored state" : ""));
}

////////////////////////////////////////////////////////////////////////////
// The minor lifecycle methods - you probably won't need these
////////////////////////////////////////////////////////////////////////////

@Override
protected void onPostCreate(Bundle savedState) {
super.onPostCreate(savedState);
if (null != savedState) restoreState(savedState);

// If we had state to restore, we note that in the log message
if (L) Log.i(CLASSNAME, "onCreate" +
(null == savedState ? " Restored state" : ""));

}

@Override
protected void onPostResume() {
super.onPostResume();
// Notification that resuming the activity is complete
if (L) Log.i(CLASSNAME, "onPostResume");
}

@Override
protected void onUserLeaveHint() {
super.onUserLeaveHint();
// Notification that user navigated away from this activity
if (L) Log.i(CLASSNAME, "onUserLeaveHint");
}

////////////////////////////////////////////////////////////////////////////
// Overrides of the implementations ComponentCallbacks methods in Activity
////////////////////////////////////////////////////////////////////////////

@Override
public void onConfigurationChanged(Configuration newConfiguration) {
super.onConfigurationChanged(newConfiguration);

// This won't happen unless we declare changes we handle in the manifest
if (L) Log.i(CLASSNAME, "onConfigurationChanged");
}

@Override
public void onLowMemory() {
// No guarantee this is called before or after other callbacks
```

continues

LISTING 1-1 *(continued)*

```
if (L) Log.i(CLASSNAME, "onLowMemory");
}

///////////////////////////////////////////////////////////////////////////
// App-specific code here
///////////////////////////////////////////////////////////////////////////


/**
 * This is where we restore state we previously saved.
 * @param savedState the Bundle we got from the callback
 */
private void restoreState(Bundle savedState) {
// Add your code to restore state here

}

/**
 * Add this activity's state to the bundle and/or commit pending data
 */
private void saveState(Bundle state) {
// Add your code to add state to the bundle here
}

/**
 * Perform initializations on creation of this Activity instance
 * @param savedState
 */
private void doCreate(Bundle savedState) {
setContentView(R.layout.main);

if (null != savedState) restoreState(savedState);

        ActionBar bar = getActionBar();
        bar.setDisplayShowTitleEnabled(false);
        bar.setNavigationMode(ActionBar.NAVIGATION_MODE_TABS);

// Initialize the tabs (Fails silently if the tab fragments don't exist)
int names[] = {R.string.item, R.string.detail };
int fragments[] = { R.id.content_frag, R.id.detail_frag };
initializeTabs(0, names, fragments);
}


}
```

The preceding code contains the method implementations for the lifecycle methods onRestart, onStart, onResume, onPause, and onStop. These callbacks are, like the other important lifecycle methods in this example, logged to illustrate when they are called. These methods inform you when this activity is becoming visible or is obscured by other activities on the screen. You may find it useful to observe these logging messages in the logcat view in the Eclipse IDE, and follow along with the diagrams in the Android documentation covering the activity lifecycle in order to see when the state transitions in those diagrams occurs. See `http://developer.android.com/training/basics/activity-lifecycle/starting.html`.

Note that you are not required to use the `Bundle` object to save state. There are three fundamental ways to save state in Android:

➤ **Recover state** — If your state is the result of a database query, you can save the query in the bundle (or even recover the query if it is, for example, based on the time of day) and re-run it.

➤ **Save state in a database** — If your state is in a database, locally, on the client device on which your app is running, you can read it from that database if your components are re-created.

➤ **Put it in the bundle** — You can, as described previously, save your state in the `Bundle` object.

In most non-trivial applications, some combination of these methods for saving state is used. The need to save state in Android applications has an influence on how they are designed. A data model that lives primarily in a SQLite database is a convenient way to minimize the state your application needs to preserve. Putting that database in a `ContentProvider` object removes it from the `Activity` object. The `ContentProvider` API enables a simple implementation of the observer pattern, and it puts your application on track with a design pattern that will be elaborated throughout this book, where local databases are synched to a network database.

Fragment: A Tool for Organizing Code and UI

In Android versions prior to Honeycomb, the typical Android application implementation placed the code for interacting with user interface widgets in subclasses of `Activity`. When Google's partners introduced tablet computers using the Android OS, Google responded by redesigning the user interface — and the APIs developers use to create a user interface — around a new class called `Fragment`.

`Fragment` is not a subclass of `Activity`, nor is it a subclass of `View`. Like an activity, a fragment can contain the code that handles user interaction. A fragment can be laid out like an Android widget, but it isn't a widget. A fragment is a container for code that interacts with the users.

The `Fragment` class includes lifecycle methods, but it isn't an Android component. The lifecycle methods in `Fragment` exist as a way for the `Activity` containing the fragment to propagate lifecycle events into the fragments contained in that activity. That is, individual fragment instances are never destroyed, but the `Activity` instances that contain them are destroyed.

In the chapter's example, the three most important things you will find are:

➤ Code for handling user interactions with Android widgets.

➤ Lifecycle method overrides, as in the `Activity` example, that enable logging, so you can see when these methods are called relative to the activity lifecycle.

➤ Some lifecycle methods that are unique to `Fragment`, mostly for implementing how a fragment object is initialized.

In addition to these aspects of this `Fragment` subclass, you will see some code for putting example data into a list.

The PickFragment Class

The code in Listing 1-2 looks very much like an `Activity` subclass would look if you were not using `Fragment`. But, unlike an `Activity`, the fragment's lifecycle is tied to the lifecycle of the `Activity` in which it is contained. In a large-screen layout, that means that all the `Fragment` objects in an `Activity` have their lifecycle methods called when the corresponding lifecycle methods of the `Activity` are called.

LISTING 1-2: PickFragment.java

```
package com.enterpriseandroidbook.fragmentframework;

import android.app.Activity;
import android.app.Fragment;
import android.content.res.Configuration;
import android.os.Bundle;
import android.util.Log;
import android.view.LayoutInflater;
import android.view.Menu;
import android.view.MenuInflater;
import android.view.View;
import android.view.ViewGroup;
import android.widget.AdapterView;
import android.widget.AdapterView.OnItemClickListener;
import android.widget.ArrayAdapter;
import android.widget.ListView;

public class PickFragment extends Fragment implements OnItemClickListener {

// String for logging the class name
private final String CLASSNAME = getClass().getSimpleName();

// Turn logging on or off
private static final boolean L = true;

public void onAttach(Activity activity) {
super.onAttach(activity);

// Notification that the fragment is associated with an Activity
if (L)
Log.i(CLASSNAME, "onAttach " + activity.getClass().getSimpleName());
}

public void onCreate(Bundle savedInstanceState) {
super.onCreate(savedInstanceState);

// Tell the system we have an options menu
this.setHasOptionsMenu(true);

if (null != savedInstanceState)
```

```
restoreState(savedInstanceState);

// Notification that
if (L)
Log.i(CLASSNAME, "onCreate");
}

// Factor this out of methods that get saved state
private void restoreState(Bundle savedInstanceState) {
// TODO Auto-generated method stub

}
```

The onCreate method calls attachAdapter and setOnItemClickListener, initializing this fragment.

```
@Override
public View onCreateView(LayoutInflater inflater, ViewGroup container,
Bundle savedInstanceState) {

final ListView list = (ListView) inflater.inflate(
R.layout.list_frag_list, container, false);
if (L)
Log.i(CLASSNAME, "onCreateView");

attachAdapter(list);
list.setOnItemClickListener(this);

return list;
}

public void onStart() {
super.onStart();
if (L)
Log.i(CLASSNAME, "onStart");
}

public void onresume() {
super.onResume();
if (L)
Log.i(CLASSNAME, "onResume");
}

public void onPause() {
super.onPause();
if (L)
Log.i(CLASSNAME, "onPause");
}

public void onStop() {
super.onStop();
if (L)
Log.i(CLASSNAME, "onStop");
```

continues

LISTING 1-2 *(continued)*

```
    }

    public void onDestroyView() {
    super.onDestroyView();
    if (L)
    Log.i(CLASSNAME, "onDestroyView");
    }

    public void onDestroy() {
    super.onDestroy();
    if (L)
    Log.i(CLASSNAME, "onDestroy");
    }

    public void onDetach() {
    super.onDetach();
    if (L)
    Log.i(CLASSNAME, "onDetach");
    }

    // ////////////////////////////////////////////////////////////////////////
    // Minor lifecycle methods
    // ////////////////////////////////////////////////////////////////////////

    public void onActivityCreated() {
    // Notification that the containing activiy and its View hierarchy exist
    if (L)
    Log.i(CLASSNAME, "onActivityCreated");
    }

    // ////////////////////////////////////////////////////////////////////////
    // Overrides of the implementations ComponentCallbacks methods in Fragment
    // ////////////////////////////////////////////////////////////////////////

    @Override
    public void onConfigurationChanged(Configuration newConfiguration) {
    super.onConfigurationChanged(newConfiguration);

    // This won't happen unless we declare changes we handle in the manifest
    if (L)
    Log.i(CLASSNAME, "onConfigurationChanged");
    }

    @Override
    public void onLowMemory() {
    // No guarantee this is called before or after other callbacks
    if (L)
    Log.i(CLASSNAME, "onLowMemory");
    }
```

```
// ////////////////////////////////////////////////////////////////////////
// Menu handling code
// ////////////////////////////////////////////////////////////////////////

public void onCreateOptionsMenu(Menu menu, MenuInflater inflater) {
    inflater.inflate(R.menu.search_menu, menu);
}

// ////////////////////////////////////////////////////////////////////////
// App-specific code
// ////////////////////////////////////////////////////////////////////////
```

The attachAdapter method is used to attach an ArrayAdapter to the ListView object in this fragment. The ArrayAdapater contains test values for this application.

```
/**
 * Attach an adapter that loads the data to the specified list
 *
 * @param list
 */
private void attachAdapter(final ListView list) {

    // Make a trivial adapter that loads an array of strings
    ArrayAdapter<String> numbers = new ArrayAdapter<String>(list
    .getContext().getApplicationContext(),
    android.R.layout.simple_list_item_1, new String[] { "one",
    "two", "three", "four", "five", "six" });

    // tell the list to use it
    list.setAdapter(numbers);
    // l.setOnItemClickListener(this);
}

// ////////////////////////////////////////////////////////////////////////
// Implementation of the OnItemClickListener interface
// ////////////////////////////////////////////////////////////////////////
```

The onItemClick method implements the onItemClickListener interface. This means that the onItemClick method is called whenever an Android item has been clicked. In this case, the whole fragment is full of one ListView, and clicking on an item in the list causes some data to be loaded into the fragments on the right side of the screen, or, in the case of small screens, in a separate Activity.

```
@Override
public void onItemClick(AdapterView<?> arg0, View view, int position,
long id) {
    // As an example of sending data to our fragments, we will create a
    // bundle
    // with an int and a string, based on which view was clicked
    Bundle data = new Bundle();
    int ordinal = position + 1;
    data.putInt("place", ordinal);
    data.putString("placeName", Integer.toString(ordinal));
    ((TabbedActivity) getActivity()).loadTabFragments(data);

}

}
```

The ItemFragment Class

When you run this application on a large-screen device, the `ItemFragment` object appears next or below the `PickFragment` object and displays the data corresponding to what the user selected in the `PickFragment` object, in Listing 1-3.

Like all the other classes that might need to respond to lifecycle methods, the methods are implemented and logged here, so you can readily see when they are called.

LISTING 1-3: ItemFragment.java

```java
package com.enterpriseandroidbook.fragmentframework;

import android.app.ActionBar.Tab;
import android.app.ActionBar.TabListener;
import android.app.Activity;
import android.app.Fragment;
import android.app.FragmentTransaction;
import android.content.res.Configuration;
import android.os.Bundle;
import android.util.Log;
import android.view.LayoutInflater;
import android.view.View;
import android.view.ViewGroup;
import android.widget.EditText;
import android.widget.FrameLayout;

public class ItemFragment extends Fragment implements TabListener,
        TabbedActivity.SetData {

// String for logging the class name
private final String CLASSNAME = getClass().getSimpleName();

//Turn logging on or off
private final boolean L = true;

public void onAttach(Activity activity) {
super.onAttach(activity);

// Notification that the fragment is associated with an Activity
if (L) Log.i(CLASSNAME, "onAttach " + activity.getClass().getSimpleName());
}

public void onCreate(Bundle savedInstanceState) {
super.onCreate(savedInstanceState);

// Notification that
Log.i(CLASSNAME, "onCreate");
}

public View onCreateView(LayoutInflater inflater, ViewGroup container,
        Bundle savedInstanceState) {
FrameLayout content = (FrameLayout) inflater.inflate(R.layout.content, container,
        false);
if (L) Log.i(CLASSNAME, "onCreateView");
```

```java
  return content;

}

public void onStart() {
super.onStart();
Log.i(CLASSNAME, "onStart");
}

public void onresume() {
super.onResume();
Log.i(CLASSNAME, "onResume");
}

public void onPause() {
super.onPause();
Log.i(CLASSNAME, "onPause");
}

public void onStop() {
super.onStop();
Log.i(CLASSNAME, "onStop");
}

public void onDestroyView() {
super.onDestroyView();
Log.i(CLASSNAME, "onDestroyView");
}

public void onDestroy() {
super.onDestroy();
Log.i(CLASSNAME, "onDestroy");
}

public void onDetach() {
super.onDetach();
Log.i(CLASSNAME, "onDetach");
}

////////////////////////////////////////////////////////////////////////
// Minor lifecycle methods
////////////////////////////////////////////////////////////////////////

public void onActivityCreated() {
// Notification that the containing activiy and its View hierarchy exist
Log.i(CLASSNAME, "onActivityCreated");
}

////////////////////////////////////////////////////////////////////////
// Overrides of the implementations ComponentCallbacks methods in Fragment
////////////////////////////////////////////////////////////////////////

@Override
```

continues

LISTING 1-3 *(continued)*

```
public void onConfigurationChanged(Configuration newConfiguration) {
super.onConfigurationChanged(newConfiguration);

// This won't happen unless we declare changes we handle in the manifest
if (L) Log.i(CLASSNAME, "onConfigurationChanged");
}

@Override
public void onLowMemory() {
// No guarantee this is called before or after other callbacks
if (L) Log.i(CLASSNAME, "onLowMemory");
}

//////////////////////////////////////////////////////////////////////////
// Implementation of TabListener
//////////////////////////////////////////////////////////////////////////
```

The following three methods implement the `TabListener` interface. They are passed a `FragmentTransaction` object, which aggregates all the actions taken when navigating between fragments. Here, you simply show or hide the fragment.

```
@Override
public void onTabReselected(Tab tab, FragmentTransaction ft) {
// TODO Auto-generated method stub

}

@Override
public void onTabSelected(Tab tab, FragmentTransaction ft) {
ft.show(this);

}

@Override
public void onTabUnselected(Tab tab, FragmentTransaction ft) {
ft.hide(this);

}

//////////////////////////////////////////////////////////////////////////
// Implementation of SetData
//////////////////////////////////////////////////////////////////////////
```

The following is the `setData` method, which implements the `SetData` interface. This interface tells this fragment what data it should display.

```
@Override
public void setData(Bundle data) {
// Display the number
EditText t = (EditText) getActivity().findViewById(R.id.editText1);
```

```
int i = data.getInt("place");
t.setText(Integer.toString(i));
}

}
```

The ItemDetailFragment Class

The `ItemDetail` fragment class is similar enough to the `ItemFragment` class that it does not merit displaying the listing in this chapter. You can find it in the file `ItemDetailFragment .java` in this chapter's downloadable files available at www.wrox.com and https://github.com/ wileyenterpriseandroid/Examples.git.

TYING TOGETHER ACTIVITIES, FRAGMENTS, AND THE ACTION BAR

The Android APIs provide you with infinite ways to design your user experiences. Your challenge is to find a consistent path through those infinite choices that can be considered "typical." One typical approach is to combine the `Activity`, `Fragment`, and `ActionBar` classes, along with the `View` class hierarchy and tabs to provide a user experience that resembles other well-designed Android applications. The `TabbedActivity` class in Listing 1-4 glues together the use of `Activity`, `Fragment`, and `ActionBar`.

The TabbedActivity Class

The `TabbedActivity` class is an abstract subclass of `Activity`. The other `Activity` subclasses in this application framework extend `TabbedActivity`, and if you go on to use this framework, the `Activity` subclasses you add to this framework will also likely extend this class.

As an abstract parent class of the concrete classes in this framework, `TabbedActivity` provides some capabilities inherited by those subclasses, specifically:

➤ Enabling tabs in the action bar to select among fragments

➤ Enabling the app to load data into fragments

➤ Abstracting whether the user interface is on one large screen, or divided across two smaller screens

---

LISTING 1-4: TabbedActivity.java

```
package com.enterpriseandroidbook.fragmentframework;

import android.app.ActionBar;
import android.app.ActionBar.Tab;
import android.app.ActionBar.TabListener;
```

continues

LISTING 1-4 *(continued)*

```
import android.app.Activity;
import android.content.Intent;
import android.os.Bundle;

public abstract class TabbedActivity extends Activity {
```

This `abstract` class is where most of the work, and most of the cleverness, resides. The `initializeTabs` method initializes the names of the tabs and connects the tabs to the fragments they control. This is called from the `onCreate` method of the `Activity`.

```
/**
 * Initialize tabs in an activity that uses tabs to switch among fragments
 *
 * @param defaultIndex
 *               The index of the Fragment shown first
 * @param nameIDs
 *               an array of ID for tab names
 * @param fragmentIDs
 *               an array of IDs of Fragment resources
 */
public void initializeTabs(int defaultIndex, int[] nameIDs, int[] fragmentIDs) {

// How many do we have?
int n = nameIDs.length;
int i = 0;

// Find at least one fragment that should implement TabListener
TabListener tlFrag = (TabListener) getFragmentManager()
     .findFragmentById(fragmentIDs[i]);

// Null check - harmless to call if there are no such fragments
if (null != tlFrag) {

// Get the action bar and remove existing tabs
ActionBar bar = getActionBar();
bar.removeAllTabs();

// Make new tabs and assign tags and listeners
for (; i < n; i++) {
tlFrag = (TabListener) getFragmentManager().findFragmentById(fragmentIDs[i]);
Tab t = bar.newTab().setText(nameIDs[i]).setTag(tlFrag).setTabListener(tlFrag);
bar.addTab(t);
}
bar.getTabAt(defaultIndex).select();
}
}
```

The `loadTabFragments` method is called whenever the user picks an item from the list on the left side of the screen. It loads the selected data into the views in the fragments on the right side of the screen. This method contains the only logic in the app that can be said to be somewhat aware of the layout of the screen. If there are tabs in this activity, the doLoad method is called. If not, something interesting happens — a new activity is started and the Bundle object containing the data is attached to the intent.

Despite the fact that there is an if statement here that, effectively, distinguishes between the one-activity case on larger screens and the two-activity case on smaller screens, none of the code has any logic that makes decisions based on screen size or pixel density. That is as it should be. Your program will always encounter new screen geometries. Code that makes decisions based on the parameters of the screen is always susceptible to being surprised by new devices. Instead, you should let the system make decisions about which layout to use, and ensure that your code accommodates all the possible choices.

```java
/**
 * If we have tabs and fragments in this activity, pass the bundle data to
 * the fragments. Otherwise start an activity that should contain the
 * fragments.
 *
 * @param data
 */
public void loadTabFragments(Bundle data) {
int n = getActionBar().getTabCount();
if (0 != n) {
doLoad(n, data);
} else {
startActivity(new Intent(this, TabActivity.class).putExtras(data));
}
}

/**
 * An interface to pass data to a Fragment
 */
public interface SetData {
public void setData(Bundle data);
}

/**
 * Iterate over the tabs, get their tags, and use these as Fragment
 * references to pass the bundle data to the fragments
 *
 * @param n
 * @param data
 */
private void doLoad(int n, Bundle data) {

// Null check - harmless if no data
if (null == data) return;

int i;
ActionBar actionBar = getActionBar();

for (i = 0; i < n; i++) {
```

continues

LISTING 1-4 *(continued)*

```
SetData f = (SetData) actionBar.getTabAt(i).getTag();
f.setData(data);
}
actionBar.selectTab(actionBar.getTabAt(0));
}


}
```

A Main.xml File for Large Tablets

If the code isn't making decisions about screen size, what is? In this framework, you harness the decisions the Android system makes about layouts to also determine the number of fragments displayed on different screen sizes.

This file (Listing 1-5) contains a layout that includes both the list fragment on the left and the information fragments on the right. It is in the directory called *layout-large*. So, whenever the system decides to find layouts in the layout-large folder, it will pick this file and all the fragments will be displayed.

LISTING 1-5: Main.xml

```xml
<?xml version="1.0" encoding="utf-8"?>
<LinearLayout xmlns:android="http://schemas.android.com/apk/res/android"
    android:id="@+id/content_layout"
    android:layout_width="fill_parent"
    android:layout_height="fill_parent"
    android:orientation="horizontal" >

    <fragment
        android:id="@+id/list_frag"
        android:name="com.enterpriseandroidbook.fragmentframework.PickFragment"
        android:layout_width="250dp"
        android:layout_height="match_parent"
        class="com.enterpriseandroidbook.fragmentframework.PickFragment" />

    <LinearLayout
        xmlns:android="http://schemas.android.com/apk/res/android"
        android:layout_width="match_parent"
        android:layout_height="match_parent"
        android:orientation="vertical" >

        <fragment
            android:id="@+id/content_frag"
            android:name="com.enterpriseandroidbook.fragmentframework.ItemFragment"
            android:layout_width="match_parent"
            android:layout_height="match_parent"
            class="com.enterpriseandroidbook.fragmentframework.ItemFragment" />

        <fragment
```

```
        android:id="@+id/detail_frag"
        android:name="com.enterpriseandroidbook.fragmentframework
.ItemDetailFragment"
        android:layout_width="match_parent"
        android:layout_height="match_parent"
        class="com.enterpriseandroidbook.fragmentframework.ItemDetailFragment"
                />
    </LinearLayout>

    </LinearLayout>
```

The code in the fragment doesn't ask which layout was chosen. It doesn't make decisions based on screen size or pixel density either. All it does is accommodate having, or not having, all the fragments on the screen. That accommodation is made in the loadTabFragments method of the TabbedActivity class.

A Main.xml and a Subsidiary Activity for Smaller Screens

This version of the main.xml file (Listing 1-6) is found in the *layout* folder, as opposed to the *layout-large* folder, where the other main.xml file is placed. This version is used for every screen size other than ones the Android system deems to be "large."

LISTING 1-6: Main.xml

```
<?xml version="1.0" encoding="utf-8"?>
<LinearLayout xmlns:android="http://schemas.android.com/apk/res/android"
    android:layout_width="fill_parent"
    android:layout_height="fill_parent"
    android:orientation="horizontal" >

    <fragment
        android:id="@+id/list_frag"
        android:name="com.enterpriseandroidbook.fragmentframework.PickFragment"
        android:layout_width="match_parent"
        android:layout_height="match_parent"
        class="com.enterpriseandroidbook.fragmentframework.PickFragment" />

    </LinearLayout>
```

Note that only the fragment that on a large screen displays the list on the left side of the screen appears in this layout. That means that an instance of that Fragment subclass is created when this layout is used. The Fragment subclasses that would on a large screen correspond to the fragments on the right side of the screen are never instantiated.

This isn't a problem because all the code that interacts with the user is in those Fragment subclasses. As long as the other code makes no assumptions about those classes, their presence (or absence) makes no difference.

The TabActivity Class

This activity, in Listing 1-7, starts when the `loadTabFragments` method finds no tabs. It is notable, as with the other `Activity` class in this example, for what it doesn't do. It exists to load the layout containing the fragments that would on a larger screen appear to the right of the list, but it makes no decisions or assumptions about screen sizes or layouts, or which `Fragment` subclasses are used in the layout.

The result is that on small screens this activity is launched, and it displays the tabs that would otherwise be on the right side of a larger screen.

LISTING 1-7: TabActivity.java

```java
package com.enterpriseandroidbook.fragmentframework;

import android.app.ActionBar;
import android.content.res.Configuration;
import android.os.Bundle;
import android.util.Log;

public class TabActivity extends TabbedActivity {

// String for logging the class name
private final String CLASSNAME = getClass().getSimpleName();

// Turn logging on or off
private static final boolean L = true;

@Override
protected void onCreate(Bundle savedState) {
super.onCreate(savedState);

// To keep this method simple
doCreate(savedState);

// If we had state to restore, we note that in the log message
if (L) Log.i(CLASSNAME, "onCreate" +
(null == savedState ? " Restored state" : ""));
}

@Override
protected void onRestart() {
super.onRestart();
// Notification that the activity will be started
if (L) Log.i(CLASSNAME, "onRestart");
}

@Override
protected void onStart() {
super.onStart();
// Notification that the activity is starting
if (L) Log.i(CLASSNAME, "onStart");
```

```java
}

@Override
protected void onResume() {
super.onResume();
// Notification that the activity will interact with the user
if (L) Log.i(CLASSNAME, "onResume");
}

protected void onPause() {
super.onPause();
// Notification that the activity will stop interacting with the user
if (L) Log.i(CLASSNAME, "onPause" + (isFinishing() ? " Finishing" : ""));
}

@Override
protected void onStop() {
super.onStop();
// Notification that the activity is no longer visible
if (L) Log.i(CLASSNAME, "onStop");
}

@Override
protected void onDestroy() {
super.onDestroy();
// Notification the activity will be destroyed
if (L) Log.i(CLASSNAME, "onDestroy"
// Are we finishing?
+ (isFinishing() ? " Finishing" : ""));
}

@Override
protected void onSaveInstanceState(Bundle outState) {
super.onSaveInstanceState(outState);
saveState(outState);

// Called when state should be saved
if (L) Log.i(CLASSNAME, "onSaveInstanceState");

}

@Override
protected void onRestoreInstanceState(Bundle savedState) {
super.onRestoreInstanceState(savedState);
if (null != savedState) restoreState(savedState);

// If we had state to restore, we note that in the log message
if (L) Log.i(CLASSNAME, "onRestoreInstanceState" +
(null == savedState ? " Restored state" : ""));
}
```

continues

LISTING 1-7 *(continued)*

```
////////////////////////////////////////////////////////////////////////
// The minor lifecycle methods - you probably won't need these
////////////////////////////////////////////////////////////////////////

@Override
protected void onPostCreate(Bundle savedState) {
super.onPostCreate(savedState);
if (null != savedState) restoreState(savedState);

// If we had state to restore, we note that in the log message
if (L) Log.i(CLASSNAME, "onCreate" + (null == savedState ?
    " Restored state" : ""));

}

@Override
protected void onPostResume() {
super.onPostResume();
// Notification that resuming the activity is complete
if (L) Log.i(CLASSNAME, "onPostResume");
}

@Override
protected void onUserLeaveHint() {
super.onUserLeaveHint();
// Notification that user navigated away from this activity
if (L) Log.i(CLASSNAME, "onUserLeaveHint");
}

////////////////////////////////////////////////////////////////////////
// Overrides of the implementations ComponentCallbacks methods in Activity
////////////////////////////////////////////////////////////////////////

@Override
public void onConfigurationChanged(Configuration newConfiguration) {
super.onConfigurationChanged(newConfiguration);

// This won't happen unless we declare changes we handle in the manifest
if (L) Log.i(CLASSNAME, "onConfigurationChanged");
}

@Override
public void onLowMemory() {
// No guarantee this is called before or after other callbacks
if (L) Log.i(CLASSNAME, "onLowMemory");
}

////////////////////////////////////////////////////////////////////////
// App-specific code here
////////////////////////////////////////////////////////////////////////


/**
* This is where we restore state we previously saved.
```

```
 * @param savedState the Bundle we got from the callback
 */
private void restoreState(Bundle savedState) {
// Add your code to restore state here

}

/**
 * Add this activity's state to the bundle and/or commit pending data
 */
private void saveState(Bundle state) {
// Add your code to add state to the bundle here
}

/**
 * Perform initializations on creation of this Activity instance
 * @param savedState
 */
private void doCreate(Bundle savedState) {
setContentView(R.layout.content_control_activity);

if (null != savedState) restoreState(savedState);

        ActionBar bar = getActionBar();
         bar.setDisplayShowTitleEnabled(false);
        bar.setNavigationMode(ActionBar.NAVIGATION_MODE_TABS);

// Initialize the tabs
int names[] = {R.string.item, R.string.detail };
int fragments[] = { R.id.content_frag, R.id.detail_frag };
initializeTabs(0, names, fragments);

// Load data if there is some
loadTabFragments(getIntent().getExtras());
}

}
```

> **NOTE** *Note that we sometimes use the words* activity, fragment, service, view, *and so on to refer to places in programs where the corresponding classes, which are named with their precise names, are used. That is, we use these nouns in place of the object names when that makes the text in this book easier to read. You will see this pattern of usage throughout this book.*

THE ANDROID TASK AND PROCESS MODEL

In the previous sections you learned how an Android process is assembled out of components, and how components work together with garbage collection in the Android managed run time to keep per-process heap size small. One reason per-process heap size needs to be small is that Android runs many instances of the run time at once, one for each process where a Java program is running in the Android environment. A "small" heap size means specifically that the total amount of memory available to all the applications in an Android device ranges between a few tens of megabytes to a few hundred megabytes. Each process is limited to between 24MB and 48MB, although some devices may have lower or higher limits. This means you cannot count on a fixed amount of memory, or on being able to use more than a small share of the total memory in the device.

Android's approach differs from most systems where per-process heap size can take up a large amount of available memory, and it is not uncommon for Java VM instances to have heap sizes in the hundreds of megabytes.

Starting Dalvik Instances

Although you don't need to know the details to write Android applications, it's still a good idea to know why you can start dozens of instances of the Dalvik virtual machine (VM), which is the basis of Android's managed language runtime environment, when trying to do the same with a conventional Java VM would bog down your computer, never mind a mobile device.

One problem with managed language runtime environments is that bytecodes, such as those used in Java VMs and Dalvik, are loaded like data, not like the machine instructions that computer processors run. Dalvik optimizes the creation and initialization of new instances of Dalvik by using a template process, or an *instance*. This template process starts, loads, and initializes many base classes, and it then waits until it needs to be "cloned," using the `fork` system call. See Figure 1-11 for an example.

When the Dalvik template instance, called the *Zygote*, is forked, it both speeds up the loading and initialization of new processes and reduces the memory footprint of every Dalvik instance. It does this by treating the pre-loaded base classes as if they were pure code and sharing this code across all the Dalvik instances forked from the Zygote.

For you, the developer, this means that you don't have to avoid starting Dalvik instances. If it makes sense to start an Activity from another app to, for example, pick an image file to load, do it, and don't worry about the overhead.

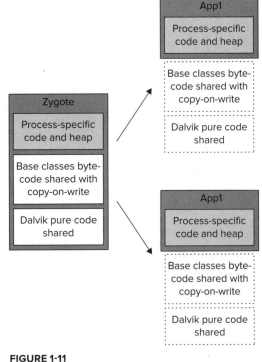

FIGURE 1-11

Death, but No Transfiguration

In the section on the `Activity` class and its component lifecycle, you saw how an activity can be destroyed and re-created. Every component in an Android process can be destroyed and, if the developer correctly handles lifecycle method calls, re-created. Every object in an Android process is contained in components. That is, there is nothing in an Android process that can hold a reference to an instance of any class that is not itself referred to only by a component. That means that whole processes could be destroyed and re-created. And they routinely are.

You can demonstrate this by running the example in this chapter and watching the logcat view in Eclipse. Note that each line in the log lists a process ID or PID. After starting the example app and observing the lifecycle method calls in the logcat view, start a large number of other applications. Eventually you will see that, when you go back to this example app, not only are the instances of every component destroyed and re-created, but the process ID (PID) has changed too! This is a bit remarkable: The user sees no difference in the operation and state of the app he is interacting with, but every object in that app has been destroyed and re-created, and it is in an entirely new process. This also illustrates that "process" and "task" are only loosely coupled in the Android task model.

This is how Android recovers memory at the granularity of a process. It also "resets" the heap size for a running app, in case the app had used a large block of memory for some purpose and then freed it. This should also convince you, if you have not already been convinced, that any attempts to thwart the Android lifecycle are futile. Occasionally, your whole process is going to get reaped by Android's memory management. There is no place to hide from the component lifecycle.

Tasks Span Applications and Processes

Android also differs from most OSs in that a task in Android isn't synonymous with a process. Android applications can, using the `startActivity` method, cause another application to be started. But that application is often part of the same task. Its capabilities are being borrowed. For example, the Gallery app is frequently used to select an image file. When this happens, another app creates an Intent object with the PICK action and asks for an image. The Gallery app has a matching intent filter, and it starts an activity enabling the user to pick an image from the gallery. While this is happening, the app that was launched and the Gallery app are part of the same task, even though they are in two separate processes.

This kind of late-binding, loosely-coupled modularity is characteristic of Android applications, and the component-based implementation of Android apps, where an Activity component is used to group Fragment objects and the View objects they contain into screens of UI work. Note in the `TabbedActivity.java` listing (Listing 1-4 earlier in the chapter) that an `Intent` object is used in the `startActivity` method call that results in a new activity being started. In this case, a class name is specified. But an `Intent` can contain a looser specification than actions and data types, instead of class names. That enables you to consume pieces of other application's UI and provide pieces of a UI to other applications.

Later in this chapter you will see how `Intent` objects are used to start applications.

MULTIPROCESSING, SECURITY, AND LIFECYCLE

Android's designers faced a difficult problem. Unlike a web server, in which all the software is controlled by one developer/administrator, a mobile device runs applications developed by multiple developers. The user has limited trust for these developers, and the developers have limited trust of one another. They all need to share memory resources, and you can't predict how many applications the user will want to run.

The Process and User ID as Security Boundary

A single runtime environment with multiple threads just isn't going to cut it for enabling a secure multiprocessing environment. Every Android application runs in its own process, which is an instance of the Dalvik managed runtime environment.

Each Android developer gets a signature (the examples you are running now are signed with a temporary signature), and every signature creates a separate user ID (UID) and group ID (GID) in the Android system. Access to each developer's application's files is limited to the UID and GID of that developer's applications.

Android processes cannot access memory in other processes, and they cannot access files with other UIDs/GIDs.

> **NOTE** *While managed language run times do enhance the robustness of systems because they run code inside a virtual machine, the Dalvik VM is not a security boundary in Android. Android applications can and do run native code.*

DECLARING APPLICATION PROPERTIES

Previously in this chapter you saw how Android components, especially the `Activity` component, are used to group elements of a user interface onto a device screen, and how the Fragment subclasses defined here are used to group View objects and the code that handles user interaction with those objects, and how declarative UI can drive the configuration of activities and fragments to adapt to a wide range of device sizes. But how did your application get started?

Components are central to starting applications. So are `Intent` objects. Manifest files are used to bring together information about all the components in your application, plus some data about names and system compatibility. Intent filter specifications are key to the loosely coupled, high-level modularity of Android applications.

You see all this information come together in the manifest file (Listing 1-8) for the framework application:

LISTING 1-8: manifest.xml

```xml
<?xml version="1.0" encoding="utf-8"?>
<manifest xmlns:android="http://schemas.android.com/apk/res/android"
    package="com.enterpriseandroidbook.fragmentframework"
    android:versionCode="1"
    android:versionName="1.0">
```

```
<uses-sdk android:minSdkVersion="15" />

<application android:icon="@drawable/icon" android:label="@string/app_name"
    android:uiOptions="splitActionBarWhenNarrow"
        android:theme="@android:style/Theme.Holo">
    <activity android:name=".MainActivity"
            android:label="@string/app_name">
        <intent-filter>
            <action android:name="android.intent.action.MAIN" />
            <category android:name="android.intent.category.LAUNCHER" />
        </intent-filter>
    </activity>
    <activity android:name="com.enterpriseandroidbook.fragmentframework
        .TabActivity" android:label="@string/data"></activity>

</application>
</manifest>
```

A file called a "manifest" lists the contents of something; in this case, it lists the contents of an Android application. Android application manifests list all the components in an application. If, in addition to the name of an activity, an intent filter is defined for an activity, that activity can be "matched" instead of being specified by name.

In this manifest, the intent filter for `MainActivity` matches the action `android.intent .action.MAIN`. It specifies that it also matches the category `android.intent.category .LAUNCHER`. These are the constants that Android launchers use to launch applications.

SUMMARY

This chapter guided you through setting up your tools and verifying that they were set up correctly.

You saw how a modern Android framework suitable for database applications is put together:

➤   It adapts to all sizes of Android devices. It's time to stop whining about "fragmentation" and write apps that adapt.

➤   It harnesses declarative UI in Android to avoid making decisions about screen configuration in code.

➤   It organizes code that interacts with the user into Fragment subclasses that can be combined into activities.

➤   It looks, acts, and interacts with the user like the latest generation of Android applications. It's up to date inside and out.

Although the example framework code in this chapter embodies how to write code for the most recent versions of Android, it can be back-ported to earlier versions of Android using the Support Package (discussed more in Chapter 11). By following the design patterns in this framework you can have code that is up to date, forward-compatible, and back-compatible as well.

2

The Relational Model and SQLite

WHAT'S IN THIS CHAPTER?

➤ Reviewing relational databases and history of the relational model

➤ Reviewing the SQL language

➤ Introducing SQLite

➤ Dealing with SQLite from the command line

WROX.COM CODE DOWNLOADS FOR THIS CHAPTER

Please note that all the code examples in this chapter are available at `https://github.com/wileyenterpriseandroid/Examples.git` and as a part of the book's code download at www.wrox.com on the Download Code tab.

Mobile enterprise applications — perhaps most mobile applications — involve synchronizing data between some large, network-accessible backend stores and a mobile device with limited resources.

The backend has lots of data. The mobile device only needs — and can only hold — a little bit of it at any given time.

This chapter begins the exploration of the datastores that are found at the two ends of an Android enterprise application: SQL engines.

If you are already acquainted with relational data systems, many of the concepts in this chapter will be familiar to you.

SQL is the language of the relational database management systems (RDBMSs) that have been a standard on the backend for many years. Since Android adopted SQLite as a way of storing structured, persistent data, SQL is, now, also found on the mobile client side.

There are entire books on the subject of SQL and even just the SQLite dialect of SQL. This chapter is not a replacement for those resources: It is not a reference manual. There are two goals:

➤   Review the main concepts of the relational model and the SQL language to set the stage for a later architectural level discussion of their suitability in specific circumstances.

➤   Review some of the key differences between SQLite, the SQL engine used in the Android system and the SQL engines with which most enterprise developers are already familiar.

DATABASES AND THE RELATIONAL MODEL

For the last 20 years or so, the relational model has dominated as the standard for large-scale data-management systems. Nearly any project that requires storing significant quantities of information for significant lengths of time uses some kind of relational engine to do it. It is possible that this period of relative stability is simply the eye of a storm.

Although SQL didn't actually become a standard until 1986, relational systems were already gaining a foothold in the late 1970s. Before that, system architects often had to confront the issue of data storage themselves. There were best practices, plenty of academic research, and even some commercial tools. Still, developers often had to build custom data storage systems using only a file system and low-level access to it.

Since RDBMSs have become a standard, though, we've had many years to get addicted to the idea that if it is data, it is the database's problem. It is only recently that system designers have begun to question the idea that RDBMSs are a generic solution to all of their data storage needs. Especially as they turn to distributed, cloud-based architectures, some developers are finding that there are all kinds of attractive alternatives to big SQL. The particular challenges of distributed data management are discussed in some detail in the second half of this book.

Mobile devices provide another environment that challenges the traditional SQL engine approach to data storage. In fact, until very recently, most mobile devices barely supported a file system, let alone a SQL engine.

It is obviously desirable that smart mobile devices continue to work — possibly with reduced functionality — even when they are not connected to a network. That implies that they must have local data storage. Certainly, it would be possible to return developers to a 1970's environment and leave them to build their own file- or record-based storage systems. That seems a bit austere, though, especially in the Android environment, which is a full Linux-based system and theoretically capable of supporting nearly any of the common RDBMS systems, open or proprietary. Most Android platforms, though, are still resource constrained: Using memory and battery to run a big SQL engine would be a waste.

The Android platform takes an interesting middle road by embedding SQLite. Very conveniently, SQLite speaks SQL, which makes it familiar and easy to use for a wide range of developers. SQLite, on the other hand, is very definitely not a full RDBMS. In some ways, it is the best of both worlds

— it looks like an RDBMS, but it doesn't cost as much. On the other hand, since it looks like an RDBMS, developers are sometimes surprised when it doesn't act like one.

The History of the RDBMS

Before digging into the specifics of SQLite and how it is used on Android, it is worth taking some time to set the stage with a little bit of history and theory. Enterprise Android applications bring together developers with a broad range of experiences. In particular, developers that have focused on mobile platforms may not be as familiar with RDBMS as their backend counterparts. While this discussion may not contribute directly to code or coding practices, it is one piece of getting mobile and server-side developers to speak the same language.

Although the relational model has roots that are pretty firmly attached to the mathematics of sets — a field that is well over a century old — it was only in 1970 that Edgar F. Codd introduced it as a foundation for data management. Codd's original proposal was an extension of a mathematically sound and well understood algebraic model. He demonstrated that it was not only sufficient for representing and manipulating datasets but that it also had some very convenient properties. Among other important features, his model provided the possibility of considering the structure of data as an entity distinct from the data itself and included the value *null* — a marker used to indicate that a given data value is missing from the database.

By the end of the 1980s, Codd's relational model became a commercial success. As extended by C. J. Date and others, RDBMS became a recognized term, and there were several implementations. Because the RDBMS model described behavior, not implementation, the developers of these systems were free to optimize them with a variety of cutting-edge, proprietary technologies, as long as the system behaved as prescribed by the model. The two main, original implementations — Ingres and System R — are the ancestors of virtually every RDBMS today, including Microsoft SQL Server and Oracle, respectively.

SQL, the standard language for RDBMS, is oddly not a descendant of ALPHA, Codd's own RDBMS language. Instead it is a descendant of SEQUEL, the language used in IBM's R Project. It was renamed SQL because the original name was already under copyright.

SQL was adopted as a standard by the National Institute of Standards and Technology (NIST) in 1986, by the International Organization for Standardization (ISO) in 1987, and has changed relatively little since. There have been fads — object-orientation and XQuery to name two — but SQL remains, pretty much unchallenged, the king of the hill.

> **NOTE** *It is an interesting mental exercise to compare this stability to the changes in other programming languages since 1986.*

The Relational Model

As mentioned previously, Codd's original model is based in mathematics, specifically a branch called *first-order predicate logic*. The model describes *relations*: unordered sets of *tuples* whose type is defined by the relation's attributes. Relations look a lot like the familiar and intuitive spreadsheet. The model also describes several operations on relations, the most important ones being *restriction, projection,* and *join (cross-product).* The relational model and the corresponding distributed database management system (DDBMS) model are illustrated in Figures 2-1 and 2-2.

The first two of these operations — restriction and projection — are very similar except that they affect relation rows and columns, respectively. Restricting a relation produces a new relation with a subset of the original's rows. Projection does almost exactly the same thing except that the new relation has a subset of the original's columns.

The cross-product operation formalizes the combination of two or more relations. The cross-product of two relations is a new relation in which each row from the first table is combined with every row from the second. Figure 2-4, included later in this chapter, shows examples of a simple cross-product and the special restriction of the cross-product, a join.

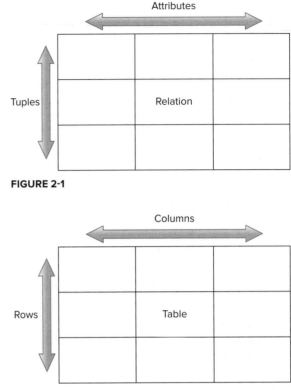

FIGURE 2-1

FIGURE 2-2

This algebra — relations and the handful of operations on them — forms the basis of the relational model. Table 2-1 shows a list of common terms used in the predicate calculus and relates them to the corresponding RDBMS vocabulary. By starting with only these simple underpinnings, and then building relations and operating on them with compositions of operators, you can manipulate data in tremendously powerful ways. You can imagine, for instance, joining the projection of a restriction of one table to the restriction of another and then performing one more restriction on the result.

TABLE 2-1

RELATIONAL MODEL	DDBMS
Relation	Table
Tuple	Row
Attribute	Column
Cross-product	Join
Projection	Select <column>,...
Restriction	Where <expression>

It is worthwhile to reiterate that, although an RDBMS presents data as tables, it does not necessarily represent them that way internally. Because the relational model is clear and specific, RDBMS designers are free to implement their products in any way they choose — probably using technologies that were completely unknown in 1970 — to make them as fast and efficient as possible.

It is also worth noting that the relational model is explicitly based on first-order predicate calculus. A first-order calculus is one in which the arguments to functions are not, themselves, functions. The notion, increasingly popular in modern programming languages, of passing functions (closures, continuations, and so on) around in code is, by definition, not possible within the relational model.

Other DBMS Features

Most RDBMS engines support — to varying degrees — other features that are not specifically part of the relational model. If a database engine is a single, monolithic entity addressed by multiple client applications, it makes a great deal of sense to make these features part of the engine, instead of leaving their implementations — and the resulting variety of bugs — to the client applications.

Strong Typing

Most database engines strictly enforce attribute types. Typically an engine defines a few native data types that describe the kind of data that can be put into a column. These types — usually various sizes of floating-point numbers, strings, integers, and so on — are specific to a particular implementation and cannot be extended. Part of defining a relation (demonstrated in the SQL language examples later in this chapter) is defining the type of data that can be placed into each of its columns. Once the relation is defined, the RDBMS will fail any attempt to put data of the wrong type into the column. An attempt, for instance, to insert a tuple that contains a string as its third attribute into a relation that specifies that that third attribute should be a floating-point number will fail and usually generate some kind of exception.

Referential Integrity

In a relational database, the native type system (the types defined by the RDBMS as described in the previous section) can be extended by declaring a column in one relation to be a reference to another relation. That is, using a special construct of the SQL language (primary and foreign keys, demonstrated later in the chapter), the data architect can declare that the contents of some column in one relation are a reference to a similarly typed column in another relation. Figure 2-3 illustrates a foreign key.

A given value in the foreign key column in Table A (the rightmost, in this particular case) is either null, or it is a link to exactly one row in Table B, the single row that contains the matching value in its leftmost column (again, leftmost in this case).

Most RDBMS engines enforce this relationship, referential integrity, for relations on which it is defined. The enforcement has two parts.

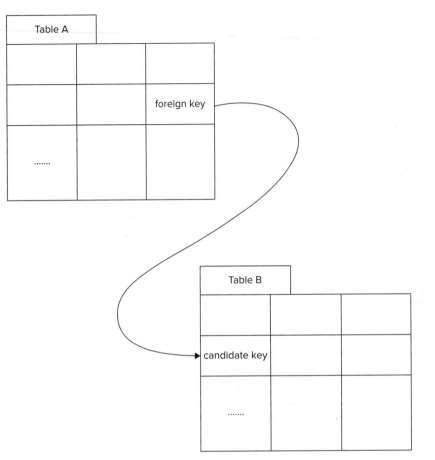

FIGURE 2-3

➤ The first part, enforcing the primary key constraint, guarantees that there is no more than one row in the target table (Table B in Figure 2-3) with the given value as primary key (in its left column in the example). A table may contain, at most, one (possibly multicolumn) primary key. A database that enforces the primary key constraint will fail an attempt to insert a new row into a table if the table already contains the key value found in the new row. For instance, if the table contains three rows with the key column values of "yes", "no", and "maybe", the attempt to add a new row with a key column value of "purple" will succeed. Attempting to add a new row whose key column contains the value "no", however, will fail.

➤ The second part of referential integrity enforcement guarantees that if the foreign key is non-null in a row in the child table (Table A in the example), there is a unique record with that key in the parent table (Table B). There are two ways that this rule might be violated, and both are forbidden. An attempt to insert a row with a foreign key whose value is not the primary key of any row in the target table will fail and usually generate an exception. So will the attempt to delete the (unique) row in the parent table that is referenced by a foreign key in the child table. If there is no information in the parent table corresponding to a given row in the child table, that row's foreign key value must be null.

Transactions

The last of the features frequently supported by RDBMS systems is the transaction. A *transaction* is a group of operations on the data that must be considered as a unit: They must either all succeed or all fail. Transaction support in a database system is frequently discussed in terms of the extent to which it supports "ACID" properties:

➤ **Atomicity** — A transaction is "all or nothing": Either the entire transaction succeeds or none of it does.

➤ **Consistency** — If the database is in a valid state before a transaction, it is still in a valid state after the transaction. A transaction cannot cause the violation of any data constraints.

➤ **Isolation** — The state of the database after a transaction is a state that could have been achieved by applying the statements in the transaction serially in some order.

➤ **Durability** — Once a transaction has completed, it can't be forgotten. Even if the power fails or the network collapses, the new state persists until it is changed by other statements.

Database engines frequently allow the data architect fairly fine-grained control over several kinds of transaction support, from permitting access to the data to only one client at a time (slow, but all transactions succeed) to allowing multiple simultaneous access, and failing the entire transaction for a client that, by chance, violates transactional rules (faster but sometimes requires retrying).

Transactions, referential integrity, strong typing, and the relational model are all core concepts of relational data systems. Now that you've re-acquainted yourself with them, it is time to turn to the specifics of their use. The canonical language for using relational systems is SQL. As an Enterprise Android developer, you will have to be fluent with SQL both to manage data within the Android platform and to use backend services effectively.

The SQL Language

SQL really is a comparatively simple language. Still, as noted earlier, it is the topic for entire books. A complete description is well outside the scope of this one. Because developers at both ends of a mobile application — the mobile side and the server backend — are likely to use SQL, it is worth taking a few moments to review its main features in general, before turning to the specifics of the SQLite dialect.

Statements in the SQL language can be divided into three large classes, the Data Definition Language (DDL), the Data Manipulation Language (DML), and queries.

Data Definition Language (DDL)

The Data Definition Language (DDL) describes the structure of the data that a database contains. The most common DDL statements are used to define a table — the number of columns it contains, the names of those columns, and the kinds of values allowed in them. This is accomplished with the CREATE TABLE statement, illustrated in Listing 2-1, along with its inverse, DROP TABLE.

LISTING 2-1: The **CREATE TABLE** statement

```
DROP TABLE contacts;
CREATE TABLE contacts (
    _id INTEGER PRIMARY KEY AUTOINCREMENT,
    name_raw_contact_id INTEGER REFERENCES raw_contacts(_id),
    photo_id INTEGER REFERENCES data(_id),
    photo_file_id INTEGER REFERENCES photo_files(_id),
    custom_ringtone TEXT,
    send_to_voicemail INTEGER NOT NULL DEFAULT 0,
    times_contacted INTEGER NOT NULL DEFAULT 0,
    last_time_contacted INTEGER,
    starred INTEGER NOT NULL DEFAULT 0,
    has_phone_number INTEGER NOT NULL DEFAULT 0,
    lookup TEXT,
    status_update_id INTEGER REFERENCES data(_id)
);
```

Listing 2-1 is an example of the definition of a moderately complex table, named `contacts`. It happens that this is, specifically, the SQLite dialect of SQL, but the definition would look nearly identical in most other dialects. The code creates the single table called `contacts` with 12 columns, each defined in one line of the code. The name of a table must be unique within a database and is frequently a plural noun, naming the objects found in the rows of the table: EMPLOYEES, NOSES, HIPPOPOTUMUSES, and so on.

> **NOTE** *A debate rages in the SQL community over whether to use singular or plural nouns to name tables. Recently the discussion seems to be favoring the singular. There is definite and strong agreement, though, that whichever scheme you choose, you should be consistent.*

The names of the columns in a table must be unique within the table. In the example, the column `_id` is an integer valued primary key for the table. The AUTOINCREMENT constraint on the `_id` column causes the db engine to create a new, unique integer for each row, automatically, as it is added.

The other columns in the table use two primitive data types — `text` and `integer`. Several of the columns — those that use the REFERENCES keyword — have complex types that are defined in other tables using foreign keys. The column `photo_file_id`, for instance, is a reference to the table `photo_files`.

> **NOTE** *Some of the other columns defined in the table have other data constraints — NOT NULL, DEFAULT 0, and so on. For more information on any of these constraints and how they work refer to a standard SQL reference like the following:*
>
> http://dev.mysql.com/doc/refman/5.0/en/language-structure.html
> http://msdn.microsoft.com/en-us/library/ms166026(v=sql.90).aspx
> http://docs.oracle.com/cd/B19306_01/server.102/b14200/toc.htm

In addition to being able to create tables, SQL DDL allows the creation of other standard RDBMS data structures like views, triggers, and indices. A typical database is likely to contain several tables, maybe an index or two, and depending on the inclinations of the designer, a few triggers or views. The collection of DDL statements that define all of the objects in a given database is called its *schema*.

Data Manipulation Language (DML)

Data Manipulation Language (DML) statements are used to add, remove, and modify data in the database. There are three DML statements — INSERT, UPDATE, and DELETE. They are all demonstrated in Listing 2-2.

LISTING 2-2: Data Manipulation Language statements

```
INSERT INTO contacts(
    name_raw_contact_id, photo_id, photo_file_id,
    last_time_contacted, status_update_id)
    VALUES(null, null, null, 1339365417, null);
UPDATE contacts SET starred=1, has_phone_number=1 WHERE _id = 3;
DELETE FROM contacts where _id = 2;
```

The INSERT statement adds a new row to the table and defines the values in some — in this case, not all — of its columns. The insert will succeed because all of the columns that are required to have values (constrained NOT NULL) have values specified or have defaults (constrained DEFAULT). The primary key for the row inserted by this statement will have an integer value automatically created by the database engine and different from any other value currently in the _id column.

The next statement in Listing 2-2, the UPDATE statement, changes the value of two columns for, at most, one row in the contacts table. It changes the value for the single row in which the value of the primary key is 3. Because the selection criteria is the primary key, there can be, at most, one such row.

The last statement in the listing, the DELETE statement, deletes (in this case) at most one row from the database. Again, this is because the selection criteria is the primary key and there can be at most one record whose primary key is 2. After this statement is executed, there exists no row whose primary key is 2 in the contacts table.

Queries

QUERY is probably the most frequently used of all the SQL statements. In relational terms, the query creates a new relation — a virtual table — that is a restriction of a projection of the cross-product of one or more other tables. Listing 2-3 shows an example of a query that illustrates an INNER JOIN.

LISTING 2-3: Query that uses INNER JOIN

```
SELECT rc.display_name, c.starred
    FROM contacts c INNER JOIN raw_contacts rc
        ON c.name_raw_contact_id = rc._id
    WHERE NOT rc.display_name IS NULL
    ORDER BY rc.display_name ASC;
```

As mentioned earlier, a join is an important restriction on the cross-product of two tables. As shown in Figure 2-4, a full cross-product of two tables combines each of the rows from the first table with every row from the second. In the query in Listing 2-3, the table `contacts` is joined with the table `raw_contacts`. There are `C(contacts) * C(raw_contacts)` rows in this cross-product, where `C(t)` is the number of rows in the table `t`. This whole cross-product probably isn't very useful. In the query, though, the `ON` clause restricts the cross-product to only rows in which the column `name_raw_contact_id` has the same value as the `raw_contacts` column `_id`. The new relation generated by the join contains the rows from `contacts`, each with the corresponding information from `raw_contacts` appended. That is definitely useful! The bottom table in Figure 2-4 illustrates a similar join.

By extension it is possible to construct joins of many tables. In RDBMS systems joins are an essential feature in almost the same way that inheritance is an essential feature in object-oriented systems.

This brief review of the SQL language completes the overview of generic relational data storage. All of the discussion in this chapter, so far, applies to both the client and server sides of a distributed mobile application. It is information with which mobile developers may be less familiar than their backend counterparts. Discussing it at such a high level serves not only to help the mobile developer understand an important local tool but also to understand the backend technology that supports her mobile application. It is now time to turn to the specifics of Android's structured data management tool, SQLite.

Relation R	
A1	B2
A2	B1
A3	B3

Relation P	
B1	X1
B2	X2
B3	X3

Cross-Product		
A1	B1	X1
A1	B2	X2
A1	B3	X3
A2	B1	X1
A2	B2	X2
A2	B3	X3
A3	B1	X1
A3	B2	X2
A3	B3	X3

Join on R.2=P.1		
A1	B2	X2
A2	B1	X1
A3	B3	X3

FIGURE 2-4

INTRODUCTION TO SQLITE

Android uses the open source database engine, SQLite. It is a small, serverless library that has several features that are extremely attractive in the mobile environment. Data stored in SQLite databases on a phone is persistent across processes, through power cycling, and, usually, across upgrades and re-installs of the system software.

SQLite is an independent, self-sustaining project. Originally developed in 2000 by D. Richard Hipp, it quickly filled a niche as a lightweight way to manage structured data. A group of dedicated developers supports a large user community and such high-profile projects as Apple Mail, the Firefox web browser, and Intuit's TurboTax.

As part of this strong support, each release of SQLite is tested very carefully, especially under failure conditions. The library is designed to handle many kinds of failures gracefully, including low memory, disk errors, and power outages. Reliability is a key feature of SQLite and more than half of the project code is devoted to testing. This is very important on a mobile platform where the environment is less predictable than it is for a device confined to a server room. If something goes wrong — the user removes the battery or a buggy app hogs all available memory — SQLite-managed databases are unlikely to be corrupted and user data is likely safe and recoverable.

> **NOTE** *There is comprehensive and detailed documentation about SQLite at the project website at* `http://www.sqlite.org/docs.html`.

The other side of the coin, though, is that SQLite is not really an RDBMS. Several of the features that you'd expect from a relational system, are completely missing. As built for Android, SQLite does support transactions and the SQL language. However, until Android API level 10 (Gingerbread), it did not support referential integrity or strong typing. In more recent versions of Android, SQLite can support referential integrity, but that support is turned off by default. It still does not support strong typing. Its own documentation suggests that one should think of SQLite "not as a replacement for Oracle, but as a replacement for `fopen()`."

SQLite from the Command Line

Perhaps the best way to introduce SQLite and its vagaries is to use it. In the interests of authenticity, this entire example was recorded on an Android emulator: an Android Virtual Device (AVD). The first line of Listing 2-4 starts an instance of the emulator, using the previously created device configuration named `tablet`. In this case, that configuration is running Android Ice Cream Sandwich, release 15, v4.0.3. The example would look nearly identical on most other versions of Android or on an actual Android device. For that matter, it would look the same from the command line of any other UNIX-like system that has sqlite3 installed.

> **NOTE** *The sqlite3 program is only available on "engineering" builds of Android. The emulator uses an engineering build, but most production devices (such as your phone) use dramatically streamlined versions of Android. Production builds have fewer debugging tools installed, thus leaving more space for user data and making them somewhat more resistant to data breaches.*

A SQLite database is a simple file. On Android devices most applications store their databases in their file system sandbox in a sub-directory named `databases`. For instance, databases for an application whose package name is `com.enterpriseandroid.contacts.webdataContacts` are most likely to be in the directory `/data/data/com.enterpriseandroid.contacts.webdataContacts/databases`. There is no reason, of course, that an application can't share access to its databases by putting them, instead, into a public storage area (anything stored on the file system named /sdcard, for instance, is publicly available to any application). As you will see in the next chapter, though, there are much better ways to share data than by making the database itself globally available.

The example also demonstrates the use of the adb tool, the Android Debugger, from the Android SDK. adb is the Swiss Army knife of Android tools. It is found in the directory platform-tools of the SDK (which, in the example, is located using the shell variable $ANDROID_HOME). When run, adb connects to a daemon on a running Android system. In this case it is connecting to the emulator started on the line above. To get a shell prompt on the emulator, use the command adb shell.

From the shell prompt, you can run the SQLite command-line utility *sqlite3*. Listing 2-4 uses the file system sandbox for an installed application whose package name is com.enterpriseandroid .contacts.dbDemo.

LISTING 2-4: Starting sqlite3

```
wiley> $ANDROID_HOME/sdk/tools/emulator -avd tablet &
wiley> $ANDROID_HOME/sdk/platform-tools/adb shell
# cd /data/data/com.enterpriseandroid.contacts.dbDemo/databases
# sqlite3 demo.db
Enter ".help" for instructions
Enter SQL statements terminated with a ";"
sqlite>
```

The first thing to remember when using sqlite3 from the command line is that each command must be terminated with a semicolon. Listing 2-5 illustrates this point.

LISTING 2-5: Ending sqlite3 commands with semicolons

```
sqlite> select * whoops typo
   ...>
   ...> ;
Error: near "whoops": syntax error
```

Until sqlite3 sees the statement-terminating semicolon, it interprets all input as part of a single SQL statement and offers the continuation prompt, ...>. Only after the semicolon does it parse and evaluate the input, delivering any necessary error messages.

There are also several meta-commands (not part of the SQL language) that are very useful when working with sqlite3. Meta-commands are commands that begin with a period. They are not interpreted as SQL but, instead, as commands to the sqlite3 command-line program. The two most important of these are .help and .exit.

➤ The .exit command exits the sqlite3 command interpreter.

➤ The .help command prints a list of other "dot" commands.

> **NOTE** *You can also terminate a SQLite command-line session by typing Ctrl+D. This will work even when the command parser is hopelessly confused.*

SQLite syntax supports a wide variety of data types: TINYINT, BIGINT, FLOAT(7, 3), LONGVARCHAR, SMALLDATETIME, and so on. As mentioned earlier, though, the type of a column is actually little more than a comment. Listing 2-6 demonstrates this by storing the string value "la" into several columns with non-text types.

LISTING 2-6: sqlite3 data types

```
sqlite> create table test (
   ...> c1 biginteger, c2 smalldatetime, c3 float(9, 3));
sqlite> insert into test values("la", "la", "la");
sqlite> select * from test;
la|la|la
```

The column type is useful only as a hint to help SQLite choose an efficient internal representation for the data stored in the column. SQLite determines the internal storage type using a handful of simple rules that regulate "type affinity." These rules are very nearly invisible except as they affect the amount of space that a given dataset occupies on disk.

> **NOTE** *There are full details at*
> http://www.sqlite.org/datatype3.html#affinity.

In practice, many developers just restrict themselves to four primitive internal storage types used by SQLite — integer, real, text, and blob — and explicitly represent timestamps as text and booleans as integers.

There are a number of constraints that can be attached to a column definition. The most important is the PRIMARY KEY constraint. A primary key column contains for each row in a table a unique value that identifies the row.

SQLite does support non-integer primary keys. It even supports composite (multi-column) primary keys. Beware, though, of primary key columns that are not integer primary keys! In addition to implying a UNIQUE constraint (described later in this chapter), the primary key constraint should also imply a NOT NULL constraint. Unfortunately, because of an oversight in early versions, SQLite allows NULL as the value of a primary key for any type except integer. Because each NULL is a distinct value (different from even other NULLs) SQLite permits a primary key column to contain multiple NULLs and thus permits multiple rows in a table that cannot be distinguished by their primary key.

As Listing 2-7 demonstrates, an integer primary key column is, by default, also set to autoincrement. That means that SQLite will automatically create a new value for that column for each new row added to the database. To make this behavior explicit, declare the column PRIMARY KEY AUTOINCREMENT.

LISTING 2-7: sqlite3 primary key autoincrement

```
sqlite> create table test (key integer primary key, val text);
sqlite> insert into test ( val ) values ("something");
sqlite> insert into test ( val ) values ("something else");
sqlite> select * from test;
1|something
2|something else
sqlite>
```

The autoincrement feature is very useful because through it the database engine itself guarantees that the key created for a new row is unique. However, it presents a problem that can lead to awkward and clumsy code. When adding a new row to the database, the code may have to read the new row immediately after creating it to discover the key that the database assigned.

Another important constraint that might appear in the column definition is FOREIGN KEY. As noted previously, by default, SQLite does not enforce foreign key constraints. Like the column type, it is essentially a comment. This is demonstrated in Listing 2-8.

LISTING 2-8: The foreign key comment

```
sqlite> create table people (
   ...> name text, address integer references addresses(id));
sqlite> create table addresses (id integer primary key, street text);
sqlite> insert into people values("blake", 99);
sqlite> insert into addresses(street) values ("harpst");
sqlite> select * from people;
blake|99
sqlite> select * from addresses;
1|harpst
sqlite> select * from people, addresses where address = id;
sqlite>
```

In a database that supported referential integrity, the first insert statement would fail with a foreign key constraint violation. In fact, the attempt to create the table in the first create table statement would fail for the same reason.

> **NOTE** *To enable referential integrity support in recent versions of Android, use the pragma:* pragma foreign_keys = true.

Although SQLite does not necessarily enforce referential integrity, the relational concept of a complex type, defined in one table and referenced from others through a foreign key, is central to well designed, easily modified, and efficient data storage. Developers are encouraged to use standard best practices (for example, normalization) when designing SQLite databases. The only difference is that the code accessing the database must be prepared to enforce referential integrity constraints itself instead of depending on the database to do it. Listing 2-9 extends the example begun in Listing 2-8 by demonstrating a simple join.

LISTING 2-9: A simple join

```
sqlite> insert into addresses(street) values("pleasant");
sqlite> insert into addresses(street) values("western");
sqlite> insert into people values ("catherine", 2);
sqlite> insert into people values ("john", 3);
sqlite> insert into people values ("lenio", 3);
sqlite> select name,street from people, addresses where address = id;
catherine|pleasant
john|western
lenio|western
```

In this example there is one person who lives on Pleasant Street but there are two who live on Western Avenue. There is, however, only one record in the addresses table for the street named western. The data is not duplicated. The foreign key in the people table refers to the single record that holds the address of the two people who live on Western Avenue.

SQLite supports several other column constraints. They are illustrated in Listing 2-10.

➤ unique: When this constraint is applied to a column, SQLite will refuse any attempt to add a row to the table that would result in some value appearing in the column more than once.

➤ not null: When this constraint is applied to a column, SQLite will refuse to perform any operation that would cause the value in the constrained row to be NULL.

➤ check(*expression*): When this constraint is applied to a column, the expression is evaluated whenever a new row is added to the table, or when an existing row is modified. If the result of the evaluation is 0 when cast as an integer, the attempt fails and is aborted. If the expression evaluates to NULL or any other non-zero value, the operation succeeds.

LISTING 2-10: Column constraints

```
sqlite>  create table test (
   ...> c1 text unique, c2 text not null, c3 text check(c3 in ("OK", "dandy")));
sqlite> insert into test values("dandy", "dandy", "dandy");
sqlite> insert into test values("dandy", "dandy", "dandy");
Error: column c1 is not unique
sqlite> insert into test values("dandy", null, "dandy");
Error: test.c2 may not be NULL
sqlite> insert into test values("dandy", "dandy", "bad");
Error: constraint failed
sqlite>
```

An Example SQLite Database

Now that you've explored some of the idiosyncrasies of SQLite, you are ready to work a complete example: a simple contacts database. First create the contacts table:

```
sqlite> create table contacts (
   ...> _id integer primary key autoincrement,
   ...> name text not null);
sqlite>
```

The name of the primary key column is determined by an Android system requirement (more about that in the next chapter). Perhaps, after a moment's consideration, it seems like a great idea to add a column to the table, to record the time at which a contact's information was last changed. That is accomplished with an additional column and a pair of triggers:

```
sqlite> alter table contacts add last_modified text;
sqlite> create trigger t_contacts_audit_i
   ...> after insert on contacts begin
   ...> update contacts set last_modified=datetime('now', 'utc')
   ...> where rowid = new.rowid;
   ...> end;
sqlite> create trigger t_contacts_audit_u
   ...> after update on contacts begin
   ...> update contacts set last_modified=datetime('now', 'utc')
   ...> where rowid = new.rowid;
   ...> end;
sqlite>
```

Now try adding a record to verify that things are working so far:

```
sqlite> insert into contacts(name) values("Dianne");
sqlite> select * from contacts;
1|Dianne|2012-06-30 08:29:18
sqlite>
```

Perfect! The contacts need addresses. You can create a table for those:

```
sqlite> create table addresses(
   ...> _id integer primary key autoincrement,
   ...> number integer not null,
   ...> unit text,
   ...> street text not null,
   ...> city integer references cities);
sqlite>
```

As noted previously, if referential integrity support had been enabled, this table definition would cause an error because the cities table does not exist. In SQLite's default configuration, however, it is not a problem: You can define it later.

What's missing is a way to connect contacts to their addresses. In order to do that, you need one more table:

```
sqlite> create table contact_addresses(
   ...> contact integer references contacts,
   ...> address integer references addresses);
sqlite>
```

You can now add data:

```
sqlite> insert into contacts(name) values("Guy");
sqlite> insert into contacts(name) values("Chet");
sqlite> insert into contacts(name) values("Tim");
sqlite> insert into addresses(number, street)
   ...> values(651, "North 34th Street");
sqlite> insert into addresses(number, street)
   ...> values(345, "Spear Street");
```

```
sqlite> insert into addresses(number, street)
   ...> values(1600, "Amphitheatre Parkway");
sqlite> select * from contacts;
1|Dianne|2012-06-30 09:46:42
2|Guy|2012-06-30 09:46:42
3|Chet|2012-06-30 09:46:42
4|Tim|2012-06-30 09:46:42
sqlite> select * from addresses;
1|651||North 34th Street|
2|345||Spear Street|
3|1600||Amphitheatre Parkway|
sqlite> insert into  contact_addresses(contact, address) values(1,1);
sqlite> insert into  contact_addresses(contact, address) values(2,2);
sqlite> insert into  contact_addresses(contact, address) values(3,3);
sqlite> insert into  contact_addresses(contact, address) values(4,2);
sqlite>
```

The contacts now have addresses. You can see those addresses using a `join` query:

```
sqlite> select name, number, street
   ...> from contacts, addresses, contact_addresses
   ...> where contacts._id = contact_addresses.contact
   ...> and addresses._id = contact_addresses.address;
Dianne|651|North 34th Street
Guy|345|Spear Street
Chet|1600|Amphitheatre Parkway
Tim|345|Spear Street
sqlite>
```

Perhaps you would like to determine how many contacts are to be found at each address. That can be done using the `count` function and the `group by` clause:

```
sqlite> select count(name), number, street
   ...> from contacts, addresses, contact_addresses
   ...> where contacts._id = contact_addresses.contact
   ...> and addresses._id = contact_addresses.address
   ...> group by number, street;
2|345|Spear Street
1|651|North 34th Street
1|1600|Amphitheatre Parkway
sqlite>
```

Perhaps, now that you know how many contacts are at each address, you want to show a new list of contacts ordered by their address. In a small database like this, that is no problem. On the other hand, if there are a lot of addresses and you are going to use the address number and street as a sort key, you should probably create an index. An index simply optimizes the process of finding a specific value in the indexed columns. It does this at the expense of the space needed to store the index and the time needed to update it on write operations. Columns (or sets of columns) that don't change often and are frequently used as selection or sort criteria are good candidates for indices. You can now create indices on both contacts' names and addresses.

```
sqlite> create index t_contacts_name on contacts(name);
sqlite> create index t_addresses_num_street on addresses(number,street);
sqlite>
```

Take a look at that list of contacts again, this time organized by address:

```
sqlite> select number, street, name
   ...> from contacts, addresses, contact_addresses
   ...> where contacts._id = contact_addresses.contact
   ...> and addresses._id = contact_addresses.address
   ...> order by number asc, street desc, name asc;
345|Spear Street|Guy
345|Spear Street|Tim
651|North 34th Street|Dianne
1600|Amphitheatre Parkway|Chet
sqlite>
```

Suppose that one of the contacts moves to a new address. Perhaps you want to keep track of your contacts' current addresses, as well as their previous ones. You might do that by adding a new column to the contact_addresses table, called moved_in, to record the date on which a contact arrives at a particular address.

```
   ...> alter table contact_addresses add moved_in text;
sqlite>
```

Notice that the type of the new field to be used as a timestamp is text. The standard way to represent a timestamp in SQLite is as a text field within which times are represented by fixed format strings.

> **NOTE** *There is more information about standard representations of time formats here:* http://www.sqlite.org/lang_datefunc.html

This code places a default value for the move in date into all of the records already in the database:

```
sqlite> update contact_addresses set moved_in=datetime(0, 'unixepoch');
sqlite> select * from contact_addresses;
1|1|1970-01-01 00:00:00
2|2|1970-01-01 00:00:00
3|3|1970-01-01 00:00:00
4|2|1970-01-01 00:00:00
sqlite>
```

Now you can move the contact Guy from Spear Street to Amphitheatre Parkway:

```
sqlite> insert into contact_addresses(contact, address, moved_in)
   ...> values(2, 3, datetime("2012-05-01"));
sqlite> select * from contact_addresses order by contact desc, moved_in asc;
4|2|1970-01-01 00:00:00
3|3|1970-01-01 00:00:00
2|2|1970-01-01 00:00:00
2|3|2012-05-01 00:00:00
1|1|1970-01-01 00:00:00
sqlite>
```

Notice that there are now two records in the `contact_addresses` table for contact 2, one much more recent than the other. A query similar to the last will show all of Guy's addresses:

```
sqlite> select name, number, street, moved_in
   ...> from contacts, addresses, contact_addresses
   ...> where contacts._id = contact_addresses.contact
   ...> and addresses._id = contact_addresses.address
   ...> order by name asc, moved_in desc;
Chet|1600|Amphitheatre Parkway|1970-01-01 00:00:00
Dianne|651|North 34th Street|1970-01-01 00:00:00
Guy|1600|Amphitheatre Parkway|2012-05-01 00:00:00
Guy|345|Spear Street|1970-01-01 00:00:00
Tim|345|Spear Street|1970-01-01 00:00:00
sqlite>
```

Using the `having` clause, you can show only contacts that have moved at least once:

```
sqlite> select name, number, street
   ...> from contacts, addresses, contact_addresses
   ...> where contacts._id = contact_addresses.contact
   ...> and addresses._id = contact_addresses.address
   ...> group by name
   ...> having count(contacts._id) > 1
   ...> order by name desc;
Guy|1600|Amphitheatre Parkway
sqlite>
```

And, finally, with a sub-select, you can show only each contact's most recent address:

```
sqlite> select name, number, street
   ...> from contacts, addresses, contact_addresses
   ...> where contacts._id = contact_addresses.contact
   ...> and addresses._id = contact_addresses.address
   ...> and moved_in = (
   ...> select max(moved_in)
   ...> from contact_addresses
   ...> where contact = contacts._id)
   ...> order by name desc;
Tim|345|Spear Street
Guy|1600|Amphitheatre Parkway
Dianne|651|North 34th Street
Chet|1600|Amphitheatre Parkway
```

At this point, the database schema looks like this:

```
sqlite> .schema
CREATE TABLE addresses(
_id integer primary key autoincrement,
number integer not null,
unit text,
street text not null,
city integer references cities);
CREATE TABLE contact_addresses(
contact integer references contacts,
address integer references addresses,
moved_in text);
CREATE TABLE contacts (
```

```
    _id integer primary key autoincrement,
name text not null, last_modified text);
CREATE INDEX t_addresses_num_street on addresses(number, street);
CREATE INDEX t_contacts_name on contacts(name);
CREATE TRIGGER contacts_audit_i
after insert on contacts begin
update contacts set last_modified=datetime('now', 'utc')
where rowid = new.rowid;
end;
CREATE TRIGGER contacts_audit_u
after update on contacts begin
update contacts set last_modified=datetime('now', 'utc')
where rowid = new.rowid;
end;
sqlite>
```

Although simple, this example demonstrates many of the concepts used in even very complex databases. The next chapter shows you how to harness these concepts in an Android application.

SUMMARY

In the first half of this chapter, you reviewed some of the essential concepts that underlie relational database systems:

➤ Relations (tables), cross-products (joins), projections, and restrictions

➤ The SQL language: data definition, manipulation, and queries

➤ Transactions, data typing, and referential integrity

Many of these concepts will be familiar to experienced enterprise system developers. Android, however, is among the first platforms to bring them to a mobile environment and they may be new even to very experienced mobile systems developers.

In the second half of this chapter you met SQLite, Android's mechanism for storing structured data. While SQLite speaks SQL, it is not at all the kind of RDBMS with which most enterprise developers are familiar. Rather, it is a library included in an application that allows the application to efficiently and safely manage structured data stored in a file. However, its support for data typing and referential integrity is limited.

3

Android Database Support

WHAT'S IN THIS CHAPTER?

➤ Learning about SQL support in Android

➤ Understanding SQL from Java: The SQLiteDatabase class

➤ Creating a database: The SQLiteOpenHelper class

➤ Understanding loaders, cursors, and adapters

WROX.COM CODE DOWNLOADS FOR THIS CHAPTER

Please note that all the code examples in this chapter are available at `https://github.com/wileyenterpriseandroid/Examples.git` and as a part of the book's code download at `www.wrox.com` on the Download Code tab.

The previous chapter introduced SQLite and demonstrated its use from a command line on the Android platform. This chapter extends the demonstration to show the use of SQLite from an application.

In order to use local, structured data from an application, it is necessary to do several things:

➤ Embed SQL commands in application code and execute them at run time.

➤ Create, initialize, and update databases as needed.

➤ Select a database lifecycle management strategy appropriate for an application.

➤ Parse the data obtained from queries for use in an application.

SQL IN JAVA: THE SQLITEDATABASE CLASS

Chapter 2 demonstrated the use of SQLite from the command line. In order to be useful as part of an application, however, it must be possible to embed SQL in the Java code that composes an application. The Android library provides the SQLiteDatabase class for this purpose.

Running SQL queries against a SQLite database, from Java code, requires an instance of the SQLiteDatabase class. You'll see in the next section how to get such an instance. This section shows the basics of how to use the instance, once you have it. Here, you will see how the instance methods provide basic, low-level access to a database.

Basic SQL Embedding

The simplest and most representative of the SQLiteDatabase methods is execSQL. It takes as an argument a single string containing arbitrary SQL and executes that string as a query against the attached database. This is, in general, how SQL code is embedded in an application: The SQL is expressed as a Java string and then passed to a synchronous method for execution. When the method returns, the SQL has been executed. Nearly all of the SQL statements demonstrated in the previous chapter can be executed in this way. Here, for example, is Java code that executes a single SQL statement that creates a database table:

```
db.execSQL("create table pets(name text, age integer)");
```

If executed successfully, this Java code will create the new table named pets with two columns in the attached database.

There are some limitations to keep in mind when using the Android SQL APIs. The first of these limitations — and this particular limitation isn't specific to the execSQL method — is that the SQLite "dot" commands introduced in the previous chapter (for example, .help, .schema, .table, and .exit) are not SQL. They are artifacts of the sqlite3 command-line interpreter and cannot be used from application code.

Another limitation that applies across the entire Android SQLite API — one that might be particularly surprising in the context of the execSQL method — is that multiple SQL statements cannot be batched in a single method call. The string passed to execSQL as an argument should contain exactly one SQL statement. If it contains more than one statement (probably separated by semicolons), all of the statements after the first semicolon are silently ignored.

A final and perhaps obvious limitation, specific to executing SQL statements from the execSQL method, is that the method has no means of returning a value. Even if it were possible to run a SQL query using execSQL, it would be pointless to do so because there is no way to get programmatic access to the query results. In fact, when a statement executed by the execSQL method does return data, the method throws a SQLiteException with an error message indicating that a query statement should be run using a different method.

The most generic method that returns a result is the rawQuery method. It can be used to execute SQL that returns a result and to recover that result programmatically. As an example, consider an application that requires the ability to determine, at run time, the structure of a table in an open database: It needs something roughly equivalent to the .schema <tablename> command implemented by the sqlite3 CLI. An implementation of this requirement might use `rawQuery` and SQLite's `pragma table_info` command, like this:

```
Cursor c = db.rawQuery("pragma table_info(" + tableName + ")", null);
```

This query is a bit far-fetched, perhaps, because applications are unlikely ever to connect to a database whose structure is not well known. The point, however, is that `rawQuery` is an analog to `execSQL`: It provides a way to execute arbitrary SQL that returns data. That data is returned — as it is from most SQLite API methods — as a cursor. Cursors are discussed in detail later in this chapter.

In general, `execSQL` and `rawQuery` are both blunt instruments. Rather than being general tools for programmatic execution of SQL, they should, instead, be used as last resorts to access infrequently used SQL that is not addressed elsewhere in the Android SQLite API. The `execSQL` method's chief use, as will become clear in a moment, is building a new database. Most developers will probably never use `rawQuery`.

Before moving away from these low-level methods, you should examine one more generic API pattern. Both execSQL and rawQuery take a third argument (it is optional for `execSQL`), called `bindArgs`. As an example of why `bindArgs` is valuable, consider this naive code — incorrect for many reasons, but intended to clean old records for a given individual from the database:

```
db.execSQL("delete from people where name='" + person
    + "' and added_date < "
    + String.valueOf(System.currentTimeMillis() - HISTORY));
```

Now consider what happens if the variable `person` contains the value `fred';`. Remember that the `execSQL` method simply ignores any text that appears after a semicolon. When executed, this code will delete all of the records for `fred` instead of just a few historical records. This is a very simple example of the problem that is at the root of the by now very familiar SQL-injection database attack.

This kind of error can be avoided by using `bindArgs`. The SQLite API provides a way of replacing parameter characters (`?` and `?NNN`) in a SQL expression with the values specified as `bindArgs`. This binding is subject to syntactical checks and is thus much less vulnerable to the kind of security issue demonstrated in this section. For more information on using SQL parameters in SQLite, see `http://www.sqlite.org/lang_expr.html#varparam`.

Syntactic SQL

Instead of embedding SQL in application code as unchecked, untyped strings, the Android SQLite API hoists the semantics of SQL into API methods. As you might expect, most of these methods fall into one of four families: insert, update, delete, and query. There are, in addition, a couple of convenience methods and several management methods.

Delete

The smallest of the families is the delete-related methods. In fact, it contains exactly one method: `delete`. It is instructive to review the arguments to the `delete` method because they establish another pattern used throughout the API.

Before reviewing the method arguments, though, you should note that the two methods on the `SQLiteDatabase` object, `create` and `delete`, are not opposites! The `create` method creates a new database. Its opposite is `deleteDatabase`. Most developers will never use either. The `delete` method executes a SQL `delete` statement that, conditionally, deletes rows from a specific table in the database. Its opposite is `insert`.

In general, again, statements in the SQL language have a syntax that defines clauses. This structure is frequently highlighted when SQL statements are pretty-printed, as were some of the examples in the previous chapter. Here is an example of a pretty-printed `delete` statement:

```
DELETE
    FROM pets
    WHERE age > 10 AND age < 20
```

The pattern within the Android `SQLiteDatabase` API is that the first part of this statement, in this case, the `DELETE`, is supplied by the method itself — the `delete` method produces a `DELETE` statement, the `insert` method produces an `INSERT` statement, and so on.

The subclauses for the statement are, each, separate arguments to the method. They are specified without the keyword that introduces them in SQL. For instance, the previous pretty-printed example could be embedded in Java as:

```
db.delete("pets", "age > 10 AND age < 20", null);
```

Aside from preventing minor misspellings (`deleet` for `delete` or something), this code isn't really a dramatic improvement over `execSQL`. It is simply a convenience method that is transformed, quite literally, into the `execSQL` version. The third argument, however, is the `bindArgs` feature, and makes the `delete` statement significantly safer. Given a table:

```
CREATE TABLE pets(name text, age integer)
INSERT INTO pets VALUES("linus", 14)
INSERT INTO pets VALUES("fellini", 15)
INSERT INTO pets VALUES("totoro", 8)
```

The following method call will successfully delete two rows from the database, leaving only the row for "totoro":

```
db.delete("pets", "age = ? OR name = ?", new String[] {"15", "linus"});
```

Although it does not support the named arguments described in the SQLite documentation, the Android API does support numbered arguments. This method call has exactly the same effect as the previous one:

```
db.delete("pets", "age = ?2 OR name = ?1", new String[] {"linus", "15"});
```

Update

The family of methods that implement database updates is also very small. It includes two methods, `update` and `updateWithOnConflict`. They introduce a new syntactic constraint in the form of a new type, `ContentValues`. `ContentValues` provides a binding from a column name to its value. For instance, the SQL statement:

```
UPDATE pets
    SET age = 99
    WHERE name = "linus" OR name = "fellini"
```

would be coded using the Android SQLite API as follows:

```
ContentValues newAges = new ContentValues();
newAges.put("age", Integer.valueOf(99));
db.update(
    "pets",
    newAges,
    "name = ? OR name = ?",
    new String[] {"linus", "fellini"});
```

Again, the interface extensions appropriately enforce structure. The SQL statement that the library actually prepares for execution looks like this:

```
UPDATE pets SET age = ? WHERE name = ? OR name = ?
bindArgs: 99, "linus", "fellini"
```

The other update method, updateWithOnConflict, supports the SQLite ON CONFLICT clause (see http://www.sqlite.org/lang_conflict.html), which controls behavior when statement execution would violate a UNIQUE or NOT NULL constraint. This can happen, for instance, when an update statement attempts to set the primary key for some row to a value that is already the primary key for some other row. Although the choice of a conflict resolution algorithm can affect the method's return value (or the exceptions it throws), it is primarily something that is passed to the SQLite engine and not explicitly handled by the Android SQLite library. In particular, calling updateWithOnConflict, specifying CONFLICT_IGNORE, does not guarantee that no SQLiteException will be thrown. The SQLiteException is an unchecked exception and can be thrown by nearly any method in the Android SQLite API. The documentation for the SQLiteDatabase class mentions it only haphazardly: There are many situations in which it could be thrown that are not described there.

Insert

The insert family of methods is nearly identical to the update family: Its methods take as arguments the name of the database they must update and a ContentValues object mapping column names to values. There are a few small differences, however. Perhaps oddly, the insert methods, alone among the statement execution methods, catch and discard any SQLiteException thrown by underlying code. They return an error value of -1 to indicate failure. To get behavior that is analogous to the behaviors of the delete and update methods, use insertOrThrow. Here is an example of an insert:

```
ContentValues newPet = new ContentValues();
newPet.put("name", "luna");
newPet.put("age", 99);
db.insert("pets", null, newPet);
```

The replace method is also a member of the insert family. It is a convenience method that is translated to a call to insert using the OR REPLACE ON CONFLICT algorithm for resolving constraint violations. The replace method will insert a new row, if the insertion does not cause a conflict. If the insertion would cause a conflict, existing rows are replaced by new values. The behavior of this method can be surprising. Consider the following dataset:

```
CREATE TABLE test(id integer primary key, key text unique, val text unique)
INSERT INTO test VALUES(1, "foo", "foo")
INSERT INTO test VALUES(2, "bar", "bar")
```

Running the following code:

```
ContentValues newTest = new ContentValues();
newTest.put("key", "bar");
newTest.put("val", "foo");
db.replace("test", null, newTest);
```

results in the following:

```
sqlite> select * from test;
3|foo|bar
```

Although this particular sample code, simple as it is, does not generate any exceptions, clearly the deletion of two rows and the disappearance of the two associated primary keys could cause all sorts of foreign key constraints to be violated. *Caveat emptor.*

Query

The query family of methods is, by virtue of being most complex, the largest. Including the `rawQuery` methods that you met earlier in the chapter and the methods on the `SQLiteQueryBuilder` class, there are a total of 13 query methods.

To begin, Listing 3-1 shows an example of a SQL query, with all of its clauses.

LISTING 3-1: A complete query

```
SELECT table1.name, sum(table2.price)
    FROM table1, table2
    WHERE table1.supplier = table2.id AND table1.type = "spigot"
    GROUP BY table1.name
    HAVING sum(table2.price) < 50
    ORDER BY table1.name ASC
    LIMIT 100
```

Each of the clauses is represented by its own argument in the query methods:

➤ `table` — The FROM clause: a table to query

➤ `columns` — A list of columns to be included in the result: the projection

➤ `selection`, `selectionArgs` — The WHERE clause and its arguments

➤ `groupBy` — The GROUP BY clause

➤ `having` — The HAVING clause

➤ `orderBy` — The ORDER BY clause

An empty or non-existent clause can be represented by a Java null value. Analogous to the `insert` and `update` statements, the WHERE clause in the query method is specified using two method arguments: `selection` and `selectionArgs`. The string passed as the selection can contain parameter tokens (such as ? or ?NNN), which are replaced by the corresponding values from the `selectionArgs` array. Here is a very simple query on the `pets` database:

GORDIE

```
sor c = db.query(
 "pets",
 new String[] { "name", "age" },
 "age > ?",
 new String[] { "50" },
 null, // group by
 null, // having
 "name ASC");
```

There are four additional arguments, available on overloaded variations of the query method. They are listed here in roughly decreasing order of normal use:

➤ limit — Maximum number of rows to be returned in the query

➤ distinct — A standard SQL keyword that causes the query to return only one instance of each row meeting the selection criteria, even if there are several such rows in the queried table

➤ CancellationSignal — An object that can cancel the query to which it is passed

➤ cursorFactory — Allows the use of custom implementations of the cursor

Even the full version of the SQLiteDatabase query method, however, with all 11 of its arguments, cannot accommodate a UNION query. To do that, it is necessary to use the SQLiteQueryBuilder.

The query builder is not an elegant tool. In the end, it basically concatenates clause strings together to build a query string. It also has several bells and whistles that can be a bit confusing. Although it is one of the few tools available for constructing generic complex queries, its API suggests that it was designed not as a general-purpose query tool but rather as a means of handling queries for a content provider (discussed in detail in Chapter 4). It does facilitate the task of constructing JOIN and UNION queries.

Consider the following database:

```
CREATE TABLE vals(id integer PRIMARY KEY, val text)
CREATE TABLE keys(key text, fk integer references ref(id))
INSERT INTO vals VALUES(1, 'bar')
INSERT INTO vals VALUES(2, 'baz')
INSERT INTO vals VALUES(3, 'zqx3')
INSERT INTO vals VALUES(4, 'quux')
INSERT INTO keys VALUES('one', 1)
INSERT INTO keys VALUES('one', 4)
INSERT INTO keys VALUES('two', 2)
INSERT INTO keys VALUES('two', 3)
```

This code uses the SQLiteQueryBuilder to construct and execute a query on a join of its two tables:

```
SQLiteQueryBuilder qb = new SQLiteQueryBuilder();
qb.setTables("keys k INNER JOIN vals v ON k.fk = v.id");
Cursor c = qb.query(db,
    new String[] {"k.key AS kk", "v.val AS vv"},
    "kk = ?",
    new String[] { "two" },
    null,
    null,
    "vv DESC",
    null);
```

The actual query run by this bit of code looks like this:

```
SELECT k.key AS kk, v.val AS vv
    FROM keys k INNER JOIN vals v ON k.fk = v.id
    WHERE (kk = ?)
    ORDER BY vv DESC
```

And its output is as follows:

```
two|zqx3
two|baz
```

Note, first of all, that this query supports the, by now familiar, separation of selection clause from the arguments to the clause. Once again, expression parameters, represented by ?NNN (a question mark followed by between 0 and 3 digits), are replaced by their corresponding values from the selectionArgs array. This substitution is performed by SQLite and is fairly resistant to misuse. The query builder actually performs one other safety check on the WHERE clause, verifying that it is syntactically correct both as given and when wrapped in parentheses (that is, both expr and (expr)). The idea is that it is extremely difficult (if not completely impossible) to construct a devious selection clause that produces a correct SQL expression both ways.

Next, note that the query builder allows the construction of complex queries. Because it is basically just concatenating strings together, it is largely agnostic as to what is in those strings. The previous query, for instance, could also be written as follows:

```
SQLiteQueryBuilder qb = new SQLiteQueryBuilder();
qb.setTables("keys k, vals v");
Cursor c = qb.query(db,
    new String[] {"k.key as kk", "v.val as vv"},
    "k.fk = v.id AND kk = ?",
    new String[] { "two" },
    null,
    null,
    "vv DESC",
    null);
```

In which case, the actual query looks like this:

```
SELECT k.key as kk, v.val as vv
    FROM keys k, vals v
    WHERE (k.fk = v.id AND kk = ?)
    ORDER BY vv DESC
```

The features demonstrated thus far make the query builder sufficient to create nearly any query needed in application code. As mentioned, there is also a facility to produce a UNION query that is not explored here. The query builder provides some measure of safety both against syntactic errors and against the injection of malicious code by a client in the SQL it constructs.

> **NOTE** *Actually, there is one more tool in the query builder suite, the* ProjectionMap. *That tool is discussed in the context in which it is most relevant, a content provider, in Chapter 4.*

Other Tools

In addition to the four main statement families, the SQLiteDatabase object supports several other methods. A significant number of these methods are used to manage transactions.

Code that must manage its own transactions will do so using something like the following template:

```
db.beginTransaction();
try {
    // sql...
    db.setTransactionSuccessful();
}
finally {
    db.endTransaction();
}
```

In other words, any transaction that is not explicitly marked as successful is rolled back. The SQLiteDatabase object supports all of the SQLite transaction types (documented here: http://www.sqlite.org/lang_transaction.html).

There is one other method that deserves some special attention: setForeignKeyConstraintsEnabled. As noted in the previous chapter, the Android build of SQLite disables foreign key constraints by default. As of API level 16, Jelly Bean, the setForeignKeyConstraintsEnabled method allows an application to enable the constraints programmatically. The new method replaces the previous means of achieving the same effect, which worked as far back as API level 7, Eclair, executing the pragma PRAGMA foreign_keys=true.

Most of the other methods on the SQLiteDatabase object manage, create, or delete the file that contains the database. The Android library has a much more convenient tool for that purpose, called SQLiteOpenHelper.

Creating a Database: The SQLiteOpenHelper Class

In a typical web service, creating a database is likely to be a distinct, infrequent, and substantial task. Designing, tuning, maintaining, and updating a database on an engine hosting several can be very specialized work. An organization might even employ an entire, separate segment of its engineering staff, database administrators, to do such work. Regardless of who does the work, creating the database is certainly part of the installation of the application and not part of its execution.

In a mobile application, things are different. When a user installs a new application, that application is going to have to bootstrap itself into existence. The application bundle is all there is. If a database is necessary, the application is going to have to create it. The SQLiteOpenHelper class is Android's hedge against this edge case.

SQLiteOpenHelper is a template class — it is abstract. To use it, you must create a subclass. There will be one such subclass for each database managed by your application.

The subclass typically has a constructor that takes only a single argument, the context. The constructor for SQLiteOpenHelper, itself, however, takes at least four arguments. In order to make this work, the subclass defines several constants — including the name of the file to contain the database and its current version — and passes them to the super constructor. For instance, an application that is currently using version 6 of a database stored in the file keyval.db, might look something like this:

```
public class KeyValHelper extends SQLiteOpenHelper {
    public static final String DB_FILE = "keyval.db";
    public static final int VERSION = 6;
    // ...

    public KeyValHelper(Context context) {
        super(context, DB_FILE, null, VERSION);
    }
    // ...
}
```

When application code requests a new instance of this database from the helper, the helper first checks to see if the database file exists. If there is no such file, it creates it, using the name passed as the second argument to the constructor (a name that, by convention, ends with the suffix .db). Next, it calls onCreate, one of its three template methods. The subclass implementation of this method is responsible for completely creating the necessary schema in the newly created database file. The code shown in Listing 3-2, for example, creates and initializes the key/value database used in the examples in the previous section of the chapter.

LISTING 3-2: The SQLOpenHelper onCreate method

```
@Override
public void onCreate(SQLiteDatabase db) {
    ContentValues vals = new ContentValues();
    db.execSQL("CREATE TABLE " + TAB_VALS
        + "(" + COL_ID + " integer PRIMARY KEY,"
        + KeyValContract.Columns.VAL +  " text)");
    vals.put(COL_ID, 1);
    vals.put(KeyValContract.Columns.VAL, "bar");
    db.insert(TAB_VALS, null, vals);
    vals.clear();
    vals.put(COL_ID, 2);
    vals.put(KeyValContract.Columns.VAL, "baz");
    db.insert(TAB_VALS, null, vals);
    vals.clear();
    vals.put(COL_ID, 3);
    vals.put(KeyValContract.Columns.VAL, "zqx3");
    db.insert(TAB_VALS, null,  vals);
    vals.clear();
    vals.put(COL_ID, 4);
    vals.put(KeyValContract.Columns.VAL, "quux");
    db.insert(TAB_VALS, null, vals);
    vals.clear();

    db.execSQL("CREATE TABLE " + TAB_KEYS + "("
        + KeyValContract.Columns.KEY + " text, "
        + COL_FK + " integer references ref(" + COL_ID + "))");
    vals.put(KeyValContract.Columns.KEY, "one");
    vals.put(COL_FK, 1);
```

```
        db.insert(TAB_KEYS, null, vals);
        vals.clear();
        vals.put(KeyValContract.Columns.KEY, "one");
        vals.put(COL_FK, 4);
        db.insert(TAB_KEYS, null, vals);
        vals.clear();
        vals.put(KeyValContract.Columns.KEY, "two");
        vals.put(COL_FK, 2);
        db.insert(TAB_KEYS, null, vals);
        vals.clear();
        vals.put(KeyValContract.Columns.KEY, "two");
        vals.put(COL_FK, 3);
        db.insert(TAB_KEYS, null, vals);
    }
```

An application should *always* use the database's helper object to obtain an instance of a database. By doing so, it guarantees that the instance it holds is complete, initialized, and ready for use.

> **WARNING** *Do not call* getReadableDatabase *or* getWriteableDatabase *from an implementation of the* onCreate *method! Suppose, for instance, that you intend to expose the ability to insert keys and values into the database from Listing 3-2 using methods like this:*
>
> ```
> void insertKey(String key, int fk) {
>     ContentValues r = new ContentValues();
>     r.put(KeyValContract.Columns.KEY, key);
>     r.put(COL_FK, Integer.valueOf(fk));
>     getWriteableDatabase().insert(TAB_KEYS, null, r);
> }
>
> void insertVal(String val, int id) {
>     ContentValues r = new ContentValues();
>     r.put(COL_ID, Integer.valueOf(id));
>     r.put(KeyValContract.Columns.VAL, val);
>     getWriteableDatabase().insert(TAB_VALS, null, r);
> }
> ```
>
> *Realizing that the extremely verbose implementation of* onCreate *could be improved dramatically by using these methods, you write:*
>
> ```
> @Override
> public void onCreate(SQLiteDatabase db) {
>     db.execSQL("CREATE TABLE " + TAB_VALS + "("
>         + COL_ID + " integer PRIMARY KEY,"
>         + KeyValContract.Columns.VAL + " text)");
>     // DON'T DO THIS!!!
>     insertVal("bar", 1);
>     // ...
> }
> ```
>
> *continues*

continued

This won't work. The call to `getWriteableDatabase` *in* `insertVal` *will cause a recursive loop. An overloaded version of the method that allows* `onCreate` *to pass on the database passed to it as a parameter solves the problem:*

```
public void addVal(int id, String val) {
    addVal(dbHelper.getWriteableDatabase(), id, val);
}
void insertVal(SQLiteDatabase db, String val, int id) {
    ContentValues r = new ContentValues();
    r.put(COL_ID, Integer.valueOf(id));
    r.put(KeyValContract.Columns.VAL, val);
    db.insert(TAB_VALS, null, r);
}
```

The fourth argument to the helper's constructor is the database version. It is an integer and must be greater than 0. When the helper creates the new database, in addition to using the `onCreate` method to initialize it, it also stores the version number in database metadata. In addition to checking for existence, when opening a database, the helper also compares the version number passed in this open attempt against the one that is stored in the metadata. If the version numbers are the same, the open succeeds without further processing. On the other hand, if the version requested by the application (the argument to the constructor) is greater or less than the version number stored in the metadata, the helper invokes the method `onUpgrade` or `onDowngrade`, respectively. These methods are responsible for converting the existing database to the schema requested by the application.

Obviously, the application user does not expect a version change to cost them their stored data. The `onUpgrade` and `onDowngrade` methods must be coded very carefully to assure that they do not corrupt or lose data. The helper object wraps the call to either method in a transaction so that any exception thrown during the transformation will cause it to be rolled back entirely. At least the data won't be completely lost.

> **NOTE** *An important technique, suggested by the documentation, consists of using an* `ALTER_TABLE` *statement to change the name of an existing table, creating a new and correctly configured table with the same name, and then copying data from the old to the new table.*

As mentioned, although foreign key constraints are disabled by default, there are programmatic means for enabling them. The helper object supports two methods that are well suited to making the necessary calls. If the design of an application includes the enforcement of foreign key constraints, your choice of which method is used to implement those constraints might hinge on how the application performs up and downgrades.

➤ The `onConfigure` method is called as soon as the connection to the database has been set up and before `onCreate`, `onUpgrade`, or `onDowngrade`. A call to `setForeignKeyConstraintsEnabled` here will enforce the constraints, all the time, for the entire database.

➤ The onOpen method is called only after onCreate, onUpgrade, and onDowngrade, leaving those methods free to play fast and loose while they rebuild the schema. The occasion in which an application must rename or recreate a table or two during an upgrade might be one of the few times that it is truly a relief that foreign key constraints are not enforced. Enabling foreign key constraints in the onOpen method causes them to be enforced only after the database has been initialized.

As must be apparent by this point, attempting to open a database can take a relatively long time. If the act of getting a database instance requires either creating the schema from scratch or copying over a substantial amount of data, the operation might take several seconds. This is far too long for an operation that runs synchronously, as part of the UI.

The SQLiteOpenHelper class guarantees that its constructor runs very quickly. It is quite safe to create the helper itself, directly, for instance, in response to the push of a button or a selection in the Action Bar. On the other hand, when it comes time to request the actual database instance, using getReadableDatabase or getWriteableDatabase, that action must be performed asynchronously and not on the UI thread.

> **NOTE** *A discussion of Android concurrency tools is out of the scope of this chapter. On the other hand, an essential part of creating a lively, responsive application is understanding those tools and how to use them correctly. Fortunately, Android provides a convenient tool for asynchronously accessing a database, the loader. It is discussed in detail later in this chapter.*

Managing a Database

Before leaving the discussion of the database, you should consider one other topic, lifecycle management. An open database is about 1KB of memory. On a device with memory restrictions, that's enough to be of interest. There are two basic strategies for managing a database from an application:

➤ Get it and keep it

➤ Get it when you need it

The first, get it and keep it, is the simpler of the two strategies and is a very reasonable choice unless there is a case for recovering memory within the application process. If there are substantial periods of time during which an application does not need access to the database — an application with multiple activities, only one of which uses the database, for instance — then holding the database means that the memory it occupies cannot be repurposed.

Don't confuse garbage collection of in-process memory, though, with the Android system's management of process lifecycle! If an application's process is terminated — perhaps because it has been in the background for too long or because too many new applications have been started in front of it — the database, any connections, and everything else that is part of the application memory space are gone. As long as you've left the database in a consistent state — no uncommitted transactions and no open file connections to large objects (BLOBs) — tweaking soon-to-be-deallocated memory is a waste of effort.

Although it is simpler, the get-it-and-keep-it strategy still requires attention. If code simply forgets about the db instance, without explicitly closing it, the garbage collector will collect the instance. That will generate an error message similar to this:

```
09-02 15:27:10.286: E/SQLiteDatabase(16433): close() was never explicitly called on
database '/data/data/net.callmeike.android.sqlitetest/databases/test.db'
09-02 15:27:10.286: E/SQLiteDatabase(16433): android.database.sqlite.
DatabaseObjectNotClosedException: Application did not close the cursor or database
object that was opened here
09-02 15:27:10.286: E/SQLiteDatabase(16433):     at android.database.sqlite.SQLiteD
atabase.<init>(SQLiteDatabase.java:1943)
09-02 15:27:10.286: E/SQLiteDatabase(16433):     at android.database.sqlite.
SQLiteDatabase.openDatabase(SQLiteDatabase.java:1007)

...

09-02 15:27:10.286: E/System(16433): Uncaught exception thrown by finalizer
09-02 15:27:10.297: E/System(16433): java.lang.IllegalStateException: Don't have
database lock!
```

Holding a reference to the database only in an instance variable of an activity will cause this error. When the activity is no longer visible, it is subject to garbage collection. If it holds the only reference to the database, the database will be finalized at the same time without having been closed.

In order to get and keep a database, it is necessary to hold a strong reference to it. To do this, keep the reference in either in a static class variable or an application instance variable. The latter policy — holding the database reference in an application object — is an excellent way to share a database instance across multiple activities. Listing 3-3 is an example of an Application subclass that does this.

LISTING 3-3: Holding a database reference in an Application object

```java
public class KeyValApplication extends Application {
    private KeyValHelper dbHelper;
    private Thread uiThread;

    @Override
    public void onCreate() {
        super.onCreate();

        // ...

        uiThread = Thread.currentThread();
        dbHelper = new KeyValHelper(this);
    }

    public SQLiteDatabase getDb() {
        if (Thread.currentThread().equals(uiThread)) {
            throw new RuntimeException("Database opened on main thread");
        }
        return dbHelper.getWriteableDatabase();
    }
}
```

Note the check in the first few lines of the getDb method that verifies the constraint described earlier in this chapter: The database must not actually be opened on the UI thread.

This code also makes use of another feature of Android's SQLite system. The database helper holds a reference to the database instance that it creates. In terms of memory management, holding a reference to a database helper is equivalent to holding a reference to the database that it opened. Further, closing the database instance (calling its `close` method) simply annoys the helper. The helper's strategy is to create and cache a single database instance and return a reference to that cached instance, in response to each request. If it notices that the instance has been explicitly closed, it must release the cached reference and open a new connection. That is hardly optimal.

You might wonder at the implementation of the `getDb` method, recalling that there are actually two methods on `SQLiteOpenHelper` for obtaining a database: `getReadableDatabase` and `getWriteableDatabase`. It might be a surprise to discover that `getReadableDatabase` usually returns a writeable database.

An application can get a reference to a read-only database only by explicitly requesting one (using `getReadableDatabase`) when for some reason the Android system cannot open a connection to a writeable database. That might happen, for instance, if the file system were full. Normally, however, both methods return a reference to the same, single, cached database object.

Further, there is an interesting corollary to this that explains the implementation of the `getDb` method in Listing 3-3. Consider that an application has, somehow, obtained a reference to a database that is actually read-only. Suppose, now, that the condition that made it impossible to acquire a writeable database clears and that, after the condition clears, the application makes a call to `getWriteableDatabase`. Under these circumstances, the helper will open a new, writeable database connection, and may close the read-only connection. If the application has cached references to the read-only database, further attempts to use them will result in errors. Given these semantics, best practice is to request and use only writeable database instances, unless there is a clear and very time-constrained reason to do otherwise. The implementation of `getDb` in Listing 3-3 does exactly this.

An application for which the second strategy, get it when you need it, is necessary must be aware of all of the objects that might hold references to the database object that it wants to release. Closing the database without releasing all of the references to it accomplishes nothing, of course, because unless the last reference is gone, the database object cannot be garbage collected and its memory re-used. As described previously, the `SQLiteOpenHelper` retains a reference to its database. Both of the classes `SQLiteQuery` and `SQLiteCursor` also retain back pointers to their owner database. It is essential to remember this, even when the query and cursor are managed by a loader, a service introduced in the next section.

CURSORS, LOADERS, AND ADAPTERS

Veterans of Java J2EE development typically find that Android has a familiar feel about it. Applications that don't have clear beginnings and endings and objects that have managed lifecycles are things they know and may even have come to appreciate, if not exactly to love. That familiarity comes to a harsh end, though, at the interface between the DB and UI tiers.

In the Android world, the DB tier is embodied in the `ContentProvider` class, the topic of the next chapter. In the UI, Android's analog for a servlet is the activity. J2EE developers — especially those who have worked for many years with Java EE version 3.0 or later and for whom Spring and Hibernate are old friends — will be expecting some kind of object-relational model as the next step. Think again. In Android, the interface between the UI and DB tiers is CRUD and cursors. The tolerant will call it "REST-like."

Cursors

Cursors are the objects returned from database-query methods, `query` and `rawQuery`. An Android cursor is an in-memory representation of a SQL relation. It is rectangular, with rows and columns. It also has a pointer to a current row, which is often, confusingly, called the cursor. There is only a single current row pointer per cursor, and its value is between -1 and the value returned by the `getCount` method (that is, just before the first row, 0, to just after the last row, count – 1). The row pointer is a mutable part of the cursor state and is accessible for both read and write from all objects with references to the cursor.

Upon return, the new cursor has a row pointer that points just before the first row. Therefore, a common idiom for reading all of the data from a cursor looks like this:

```
while (c.moveToNext()) {
    // get data from a single row
}
```

Because the method `moveToNext` returns `false` if it is pointing at the last row of data in the cursor, this code will loop through all of the rows in the cursor and then terminate. Because the cursor method `getCount` returns the number of rows in the cursor, this same loop could be written, perhaps less expressively, as follows:

```
for (int i = 0; i < c.getCount(); i++) {
    c.moveToPosition(i);
    // get data from a single row
}
```

There are several other methods available for managing the row pointer. The methods `getPosition`, `isFirst`, `isLast`, `isBeforeFirst`, and `isAfterLast` all can be used to find the current location of the row pointer. The methods `moveToPrevious`, `moveToFirst`, `moveToLast`, `moveToPosition` and `move` all set the location of the row pointer. The last two, `moveToPosition` and `move`, set the new position absolutely and with reference to the current position, respectively.

Once the row pointer is set to the row currently of interest, data are extracted from particular columns using their column indices. The columns in a cursor will, in most cases, be exactly those from the projection specified in the call to the `query` method — in most cases, in the order in which they were specified in the query. Nonetheless, the best practice for minimizing the possibility of hard-to-find protocol errors is to use symbolic column names. Reasonably safe code might look something like this:

```
private void getValues(SQLiteDatabase db) {
    Cursor c = db.query(
            KeyValContract.TABLE_KEYVAL,
            new String[] {
                    KeyValContract.Columns.ID,
```

```
                    KeyValContract.Columns.KEY },
                    null, null, null, null, null);
        int idIdx = c.getColumnIndex(KeyValContract.Columns.ID);
        int keyIdx = c.getColumnIndex(KeyValContract.Columns.KEY);
        while (c.moveToNext()) {
            Integer id = getInt(c, idIdx);
            String key = c.getString(keyIdx);
            // ... process the extracted value
        }
    }

    private Integer getInt(Cursor c, int idx) {
        if (c.isNull(idx)) { return null; }
        long n = c.getLong(idx);
        if ((Integer.MAX_VALUE < n) || (Integer.MIN_VALUE > n)) {
            throw new RuntimeException("Not an integer: " + n);
        }
        return Integer.valueOf((int) n);
    }
```

Note the getInt method, which checks to make sure that the value of the numeric column is neither null nor out of range. The official documentation for the cursor object notwithstanding, the data-extraction methods that return primitive types (getDouble, getInt, and so on) do not throw exceptions when the value in a source column is null. Instead they return a zero value. The SQLiteCursor object is implemented using a CursorWindow, and an accurate description of its behavior can be found in the description of that object (http://developer.android.com/reference/android/database/CursorWindow.html). In order to distinguish between missing and actual zero-valued data, the null check is necessary.

In fact, the SQLiteCursor data-extraction methods cannot be trusted to throw exceptions on data conversion errors, either. Although the various methods that extract the data are typed — getString returns a string, getDouble a double, and so on — extracting data from the column is not type-checked. Any value can be retrieved as a string, for instance. An attempt to retrieve an integer value from a column that contains a value greater than Integer.MAX_VALUE will simply cause the actual value to be truncated.

The cursor method getType might be of some help in verifying that the data in a column is of the expected type: It separates values into four categories — null, integer, float, and string. Because it does not distinguish between the integer value 99 and the long value 9999999999, but does distinguish between 99 and its perfectly convertible string representation "99", other means of type-checking, especially for foreign data, are likely to be necessary.

> **NOTE** *Note that cursors do need to be closed. They, like databases, are closeable objects and expect an explicit call to close. Be sure that there is some strategy for managing a cursor's lifecycle. Either close it explicitly, when the required values have been recovered, or make sure that it is managed.*

There is one other important family of methods on the cursor, those concerned with notification and content observers. They are discussed in Chapter 4 in context of content providers and content resolvers.

Adapters and View Binders

The most common means of viewing cursor-based data in the UI is through a list view. The Android `ListView` and its associated convenience classes, `ListActivity` and `ListFragment`, abstract the process of displaying homogenous data from the particular data being displayed. In order to do this they depend on *adapters* and *view binders.*

An adapter maps columns in a cursor to views in a cell of a list view layout. Figure 3-1 illustrates its role.

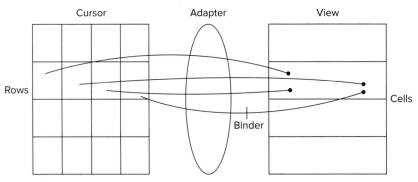

FIGURE 3-1

The Android-supplied `SimpleCursorAdapter` is quite flexible and very easy to use. It is probably sufficient for most applications. To use it, simply create the adapter and pass it to the list view by using the `setAdapter` method. The list view will use the adapter both to identify the values that should be visible in a particular list view cell and also to identify the row in the attached cursor that corresponds to clicks and edits in the view.

The `SimpleCursorAdapter` constructor takes five arguments:

➤ `context` — Usually the activity from which this list is visible.

➤ `layout` — The ID of standard XML layout for a single cell in the list view. This is the target for the cursor data.

➤ `cursor` — The source cursor from which data is obtained. Each row in this cursor corresponds to a cell in the list view and each column to a subview in the cell's layout.

➤ `from` — An ordered list of column names.

➤ `to` — An ordered list of IDs for corresponding subviews of the list cell layout. The contents of column `from[0]` will be placed in view `to[0]`, `from[1]` in `to[1]`, and so on.

For example, the code in Listing 3-4 will generate the screen shown in Figure 3-2, assuming that `keyvalCursor` is the result of querying the database used as an example elsewhere in this chapter.

LISTING 3-4: A simple list view

RES/LAYOUT/KEYVAL_ROW.XML

```xml
<?xml version="1.0" encoding="utf-8"?>
<RelativeLayout
    xmlns:android="http://schemas.android.com/apk/res/android"
    android:layout_width="fill_parent"
    android:layout_height="wrap_content" >

    <TextView
        android:id="@+id/listview_key"
        android:layout_width="wrap_content"
        android:layout_height="wrap_content"
        android:layout_alignParentTop="true"
        android:layout_alignParentLeft="true"
        android:textSize="18sp">
    </TextView>

    <TextView
        android:id="@+id/listview_id"
        android:layout_width="wrap_content"
        android:layout_height="wrap_content"
        android:layout_alignParentTop="true"
        android:layout_alignParentRight="true"
        android:textStyle="bold" >
    </TextView>

    <TextView
        android:id="@+id/listview_val"
        android:layout_width="fill_parent"
        android:layout_height="wrap_content"
        android:layout_below="@id/listview_key"
        android:layout_alignParentLeft="true"
        android:paddingLeft="12dp">
    </TextView>
</RelativeLayout>
```

KEYVALACTIVITY.JAVA

```java
private static final int LOADER_ID = 6;
private static final String[] FROM = new String[] {
    KeyValContract.Columns.ID,
    KeyValContract.Columns.KEY,
    KeyValContract.Columns.VAL
};

private static final int[] TO = new int[] {
    R.id.listview_id,
    R.id.listview_key,
    R.id.listview_val
```

continues

LISTING 3-4 *(continued)*

```
    };

    // ...

    @Override
    protected void onCreate(Bundle savedInstanceState) {
        super.onCreate(savedInstanceState);
        setListAdapter(
            new SimpleCursorAdapter(this, R.layout.row, null, FROM, TO, 0));
        // ...
    }
```

If an adapter is the wiring between the source cursor and the target view, a view binder is a transformation along a wire. By default, an adapter tries to do something sensible with the data it maps. If the target view is a text view, it is easy (recall that the value of any column can be retrieved as a string). Adapters make reasonable choices, as well, if the target is an image view and the source can be interpreted as the resource ID of an image. If the data represents a time since the epoch and needs to be translated into a real date, or a 32-bit ARGB hue representation to be displayed as a color, a custom view binder is the tool for the job.

A quick note about the implementation of a view binder is in order. Remember that the view binder's `setViewValue` method will be called for every sub-view of every cell in the target list. If the list view is to be fast, smooth, and responsive, it is essential that the view binder do its work very quickly. This is one of the few places that extreme optimization is appropriate.

In order for an adapter to work correctly, the cursor to which it is a view must have an integer primary key named `'_id'`. The adapter uses the canonically named column to map view rows to cursor rows. If it cannot find the column, it will throw an exception like this:

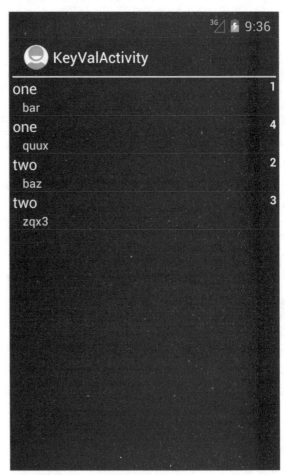

FIGURE 3-2

```
09-03 14:27:50.285: E/AndroidRuntime(2289): FATAL EXCEPTION: main
09-03 14:27:50.285: E/AndroidRuntime(2289): java.lang.IllegalArgumentException:
column '_id' does not exist
```

```
09-03 14:27:50.285: E/AndroidRuntime(2289):    at android.database.AbstractCursor.
getColumnIndexOrThrow(AbstractCursor.java:267)
09-03 14:27:50.285: E/AndroidRuntime(2289):    at android.database.CursorWrapper.
getColumnIndexOrThrow(CursorWrapper.java:78)
```

This does not imply that all tables viewed through list views must have a column named '_id'. There are several alternatives.

If the relation to be viewed has an integer primary key column, my_pk, for instance, that column can be aliased in the query, using a SQL column alias: SELECT my_pk AS _id FROM ....

If the viewed relation does not have an integer primary key, a little SQLite skill may solve the problem. It turns out that rows in SQLite data tables have an implicit column, rowid. The rowid is integer-valued and unique to a row. In most circumstances — anything except many-to-many joins — adding rowid to the projection and renaming it in the query, SELECT rowid AS _id, . . ., makes it possible to view the resulting cursor through a list view.

Loaders

As mentioned earlier, database operations cannot be performed on the UI thread. A slow query, a contended transaction, or a database update might require an amount of time that would cause an intolerable stall in the UI. Recall that the code in Listing 3-3 explicitly checks to see whether a database instance is being requested from the UI thread. It throws an exception if so. The standard Android tool for avoiding such problems, by moving queries off the UI thread is the *loader*.

Loaders appeared in Honeycomb to replace the managed query interface. They are an abstraction of a process that loads data in the background. The subclass of interest here is the CursorLoader, which, given some parameters that specify a database and a query to be made against that database, runs the query on a daemon thread and then publishes the result. Loaders are used in activities or fragments by passing them to the loader manager.

Implementing and using a loader can seem like a study in indirection. What the code actually needs is a cursor to the data. It can't simply ask for the cursor, though, because it might take a significant amount of time to get it and that would excessively delay the UI thread. Instead, it asks the loader manager to initialize a new load process. Again, instead of simply describing the process of getting the cursor to the loader manager, when it requests initialization, the code must pass a reference to an observer. Figure 3-3 diagrams the process.

At some point, the loader manager calls the observer. It is the observer's responsibility to create and return the correct loader. The loader is the object that implements the process of obtaining the cursor. The loader manager runs the loader and, when it completes, again calls the observer, this time with the cursor that the loader returned.

This surprising amount of complexity is necessary, in short, because there is no telling when an activity is suddenly going to become unimportant. Users looking at their contacts might suddenly recall the phone number of the person they intended to call and navigate directly to the phone app. If the loader continues running when that happens, it is wasting battery. Solving this problem of incongruous lifecycles is not impossible but it can be tricky and difficult. Representing the entire load process as an object and letting the loader manager manage its execution is a big win.

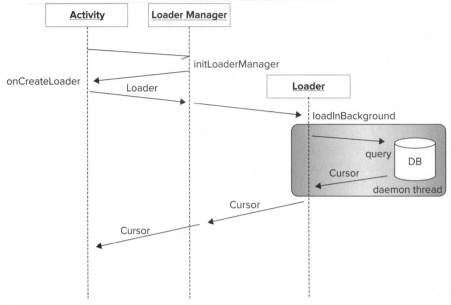

FIGURE 3-3

Here's a simple example of the use of a loader:

```
public class KeyValActivity extends ListActivity
    implements LoaderManager.LoaderCallbacks<Cursor>
{
    private static final int LOADER_ID = 6;
// ...
@Override
    public Loader<Cursor> onCreateLoader(int arg0, Bundle arg1) {
        return new CursorLoader(
                this,
                KeyValContract.URI,
                null, null, null, null);
    }
@Override
    public void onLoadFinished(Loader<Cursor> loader, Cursor c) {
        ((SimpleCursorAdapter) getListAdapter()).swapCursor(c);
    }
@Override
    public void onLoaderReset(Loader<Cursor> arg0) {
        ((SimpleCursorAdapter) getListAdapter()).swapCursor(null);
    }
@Override
    protected void onCreate(Bundle savedInstanceState) {
        // ...
        getLoaderManager().initLoader(LOADER_ID, null, this);
    }
}
```

The onCreate method in the ListViewActivity gets the loader manager and asks it to initialize a new load process. The important thing to note here is the unique identifier, LOADER_ID. The Android system guarantees that there will never be more than one loader with that identifier. This is essential, because if onCreate (or any other lifecycle method) is called again while the loader still exists (remember that their lifecycles are not the same), it would be possible to have multiple loaders in different phases of execution completing the same load process. The unique, per-process identifier eliminates this possibility.

The third argument to initLoader is a reference to the observer that will actually create the loader. In this example, the activity itself will serve as the observer. This is a reasonable consolidation because it is the activity's lifecycle that needs to be synchronized with that of the loader. The second argument to initLoader is a bundle that can be used to supply arguments to the loader, on its creation.

In order to be an observer to the LoaderManager, the ListViewActivity must implement LoaderManager.LoaderCallbacks<Cursor> (Cursor, because the loader will return a cursor). Implementing that interface requires that it implement the three new methods — onCreateLoader, onLoaderFinished, and onLoaderReset.

The first of these methods, onCreateLoader, simply creates the new loader and returns it. The loader that is created in this example is a CursorLoader that requests data from a content provider. The specifics of this request are the subject of the next chapter. For the moment, presume that its interface is very similar to the interface for the database query method: It takes similar arguments and returns a cursor on completion.

The loader manager executes the returned loader asynchronously. When it eventually completes, it returns its cursor. The loader manager then calls the second of the observer's methods, onLoaderFinished, with that cursor. The implementation of the callback quite simply replaces the cursor visible from the list view. If, for some reason — perhaps a phone call or a navigation event — the activity no longer needs to populate the view, the manager calls onLoaderReset. onLoaderReset replaces the cursor with null. Since the loader manager executes the loaders, it can manage the cursors that they return. When onLoaderReset is run the replaced cursor is also closed as necessary.

SUMMARY

In this chapter, you have explored the essentials of using SQL from code. The chapter introduced:

➤ The low-level methods required to execute SQL commands

➤ The tools necessary to create and manage the lifecycle of a database

➤ The cursor object that manages query results

➤ Asynchronous queries, the tools to manage them, and display them in an activity

You now have the tools to manage persistent data on an Android device. Information that must survive even power-cycling can be stored into a SQLite database and recovered quickly and correctly using Android built-in tools like cursors, loaders, adapters, and view binders. Sharing that data across an enterprise, though, requires additional tools. The next chapter introduces the content provider, the architectural component used to share data.

4

Content Providers

WHAT'S IN THIS CHAPTER?

- ➤ Using content providers
- ➤ Publishing a contract: URIs and types
- ➤ Implementing a content provider
- ➤ Controlling access to your content provider with permissions and registration
- ➤ Understanding content provider file operations

WROX.COM CODE DOWNLOADS FOR THIS CHAPTER

Please note that all the code examples in this chapter are available at `https://github.com/wileyenterpriseandroid/Examples.git` and as a part of the book's code download at `www.wrox.com` on the Download Code tab.

Content providers are the foundation for the rest of this book. In this chapter you will meet content providers and the tools used to build them. In addition you are introduced to the REST-like architecture they support and how that architecture enables the use of Android in the enterprise. The application created in this chapter can be found in the project KeyValCP.

The techniques introduced in the previous chapter — creating a globally accessible reference to a database object — might be appropriate for a small application. In more complex applications, however, developers will require better architectural separation between data management and other components of their application.

The Android content provider framework has several parts:

➤ **Contract** — A Java source file that publishes symbols and constants that external processes need to access the provider. External applications include this file as part of their source.

➤ **Content Resolver** — A part of the Android library that uses system-level services to identify the single content provider currently registered as the manager of the dataset corresponding to a given URI. The URI is typically obtained from the contract.

➤ **Content Provider** — The content resolver forwards requests to a content provider. The provider manages a dataset, supplying clients with a consistent view of the data and managing their access to it.

➤ **Content Observer** — The content observer API supports a URI-based notification system, which makes it possible for clients to discover changes in the dataset.

The investigation of content providers starts with a review of their use. Approaching the new component from the top down reveals some interesting architectural issues and motivates the discussion of its implementation that comprises the remainder of the chapter.

USING A CONTENT PROVIDER

The final example in Chapter 3 quietly introduced a content provider: It is the source of the data that is displayed through the simple cursor adapter in the list view. The example code is deceptively simple — it slides the content provider into the example with very little comment. Reexamining the code carefully, though, you can infer some of the essential architectural details of the content provider. There are four of them, as follows.

URIs as Names for Virtual Datasets

Listing 4-1 shows an excerpt from the "Loaders" section of the previous chapter. It's just the snippet in which the cursor loader is created.

LISTING 4-1: Creating a CursorLoader

```
@Override
public Loader<Cursor> onCreateLoader(int id, Bundle params) {
    return new CursorLoader(
        this,
        KeyValContract.URI,
        null, null, null, null);
}
```

There must be a query to the content provider hidden inside the cursor loader created here, because the loader eventually produces a cursor. In order to understand how that might work, let's review the formal parameters for the CursorLoader constructor. They are:

```
CursorLoader(
    Context context,
    Uri uri,
    String[] projection,
    String selection,
    String[] selectionArgs,
    String sortOrder)
```

This should look familiar. Most of the parameters are very similar to those shown in Chapter 3, Listing 3-1. They are the parameters required by the database query method. This cursor loader has — as you might expect — enough information to identify some data source and to perform a query against it. Chapter 3 demonstrated that the cursor created by the loader is passed as the argument to the callback method `onLoadFinished`. In the `KeyVal` example that returned cursor was used to power the list view that is the application's main screen.

While most of the parameters to the two methods (the loader constructor and the database query method) are identical, notice that the database query method (shown in Chapter 3) is a method on a SQLite database object. It takes as its first argument the name of a database table. The first parameter to the loader constructor is instead a URI. If the cursor loader is going to be able to construct a complete query from its parameters, there must be some way for it to identify a database — and a table within that database — from the URI.

This is the first important architectural feature of the content provider: URIs are used as abstract names for virtual datasets. Content providers are identified indirectly, using the URIs that name them. Android reserves URIs with the canonical scheme `content://` for this purpose. The protocol by which a content provider registers the owner of a particular group of URIs is discussed in detail later in this chapter. For now, let's return to exploring the behavior of a content provider by observing it in use.

> **NOTE** *The type hierarchy of the* `CursorLoader`, *a subtype of* `AsyncTaskLoader<D>`, *suggests the creation of other custom loader types. Although this is possible, it is equally clear that the* `CursorLoader` *is more mature than its potential cousins. This long-standing issue:*
>
> `http://code.google.com/p/android/issues/detail?id=14944`
>
> *unresolved at the time of this writing, demonstrates the kinds of problems that developers may encounter when creating custom loaders.*

Content Resolvers: The Link between Clients and Providers

In the example code as it stands, the content provider is used entirely behind the scenes in the cursor loader. All of the details are hidden in its implementation. Adding a new feature to the application will help to reveal some of those details. The implementation of this new feature, a data insert, is very similar to the implementation of the query, shown previously. It moves one step closer to the content provider, though, and requires writing code that was hidden in the loader in that example.

To the application UI, add a pair of text fields and a button, which, when pushed, inserts the contents of the text fields into the database as a new key/value pair. Listing 4-2 shows the essentials of the implementation of the new feature. Only the snippet of code that actually uses the content provider is shown here — as noted, the complete code for all of the examples in the chapter, as well as the rest of the book, are available as a part of this book's download at www.wrox.com.

LISTING 4-2: Using ContentResolver insert

```
private static class AsyncInsert extends AsyncTask<Void, Void, Void> {
    private final Context ctxt;
    private final String key;
    private final String val;

    public AsyncInsert(Context ctxt, String key, String val) {
        this.ctxt = ctxt;
        this.key = key;
        this.val = val;
    }

    @Override
    protected Void doInBackground(Void... params) {
        ContentValues values = new ContentValues();
        values.put(KeyValContract.Columns.KEY, key);
        values.put(KeyValContract.Columns.VAL, val);

        try {
            ctxt.getContentResolver()
                .insert(KeyValContract.URI_KEYVAL, values);
        }
        catch (Exception e) { Log.w("INSERT", "Insert failed", e); }

        return null;
    }
}
```

Because database access is a relatively slow operation, it cannot be performed from the UI thread. The implementation of the new feature must call the content resolver's — and thereby the content provider's — insert method from a non-UI thread. The cursor loader, in its implementation, does exactly the same thing for the query method. AsyncInsert, the class from which the insert call is performed, is based on an AsyncTask, as is the loader.

The new feature uses a new button, added to the view, to submit the new key/value pair for insertion into the database. The code in the button's onClick method (not shown) creates a new instance of the AsyncInsert task and executes it. Unlike the query example, this simple insert is fire-and-forget. The insert task does not return a result and, unlike the loader, does not need a way to notify anyone of its completion. The code in AsyncInsert.doInBackground — the business end of the AsyncInsert class — should look entirely familiar. It is nearly identical to the database insert method, described in Chapter 3. As in the previous examination of the cursor loader, you can infer that the name of the table into which the new values are to be inserted must be encoded in the URI passed as the first argument to the insert method. The new tool introduced here is the

`ContentResolver`. It is obtained from the context. The `insert` method used to add the new key/value pair to the database is a method on this new object.

From this new feature you might deduce that content providers are not, typically, used directly through object references. You do not normally obtain a reference to a content provider object and then call methods on it. Instead, as demonstrated in this code, you obtain a content resolver object from the context and then use it to forward requests to the content provider.

If you were to examine the code for the `CursorLoader`, you would find that, internally it uses the parameters passed to its constructor to make an analogous call to `ContentResolver.query`. This is the second important architectural artifact in the content provider framework. The content resolver is the tool that resolves a content URI into a connection to a specific content provider.

Content Observers: Completing the Loop

The next important architectural feature of a content provider is also already part of the example application and is also hidden in the loader. The application as implemented thus far looks like Figure 4-1 when it's run.

Pressing the Add button causes the display to update so that it looks like Figure 4-2.

FIGURE 4-1

FIGURE 4-2

This is exactly what should happen. On the other hand, it is a little surprising that it does! Consider that the example code obtained one specific cursor from one specific query to the database and then associated that cursor with the displayed list view. That cursor contains data from a query that was made before the new key and value were added to the database. Why did the new database row become visible in the list view? How did the list view discover that something had changed and that an update was necessary?

The answer is another content resolver method called `registerContentObserver`. The parameters to this method are:

```
registerContentObserver(
    Uri uri,
    boolean notifyForDescendents,
    ContentObserver observer))
```

By this time, you may be expecting the URI argument. Its meaning here, though, is quite ingenious. The `registerContentObserver` method allows an object to register as a listener for changes, but not changes to a particular database, a particular table, or even a particular content provider. Instead, it registers the listener for notification of any changes that affect a particular URI. Using a URI to represent a dataset is a very powerful concept. Listing 4-3 shows how to add a little bit more code to the example application to demonstrate the function of a content observer.

LISTING 4-3: Registering a content observer

```
getContentResolver().registerContentObserver(
    KeyValContract.URI,
    true,
    new ContentObserver(null) {
        public void onChange(boolean selfChange) { toast.show(); }
    });
```

This new snippet registers a new content observer with the context's content resolver. Notice that, unlike many of the callback registration methods in the Android framework (such as `setOnClickListener`), the `registerContentObserver` method supports the registration of multiple observers.

This new code uses a `Toast` — Android's simple means of briefly displaying a small asynchronous message — to provide notification when it receives the `onChange` callback. When this code is added to the example, pressing the Add button causes the display, after a very brief pause, to look like Figure 4-3.

Notice the little "update!" message at the bottom of the display. It was generated in the newly added observer.

The new observer is registered to listen to the same URI that is the target of both the query and insert calls already part of the example. The call to insert changes the dataset that backs that URI and that causes the new observer to be notified.

A similar observer, registered by the cursor loader, causes the list view to be updated. If you were to examine the internals of the cursor loader, you would find that when it obtains a cursor from the database, it registers through a chain of listeners (loader manager to loader, to cursor, to content resolver) as an observer for this same URI. Any change to the underlying dataset that generates a notification to that URI will alert the loader manager that it must requery the database and create a new cursor with the updated data.

FIGURE 4-3

Here is a partial log from a run of the example program. It provides a little more insight into what is going on:

```
10-09 18:18:58.812: D/LOADER(768): onCreateLoader
10-09 18:18:59.663: D/LOADER(768): onLoadFinished
10-09 18:20:16.723: D/INSERT(768): button click!
10-09 18:20:16.843: D/LOADER(768): onLoadFinished
```

The first line shows the loader manager calling the example activity's onCreateLoader method to create a loader. The manager uses the new loader to get a cursor from the content provider (the loader's query method is run in the background and returns the cursor). Once it has the cursor, the manager calls the activity's onLoadFinished method, creating the second line in the log. The entire process — creating the loader and using it to obtain a cursor — takes almost a second on an emulator. At this point, the load is complete and the cursor data is visible through the list view.

Almost a minute later, the log registers a click on the Add button. About a quarter of a second later, there is second call to onLoadFinished. This second call is the result of the following steps:

1. When the user clicks the button and its handler's onClick method is called, a new AsyncInsert object is created and started.

2. The AsyncInsert object's doInBackground method is scheduled to run asynchronously on a daemon thread. When it runs, it obtains a content resolver object and uses it to invoke the insert method on the content provider.

3. The content provider updates its data (inserts rows into its database tables, in this case) and notifies observers that a change has taken place in the data underlying the URI that represents the dataset.

4. The observer registered by the loader manager as part of the process of creating the loader receives the notification.

5. When it receives the notification of a change in the dataset, the loader manager runs the loader again. The loader is an async task and is also scheduled and run on a daemon thread.

6. When its doInBackground method runs, the loader obtains a content resolver object and uses it to run a new query with the parameters passed to it at its creation. This is exactly the same query it ran last time but the results will now be different; they will include the newly added rows.

7. When the query returns a new cursor, the loader passes the cursor back to the loader manager. The loader manager in turn calls onLoadFinished (a second time, shown as the fourth line in the log), passing it the updated cursor.

8. The activity's onLoadCursor method attaches the updated cursor to the list view's adapter and the updated contents of the query become visible through it.

IPC: System-Wide Accessibility

The last important architectural feature supported by content providers is perhaps the most significant. It is the ability to use them no matter where they are on the system. All of the previous examples use URIs to identify specific content providers. They interact with a specific dataset: obtaining or updating data or receiving update notifications based solely on the URI. At no time does anything in the code indicate whether the target content provider is bundled as part of the activity's application, part of some other application, or a part of some system service.

This exact code works equally well regardless of which application, user, or process owns the content provider. This ability to identify data by its name instead of by the specific object that happens to provide it makes the content provider a powerful tool for extensibility in the enterprise environment. The example code for this chapter includes a second application, the KeyValClient, which is nearly an exact copy of the UI sections of the KeyVal application. It does not, however, include any of the data management sections. As long as the KeyVal application — the app that registers the content provider — is installed on a target device, KeyValClient will also run. It uses the content provider from the other application.

Now that you've seen what a content provider looks like from the client side, it's time to implement one. There are four key parts to a content provider:

➤ The contract

➤ CRUD methods and database management

➤ Content observers

➤ Registration and permissions

THE CONTRACT: URIS AND TYPES

Because content providers are intended for use across application — and here the term *application* is intended to mean a compilation unit — there must be some way of describing the provider's protocol to all of its clients. In order for other applications to interact with a given content provider, they must know its URI at the very least. By convention, they do this by including a small source file called the *contract*.

A contract is a Java source file that simply defines some global symbols (constants) needed by clients that want to use the provider. The file usually contains no methods and is based on the standard Java idiom for a namespace used only for symbol definition — an uninstantiable class with a private constructor. Also by convention, a content provider's contract has the name of the content provider, with the suffix Contract.

The example content provider, the KeyValContentProvider, has a contract called KeyValContract. It is shown in its entirety in Listing 4-4.

LISTING 4-4: The contract

```
public final class KeyValContract {
    private KeyValContract() {}
    public static final int VERSION = 1;

    public static final String AUTHORITY
        = "com.enterpriseandroid.database.keyval";

    private static final Uri URI_BASE
```

```
        = new Uri.Builder()
            .scheme(ContentResolver.SCHEME_CONTENT)
            .authority(AUTHORITY)
            .build();

    public static final String TABLE_VALS = "vals";
    public static final Uri URI_VALS
        = URI_BASE.buildUpon().appendPath(TABLE_VALS).build();
    public static final String TYPE_VALS
        = ContentResolver.CURSOR_DIR_BASE_TYPE
            + "/vnd.com.enterpriseandroid.database.val";
    public static final String TYPE_VAL
        = ContentResolver.CURSOR_ITEM_BASE_TYPE
            + "/vnd.com.enterpriseandroid.database.val";

    public static final String TABLE_KEYVAL = "keyval";
    public static final Uri URI_KEYVAL
        = URI_BASE.buildUpon().appendPath(TABLE_KEYVAL).build();
    public static final String TYPE_KEYVALS
        = ContentResolver.CURSOR_DIR_BASE_TYPE
            + "/vnd.com.enterpriseandroid.database.keyval";
    public static final String TYPE_KEYVAL
        = ContentResolver.CURSOR_ITEM_BASE_TYPE
            + "/vnd.com.enterpriseandroid.database.keyval";

    public static final class Columns {
        private Columns() {}

        // vals table columns
        public static final String ID = BaseColumns._ID;
        public static final String VAL = "val";

        // the keyval table has the following columns,
        // in addition to those above
        public static final String KEY = "key";
        public static final String EXTRA = "extra";
    }

    public static final class Permission {
        private Permission() {}

        public static final String READ
            = "com.enterpriseandroid.database.keyval.READ";
        public static final String WRITE
            = "com.enterpriseandroid.database.keyval.WRITE";
    }
}
```

Authority

The first item to notice — the most important part of the contract — is the *authority* string. The authority is the namespace for the data owned by this content provider. Although it can be any string at all as long as it is unique, by convention it starts with the reversed Internet domain name of the owner.

The Android system will not allow two content providers to be registered simultaneously as authorities for any single data namespace. The process by which content providers register their authority is described later in this chapter in the section on registration and permissions. An attempt to register a second content provider as authority for the same namespace will cause an error.

Here, for instance, is what happens to an attempt to use Android's standard debugging tool, adb, to install a second application that contains a conflicting registration for the authority already registered by the previously installed KeyVal example:

```
adb install KeyValConflict.apk
1790 KB/s (29937 bytes in 0.016s)
        pkg: /data/local/tmp/KeyValConflict.apk
Failure [INSTALL_FAILED_CONFLICTING_PROVIDER]
```

> **NOTE** *Note that the authority for which a content provider registers is an absolute string, not a prefix. It is perfectly acceptable for one content provider to register for the authority* com.fortunefivecompany.data *and for a second, unrelated content provider to register for the authority* com.fortunefivecompany .data.blackhat.

Within the namespace, a content provider may maintain any number of virtual tables. A table is simply the relation described in Chapter 2 — a rectangular array of data in which each tuple (row) contains data for each of the table's attributes (columns). As noted previously, the Android architecture does not include the ORM layer that developers accustomed to enterprise programming might expect. Instead of an object model for data, Android uses the relational model consistently from its backend persistent storage mechanisms, all the way up to the UI.

A discussion of relational table model and contract API is as good a place as any to pause and revisit Android's use of the relational model. Architecturally, it is certainly a plausible decision. The relational model of data is sound, flexible, and well understood. Using it from the bottom of the stack all the way through to the top clearly reduces copy costs. On the other hand, experienced backend developers will smell a rat.

The most compelling arguments against the pervasive use of the relational model have to do with the specific implementation: the mutability of the cursor object. Moving the cursor's row pointer (its cursor) is an essential part of using it. At the very least, client code must have a protocol establishing ownership of the cursor's row pointer. Perhaps more important, it is essentially impossible to make a cursor thread-safe. Android's creators apparently felt the trade-off was worth it.

It is certainly possible to layer an ORM over the Android relational model. Just as certainly, there are commercial and OSS frameworks that do exactly that. Under some circumstances this may be desirable. There are, however, two fairly strong arguments against the general use of this type of architecture.

The first argument is that the cursor is very well integrated into Android's super-fast interprocess communication mechanism. Although implementing your own cross-process data communication mechanism is simply a matter of programming, it is a matter of a lot of programming. More important, only applications that embed the entire client half of your custom mechanism have access to the data. Content resolvers support content providers and cursors, not their extensions.

A second reason for learning to live with the relational model is that the environment around cursors and the relational model they represent is well used. Chapter 3 demonstrated a very typical list view: It used a cursor all the way up to the UI glass. This architecture helps make the list view quick and responsive. We noted, at the time, that it isn't absolutely necessary to hand the list view a cursor. We also noted, though, that the tools for working with cursors, the `CursorLoader` and the `SimpleCursorAdapter`, are mature and well documented even if the super-classes they specialize in are not. We do not recommend replacing, subclassing, or wrapping cursors.

The contract contains an internal namespace, `Columns`, that defines the names of the columns in the virtual tables. These are the names of the columns that will appear in a cursor obtained from the content provider. As usual, these names need not be the names of actual columns in any actual database. There is a pretty good argument that revealing the actual names of your tables gives clients too much information about the internal implementation of the content provider.

The `KeyVal` example is very simple and does expose actual column names. It also has only one set of column names that apply to the columns in both of its virtual tables. Were this not the case, it might have been necessary to define separate inner namespaces for each of the tables or perhaps to define two entirely separate contracts.

Virtual Table URIs

The next important item in the contract is the URI. By convention, a content provider URI looks like Figure 4-4.

scheme   authority   path id

content://com.enterpriseandroid.database.keyval/keyvals/3

FIGURE 4-4

The first portion of the URI, the scheme, is always `content://`. As noted previously, Android reserves this scheme for content providers and all content provider URIs must use it.

The next portion of the URI is the authority. It is the unique name for the dataset, as described previously.

The last section of the URI, the path, is typically the name of a virtual table maintained by the content provider. The virtual table named by a path need not correspond to a physical table in a SQLite database. There is no reason that it needs to correspond with anything in any particular database. A content provider is free to use any convenient storage mechanism — SQLite tables, a directory tree on the file system, or even values obtained from some external hardware sensor — to back its virtual table.

The content provider in the `KeyVal` example supports two virtual tables: `vals`, which maps directly to a SQLite table, and `keyval`, which is a virtual table created from a join of the SQLite `keys` and `vals` tables. The URIs for the two virtual tables are:

```
content://com.enterpriseandroid.database.keyval/vals
content://com.enterpriseandroid.database.keyval/keyvals
```

In the `KeyVal` contract these URIs are constructed from the base URI using the handy `URI.Builder` class.

The ID portion of a content provider URI is an integer. If a URI contains an ID, the URI refers to a specific, single row in the virtual table named in the path. The ID is meant to act as a primary key into the virtual table.

The path/ID portion of a URI may be arbitrarily complex. One can imagine, for instance, a URI that looks like this:

```
content://com.android.contacts/contacts/52/phone/2
```

a request for the second phone number of the contact whose ID is 52. Although convention — and even some past documentation — suggest this kind of path, the tools to support it are at best immature.

Return Value MIME Types

A content provider's virtual table contains data of a particular type, defined by the relational attributes — the columns — in the cursor it returns. The content provider framework includes a protocol that allows providers to specify that type and a provider's contract should define them for each of its tables. Content provider types are simply MIME types (strings that have the format type/subtype).

The type portion of a content provider MIME type is determined by a strong convention. If the query specifying the returned data is semantically constained so the the returned cursor contains 0 or 1 rows — it is a query that specifies a unique row — the major type of the returned value must be vnd.android.cursor.item. For example, a query that specifies a primary key for the table it references cannot return more than one row. It should, therefore, return the item type. If, on the other hand, the cursor might contain any number of rows (0 to n), the returned major type is vnd.android.cursor.dir. A content provider should be able to tell, simply by examining a URI, whether that URI is legal and whether it is bound to return at most one row from the database.

The subtype portion of the type is defined, entirely, by the service providing the data. For very simple one column data, it might make sense to use one of the standard MIME subtypes: html, jpeg, mpeg3, and so on. By convention, however, any complex (multi-column) data should have its own unique type and that type should begin with the string "vnd.". The KeyVal example defines two tables and, therefore, four MIME types: item and dir for each. Since the contents of the dir and item cursors are the same for a given table, the subtypes for both of the MIME types for that table are also the same.

Permissions

The last set of definitions in a contract comprises the permissions that a client application must request, in order to get access to the provider's dataset. As you will see toward the end of this chapter, permissions are simple strings used in the application's manifest file. They do not typically appear in code. It might be perfectly reasonable to document the permissions in a comment, instead of as symbol definitions.

One reasonable approach — used in the actual code for the KeyValContract but excluded here to save space — is to include in the contract the excerpt from the manifest that declares, defines, and applies permissions to the content provider.

Publishing the Contract

It probably goes without saying that designing a content provider's API and the contract that defines it can be a tricky job. There are no constraints and barely any conventions controlling what a content provider can or can't do when it translates URIs into references to the dataset it controls. As usual, APIs that take full advantage of the flexibility of the interface tend to be less useful, in the long run, than those that are simpler and more consistent. The architect of a content provider API could do much worse than to take advice from two specific sources:

➤ **Android's Contacts API** — The first design for the Contacts API is an excellent example of a pretty good interface that simply did not support the flexibility that was eventually necessary. The new API is considerably more complex but quite flexible.

➤ **RESTful client/service architecture** — The construction and use of APIs that support scalable, stateless, and cacheable data communications are the topic of the rest of this book.

No matter how you choose to implement your contract, remember that it is the only means you have for communicating to potential clients the API that your content provider exposes. The contract file is the place to document exactly how your content provider works. It should contain comments describing the details of your API, including what exceptions it might throw and under what conditions it might throw them, use cases you do not intend to support, even in the long run, and so on.

The Android content provider framework doesn't really support API versioning in any meaningful way. If you ever have to change the contact provider's API, you will probably have to create a new authority and support both the old and the new, distinguishing them by URI.

Once you have a well-designed and documented contract, publish it. If you are targeting a specific enterprise, you will use the internal source control system or repository to publish the contract file. If you are targeting a general audience, you might use one of the popular code-sharing sites like GitHub or SourceForge.

IMPLEMENTING THE CONTENT PROVIDER

You've now seen how to use a content provider and how to publish its API. The next step it to implement its CRUD methods — create, insert, update, and delete. This section examines the code that does that for the content provider you've been considering so far in this chapter — KeyVal.

In the process of creating the content provider CRUD methods, there are a few architectural issues that a developer must keep in mind. As usual when building Android components, one of the most important of these is understanding the component lifecycle and which methods are run on which threads.

A content provider's onCreate method is always run on the UI thread of the application to which it belongs. This means that it must not undertake any long-running initialization. Fortunately, the framework guarantees that creating a SQLiteDatabaseHelper object is a fast operation — the onCreate method may create an instance of the helper.

It may not, however, use the instance to obtain a database instance! As noted previously, obtaining the actual database instance may require rebuilding a database's entire schema and repopulating it with data. That is an operation far too slow to be run on the UI thread.

All of the other externally visible methods in the content provider may be called from multiple threads. When used from the application that defines the provider, they will probably be invoked from an AsyncTask – perhaps explicitly, or perhaps using a loader — and thus run on one of several daemon threads in the AsyncTask's executor's thread pool. When called from other applications, content provider methods are run on *Binder* threads, which are threads allocated explicitly for interprocess communications. In either case, because it is the client's responsibility to make sure they are not run on the UI thread, the externally visible content provider methods may perform long running operations.

Finally, remember to keep the content provider thread safe. Although onCreate is called from a single thread — the UI thread — the other methods in the class may each be called from multiple threads. If onCreate shares data with other methods, it must share it safely. Those other methods must synchronize even to share data across multiple executions.

Creating the Content Provider

Listing 4-5 shows the initialization of the example content provider. Note that the onCreate method returns a boolean indicating whether initialization was completed successfully or not.

LISTING 4-5: Initializing a content provider

```
public class KeyValContentProvider extends ContentProvider {
    // code elided...

    private volatile KeyValHelper helper;

    @Override
    public boolean onCreate() {
        helper = new KeyValHelper(getContext());
        return null != helper;
    }
}
```

Earlier in this chapter, you read that the virtual tables provided by a content provider are identified by their URIs. The section "Virtual Table URIs" earlier in the chapter explored the syntax of those URIs. A content resolver forwards a data request to the appropriate content provider based on the authority section of the URI in the request. The task of parsing the rest of the URI, however, falls to the content provider. It must identify the table to which the request refers and must extract path and ID sections, if they are present.

Fortunately, the Android framework supplies a simple but very convenient URI parsing tool, called the URI Matcher. Listing 4-6 shows the construction of the URI matcher for the KeyVal example program.

LISTING 4-6: Defining a URIMatcher

```
private static final int STATUS_VAL_DIR = 1;
private static final int STATUS_VAL_ITEM = 2;
private static final int STATUS_KEYVAL_DIR = 3;
private static final int STATUS_KEYVAL_ITEM = 4;

private static final UriMatcher uriMatcher;
static {
    uriMatcher = new UriMatcher(UriMatcher.NO_MATCH);
    uriMatcher.addURI(
        KeyValContract.AUTHORITY,
        KeyValContract.TABLE_VALS,
        STATUS_VAL_DIR);
    uriMatcher.addURI(
        KeyValContract.AUTHORITY,
        KeyValContract.TABLE_VALS + "/#",
        STATUS_VAL_ITEM);
    uriMatcher.addURI(
        KeyValContract.AUTHORITY,
        KeyValContract.TABLE_KEYVAL,
        STATUS_KEYVAL_DIR);
    uriMatcher.addURI(
        KeyValContract.AUTHORITY,
        KeyValContract.TABLE_KEYVAL + "/#",
        STATUS_KEYVAL_ITEM);
}
```

Return Types and the URI Matcher

The URI matcher is, essentially, a map of regular expressions to integers. It supports replacing long chains of if-then-else statements with a terser, more compact implementation based on a single switch statement.

In order to see a URI matcher in use, first recall from the section called "Return Value MIME Types" earlier in the chapter that a content provider defines MIME types for the data it manages. There are different types for different tables and different types for cursors that contain single and multiple rows. An implementation of a content provider must define the method getType, which clients use to determine what kind of data will be returned for a request from a particular URI. Because the getType method must determine the return type from the URI, it provides an excellent example of the use of the URI matcher.

The example content provider returns one of four MIME types, a dir, and an item type for each of its two tables. The URI matcher contains the four corresponding regular expressions, two for each table, one ending with the table name, and one ending with the table name followed by /#. Each of these four expressions is mapped to one of the unique integers defined in the symbols STATUS_VAL_DIR, STATUS_VAL_ITEM, STATUS_KEYVAL_DIR, and STATUS_KEYVAL_ITEM. A properly formed URI for this content provider will match exactly one of the expressions and thus be mapped to one of the unique integers.

Consider the URI:

```
content://com.enterpriseandroid.database.keyval/vals
```

This is a valid URI for the `KeyVal` content provider. It matches only one entry in the URI matcher, the first. An attempt to match this URI will therefore return the value `STATUS_VAL_DIR`.

On the other hand, the following URI:

```
content://com.enterpriseandroid.database.keyval/vals/47
```

matches only the second entry in the matcher. The second entry is very like the first — matching the same authority and the same table name — but ends with the token #, which matches any string of numerals (the * matches any string). The attempt to match this URI will return the value `STATUS_VAL_ITEM`.

The following are all examples of URIs that will not match any of the expressions in the URI matcher:

```
content://com.enterpriseandroid.database.keyval/vals/val
content://com.enterpriseandroid.database.keyval/mango
content://com.enterpriseandroid.database.keyval/47
```

All three of these URIs will be mapped to the URI matcher's default value, specified in its constructor, called `UriMatcher.NO_MATCH`.

As shown in Listing 4-7, the implementation of the `getType` method need only use the URI matcher to categorize a URI into one of the five classes and return the MIME type for the corresponding class, or null, when the URI cannot be matched.

LISTING 4-7: Using a URIMatcher

```java
@Override
public String getType(Uri uri) {
    switch (uriMatcher.match(uri)) {
        case STATUS_VAL_DIR:
            return KeyValContract.TYPE_VALS;
        case STATUS_VAL_ITEM:
            return KeyValContract.TYPE_VAL;
        case STATUS_KEYVAL_DIR:
            return KeyValContract.TYPE_KEYVALS;
        case STATUS_KEYVAL_ITEM:
            return KeyValContract.TYPE_KEYVAL;
        default:
            return null;
    }
}
```

Writing the Database

The content provider in `KeyVal`, a simplified example application, implements only one of the three possible write methods. Of insert, update, and delete, it supports only insert and supports that on only one of the two tables it maintains. Insert is only legal on the `keyval` table. It is neither legal to insert a key with no value nor a value with no key. As shown in Listing 4-8, the URI matcher handles this constraint nicely.

LISTING 4-8: Implementing insert

```
@Override
public Uri insert(Uri uri, ContentValues vals) {
    long pk;
    switch (uriMatcher.match(uri)) {
        case STATUS_KEYVAL_DIR:
            pk = insertKeyVal(vals);
            break;

        default:
            throw new UnsupportedOperationException(
                "Unrecognized URI: " + uri);
    }

    getContext().getContentResolver().notifyChange(uri, null);
    return uri.buildUpon().appendPath(String.valueOf(pk)).build();;
}
```

The call to the content resolver method `notifyChange` is an essential part of the content observer feature discussed in the section entitled "Content Observers: Completing the Loop" earlier in the chapter. You'll see it again shortly in the section "Content Observers (Again)."

The insert method returns a URI for the newly added row. It is the URI for the table into which the row was inserted with the primary key for the new row appended.

Listing 4-9 shows the implementation of the insert.

LISTING 4-9: Insert using a transaction

```
private long insertKeyVal(ContentValues vals) {
    SQLiteDatabase db = helper.getWritableDatabase();
    try {
        db.beginTransaction();
        long id = helper.insertVal(
            db,
            vals.getAsString(KeyValContract.Columns.VAL));
        long pk = helper.insertKey(
            db,
            vals.getAsString(KeyValContract.Columns.KEY),
            id);
        db.setTransactionSuccessful();
        return pk;
    }
    finally { db.endTransaction(); }
}
```

The use of the transaction in this method is worthy of note. By default, SQLite wraps each write operation (two inserts, in this case, performed within the helper methods `insertKey` and insertVal) in its own transaction. In order to implement a transaction, SQLite must open, write, and then close the database's journal file. This can be incredibly expensive for operations that require multiple writes to the database. In addition to providing the atomicity necessary to preserve referential integrity, explicitly wrapping the two operations in the code in a single transaction can substantially improve performance.

As noted previously, a content provider exposes a virtual relation. Even if there is a real SQLite table backing it, there is no reason that either the name of that virtual table or the names of its virtual columns should match their actual counterparts. To the contrary, best practice suggests that exposing the internal implementation of the content provider, by tying virtual and actual names together, is a bad idea. It both cracks the layer of abstraction between the content provider contract and its implementation and may even allow clients to breach the provider's security.

The code in Listing 4-9 uses explicit methods on the helper class to insert data into the database. Listing 4-10 demonstrates another means of converting between virtual and actual column names, using a small utility class, ColumnDef, and a static map.

LISTING 4-10: Converting virtual column names to real

COLUMNDEF.JAVA

```java
public class ColumnDef {
    public static enum Type {
        BOOLEAN, BYTE, BYTEARRAY, DOUBLE, FLOAT, INTEGER, LONG, SHORT, STRING
    };

    private final String name;
    private final Type type;

    public ColumnDef(String name, Type type) {
        this.name = name;
        this.type = type;
    }

    public void copy(String srcCol, ContentValues src, ContentValues dst) {
        switch (type) {
            case BOOLEAN:
                dst.put(name, src.getAsBoolean(srcCol));
                break;
            case BYTE:
                dst.put(name, src.getAsByte(srcCol));
                break;
            case BYTEARRAY:
                dst.put(name, src.getAsByteArray(srcCol));
                break;
            case DOUBLE:
                dst.put(name, src.getAsDouble(srcCol));
                break;
            case FLOAT:
                dst.put(name, src.getAsFloat(srcCol));
                break;
            case INTEGER:
```

```
                        dst.put(name, src.getAsInteger(srcCol));
                        break;
                    case LONG:
                        dst.put(name, src.getAsLong(srcCol));
                        break;
                    case SHORT:
                        dst.put(name, src.getAsShort(srcCol));
                        break;
                    case STRING:
                        dst.put(name, src.getAsString(srcCol));
                        break;
                }
            }
        }
```

KEYVALCONTENTPROVIDER.JAVA

```
private static final Map<String, ColumnDef> COL_MAP;
static {
    Map<String, ColumnDef> m = new HashMap<String, ColumnDef>();
    m.put(
        KeyValContract.Columns.KEY,
        new ColumnDef(KeyValHelper.COL_KEY, ColumnDef.Type.STRING));
    m.put(
        KeyValContract.Columns.VAL,
        new ColumnDef(KeyValHelper.COL_VAL, ColumnDef.Type.STRING));
    COL_MAP = Collections.unmodifiableMap(m);
}

// code omitted...

private ContentValues translateCols(ContentValues vals) {
    ContentValues newVals = new ContentValues();
    for (String colName: vals.keySet()) {
        ColumnDef colDef = COL_MAP.get(colName);
        if (null == colDef) {
            throw new IllegalArgumentException(
                "Unrecognized column: " + colName);
        }
        colDef.copy(colName, vals, newVals);
    }

    return newVals;
}
```

Although it is not used in the KeyVal example, the ColumnDef utility class is a very handy tool.

There is yet one more tool for making this virtual to actual mapping. It is a class introduced back in Chapter 3, the QueryBuilder. It works only for queries, not any of the write methods. As a tool for managing queries against the virtual tables exposed by a content provider, though, the query builder's full power becomes evident.

Database Queries

All that remains to complete the implementation of this content provider is to implement the query methods. The KeyVals example supports queries on either of its two tables, keys and keyvals.

Because they are very similar, this section examines only the implementation of the more complex of the two, keyvals, in detail. Listing 4-11 shows the first of the two methods that, together, handle queries to the keyvals table.

LISTING 4-11: Implementing query

```
@Override
public Cursor query(
    Uri uri,
    String[] proj,
    String sel,
    String[] selArgs,
    String ord)
{
    Cursor cur;

    long pk = -1;
    switch (uriMatcher.match(uri)) {
        case STATUS_VAL_ITEM:
            pk = ContentUris.parseId(uri);
        case STATUS_VAL_DIR:
            cur = queryVals(proj, sel, selArgs, ord, pk);
            break;

        case STATUS_KEYVAL_ITEM:
            pk = ContentUris.parseId(uri);
        case STATUS_KEYVAL_DIR:
            cur = queryKeyVals(proj, sel, selArgs, ord, pk);
            break;

        default:
            throw new IllegalArgumentException(
                "Unrecognized URI: " + uri);
    }

    cur.setNotificationUri(getContext().getContentResolver(), uri);

    return cur;
}
```

Again, the URI matcher manages the work of sorting query URIs into five classes: those with and without specified primary keys for the two tables, respectively, and those that are unrecognized and illegal. If a primary key is specified in the URI, it is parsed out and passed to the query method for a specific table as the final parameter.

Note, again, the call to setNotification. You'll return to it in the section called "Content Observers (Again)." This time, the notification URI is the URI that specified the table to be queried.

Listing 4-12 shows the use of a QueryBuilder to construct and run the join query underlying the content provider's keyval table.

LISTING 4-12: Using the QueryBuilder

```java
private Cursor queryKeyVals(
    String[] proj,
    String sel,
    String[] selArgs,
    String ord,
    long pk)
{
    SQLiteQueryBuilder qb = new SQLiteQueryBuilder();
    qb.setStrict(true);

    qb.setProjectionMap(KEY_VAL_COL_AS_MAP);

    qb.setTables(
        KeyValHelper.TAB_KEYS
        + " INNER JOIN " + KeyValHelper.TAB_VALS
        + " ON(fk=id)");

    if (0 <= pk) { qb.appendWhere(KeyValContract.Columns.ID + "=" + pk); }

    return qb.query(
        helper.getWritableDatabase(),
        proj,
        sel,
        selArgs,
        null,
        null,
        ord);
}
```

The `QueryBuilder` method `setTables` creates the join and the `appendWhere` method adds the primary key match, if it was specified. Be careful using `appendWhere` to add multiple constraints. Although anything added using `appendWhere` is added to the selection clause specified in the call to query — using parentheses and an AND — multiple calls to `appendWhere` are simply concatenated. Thus, although:

```java
qb.appendWhere("cond1");

//...

qb.query(
    //...
    "condSel",
    //...
    );
```

produces:

```
(cond1) AND (condSel)
```

perhaps unexpectedly:

```java
qb.appendWhere("cond1");
qb.appendWhere("cond2");
```

```
//...

qb.query(
    //...
    "condSel",
    //...
    );
```

produces:

```
(cond1cond2) AND (condSel)
```

If you specify multiple `appendWhere` constraints, you must add your own conjunctions and parentheses as needed.

The most interesting thing in this code is the use of the query builder's projection map feature. If a projection map is specified, the query builder parses the select clause and replaces column names it finds there with the names to which they are mapped in the projection map. There is a trick to this! If you simply map each virtual name to its actual counterpart, other clauses specified by the client will fail. For instance, if the projection map contains:

```
clave => key
valer => val
```

and the query built from client arguments is:

```
SELECT clave, valer FROM keys INNER JOIN vals ON(fk=id) ORDER BY clave;
```

then after translation by the query builder the query will look like this:

```
SELECT key, val FROM keys INNER JOIN vals ON(fk=id) ORDER BY clave;
```

which will, of course, fail because there is no column named `clave` on which to sort. Listing 4-13 shows the projection map used for the `keyval` table. It works because, instead of mapping the virtual name to the actual name, it instead maps the virtual name to *<actual_name>* AS *<virtual_name>*. The previous query, after a similar translation, would look like this:

```
SELECT key as clave, val as valer
    FROM keys INNER JOIN vals ON(fk=id) ORDER BY clave;
```

LISTING 4-13: Creating a ProjectionMap

```
private static final Map<String, String> KEY_VAL_COL_AS_MAP;
static {
    Map<String, String> m = new HashMap<String, String>();
    m.put(KeyValContract.Columns.ID,
        KeyValHelper.TAB_KEYS + "." + KeyValHelper.COL_ROWID
            + " AS " + KeyValContract.Columns.ID);
    m.put(KeyValContract.Columns.KEY,
        KeyValHelper.COL_KEY + " AS " + KeyValContract.Columns.KEY);
    m.put(KeyValContract.Columns.VAL,
        KeyValHelper.COL_VAL + " AS " + KeyValContract.Columns.VAL);
    KEY_VAL_COL_AS_MAP = Collections.unmodifiableMap(m);
}
```

Using a query builder projection map provides an additional layer of security for a content provider. If, in the process of mapping virtual column names to their actual counterparts, the query builder encounters a request for a column that is not a key in the projection map, it throws an IllegalArgumentException. The KeyVal content provider, for instance, protects the two columns keys.fk and vals.id from exposure, simply by not including them in the projection map.

The query builder also supports a default projection. Because an empty projection — the list of columns to include in the result — doesn't make any sense, when a null is passed to the query method, the value of the projection parameter the query builder uses is a default projection that contains all of the actual columns (the map values). If your content provider supports this default value or any other default, for that matter, be sure to document it in the provider's contract.

As of the Ice Cream Sandwich release, the QueryBuilder supports a strict mode, which is enabled by calling setStrict(true). By default (and in an earlier version of Android), strict mode is off. In this state, a client-supplied column specifier that contains the word as (upper- or lowercase) is allowed, whether or not it is in the projection map. It is best practice to set strict mode if possible.

Content Observers (Again)

In the section earlier in the chapter entitled "Content Observers: Completing the Loop," you examined content observers from the client side in some detail. During the implementation of the example content provider there were two additional places that the subject of content observers arose. The first of these was near the end of the insert method, when writing to the database. The code uses the content resolver method called notifyChange. Similarly, the cursor method called setNotificationUri is used near the end of the query method, after a database read. It sets a URI as the notification target for the cursor.

These two methods really do complete the content observer loop. Ensuring that your content provider uses them correctly is an important key to making it useful, both within your application and to external clients.

In the query method, the cursor returned from the query is registered as an observer for changes posted for the URI that represents the dataset onto which it is a view. It is because it receives these notifications that it can, as you saw, notify the loader manager that a change has occurred and an update is necessary. Unless the cursor in the example application is registered to receive these notifications, the view will not update when the database changes.

The insert method contains the call to notifyChange, which actually broadcasts the notification to all observers. The URI chosen as the notification target deserves some thought. The second argument to registerContentObserver, which is notifyForDescendents, was not discussed when it was first shown in Listing 4-3. The code in that listing demonstrates registering an observer that posts a toast when a database update occurs. That second argument controls whether the observer is notified only for exact matches to the target URI (false) or whether, instead, it is notified for any URI for which the target URI is a prefix (true). As with all API design decisions, best practice suggests defining a policy and sticking to it.

For instance, it might make sense for the insert method's notification target to be exactly the URI for the newly inserted row. The code would look like this:

```
uri = uri.buildUpon().appendPath(String.valueOf(pk)).build();
getContext().getContentResolver().notifyChange(uri, null);
return uri;
```

causing the URIs on which it notified to look like this:

```
content://com.enterpriseandroid.database.keyval/keyvals/42
```

This finer-grained notification might be preferable. Clients can use the `notifyForDescendents` parameter when registering their observers if they require notification of any change in the dataset (as the list view in the example does). Remember, though, that more frequent, smaller notifications may be less efficient than broader and less specific ones. Consider your use patterns and design accordingly.

PERMISSIONS AND REGISTRATION

Like all of the other major managed Android components, a content provider must be registered in the manifest. Listing 4-14 shows a typical registration, the one used for the example program.

LISTING 4-14: Registering a content provider

```
<provider
    android:name=".data.KeyValContentProvider"
    android:authorities="com.enterpriseandroid.database.keyval"
    android:grantUriPermissions="true"
    android:readPermission="com.enterpriseandroid.database.keyval.READ"
    android:writePermission="com.enterpriseandroid.database.keyval.WRITE" />
```

This registers the content provider defined in the class `com.enterpriseandroid.database` `.keyval.data.KeyValContentProvider` — the class that has been the subject of the chapter — as authority for the namespace `com.enterpriseandroid.database.keyval`. All content URIs for that authority will now be directed to an instance of this content provider. Again, note that this authority is simply a string and that clients must match it exactly. There is no semantic information in the string. Your personal application could probably register as authority for the string `"com.google.zqx3"`.

The declaration also uses permissions to define access rights for the content provider.

> **NOTE** *This section discusses only the mechanics of using permissions with a content provider. There is a more complete discussion of permissions and why they are necessary in Chapter 12.*

Using permissions in Android is a three-step process:

1. A service provider defines the permission.

2. The service provider uses the permission to protect a component.

3. Clients request the permission.

Listing 4-15 shows the definitions for the permissions used by the `KeyVal` content provider. Although any component — including a content provider — can be protected with the `android:permissions` attribute, the content provider allows somewhat finer grained control; there are separate read and write permissions.

LISTING 4-15: Defining permissions

```
<permission
    android:name="com.enterpriseandroid.database.keyval.READ"
    android:description="@string/content_read_desc"
    android:permissionGroup="com.enterpriseandroid.database.keyval"
    android:protectionLevel="dangerous" />
<permission
    android:name="com.enterpriseandroid.database.keyval.WRITE"
    android:description="@string/content_write_desc"
    android:permissionGroup="com.enterpriseandroid.database.keyval"
    android:protectionLevel="signature" />
```

The most significant feature of a permission is probably its name. The usual warnings apply — a permission name is simply a string that uniquely identifies the permission and contains absolutely no semantic information about the permission. A close second in importance is `android:protectionLevel`. The protection level determines how difficult it is to obtain the associated permission. The possible values for permission level are:

➤ **Normal** — A permission that is granted if requested.

➤ **Dangerous** — If an application requests a dangerous permission, the user is offered the opportunity to approve granting the permission to the application before the application is installed. If the user approves, the permission is granted, and the application is installed. If the user does not approve, the application is not installed.

➤ **Signature** — Like normal, a signature permission is granted without notifying the user, but only if the application requesting the permission is signed with the same certificate as the application using it to protect a component.

> **NOTE** *There are actually three other permissions,* signatureOrSystem, system, *and* development, *all described in Chapter 12. None of them are relevant to normal application development.*

Permissions may be grouped together into collections of permissions that control related capabilities. Permission groups have no effect on permission function. They may affect the way they are displayed to a user when installing the application. In the case of the `KeyVal` example, the two permissions controlling read and write access to the content provider belong to a single permissions group. The definition for that group is shown in Listing 4-16

LISTING 4-16: Defining a permission group

```
<permission-group
    android:name="com.enterpriseandroid.database.keyval"
    android:description="@string/content_group_desc"
    android:label="@string/content_group_label" />
```

Once the permissions have been defined, they must be applied, as demonstrated in Listing 4-14. As used in that listing, applications that request the permission named:

```
android:readPermission="com.enterpriseandroid.database.keyval.READ"
```

are allowed to perform queries against the `KeyVal` content provider, if the end user approves the capability.

Only applications that request this permission:

```
android:readPermission="com.enterpriseandroid.database.keyval.WRITE"
```

and that are signed with the same key that was used to sign the `KeyVal` app itself will be granted the capability to write to the `KeyVal` content provider. Listing 4-17 shows an example of requests for both permissions taken from the `KeyValClient` application.

LISTING 4-17: Requesting permissions

```
<uses-permission
    android:name="com.enterpriseandroid.database.keyval.READ" />
<uses-permission
    android:name="com.enterpriseandroid.database.keyval.WRITE" />
```

The `grantUriPermissions` attribute in the provider declaration in Listing 4-14 is also of interest. A full description of this attribute is outside the scope of this section. Documentation can be found on the Android Developer website:

```
http://developer.android.com/guide/topics/manifest/grant-uri-permission-element.html
```

In short, this permission allows the application defining the content provider to grant extremely fine-grained access permissions to clients a single URI at a time. The following code, for instance in the application defining the content provider, passes a single, explicit URI to the activity responding to the implicit intent named in the symbol `KEYVAL_CLIENT`.

```
Intent i = new Intent(KEYVAL_CLIENT);
i.setData(KeyValContract.URI_KEYVAL.buildUpon().appendPath("2").build());
i.addFlags(Intent.FLAG_GRANT_READ_URI_PERMISSION);
startActivity(i);
```

Presuming the content provider's manifest declaration sets the `grantUriPermissions` to `true`, the client application will, regardless of other permissions, be able to perform a query against the provider, using the single passed URI.

CONTENT PROVIDERS AND FILES

There is one more issue to address, before leaving the discussion of content providers: storing large data objects. Imagine for instance that you are designing an application that will allow doctors to review and comment on patient records. The problem changes dramatically if the records include digitized x-rays, each of which is several megabytes.

To demonstrate solutions to the issue, consider a new feature for the `KeyVal` application that allows values to be associated with arbitrarily large text "extras." A key is associated with a value, as is already the case. The new feature adds the ability to associate a value with a very large amount of text.

In the UI, a value that has extras available shows in the list view with a green check to its left. If there is no blob available, the item has a red X, as shown in Figure 4-5.

Clicking on one of the items with a green check starts a new activity that displays the contents of the value's associated extras, as shown in Figure 4-6.

FIGURE 4-5

FIGURE 4-6

The details of implementing the UI are left to the curious. The concern here is how to implement a content provider that efficiently stores the large text objects.

Like most database systems, SQLite supports blobs — binary large objects. There are several ways to use SQLite blobs from within the Android framework. For instance, either of the code fragments shown in Listing 4-18 will work.

LISTING 4-18: Using blobs

```
// blob is a byte array
ContentValues vals = new ContentValues();
vals.put("image", blob);
db.insert(TAB_KEYS, null, vals);

SQLiteStatement ins = db.compileStatement(
    "INSERT INTO " + TAB_KEYS + "(image) VALUES(?)");
ins.bindBlob(1, blob);
```

Although this is a plausible solution for small byte arrays — hundreds of bytes or fewer — it is quite inefficient when the arrays get large. There are two reasons for this.

The first reason has to do with the implementation of SQLite. As a database file gets bigger and the widths of columns get larger, operations just get slower. Even for SQLite, with all its clever optimizations, size matters.

There are several ways to optimize blob storage, if necessary.

➤ One useful trick is to keep the blobs in a separate database file — not a separate table in the same file, but an entirely separate file. A table in the main file holds only the primary key (and other small columns). One or more tables in the second file hold the blobs themselves. There is evidence that this scheme helps SQLite handle database fragmentation caused by deletes, and that it can speed queries. Certainly it will speed up any query that doesn't actually require recovering a blob.

➤ There is also evidence that the efficiency of blob storage can be improved by appropriate use of the page size pragma. SQLite stores blobs in blocks called pages. Adjusting the page size for a database file to correspond with the size of the blobs being stored in its tables can significantly improve efficiency. Of course, this may require separate database files for blobs of different sizes.

➤ Finally, especially when dealing with large data objects, it's useful to remember that in order to recover file system space after deletes, it may be necessary to use the SQLite VACUUM command:

```
db.execSQL("VACUUM")
```

A second reason for avoiding blobs in database tables is much more important. When using a content provider from an external application — an application that runs in a different process — the blob data must be transferred across the interprocess communications channel. Clearly, for large data objects, this is inefficient. Fortunately, the Android framework provides a very slick way to avoid the problem.

Among the kinds of data that can be transferred through Binder, Android's interprocess communication framework, is a file descriptor. It is possible for one application to open a file and then pass the open file descriptor to another application. The second application may then use the file as if it had opened it itself (constrained, of course, by the read/write permissions on the descriptor). The data contained in the file does not have to cross the IPC boundary! This mechanism, in addition, allows the serving application to share the contents of a file without ever giving the client application access to it on the file system. The client cannot open it, or even find it without the content provider's help.

This suggests an alternative means of storing large data objects as files. Content providers support this scheme using the methods `ContentResolver.openInputStream(URI)`, `ContentResolver` `.openOutputStream(URI)`, and `ContentProvider.openFile(URI, mode)`.

As usual, the URI must be a content URI (its scheme must be `content://`). It is forwarded to the content provider registered as owner of the URI's authority section. A content provider implements the `openFile` method to handle these requests. It is free to handle the URIs it receives in any way it chooses.

File requests might, for instance, be modeled as an entirely new virtual table. A content provider implemented in this way will have to handle URIs naming the new table, appropriately, in the previously described CRUD methods. This probably means throwing exceptions.

Listing 4-19 is the beginning of another way to handle file requests.

LISTING 4-19: Implementing openFile

```
@Override
public ParcelFileDescriptor openFile(Uri uri, String mode)
    throws FileNotFoundException
{
    switch (uriMatcher.match(uri)) {
        case STATUS_VAL_ITEM:
            if (!"r".equals(mode)) {
                throw new SecurityException("Write access forbidden");
            }
            return readExtras(uri);

        default:
            throw new UnsupportedOperationException(
                "Unrecognized URI: " + uri);
    }
}
```

Again, the URI Matcher manages parsing the passed URI. In this case, it rejects any requests that are not against the values table. Because this is a simplified example, it also rejects any requests for write permission. All legal requests are passed to the `readExtras` method.

What does `readExtras` do? It must open a `ParcelFileDescriptor` — a file descriptor that can be passed over the IPC channel — and return it. You need a place in the Android file system to create, read, and write those files.

A complete review of the Android file system is out of the scope of this book. Before creating and using files, it's worthwhile to review the documentation. At the very least, you should understand the implications of the various possible locations for saving a file — the application sandbox and the SD card.

The example program will create files in the sandbox, the directory /data/data/
<application-package>. Android puts files it creates on your behalf into a directory
just beneath the sandbox named files.

Of course, there are many ways to implement readExtras. Since the feature specification dictates
that there can be no more than one file associated with a particular value — and values are
unique — the implementation might construct a file name from the value itself. Another possibility
might add a new column to the virtual keyval table, containing the URI of the file that holds
a value's extras. Especially if there were multiple blobs associated with a keyval record, an
implementation along these lines might work well.

> **NOTE** *Recall that the column contents should be virtual. There is no reason to
> reveal actual file locations to the client. Doing so exposes implementation details
> that are better kept private.*

Once the code has determined a pathname for the file containing the extras, it will use the
framework method ParcelFileDescriptor.open(path, modeBits) to create file handle that can
be passed back to the client over the IPC channel. The client reads (or possibly writes) and closes the
file normally.

Instead of any of these strategies, the KeyVal implementation of readExtras makes use of yet
another feature in the Android framework, the openFileHelper. The complete readExtras method
is shown in Listing 4-20.

LISTING 4-20: Using the openFileHelper

```
private ParcelFileDescriptor readExtras(Uri uri)
    throws FileNotFoundException
{
    return openFileHelper(uri, "r");
}
```

You might ask what is going on. How can it be so simple? It turns out that the framework supports
a special database column named _data. If a normal query to a content provider for the column
_data returns a cursor that contains a single row, the single value in that column is used as the full
pathname for the file to be opened.

Making this work in KeyVal requires changes to both of the virtual tables managed by the content
provider. First, there are some simple changes necessary for the values table. It will need a _data
column that contains either null if there are no related extras, or else the full pathname of the
file containing the extras if there are. Because openFileHelper makes a normal call to the query
method, the new column must be visible. To make it visible, it must be added to the projection map
for the values virtual table. That, in turn will make it visible to all clients. The new column is not
mentioned in the contract file. That may not be sufficient to ensure security but it at least makes it
clear that it is not part of the KeyVal API.

The changes to the `keyval` table are more interesting and do require a change in the contract. You need to expose a new column that can be used to locate the extras associated with a key's value, if one exists. The new column must be added to the contract and exposed through the projection map. The right value to use in that column is the primary key of the value that has the extras.

Listing 4-21 shows the definition for the new virtual column.

LISTING 4-21: Using CASE to define a virtual column

```
m.put(KeyValContract.Columns.EXTRA,
    "CASE WHEN " + KeyValHelper.COL_EXTRA
    + " NOT NULL THEN " + KeyValHelper.COL_ID
    + " ELSE NULL END AS " + KeyValContract.Columns.EXTRA);;
```

This definition makes use of the SQL CASE statement to produce the new virtual column. If a value has no associated extra data, this virtual column contains a null. If the value does have associated extras, however, the column contains the primary key for the value from the values table. In order to get the file data, now the client needs to request a file from the content provider. The client does this using the URI for the values virtual table and restricts it with the primary key from this new column. Listing 4-22 is an example of code that does just that.

LISTING 4-22: Reading a file from a content provider

```
InputStream in = null;
try {
    in = getContext().getContentResolver().openInputStream(
        KeyValContract.URI_VALS.buildUpon()
            .appendPath(String.valueOf(extra))
        .build());

    // process the file contents
}
catch (FileNotFoundException e) {
    Log.w("CONTENT", "File not found: " + extra, e);
}
catch (IOException e) {
    Log.w("CONTENT", "Failed reading: " + extra, e);
}
finally {
    if (null != in) { try { in.close(); } catch (IOException e) { } }
}
```

There is just one other detail necessary to make the application work. Recall that `ParcelFileDescriptor.open(path, modeBits)`, the method used to open the extras file, requires a full pathname for the file it opens. It follows that the _data field in the values database must contain a full pathname.

The method `Context.openFileOutput` is a convenient way to create private files. As described, it creates files in a subdirectory of an application's private sandbox. In order to programmatically obtain the name of that directory, to construct the full pathname for the _data column, use the method `Context.getFilesDir`. The name of the file stored into the _data column is:

```
context.getFilesDir() + "/" + filename
```

SUMMARY

This chapter examined the Android content provider component in thorough detail.

➤ Starting with a client's point of view, the chapter uncovered the content provider's essential behavior.

➤ Next, it introduced the contract file, an exportable definition of a content provider's API.

➤ The chapter took a deep dive into the specifics of content provider implementation, exploring tools like the URI matcher, transactions, the query builder, and a couple of handy tools for implementing a virtual table space.

➤ It described registering a content provider in the application manifest and the types of permissions used to control access to it.

➤ As a recurring theme, the chapter discussed one of Android's most brilliant features, the content observer. The content observer uses a URI as a rendezvous point for the dataset it represents. Notifications sent by clients that change the backing dataset are broadcast to all clients subscribed to those notifications.

➤ Finally there was a discussion of an advanced topic, using a content provider to facilitate access to large data objects, including the ability to efficiently transfer files.

This chapter completes a low-level foundation upon which you can build an architecture for enterprise application. It steps away from the generic programming concerns of the preceding chapters and introduces one of Android's key architectural components. The content provider is the basis for Android's approach to mobile architecture: a RESTful cache pulled up out of the Internet, right onto the mobile device.

The rest of this book explores effective use of this cache.

5

REST, Content Providers, Concurrency, Networking, and Sync Adapters

WROX.COM CODE DOWNLOADS FOR THIS CHAPTER

Please note that all the code examples in this chapter are available at `https://github.com/wileyenterpriseandroid/Examples.git` and as a part of the book's code download at `www.wrox.com` on the Download Code tab.

Mobile developers — including Android developers — face common challenges when communicating with remote services. Tasks that are straightforward on a local network or even the wired Internet — using a remote service or requesting remote data — can have all sorts of subtle pitfalls in a mobile environment. Attempting to use the network efficiently while synchronizing data between mobile platforms and backend web services adds additional headaches. Among the key challenges that Android developers face are these:

➤ Data synchronization between a mobile client and a web service

➤ Handling large datasets

➤ Using Android APIs to solve these problems in such a way that the solutions can be reused across application domains

➤ Android MVC and correct handling of the UI thread during remote requests

The previous chapters built the foundation for Android applications, setting the stage by describing the Android user interface, database programming and, most important, content providers. This chapter builds on that foundation — which, so far, is entirely local — to introduce client-side network programming. Here you step off the isolated mobile device and expand your horizons to a *connected* mobile device.

This chapter introduces REST (Representational State Transfer) as a powerful architectural style. It demonstrates this style with two example clients that store information about contacts in a RESTful server. The next chapter illustrates the construction of the server with which the clients communicate. Together, these two chapters provide the model for a generic, functional, end-to-end mobile platform based on sound principles for robust Android programming.

> **NOTE** *Note that in order to run the client application created in this chapter it is necessary, also, to run a server like the one described in the next chapter. The material presented here follows logically from the discussion of content providers in Ch. 4 and, thus, appears here, before the description of the server on which it depends.*

The Android platform creates an issue of particular concern to developers creating networked applications: How do well behaved networking and data management interact with Android's process model — the lifecycles of activity and service components? This chapter describes three rock-solid architectural approaches that answer that question.

➤ **Service-centric** — Based on an Android `IntentService`

➤ **ContentProvider-centric** — Based on an Android `ContentProvider`

➤ **SyncAdapter-centric** — Based on Android's sync adapter framework

BASIC REST

The exploration of external data management on Android starts with a primer on what has become a standard set of architectural constraints for designing communication protocols between Internet services and their clients — Representational State Transfer or REST. Although REST has roots that go well back into the mid-1990s, the name was introduced and formalized by Roy Fielding in his doctoral dissertation in the year 2000. One of the designers of HTTP, Fielding used REST as a way of formalizing an architectural style that meets the goals of the web, among them extreme, anarchic scalability.

Why REST?

As far back as 1990, Sun Fellow Peter Deutsch codified a list of assumptions that engineers were making at the time in their distributed computing architectures that doomed the resulting products to failure. Dubbed by Deutsch as the "Fallacies of Networked Computing," the first four are attributed to Bill Joy and Dave Lyon and the last to James Gosling. They are:

1. The network is reliable.
2. Latency is zero.
3. Bandwidth is infinite.
4. The network is secure.
5. Topology doesn't change.
6. There is one administrator.
7. Transport cost is zero.
8. The network is homogenous.

Engineers at the time assumed — sometimes implicitly — that multiple computers connected together by a network would behave as an analog of multiple components connected in a computer. They expected, in other words, that a network would behave like a single, huge machine. As is so often the case in engineering, size matters. The early attempts to scale architecture linearly, from a single machine to a network, were largely disappointing.

Enter REST and a radical change in point of view. Instead of hiding the vagaries of the underlying network, the REST style focuses on them. The architectural constraints imposed by the RESTful style assume the contradictions of Deutsch's fallacies and provide elegant tools for designing consistent, resilient, and highly scalable client-server systems.

RESTful style architectures are particularly relevant in the world of mobile computing. The network as perceived from a mobile device is even less reliable than that perceived by the pioneers of distributed architecture. In the course of a normal day, a mobile device might be powered down abruptly, lose its signal in a subway tunnel, switch from a 3G to a WiFi network, and so on. An architectural style that frankly acknowledges this environment and offers the developer ways to thrive in it means the difference between applications that constantly and mysteriously fail and those that work. As you will see, the constraints imposed by the Android-managed container are yet another reason to prefer the RESTful style.

The exact definition of REST and whether a particular API is RESTful can be the source of lengthy and heated discussions. This chapter makes every attempt to avoid those discussions, focusing instead on what distinguishes the REST style from others, and how REST is particularly suited for use in Android.

An API that is RESTful will tend to have the following attributes:

➤ **It is client/server.** A RESTful API clearly distinguishes the role of a client, the entity that makes requests for services, from a server, the entity that listens for those requests and supplies the services.

➤ **It is stateless.** In a RESTful API a client cannot expect a server to hold context between requests. Each client request must contain all of the information necessary for the server to process it completely.

➤ **It describes the exchange of representations of named resources, not the exchange of those resources themselves.** This is a bit subtle, but fairly important — it acknowledges a layer of abstraction between internal and external representations of objects. A resource is any object that can be named, commonly with a URI. A representation is simply a transferable document that describes the current state of some resource. A trivial example of this distinction is a server that is willing to describe the single resource named by a given URI using either JSON or XML: a single resource with multiple representations. A more technical example is a protocol in which a representation includes a version number. This representation is a snapshot of the resource at some particular moment in time and, clearly, not the resource itself.

➤ **It has a uniform interface.** This is probably the best known and most significant of the REST constraints. A RESTful API will, typically, support only the four standard CRUD methods, insert, update, delete, and query (PUT, POST, DELETE and GET, respectively, in HTTP) regardless of the application's functional API. This design choice represents a focus on the nature of the infrastructure that supports client/server transactions: an unreliable, asynchronous network. This is dramatically different from the APIs typical of other remote technologies such as COM, CORBA, and SOAP that have a set of operations that is much richer and more tightly coupled to the behavior of the specific service.

> **NOTE** *For the curious, there are lengthy discussions of REST online:*
> ```
> http://en.wikipedia.org/wiki/Representational_state_transfer
> http://www.ics.uci.edu/~fielding/pubs/dissertation/evaluation.htm
> ```

These attributes lead to protocols that have some very nice characteristics. First of all, because the interface is uniform, it is possible to create generic proxies for RESTful APIs. That means that a proxy for one RESTful API is a proxy for any RESTful API. The client of a RESTful API cannot tell whether it is talking to the origin server or to some local cache that is ignorant of the service it is caching. RESTful APIs automatically scale with the network.

The REST constraints for idempotency, the transfer of resource representations rather than objects, and against server-side session state also facilitate the caching of RESTful protocols. Although a particular representation of a resource may be out of date, it is probably consistent forever. A service and its clients can negotiate the degree of staleness that is tolerable. Many RESTful APIs include specific metadata that describes what can be cached and for how long.

By recognizing and embracing the vagaries of the medium — a slow, unreliable network with changing, anarchic topology — REST insulates a client from the concerns of the server.

REST over HTTP

Although the REST style can be used with nearly any protocol, in the Internet, HTTP is the vehicle of choice because it is RESTful in itself. The combination of a URI to name a target resource; the four methods PUT, POST, DELETE, and GET; and the request content provide a transport that most RESTful services simply adopt. Let's take a minute to review a few of the details of the mapping from REST to HTTP.

URIs

Almost all RESTful APIs in the Internet use URIs to name their resources. These URIs have a predictable structure that is defined in RFC 3986. Here is an abbreviated version of that structure:

```
http[s]://<host>[:<port>]/(<path-seg>/)*<path-seg>[?<param>=<value>(&<param>=<value>)*]
```

This proto-typical URI has four parts — a scheme, an authority, a path, and a query. In detail:

➤ The scheme for a URI used in a RESTful protocol is very likely to be either `http://` or `https://`.

➤ The authority for a URI used by a RESTful protocol is likely to be the DNS name of the origin server for the service that is the target of the request. In addition to the hostname, the URI may contain the port number on the target host at which the server is accepting connections.

➤ The path portion of a URI used by a RESTful protocol is a standard slash-separated (/), hierarchical namespace. Just as the scheme and authority sections of the URI probably identify a service, so the path portion identifies a specific resource maintained by that service.

➤ A URI used in a RESTful protocol may have a query section. If the section exists, it begins with a question mark (?). Following the question mark is a list of one or more key/value pairs separated by ampersands (&). The key/value pairs are given as a key followed by an equals sign (=) and then its value.

> **NOTE** *There is more information on the full syntax of a URI at:*
> `http://tools.ietf.org/html/rfc3986`

Although the similarity is only partial, a URI in a RESTful API might be understood as a reference to an object in much the same way that a Java variable is a reference to an object. In a well-designed Java program, it is likely that you have no idea what, actually, is at the end of a Java reference. You can ask for information about the referenced object's state, and you may even be able to change that state. You should not take the liberty, though, of guessing at the object's actual implementation.

In a RESTful protocol, the URI functions in much the same way. The client program can ask about the resource to which the URI refers and may, similarly, be able to ask the service to update that resource. However, it never touches the actual resource and is not free to infer the resource's implementation.

Contents

In addition to containing a URI, an HTTP request may contain a typed data payload. For example, the payload often is structured application data. When this is the case, the data is typically represented either as XML or, more popular in recent history, JSON.

An HTTP request has a header section that contains metadata about the request. Among other things, the header for a request containing a payload will specify a `Content-Type`. The value for the content type header field is a MIME (Multipurpose Internet Mail Extension) type that describes how the payload should be interpreted.

MIME is an Internet standard for describing content type. If the payload data is structured application data, XML or JSON, as described previously, the `Content-Type` field will contain `application/xml` or `application/json`. If the content is something else entirely — perhaps an audio file — the MIME type will identify it accordingly (`audio/mp3`, for instance).

> **NOTE** *There is more information on MIME and HTTP at the following sites.*
>
> *MIME* — `http://tools.ietf.org/html/rfc2045` *through* `2049`
> *HTTP* — `http://tools.ietf.org/html/rfc2616`

An Example REST API

To make this discussion of REST more concrete, let's look at a simplistic web service API. This API is the basis for the example code — clients and a backend service — implemented in this and the next chapter. The API supports persistent operations on a collection of contact resources. Although the example is simplistic in several respects — respects that will be discussed in detail later in the chapter — the general concept is entirely realistic. Any mobile application that has a social aspect will have to track relationships between entities that are similar to the contacts used in this example. Developers familiar with the Android platform will know that it already supports a rich and extensible framework for contacts. Creating a useful social application will require, at best, understanding and integrating with that framework. At least as likely, though, it will require a custom implementation such as the one discussed here.

Contact Representation

The example API supports a set of contact resources. These resources will be represented in messages between the client and the server as JSON documents described by the following schema:

```json
{
    "title": "RESTfulContacts",
    "type": "object",
    "properties": {
            "id": {
                    "type": "integer"
            },
            "firstName": {
                    "description": "first name",
                    "type": "string"
            },
            "lastName": {
                    "description": "last name",
                    "type": "string"
            }
```

```
            "phone": {
                    "description": "phone number",
                    "type": "string"
            }
            "email": {
                    "description": "email address",
                    "type": "string"
            }
            "version": {
                    "description": "version id",
                    "type": "integer",
                    "minimum": 0
            }
            "updateTime": {
                    "description": "time of last sync",
                    "type": "integer",
                    "minimum": 0
            }
            "deleted": {
                    "description": "contact has been deleted",
                    "type": "boolean",
            }
        }
    }
}
```

> **NOTE** *This document is in a format called json-schema. JSON schema is the JSON analog for XML Schema; it is used to describe the format of a family of JSON documents. The rest of this book will use it, frequently, for that purpose. There is more documentation on JSON schema at:*
>
> `http://json-schema.org/`

Remember that since this is a RESTful API, the previous schema describes only a representation of the actual resource. The `version`, `updateTime`, and `deleted` attributes, for instance, are metadata that describe a resource. The client and server may use that metadata to synchronize their respective versions of the resources.

In order to exchange information about those internal representations — however they are implemented — the client and the server must be able to describe those resources in a way that fits into the JSON schema. This process — creating a transferable representation from a resource — is called *marshaling*. For example, here is the marshaled representation of the resource for John Smith:

```
{
    "firstName": "john",
    "lastName": "smith",
    "phone:": "781-123-4567",
    "email": "john.smith@gmail.com"
}
```

Contact Methods and URIs

The JSON schema describes the payload for the HTTP requests that the client sends to the server. Defining the schema is analogous to defining parameters for API methods. In this simple example, the schema is the union of the parameters for all of the API methods. You might think of it is as if all of the arguments to all of the methods supported by the server were combined into a single parameter, passed to each of those methods. To complete the definition of the RESTful Contacts API, you also need a catalog of the small set of methods that the server supports. Here it is:

➤ A request for the states of all contacts:

```
GET /Contacts
```

➤ A request for the state of a specific contact, the contact with id 1:

```
GET /Contacts/1
```

➤ A request to create a new contact. The payload describes the new contact:

```
POST Contacts
```

payload:

```
{
    "firstName": "john",
    "lastName": "smith",
    "phone:": "781-123-4567",
    "email": "john.smith@gmail.com"
}
```

➤ A request to update the phone number associated with a contact, which is contact #1 again. As with the preceding example, the payload contains a description of the contact fields to be changed, along with their new values:

```
PUT /Contacts/1
```

payload:

```
{
    "phone:": "781-123-4567"
}
```

➤ A request to delete all of the information about the contact whose phone number was changed:

```
DELETE /Contacts/1
```

➤ A request to synchronize information about multiple contacts. The payload (not shown here) is a list of one or more contacts that have been changed on the client and that must be updated on the server:

```
POST /Contacts/sync
```

Contact Transactions

This section puts this API, as specified so far, into practice. You can try out a few HTTP transactions by issuing requests from the command line using the command-line tool `curl`. Exercising the server in this way will reveal its behavior.

> NOTE *The backward-slash (\) character in the command line examples below, is the line continuation character. It is used by UNIX command line interpreters (shells) to indicate that a single command spans several lines. It is used here simply for formatting purposes: It is not actually part of the curl command. This session may look slightly different in other command-line interpreters.*

First, let's create a new contact:

```
> curl -X POST \
    -H "Content-Type: application/json" \
    -d '{"firstName":"mike","email":"mlayton@dartmouth.edu",
        "lastName":"layton","phone":"826-9027"}' \
    http://wileycontacts.com:8080/springServiceContacts/Contacts
```

```
POST /springServiceContacts/Contacts HTTP/1.1
User-Agent: curl/7.28.0
Host: wileycontacts.com:8080
Accept: */*
Content-Type: application/json
Content-Length: 91
{
    "firstName":"mike",
    "lastName":"layton",
    "email":"mlayton@dartmouth.edu",
    "phone":"826-9027"
}

HTTP/1.1 200 OK
Server: Apache-Coyote/1.1
Content-Type: application/json;charset=UTF-8
Transfer-Encoding: chunked
Date: Sun, 06 Jan 2013 05:56:31 GMT
{
    "location":"http://wileycontacts.com:8080/springServiceContacts/Contacts/28"
}
```

That seems to have worked! The 200 return status indicates that the server successfully processed the request. The returned payload appears to be the URI for the newly created contact. Excellent! You should now be able to retrieve this newly created resource:

```
> curl -X GET http://wileycontacts.com:8080/springServiceContacts/Contacts/28
```

```
GET /springServiceContacts/Contacts/28 HTTP/1.1
User-Agent: curl/7.28.0
Host: wileycontacts.com:8080
```

```
Accept: */*

HTTP/1.1 200 OK
Server: Apache-Coyote/1.1
Content-Type: application/json;charset=UTF-8
Transfer-Encoding: chunked
Date: Sun, 06 Jan 2013 06:21:36 GMT

{
    "id":28,
    "firstName":"mike",
    "lastName":"layton",
    "phone":"(802) 826-9027",
    "email":"mlayton@dartmouth.edu",
    "version":1,
    "updateTime":1357451791659,
    "deleted":false
}
```

That worked too. The service is holding version "1" of the resource.

This demonstrates the basic functionality of the API. Tidy up by deleting the test resource:

> **curl -X DELETE http://wileycontacts.com:8080/springServiceContacts/Contacts/28**

```
DELETE /springServiceContacts/Contacts/28 HTTP/1.1
User-Agent: curl/7.28.0
Host: wileycontacts.com:8080
Accept: */*

HTTP/1.1 200 OK
Server: Apache-Coyote/1.1
Content-Type: text/plain;charset=ISO-8859-1
Content-Length: 3
Date: Sun, 06 Jan 2013 06:35:55 GMT
```

Again, this seems to have worked. The 200 status confirms that the server successfully processed the request. To verify that the test resource is gone, you can query for it again.

> **curl -X GET http://wileycontacts.com:8080/springServiceContacts/Contacts/28**

```
GET /springServiceContacts/Contacts/28 HTTP/1.1
User-Agent: curl/7.28.0
Host: wileycontacts.com:8080
Accept: */*

HTTP/1.1 404 Not Found
Server: Apache-Coyote/1.1
Content-Type: text/html;charset=utf-8
Content-Length: 952
Date: Sun, 06 Jan 2013 06:50:45 GMT
```

The resource is gone. The 404 status indicates that it no longer exists on the server.

As this section demonstrates, a basic RESTful interface can be a very simple thing. It does not require complex clients — in this case you used a simple HTTP command-line tool — and both the queries from the client and the responses from the server are straightforward and understandable. REST can get quite complex, but it doesn't start that way.

ANDROID NETWORKING

Before we turn to creating client code for this RESTful API, this section reviews some basic networking and how applications implement HTTP connections on the Android platform.

Network connections and their attributes can be finicky and time-consuming to debug. Trying to turn around even the simplest REST request can be maddening when a tight-lipped server returns nothing more informative than a 400 status in response to a request. The fault can be in the request headers (unexpected or multiple content types, an unsupported encoding, or a missing response type), or in the payload (bad JSON or XML syntax, or possibly something wrong in the payload semantics, such as a missing attribute). Because REST syntax is so generic, it can be difficult to determine the root cause of a failure.

As always, an excellent strategy for dealing with this sort of problem is to start with working code. There are many example RESTful HTTP client implementations to be found with simple web searches. There are also two good examples in this section. Copy them and tweak them until they meet your needs.

Better yet, if there is a client that already works with the specific server that is your target, use it! If it is in a different language, translate it. If that is impractical, use a network monitor like tcpdump or Wireshark to determine exactly what it is sending and make sure your client sends the same thing. Of course, if you have access to the server itself, you may be able to use its log to understand what is going on. Once you have something that works, it is easy to modify and refactor it, backing out changes when it breaks.

The Apache Libraries

Android contains two entirely different networking libraries, found in the packages `java.net` and `org.apache.http`, respectively. Until about 2011, the word (some of it from Google insiders) seemed to be that Apache framework was a better choice. Listing 5-1 shows the implementation of a method that does an HTTP POST using the Apache framework.

LISTING 5-1: HTTP POST implemented using the Apache libraries

```
public void post(Uri uri, String payload, ResponseHandler hdlr) {
    HttpPost req = new HttpPost(uri.toString());
    req.setHeader(HTTP.USER_AGENT, USER_AGENT);

    if (null != payload) {
        StringEntity s = new StringEntity(payload);
```

continues

LISTING 5-1 *(continued)*

```
            s.setContentType(MIME_JSON);
            req.setEntity(s);
        }

        if (null != hdlr) { req.setHeader(HEADER_ACCEPT, MIME_JSON); }

        HttpParams httpParams = new BasicHttpParams();
        HttpConnectionParams.setConnectionTimeout(httpParams, TIMEOUT);
        HttpConnectionParams.setSoTimeout(httpParams, TIMEOUT);
        DefaultHttpClient client = new DefaultHttpClient(httpParams);

        HttpResponse resp = client.execute(req);

        if (null != hdlr) {
            Reader in = new InputStreamReader(resp.getEntity().getContent());
            try { hdlr.handleRepsonse(); }
            finally {
                try { in.close(); } catch (Exception e) { }
            }
        }
    }
}
```

The java.net Libraries

Recently, though, the tune has changed. The Android development team devoted considerable effort to the `java.net` libraries and is now recommending them as the preferred choice. The timing of the change correlates pretty well with the release of Gingerbread. The Android Developer website says:

Apache HTTP client has fewer bugs in Android 2.2 (Froyo) and earlier releases. For Android 2.3 (Gingerbread) and later, HttpURLConnection is the best choice.

At the time of this writing, Froyo comprises less than 10 percent of the Android installed base — and even that share is shrinking. Unless there is a clear, specific reason for choosing the Apache frameworks, Android developers should choose the `java.net` HTTP library classes.

An implementation of a fairly general HTTP request processor using the `java.net` libraries looks like Listing 5-2. This is the one you want.

LISTING 5-2: HTTP POST implemented using the java.net libraries

```
    private int sendRequest(
        HttpMethod method,
        Uri uri,
        String payload,
        ResponseHandler hdlr)
        throws IOException
    {
        HttpURLConnection conn
            = (HttpURLConnection) new URL(uri.toString()).openConnection();
```

```
    int code = HttpURLConnection.HTTP_INTERNAL_ERROR;
    try {
        conn.setReadTimeout(HTTP_READ_TIMEOUT);
        conn.setConnectTimeout(HTTP_CONN_TIMEOUT);
        conn.setRequestMethod(method.toString());
        conn.setRequestProperty(HEADER_USER_AGENT, USER_AGENT);
        conn.setRequestProperty(HEADER_ENCODING, ENCODING_NONE);

        if (null != hdlr) {
            conn.setRequestProperty(HEADER_ACCEPT, MIME_JSON);
            conn.setDoInput(true);
        }

        if (null != payload) {
            conn.setRequestProperty(HEADER_CONTENT_TYPE, MIME_JSON);
            conn.setFixedLengthStreamingMode(payload.length());
            conn.setDoOutput(true);

            conn.connect();
            Writer out = new OutputStreamWriter(
                new BufferedOutputStream(conn.getOutputStream()),
                "UTF-8");
            out.write(payload);
            out.flush();
        }

        code = conn.getResponseCode();

        if (null != hdlr) {
            hdlr.handleRepsonse(new BufferedReader(
                new InputStreamReader(conn.getInputStream())));
        }
    }
    finally {
        if (null != conn) {
            try { conn.disconnect(); } catch (Exception e) { }
        }
    }

    return code;
}
```

> **NOTE** *The best reference material for the Android network frameworks is the following:*
>
> http://d.android.com/reference/java/net/HttpURLConnection.html
>
> *Should you need it, there is additional information about the Apache framework here:*
>
> http://hc.apache.org/

Permissions

Remember that on Android platforms, network access is a restricted privilege. An application must request permissions to gain access. In order for any of this code to work, you need to include the following request in your Android manifest:

```
<uses-permission android:name="android.permission.INTERNET"/>
```

Chapter 12 describes permissions, security, and access control, in detail.

CONSIDERING CONCURRENCY AND LIFECYCLES

There is an old adage in some developer circles: "The novice programmer believes concurrency is hard but the journeyman programmer does not fear it. The master programmer believes that concurrency is hard." Concurrency is a very important issue in Android and most developers embarking on an Android project can benefit from a review. While a complete discussion of Java concurrency is well outside the scope of this book, reviewing some of the key issues is well worth the time. The beginning of this chapter alluded to the fact that on the Android platform invoking a network request can be a minefield of subtle problems for which even developers with substantial mobile and Java experience may not be prepared. To illustrate these issues, this section tours a series of code snippets, each of which will highlight one or more problems that Android developers may encounter.

The Android Concurrency Architecture

To begin the discussion, we want to review a few of the basics of Android's concurrency architecture.

An Android application is a single Linux process. It has its own address space — other applications cannot accidentally change its state — and one or more of its own threads of execution.

An Android application is also a managed container. Unlike the applications that run on a common laptop or even an iPhone, an Android application does not usually control how the application process is started or stopped. Instead, an Android app is a set of special objects, declared to the framework in the manifest file, each of which can be created and used at the framework's whim. Server-side developers who have experience with JEE containers and managed beans will find this concept familiar.

The main thread in an Android application's process is usually called the UI thread, sometimes the main looper or just the main thread. Unless there is a specific arrangement to execute code on some other thread, the UI thread powers all an application's components — activities, services, content providers, and so on. All run on the UI thread.

This poses a problem because the UI thread eponymously powers the UI. Any task that occupies it for any significant period of time will cause the UI to become unresponsive. That is intolerable: Long-running tasks must run on a different thread. The Android framework will terminate your program with prejudice — with an Application Not Responding error — if it hangs the UI thread.

There is a related issue that also stems from the single threaded nature of Android's UI. The UI code is not thread safe and verifies, during method calls, that it is running on the UI thread. If a UI object discovers that one of its methods is being called from something other than the UI thread, it immediately throws an exception, killing the application. When a long-running task produces results on a non-UI thread, it must safely communicate those results back to the UI thread for presentation in the UI.

As if it were not enough that an Android developer must constantly confront one of the most difficult things to do in Java — publishing objects between threads — there is another concern. The Android framework controls the lifecycle of component objects: activities, services, and so on. It does not, on the other hand, control the lifecycle of asynchronous threads spawned to handle long-running tasks. This leads to two more unsatisfactory consequences.

First of all, if a long-running task holds a reference — a Java variable — to a managed object, it can prevent that object from being garbage collected. Spawning a thread that holds a reference to an activity, for instance, might easily keep that activity object around long after the Android framework has no use for it. The activity has been leaked — its memory cannot be reclaimed.

The second unsatisfactory consequence of the clash between objects with managed and unmanaged lifecycles is that the object with the managed lifecycle may be in an inconsistent state when a long-running task tries to use it. In the previous example, an attempt to draw on the device screen using the reference to the destroyed activity is likely to result in unpredictable behavior.

This conundrum — getting long-running tasks off the UI thread and getting the results back onto the UI thread, while keeping object lifecycles congruent — is a key force that drives the architecture of Android applications, especially ones that participate in an enterprise system.

A Naive Request

You might think that it's straightforward to invoke a RESTful operation from an Android application. It is as simple as adding one of the example clients in Listings 5-1 and 5-2 to your code and then calling it as necessary, right? After considering the threading problem, though, it should be clear that such an extremely naïve approach is not sufficient.

Developers with some UI experience might address the issue by spawning a worker thread to make the remote call and then notifying the UI thread when the call completes. As the previous section notes, this solves some problems but creates others. Developers with Android experience may even use the framework's scheduling tool, AsyncTask, to manage long-running tasks without spawning lots of expensive, heavy-weight thread objects. Truly savvy disciples of the robot may use the powerful asynchronous tool introduced in the previous chapter, the Loader. Alas, none of these solutions, depicted schematically in Figure 5-1, is sufficient.

What's wrong with these simple and seemingly reasonable approaches? Unfortunately, plenty:

➤ The Android framework might shut down a long-running network process.

➤ The managed object to which the result of the transaction must be reported might be destroyed before the transaction is complete. The application recovers but discards the result. This is an unacceptable waste of the battery and network bandwidth.

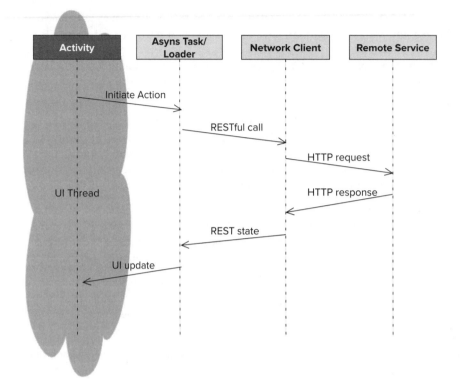

FIGURE 5-1

➤ After sending the request, the device might enter a network dead spot and be unable to communicate with the server. The request has been sent but might not succeed.

➤ The device might be powered down (or, worse yet, the battery suddenly removed). The request was never sent and there is no indication that it failed.

➤ The Android framework might need space for a new application and might terminate the process for the application running the task. All of the threads, including the one running the long-running task, are ended.

The problem here is structural. Users see an application as a collection of contracts. When, for instance, users press a Send button, they believe that they have entered into a contract with the application to send something. If the application fails to send the data, that's bad enough. If it fails to do so without notification, the user experience is very bad. When the user demands a contract on one side, and the network is unreliable on the other, that's a problem.

A mobile application that represents the state of its contract with the user as an in-memory command object is doomed to failure. In order to meet the user's expectations, it is essential to record those contracts in some persistent way.

AN ARCHITECTURE FOR ROBUST NETWORKING

How, then, can an Android application call a remote server safely and efficiently? There are three approaches that vary from one another, slightly, in their implementations. Although the three approaches differ in their implementation, they share common themes. All of the approaches are based on RESTful architecture. All depend on the fact that a query to a content provider is similar to the query to the remote service for which the content provider is a proxy. In all three, resource state, including whether the resource has changed since the last time it was synchronized with the remote service, is stored locally in a content provider (probably backed by a SQLite database). Finally, in all three, the task of synchronizing the data held locally in the content provider with the parallel data on the remote server, is implemented in an Android service, not an activity.

> **NOTE** *The discussion in this chapter — and, indeed, the rest of this book — is based in part on an architecture proposed in a presentation by Google Engineer, Virgil Dobjanschi, at the 2010 Google I/O. The presentation is available on YouTube:*
>
> `http://www.youtube.com/watch?v=xHXn3Kg2IQE`

The three resulting approaches, detailed in the next several sections are:

➤   Service-centric

➤   ContentProvider-centric

➤   SyncAdapter-centric

An architectural-level examination of these three approaches may make them seem top-heavy and over-engineered. As you review this section remember that, just because a functional component appears in a schematic does not necessarily mean that it requires a substantial amount of code. Depending on the underlying complexity of the application in which these abstract architectures are used, a diagram component may represent a Java class, a method, or even just a few lines of code somewhere.

Approach 1: Service-Centric

Although this approach may be the simplest of the three, it is also the least malleable. This section looks at it quickly, as you can see in Figure 5-2.

When an activity must perform an asynchronous task, it makes what looks like straightforward method calls to a service helper. The service helper is nothing more than a proxy that translates the arguments to the method call into extra data in an intent. When the service helper fires the intent, the service catches it in its `onStartService` method. Listing 5-3 shows what this might look like in an implementation of a client for the simple contacts API.

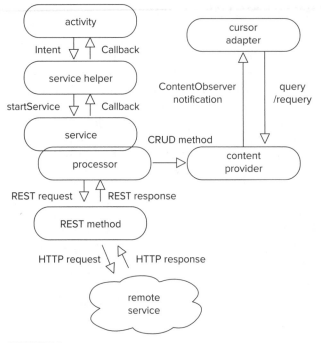

FIGURE 5-2

LISTING 5-3: A service helper

```
public void createContact(
    Activity ctxt,
    String fname,
    String lname,
    String email,
    String phone)
{
    Intent intent = new Intent(ctxt, ContactsService.class);
    intent.putExtra(ContactsService.FNAME, fname);
    intent.putExtra(ContactsService.LNAME, lname);
    intent.putExtra(ContactsService.PHONE, phone);
    intent.putExtra(ContactsService.EMAIL, email);
    ctxt.startService(intent);
}
```

NOTE *There is a complete explanation of intents and intent services in the Android developer documentation:*

http://developer.android.com/guide/components/intents-filters.html
http://developer.android.com/reference/android/app/IntentService.html

When the service receives the intent, it is responsible for several things. Its first order of business is to move the process of handling the intent off the UI thread. Recall that even in an Android service, class methods are run on the UI thread, by default. The Android IntentService is a perfect tool for scheduling tasks on background threads. Each call to an intent service's onStartService method results in a call to the service onHandleIntent method running on a daemon thread.

On the daemon thread the service implementation must:

➤ Create the new resource in the database.

➤ Mark the new resource as "dirty" — which means it's not yet synchronized with the service.

➤ Initiate a transaction with the remote service to update the remote resource.

➤ Record the ID for the update transaction in the database.

A single call to a content provider handles three of these four requirements.

To initiate the transaction with the remote server, the service object uses another architectural abstraction that is simpler than it sounds, the REST method. A REST method is very similar to the service helper. It is simply a proxy that translates a method call, from the service, into an HTTP request to the remote server.

When the remote server returns its HTTP response, processing proceeds back up the stack. The REST method returns to the service. The service interprets the response. Response processing must *always* clear the ID of the outstanding request, recorded when the request was initiated (because the transaction has completed). Depending on whether the request was successful, it may also clear the "dirty" flag and record other metadata — the time of last sync or a version number — in the resource.

If the response from the remote server forces the content provider to change a resource in any way that is visible from the UI, the content provider will use the content observer protocol to notify listeners that they need to re-query.

Notice that the burden of communicating inbound data — new information sent by the server — back to the UI thread, is handled by the content provider. Instead of explicitly publishing the new data into the UI thread, in order to make it available for display in view components, updates are pushed into the content provider. The content provider notifies the view that the data has changed, and the view makes a normal, loader-driven query to refresh the display.

Even at this crude level of detail, the appeal of this multi-tier architecture is apparent. The activity does not create or manage any AsyncTasks. The state of requests to the remote server is kept in the database. The state information may even be useful to the user and, therefore, reflected in the UI. The processor component may be somewhat complex, but it is complexity that is intrinsic in the problem and ignored by less sophisticated solutions.

Approach 2: ContentProvider-Centric

This approach is very appealing because of its homogeneity. It has a fractal-like design in which the small components look very much like the larger components that they comprise (see Figure 5-3). This is the architecture used to implement the example client in the next part of this chapter.

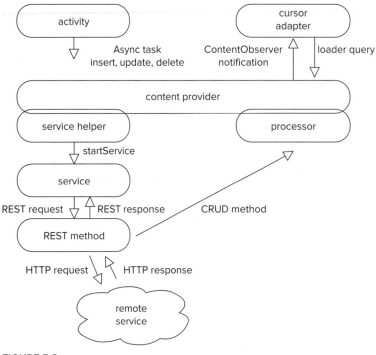

FIGURE 5-3

The components in this approach are similar to those in the previous one. The significant difference is that here the activity makes RESTful calls to a content provider as if all of the data were local. Hidden behind the content provider is a service helper that forwards requests to a service. The service is responsible, as it was in the previous approach, for synchronizing local resources with their counterparts on the remote server and doing so on a thread other than the UI thread. It uses a REST method, also similar to that in the previous style, to communicate with the remote server.

When the remote server returns a response, a processor component updates the content provider, which notifies content observers as necessary.

Notice that this style does require AsyncTasks in the activity. Content provider operations may take significant time and cannot be performed on the UI thread. On the other hand, this adds a certain symmetry to the architecture. The queries that populate the cursor adapter were, even in the previous approach, performed from a loader. A loader is, essentially, an AsyncTask.

In this style, both outbound updates and inbound queries use AsyncTasks. Note, though, that these AsyncTasks perform only *local* operations. The lifetime of one of these tasks is only the time necessary to read or write a SQLite database.

At this point the origin of a second name for these architectural styles, "figure-eight," should become apparent. In addition to the UI thread, there are two asynchronous processes. One of them — the lower lobe — synchronizes the content provider with the remote server. The second — the upper lobe — obtains information from the content provider and publishes it into the UI. AsyncTasks and loaders comprise the upper lobe, asynchronously synchronizing the UI with the data model in the content provider. In both this and the preceding approach the lower lobe is an intent service thread. It pushes data to the network or publishes it to the UI by storing it directly into the content provider.

You'll revisit this architecture in more detail later in the chapter, when you build the `restfulCachingProviderContacts` project.

Approach 3: SyncAdapter-Centric

This final style is very similar to the previous approach. The essential difference is that it uses the Android sync adapter framework, instead of a custom service, to manage the remote synchronization process. See Figure 5-4.

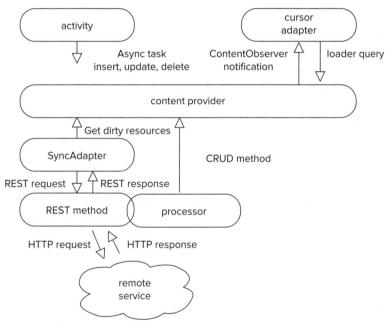

FIGURE 5-4

Sync adapters are resilient, persistent, and very efficient. They are complex and are discussed separately, in detail, in the next section of this chapter.

REST within Android

You may have noticed the parallels between the discussion of content providers in the previous chapter and the discussion of REST in this one. The relationships between the managed components within an Android application are a microcosm of the relationships between objects outside the application on the greater network. As on the Internet, client and service components have disparate lifecycles, different owners, and scale unpredictably.

Further, as you saw in Chapter 4, Android content providers support inter-process communication (IPC). The `KeyValClient` demonstrated a content provider that is part of one application and used by client code that is running in a completely different Linux process as part of a separate application. The details of how this works — an Android technology called *Binder* — are only partially addressed in this book. Note, however, that the Android framework implements communication between a client application and a content provider running as part of a different application by handing the client application a proxy for the serving content provider. In other words, the client holds a proxy to the serving content provider, and that proxy is indistinguishable from that content provider. Sound familiar?

The fact that an Android system looks a lot like a network, internally, gives rise to the architectural choice, noted in Chapter 4, that may surprise and even disturb developers with experience in back-end server-side development. Although most Enterprise Java developers (JEE) are at home using REST as an external architectural style, they are typically used to using object-relational mapping (ORM) technologies for moving data internally.

Android is much more homogeneous — the REST style is pervasive. UI components like activities use loaders to run RESTful queries against content providers, and receive cursors in return. Most JEE developers would shudder at the server-side equivalent, running a SQL query from a servlet and pushing a cursor into the JSP. In Android, however, this is a sensible choice. Using a standardized cursor API to manage relational data is useful, because client code cannot distinguish between a simple cursor, delivered from another component of the same application, or a cursor wrapper, constructed by Binder and delivered across an IPC connection from a completely different application. A fluent Android developer is comfortable using REST not only for requests to external services, but also for requests to internal services.

The restfulCachingProviderContacts Project: An Example Client

In this section, you'll see how to build a client for the RESTful API discussed so far. The full project containing all code and metadata for the client application in this chapter is available from `https://github.com/wileyenterpriseandroid/Examples.git` and as a part of the book's code download at `www.wrox.com` on the Download Code tab. This section analyzes only the highlights. The project is called `restfulCachingProviderContacts` and it produces an application, RESTfulContacts, that demonstrates basic REST techniques and the architectural style discussed in this chapter. It is based on the second architectural style, the content provider-centric API backed by a custom service.

This application is by no means industrial strength or ready for release. Although it is a good start, it has shortcomings that will provide motivation for the more mature architectures discussed in the second half of this book.

The application presents a typical list view that displays contact information, as you can see in Figure 5-5. List cells contain the contact attributes, as described in the RESTful API: first name, last name, phone number, and e-mail address. In addition — though you can't see the color in this black-and-white figure — there is a small bar on the left of each row that shows the synchronization status of a contact. The status bar is green if the contact is fully synchronized with the server side. It is yellow if there is a synchronization transaction outstanding. It's red if the contact is out of sync and there is no active transaction to sync it.

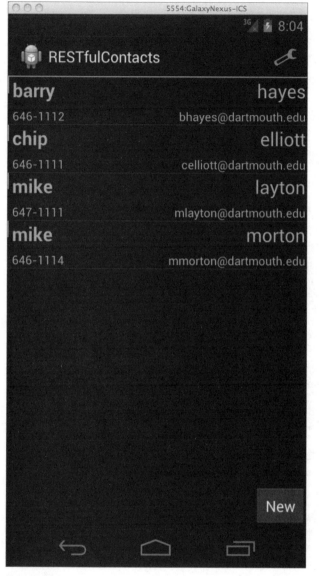

FIGURE 5-5

Clicking on the row for an individual contact or on the New button at the bottom of the page brings up a detail view. The view is populated with contact details, in the former case, and empty, in the latter. Again, there is a narrow status line at the top of the page that reflects that contact synchronization status — green, yellow, or red.

The delete button at the bottom of the page deletes an existing contact. The submit button submits changes to an existing contact or creates a new one. See Figure 5-6.

FIGURE 5-6

The wrench icon in the Action Bar brings up a preferences page from which users can enter the base URI for the server with which the client will communicate. The README file in the project's source describes how to configure an endpoint for a demo server.

Adding a Contact

Start examining the program by tracing the process of adding a new contact. This process begins when a user uses the New button to navigate to the details page, fills it out, and then presses the Submit button.

The implementation of the Submit button handler is shown in Listing 5-4. The button onClickListener calls the update method. The update method makes a sanity check (to make sure that the user hasn't mistakenly submitted an empty form) and then creates a ContentValues object to hold the user's input. Again, note that there is no intermediate POJO (Plain Ole Java Object) representation of the contact. Instead, the UI represents that data as an instance of the standard, pervasive ContentValues object.

When it has constructed the ContentValues object, it passes it to an AsyncTask called UpdateContact that posts the new values to the content provider. Remember that in order to pass the mutable content values object safely to the AsyncTask thread, the calling activity must guarantee that it no longer holds any references to it.

When the user is creating a new contact, the URI used to name the contact whose information should be edited is null. The task can determine whether an insert or an update is required by checking the URI.

The UpdateContact asynchronous task is quite safe. It is fire-and-forget, runs quickly, does not directly report results, and does not hold references to managed components.

> **NOTE** *It is best practice to make all AsyncTasks static. Because Java is a block-structured language, variables declared in a surrounding block are visible from within inner blocks. Java implements this for nested classes by manufacturing an implicit pointer, a reference to the outer class that is not visible to the programmer. A non-static AsyncTask declared inside an activity always has a reference to that activity. That reference will cause all of the problems described earlier in this chapter.*

LISTING 5-4: Adding a contact, the UI

```java
static class UpdateContact extends AsyncTask<Uri, Void, Void> {
    private final ContentResolver resolver;
    private final ContentValues vals;

    public UpdateContact(ContentResolver resolver, ContentValues vals) {
        this.resolver = resolver;
        this.vals = vals;
    }

    @Override
    protected Void doInBackground(Uri... args) {
        Uri uri = args[0];
        if (null != uri) { resolver.update(uri, vals, null, null); }
        else { resolver.insert(ContactsContract.URI, vals); }
        return null;
    }
}
```

continues

LISTING 5-4 *(continued)*

```
// code elided...
void update() {
    String s = fnameView.getText().toString();
    if (TextUtils.isEmpty(s)) {
        Toast.makeText(
            this,
            R.string.name_required,
            Toast.LENGTH_SHORT)
            .show();
        return;
    }

    ContentValues vals = new ContentValues();
    addString(fnameView, fname, vals, ContactsContract.Columns.FNAME);
    addString(lnameView, lname, vals, ContactsContract.Columns.LNAME);
    addString(phoneView, phone, vals, ContactsContract.Columns.PHONE);
    addString(emailView, email, vals, ContactsContract.Columns.EMAIL);

    new UpdateContact(getContentResolver(), vals).execute(contactUri);

    goToContacts();
}
```

Upon receiving the insert request that the UI sends to create a new contact, the content provider does a couple of things, as shown in Listing 5-5.

The Contacts content provider maintains a virtual table, as described in Chapter 4. Its first job is to convert virtual columns to physical columns.

The next step, although only a couple of lines of code, is the key point of this entire chapter. The fact that this newly created record is out of sync with the backend service is not represented as a running task. Instead it is represented as state in the database.

To do this, the code first calls the sendInsert method. In this implementation, sendInsert is the embodiment of the service helper architectural component. It creates a unique transaction ID and forwards the request to the service component as an intent. Marshalling method parameters as an intent in this way was first shown in Listing 5-3. The service will process the intent asynchronously, initiating a transaction with the remote server (as will be described shortly). The sendInsert method returns immediately with the transaction ID.

When the sendInsert method returns, having scheduled the remote transaction, the insert method completes its work by calling localInsert. localInsert adds the newly created record to the database, including the "dirty" flag, marking it as unsynchronized, and the transaction ID, identifying the transaction that has been scheduled to synchronize it.

The localInsert method also notifies any observers that the dataset backing the content provider's URI has changed. For example, if the user is now looking at the list of all contacts — quite likely, since creating a new contact causes the UI to navigate back to the list view — that list displays the newly entered, but out of sync, contact. Because it is out of sync but has a transaction scheduled to synchronize it, the status bar at the left of the row should be yellow. The notification generated in the localInsert method will cause the UI to update to show the yellow status bar.

LISTING 5-5: Adding a contact, the content provider

```java
@Override
public Uri insert(Uri uri, ContentValues vals) {
    switch (uriMatcher.match(uri)) {
        case CONTACTS_DIR:
            break;

        default:
            throw new UnsupportedOperationException(
                "Unrecognized URI: " + uri);
    }

    vals = COL_MAP.translateCols(vals);
    vals.put(ContactsHelper.COL_DIRTY, MARK);

    String xact = sendInsert(vals);
    vals.put(ContactsHelper.COL_SYNC, xact);

    return localInsert(uri, vals);
}

public Uri localInsert(Uri uri, ContentValues vals) {
    long pk = helper.getWritableDatabase().insert(
        ContactsHelper.TAB_CONTACTS,
        ContactsContract.Columns.FNAME,
        vals);

    if (0 > pk) { uri = null; }
    else {
        uri = uri.buildUpon().appendPath(String.valueOf(pk)).build();
        getContext().getContentResolver().notifyChange(uri, null);
    }

    return uri;
}

private String sendInsert(ContentValues vals) {
    Intent intent
        = RESTService.getIntent(getContext(), RESTService.Op.CREATE);

    putContentValues(vals, intent);

    getContext().startService(intent);

    return intent.getStringExtra(RESTService.XACT);
}
```

The application's intent service will eventually get around to processing the request that was posted from the sendInsert method. Since the service is an intent service, that processing automatically takes place on a daemon thread. Again, remember that this is not true for subclasses of a standard service.

The implementation of the request processor section of the intent service is shown in Listing 5-6. The `sendRequest` method used to post an HTTP request to the network is the embodiment of the HTTP method architectural component, and is the network client shown in Listing 5-2. The `MessageHandler` object marshals the content values object to JSON, and the resulting message is passed on as the payload for the HTTP request.

When the server returns its response, the contents are passed to the response handler. It simply unmarshals that content into another new, content values object. If the request is successful, the new contact has been synchronized and no longer dirty.

Whether or not the request was successful, there is no longer an outstanding transaction to synchronize the data. Once the service receives the transaction response, it is obliged to update the content provider when the transaction completes. This update is handled in the `cleanup` method, the embodiment of the processor component in this implementation.

The `cleanup` method calls the content provider to update the record on which the transaction is outstanding. The implementation is a little flabby here; it uses the ID of the transaction to identify the record requiring update. This requires exposing columns in the provider contract that really should be private. A more complete application might describe a second virtual table to be used only by the service and in which the transaction ID was the primary key.

The content provider receives the update, stores it in the database, and notifies the UI. The color of the status bar next to the new contact will change to green if the request was successful or to red if it was not.

LISTING 5-6: Adding a contact, the service

```
private void createContact(Bundle args) {
    if (args.containsKey(ID)) {
        throw new IllegalArgumentException("create must not specify id");
    }
    Uri uri = ((ContactsApplication) getApplication()).getApiUri();

    final ContentValues vals = new ContentValues();
    try {
        String payload = new MessageHandler().marshal(args);

        sendRequest(
            HttpMethod.POST,
            uri,
            payload,
            new ResponseHandler() {
                @Override
                public void handleRepsonse(BufferedReader in)
                    throws IOException
                {
                    new MessageHandler().unmarshal(in, vals);
                } });

        vals.putNull(ContactsContract.Columns.DIRTY);
    }
```

```
            catch (Exception e) {
                Log.w(TAG, "create failed: " + e, e);
            }
            finally {
                cleanup(args, vals);
            }
        }

        private void cleanup(Bundle args, ContentValues vals) {
            if (null == vals) { vals = new ContentValues(); }

            vals.putNull(ContactsContract.Columns.SYNC);
            if (BuildConfig.DEBUG) {
                Log.d(TAG, "cleanup @" + args.getString(XACT) + ": " + vals);
            }

            getContentResolver().update(
                ContactsContract.URI,
                vals,
                ContactsProvider.SYNC_CONSTRAINT,
                new String[] { args.getString(XACT) });
        }
```

While still raw and unfinished, this program is a much firmer architectural grounding on which to base mobile applications. The code is not significantly more complex than a naïve implementation. Once you grasp the concept of storing synchronization state in the database, it is easy to read and understand.

This implementation is so much more robust! Unlike the naïve implementation, this application could be extended to recognize and handle records that have not been successfully synchronized: They are the records that are still marked as dirty and that do not have pending synchronizing transactions.

Extending it to notify the user when synchronization succeeds or when new data arrives is similarly straightforward. This is a solid basis for applications that delight their users.

USING SYNC ADAPTERS

The RESTfulContacts client, as described so far, is a major step toward an enterprise-enabled application. It not only uses the network, but also uses it in a safe and robust way. Its RESTful architecture, internal and external, elegantly navigates the minefield of Android concurrency and lifecycle management issues. It is, to paraphrase Albert Einstein, as simple as possible, and no simpler.

There are, however, still some significant problems. Displaying a contact's synchronization status in the UI might be interesting, perhaps even useful, if done well. RESTfulContacts as it stands, though, is an excellent example of a horrible user experience. When a contact's synchronization status turns red, there is no hope that it will ever turn green again by itself. Worse than that, there is very little that users can do to remedy the situation.

The bad UI experience actually reflects a deeper architectural problem. Imagine the following scenario. Suppose that the user chooses a contact for editing and mistypes the telephone number. After submitting the edit, she immediately notices the misspelling in the list view and edits the contact information a second time. If she manages to submit the second edit before the first one completes, the ID for the first transaction will be overwritten in the database. Although this might just work accidentally, it certainly seems unreliable.

There is an even broader consideration. As it stands, the server-side database is wide open. Even if you and I have different base URIs to keep our contacts separate, there is nothing to stop me from using your URI and discovering all of your contacts. This is intolerable. Users need to be able to control access to their personal information. Adding authentication to the RESTfulContacts application would be quite a chore. Fortunately, the Android framework provides a tool that addresses many of these issues, the sync adapter. This section will develop a new application, based on it. The full project containing all code and metadata for the client application in this chapter is available from `https://github.com/wileyenterpriseandroid/Examples.git` and as a part of the book's code download at `www.wrox.com` on the Download Code tab. This section analyzes only the highlights. The project is called `syncAdapterContacts`, and it produces an application, SyncContacts.

The Android Synchronization service, frequently referred to by the term *sync adapter* is made up of two components. One of the components is responsible for synchronizing data between a local content provider and a backend data service. The other component manages the accounts that the synchronization service uses when authenticating itself with the backend service.

In the Android system, synchronization is organized around accounts. While one can imagine other, more data-oriented units of synchronization — a database, tables within a database, and so on — in Android it is an account that is synchronized.

Android Account Management

Account management in Android is a large, complex and ill-documented space. Much of it is also outside the scope of this book. Because accounts are the unit of synchronization, however, it will be necessary to create one in order to give the client application something to synchronize.

In order to create an account, an application must do several things:

➤ Request the permissions necessary to manage accounts.

➤ Declare an account authentication service component in its manifest.

➤ Within the service declaration, create a metadata declaration that refers to a resource describing the application's account type.

➤ Create a Java implementation of the declared service that returns an instance of a subclass of Android's account authentication template class.

➤ Optionally, implement preference pages for the account.

This section examines these requirements.

Declaring an Account Authenticator

Much of the work involved in getting account creation to work takes place in the manifest. Be warned that configuring an account authenticator is meticulous work. Android discussion forums are full of descriptions of how minor mistakes in these declarations have caused the entire Android system to crash and reboot. You would be well advised to start with working code and to make small, incremental changes to it to make it meet your specific needs.

Listing 5-7 shows the essential portions of a manifest declaring an account authentication service:

LISTING 5-7: Adding an account management service to the manifest

```
<?xml version="1.0" encoding="utf-8"?>
<manifest xmlns:android="http://schemas.android.com/apk/res/android"
    package="com.enterpriseandroid.syncadaptercontacts"
    android:versionCode="4"
    android:versionName="1.0RC5" >

    <uses-sdk
        android:minSdkVersion="11"
        android:targetSdkVersion="17" />

    <!-- Network -->
    <uses-permission android:name="android.permission.INTERNET" />

    <!-- Accounts -->
    <uses-permission android:name="android.permission.AUTHENTICATE_ACCOUNTS" />
    <uses-permission android:name="android.permission.WRITE_SYNC_SETTINGS" />

    <application
        android:name=".ContactsApplication"
        android:allowBackup="true"
        android:icon="@drawable/ic_launcher"
        android:label="@string/app_name" >

<!-- ... component declarations omitted -->

        <service
            android:name=".sync.AccountService"
            android:exported="false" >
            <intent-filter>
                <action android:name="android.accounts.AccountAuthenticator" />
            </intent-filter>

            <meta-data
                android:name="android.accounts.AccountAuthenticator"
                android:resource="@xml/account" />
        </service>
    </application>

</manifest>
```

First, note that the application uses the two permissions android.permission.AUTHENTICATE_ ACCOUNTS and android.permission.WRITE_SYNC_SETTINGS. The first of these permissions controls the ability of an application to create an account at all. The Android system distinguishes between the ability to create a new account and the ability to change the configuration of that account. Without the second permission, an application cannot modify an account it has just created.

There are two other permissions that may be necessary to an application that manipulates accounts (note that managing accounts is different than authenticating them). The permission `android .permission.GET_ACCOUNTS` allows an application to view the list of accounts known to the account service. If an application wishes to make use of an existing account — an account that it did not itself create — it may need to request this permission. The permission `android.permission .MANAGE_ACCOUNTS` allows an application to create and edit accounts.

As you design your account system, recall that these are fairly powerful permissions you are requesting. As anyone who has seen *Spider-Man* knows, "With great power comes great responsibility." Your application is responsible, not only for using these permissions only for honorable purposes but also for making sure that any code that actually uses them is secure from attack. This is code that should be written carefully and, if at all possible, reviewed by a security professional.

In Android, accounts of a given *account type* are defined by the existence of a service component that meets several rigid requirements. The service declaration identifies the component that Android will use to create, configure, and authenticate one or more accounts of the declared account type. In order for Android to recognize a service as an account authenticator, its declaration must have all of the following elements:

➤ It must declare a service that, on bind, returns an instance of `AbstractAccountAuthenticator`.

➤ The declaration must contain a filter for the intent `android.accounts .AccountAuthenticator`.

➤ The declaration must contain a reference to a metadata file.

➤ The referenced metadata file must contain an `account-authenticator` element.

➤ The `account-authenticator` element in the metadata file must contain an `android:accountType` attribute.

Unless the account authenticator (the service, the intent filter, the metadata declaration and the account type) exists, there is no account type. Without an account type, there are no accounts. Unless there is an account, there is nothing for the synchronization service to synchronize.

Recall that, by default, adding an intent filter to a service causes that service to be accessible to external applications that send the filtered intent: The service is exported. That makes sense in most cases. Providing external applications access to an application component is one of the most common reasons for declaring an intent filter. For an account authenticator, however, the fewer access patterns, the better. Perhaps surprisingly, an account authentication service does not have to be exported. The service in Listing 5-7 has its "exported" attribute explicitly set to false. It cannot be used from other applications.

This is certainly the safest way to configure an authenticator. If it is necessary to allow some external access — perhaps there are multiple applications that need to use the same authenticator — it is also possible to use permissions to control access (permissions are discussed in detail, in Chapter 12).

The next absolute requirement in the declaration of an account authentication service is a metadata reference. The metadata element must have a name attribute whose value is `android.accounts` `.AccountAuthenticator` (this is also the name of the intent accepted by the service intent filter). The metadata attribute must refer (using an `android:resource` attribute) to a correctly built `account-authenticator` resource. Listing 5-8 shows a very simple example of such a resource.

LISTING 5-8: An account authenticator metadata resource

RES/XML/ACCOUNT.XML

```
<?xml version="1.0" encoding="utf-8"?>
<account-authenticator xmlns:android="http://schemas.android.com/apk/res/android"
    android:accountPreferences="@xml/account_prefs"
    android:accountType="@string/account_type"
    android:icon="@drawable/ic_launcher"
    android:label="@string/app_name"
    android:smallIcon="@drawable/ic_launcher" />
```

RES/VALUES/STRINGS.XML

```
<?xml version="1.0" encoding="utf-8"?>
<resources>

<!-- ... string declarations omitted -->

    <!-- Sync -->
    <string name ="account_type"
        >com.enterpriseandroid.syncadaptercontacts.ACCOUNT</string>

</resources>
```

This resource appears to be fairly fault-tolerant in recent versions of Android. As mentioned previously, though, in older versions of Android, seemingly trivial errors could cause a reboot of the entire Android system. If your application targets older Androids, be sure to test thoroughly on each specific, targeted version to make sure that your implementation is sound.

The meanings of most of the attributes in the metadata file are self-evident. There are two that require additional explanation. The first of these is the `android:accountType`.

The account type is — as are most of the definable tokens used in the Android system: permissions, content provider authorities, and so on — simply a bag of characters. There are no semantic constraints. You could probably define a new account type for your application `gov.whitehouse` `.zork` if you chose to do so. By convention, of course, you will probably use the package name for your application or the reversed domain name of the remote service to be synchronized. In the example, the account type is a reference to a string resource whose value is `com.enterpriseandroid.syncadaptercontacts.ACCOUNT`.

The second attribute in the metadata file that requires some discussion, is `android:accountPreferences`. This attribute points to yet another resource, this time a file defining the preferences page that will be used to configure the account. It is likely that the page that you want to use here — preferences that configure the account — will also be part of your application's standard preferences. They are probably available, from your application, through an action bar item.

If you have already built preferences pages for your application, you may be tempted to refer here to one of the preference definition resources you've already created. Unfortunately, that won't work. You cannot simply use a standard permissions definition resource (`preference-headers`, `PreferenceScreen`). Instead you need a special resource, like the one shown in Listing 5-9, that uses an intent to launch your application's preferences activity.

LISTING 5-9: Account authenticator preferences

```xml
<?xml version="1.0" encoding="utf-8"?>
<PreferenceScreen xmlns:android="http://schemas.android.com/apk/res/android" >

    <Preference
        android:key="account_settings"
        android:summary="@string/prefs_sync_summary"
        android:title="@string/prefs_sync_title" >
        <intent
            android:targetClass
                ="com.enterpriseandroid.syncadaptercontacts.PrefsActivity"
            android:targetPackage
                ="com.enterpriseandroid.syncadaptercontacts" >
            <extra
                android:name=":android:no_headers"
                android:value="true" />
            <extra
                android:name=":android:show_fragment"
                android:value
            ="com.enterpriseandroid.syncadaptercontacts.PrefsActivity$SyncPrefs"
            />
        </intent>
    </Preference>
</PreferenceScreen>
```

This declaration will cause your application to be started, and your preferences activity to be run, exactly as if you'd navigated there from the application menu. The intent declaration in the example uses intent extras to navigate directly to the sync prefs page (":android:show_fragment" mimics the behavior of the `PreferenceActivity.EXTRA_SHOW_FRAGMENT` flag).

> **NOTE** *Re-using application preferences can be a can of worms. To begin, the documentation of XML specification of intents is not very good. There is another issue, though.*
>
> *While the example code nicely navigates directly to the sync prefs page, the bad news is that, if your application is started from preferences like these, then it is running, and its top activity is the sync prefs page. If you, subsequently, launch it from the launcher, you will find yourself in preferences, not in your launch page. Consider setting the* `android:clearTaskOnLaunch` *attribute to true in your launch activity to correct this.*

This completes the declaration of a very simple authentication service. While there are many possible variations and extensions on this minimal example — some documented and some not — this declaration is sufficient to allow the creation of an account that can be synchronized with the Android synchronization service.

The manifest declarations define a new account type, `com.enterpriseandroid`
`.syncadaptercontacts.ACCOUNT`, in the metadata for a service component. The implementation of that service component, the class `com.enterpriseandroid.syncadaptercontacts.sync`
`.AccountService`, is responsible for managing and authenticating accounts of the new type. You can now turn to the implementation of that service.

Using an Account Authenticator

In order to understand the implementation of the account authenticator it will be very useful, first, to understand what happens when an application wants to manage an account. Consider then what happens when some application unrelated to SyncContacts want to manage SyncContacts accounts. It turns out that, there is no need to simply imagine such an application! The ubiquitous Settings application, pre-installed as part of the Android's system, does exactly that. Without any loss of generality — another application would implement the same behavior in the same way — the example will use the Settings application for demonstration.

When started, the Settings (this example is taken from Android V4.0.3, Ice Cream Sandwich) application displays a page similar to the one shown on the left in Figure 5-7.

Selecting the "Accounts & sync" item invokes a page like the one shown in the center of the figure. Finally, selecting "ADD ACCOUNT" from the bottom of the page presents a page like the one on the right of the figure.

When the SyncContacts application is installed on a device, the Android framework on that device discovers the new account type declared in its manifest as part of the installation process. It remembers it. When the Settings application requests a list of all account types present on the device, the new type is included in the list, along with its icon and label, and they are displayed, as shown on the right side of Figure 5-7. Clicking the corresponding item will cause the Settings application to initiate the process of creating a new account.

When the Settings application needs to create a new account, it obtains an instance of the Android framework's `AccountManager` object. It calls the method `addAccount` on the object. This call

FIGURE 5-7

initiates an inter-process communications connection that, eventually, binds the SyncContacts authenticator, `AccountService`. The framework knows that it should bind this particular service because one of the arguments to the `addAccount` method is the account type for the account to be added, the SyncContacts account type. The framework starts the SyncContacts application if it is not already running, binds the service, and forwards the request to its `onBind` method.

> **NOTE** *The creation of inter-process communication channels is what bound services are all about. Briefly, the process goes like this: A client running in one process calls* `Context.bindService` *with an intent identifying the service to which it wants to connect. For each such request, the service process receives a call to its* `onBind` *method and returns an* `IBinder` *object. The client back in its process receives a corresponding* `IBinder` *object that connects the two processes through Binder, Android's IPC kernel extension.*
>
> *For further information on the use of Android bound services, see:*
>
> `http://developer.android.com/guide/components/bound-services.html`

Implementing an Account Authenticator

The `AccountService`, the service that supports SyncContacts' implementation of an account authentication service, is shown in its entirety in Listing 5-10. As is frequently the case for an

Android bound service, the implementation of the service itself is trivial. It is simply a named factory that returns the IBinder object that supports inter-process communication — in this case, between Android's account manager service and the account authenticator. The object that the service returns in its onBind method, the AccountMgr, is the thing that actually manages the accounts of the type declared in the manifest.

LISTING 5-10: The account service

```java
public class AccountService extends Service {
    private volatile AccountMgr mgr;

    @Override
    public void onCreate() {
        super.onCreate();
        mgr = new AccountMgr(getApplicationContext());
    }

    @Override
    public IBinder onBind(Intent intent) {
        return mgr.getIBinder();
    }
}
```

An implementation of an account authenticator must be a subclass of the abstract class AbstractAccountAuthenticator. AbstractAccountAuthenticator wraps an IAccountAuthenticator, which is the IBinder object that forms the IPC connection to the account manager. IAccountAuthenticator, though, is a hidden type and is not exposed by the Android API. The only way to use it is to subclass AbstractAccountAuthenticator.

As a subclass of the abstract type, an authenticator implementation must define seven methods: addAccount, getAuthToken, updateCredentials, hasFeatures, confirmCredentials, editProperties, and getAuthTokenLabel. Each of these methods can be quite complex. An authenticator's implementation of the addAccount method, might, for instance, require a user to enter data from a security token, send that data to a remote service, wait for the remote service to send a one-time passphrase via SMS to a pre-determined phone number, and then confirm the password with the remote service.

An authenticator may also be very simple. In the example explored here, most of the methods simply throw an UnsupportedOperationException. The implementation of the addAccount method here actually does no authentication at all. It creates a one account per application installation and uses that account for all communications with the upstream contacts server. In order to accommodate such a broad range of policies, most of the methods in AbstractAccountAuthenticator operate in three different modes, identified here as *immediate*, *intent*, and *delayed*.

Listing 5-11 demonstrates an implementation of the immediate mode.

LISTING 5-11: Simple account creation

```java
@Override
public Bundle addAccount(
        AccountAuthenticatorResponse response,
        String accountType,
        String authTokenType,
        String[] requiredFeatures,
        Bundle options)
{
    Bundle reply = new Bundle();

    String at = ctxt.getString(R.string.account_type);
    reply.putString(AccountManager.KEY_ACCOUNT_TYPE, at);

    if (!at.equals(accountType)) {
        reply.putInt(AccountManager.KEY_ERROR_CODE, -1);
            reply.putString(
                    AccountManager.KEY_ERROR_MESSAGE,
                    "Unrecognized account type");
        return reply;
    }

    Account account = new Account(ctxt.getString(R.string.app_name), accountType);
    if (!AccountManager.get(ctxt).addAccountExplicitly(account, null, null)) {
        reply.putInt(AccountManager.KEY_ERROR_CODE, -1);
            reply.putString(
                    AccountManager.KEY_ERROR_MESSAGE,
                    "Unable to create account");
        return reply;
    }
    reply.putString(AccountManager.KEY_ACCOUNT_NAME, account.name);

    String provider = ctxt.getString(R.string.contacts_authority);
    ContentResolver.setIsSyncable(account, provider, 1);
    ContentResolver.setSyncAutomatically(account, provider, true);

    String token = obtainToken(authTokenType);
    if (null == token) {
        reply.putInt(AccountManager.KEY_ERROR_CODE, -1);
            reply.putString(
                    AccountManager.KEY_ERROR_MESSAGE,
                    "Unrecognized token type");
        return reply;
    }
    reply.putString(AccountManager.KEY_AUTHTOKEN, token);

    return reply;
}
```

In immediate mode, an authenticator methods return a bundle that contains any values the authenticator wants to return to its caller. The implementation of the addAccount method in Listing 5-11, for instance, has enough information so that when it is run, it can create the account on the spot (using AccountManager.addAccountExplicitly). The type and name for the single account it will create are simply resource values that it looks up.

In the bundle, the authenticator returns the account type for which the caller requested an account. If it successfully creates an account of that type, it makes the new account synchronizable, sets it up to sync automatically, and returns the account name and an authorization token for it.

Understanding the other two modes, intent and delayed, requires revisiting the client side of account management. Most of the methods on the account manager — the client-side framework that an application, Settings, in this example, uses to manage accounts — return values that are Java `Future` objects (`AccountManagerFuture<Bundle>` specifically). A method that creates an IPC connection and proxies its request to another process cannot provide its return values immediately. Instead it returns a future, a token that represent an asynchronous computation. The future can be redeemed for the value of that computation when the computation completes.

In the example, the Settings program calls the account manager's `addAccount` method to manage a SyncContacts account. The method returns a `Future` object that represents the computations being done by the bound account authenticator at the other end of the connection. If the Settings program needs to obtain a result from that remote computation, it calls the future's `getResult` method. This method blocks until the asynchronous computation is complete and then returns the bundle that is forwarded across the IPC connection from the authenticator's `addAccount` method.

In immediate mode, the authenticator returned its result relatively quickly. The future's `getResult` method on the client side of the connection would block only briefly (still too long to be called from the UI thread, however).

In intent mode, however, instead of returning values to be forwarded to the client application, the authenticator instead returns a bundle with string value for the key `KEY_INTENT` like this:

```
Intent intent = new Intent(ctxt, AuthenticatorActivity.class);
intent.putExtra(AccountManager.KEY_ACCOUNT_AUTHENTICATOR_RESPONSE, response);
reply.putParcelable(AccountManager.KEY_INTENT, intent);
```

The returned bundle may contain other content, as necessary. Instead of returning this bundle directly to the client, though, the framework processes it specially. If the bundle contains a `KEY_INTENT` key, the framework extracts the intent that is its value and uses it to start the activity it identifies (`AuthenticatorActivity.class` in this case). When the activity runs, it can take as much time as it likes and is free to interact with the user, the network, biometrics sensors, goat entrails, or anything else necessary to authenticate a new account. Frequently this means collecting some data from the user and forwarding them to a backend server. The Android framework provides the handy activity subclass `AccountAuthenticatorActivity` as a base class for activities that support an account authenticator.

When the activity eventually completes, it (or one of its delegates) retrieves the response object, also in the bundle returned by the authenticator, and calls its `onResponse` method.

Remember the calling client? It is still waiting for the `getResult` method of the future object returned from its call to unblock and return a value! It is only when the `onResponse` method of the response object — it was passed to the account authenticator in the original client call — is invoked, that the client's `getResult` method finally unblocks and returns the bundle that the authenticator supplied as parameter to the `onResponse` method. Obviously, if the authenticator is operating in intent mode, the client can wait for a very long time, to get its response. It must be designed to accommodate that eventuality.

Delayed mode is similar to intent mode, except that the account authenticator returns null instead of a bundle. When the framework observes the null response, it, again, does not unblock the caller's `getResult` method. Unlike intent mode, though, it does not take any other action. In this mode, it is the authenticator's responsibility to make sure that the response object's `onResponse` method gets called. The authenticator is free to take action itself or to pass the response object along to any delegate it chooses. Eventually, though, it must make a decision and allow the client to proceed.

> **WARNING** *Beware! It is quite possible for an account authenticator to unintentionally block a client for a very, very long time by incautiously returning null from one of its methods!*

Creating an Account

With the implementation of the account authenticator, as shown in Listings 5-10 and 5-11, it is now possible to create an account. Returning to the window shown on the right of Figure 5-7 and selecting the SyncContacts item from the list results in a window similar to that shown in Figure 5-8.

FIGURE 5-8

An account has been created! Clicking on the SyncContacts item on the left of Figure 5-8 brings up the window shown on the right. Selecting the Sync Prefs entry on the setting page (the right-hand window) navigates to the SyncContacts application preferences page.

It is also possible to initiate account creation from within an application. Listing 5-12 shows an application menu item that has the same effect as the interactions in Figures 5-7 and 5-8. In order to run this code an application must request the permission `android.permission.MANAGE_ACCOUNTS`.

Notice that that the code does not expect a response from the call to `addAccount`. An examination of the Android source reveals that the Settings application works the same way. Neither calls `getResponse` on the future object returned by the call to `addAccount`. This suggests that it is probably safe to return null from the corresponding call in the account authenticator.

LISTING 5-12: Using the account manager within the application

```
@Override
public boolean onOptionsItemSelected(MenuItem item) {
    switch (item.getItemId()) {
        case R.id.item_prefs:
            startActivity(new Intent(this, PrefsActivity.class));
            break;

        case R.id.item_account:
            AccountManager.get(this).addAccount(
                    getString(R.string.account_type),
                    getString(R.string.token_type),
                    null,
                    null,
                    null,
                    null,
                    null);
            break;

        default:
            Log.i(TAG, "Unrecognized menu item: " + item);
            return false;
    }

    return true;
}
```

Finally, notice that the sync icon in the left window of Figure 5-8 is dimmed (whether the account was created from within the application or from Setting) and that there is no information in the "DATA & SYNCHRONZATION" section of the window on the right of the figure. That is because there is no service to synchronize the account. That's the project for the next section.

Creating a Sync Adapter

Creating a sync adapter is quite a bit simpler than creating the code to manage an account. To begin, a sync adapter service must be declared in the manifest, as shown in Listing 5-13.

LISTING 5-13: Adding synchronization service to the manifest

```xml
<?xml version="1.0" encoding="utf-8"?>
<manifest xmlns:android="http://schemas.android.com/apk/res/android"
    package="com.enterpriseandroid.syncadaptercontacts"
    android:versionCode="4"
    android:versionName="1.0RC5" >

    <uses-sdk
        android:minSdkVersion="11"
        android:targetSdkVersion="17" />

    <!-- Network -->
    <uses-permission android:name="android.permission.INTERNET" />

    <!-- Accounts -->
    <uses-permission android:name="android.permission.AUTHENTICATE_ACCOUNTS" />
    <uses-permission android:name="android.permission.WRITE_SYNC_SETTINGS" />

    <!-- Account extra -->
    <uses-permission android:name="android.permission.MANAGE_ACCOUNTS" />
    <uses-permission android:name="android.permission.GET_ACCOUNTS" />

    <!-- Sync -->
    <uses-permission android:name="android.permission.USE_CREDENTIALS" />

    <application
        android:name=".ContactsApplication"
        android:allowBackup="true"
        android:icon="@drawable/ic_launcher"
        android:label="@string/app_name" >

<!-- ... component declarations omitted -->

        <provider
            android:name=".data.ContactsProvider"
            android:authorities="@string/contacts_authority"
            android:exported="false" />

        <service
            android:name=".sync.SyncService"
            android:exported="false" >
            <intent-filter>
                <action android:name="android.content.SyncAdapter" />
            </intent-filter>

            <meta-data
                android:name="android.content.SyncAdapter"
                android:resource="@xml/sync" />
        </service>
    </application>

</manifest>
```

This listing is similar to Listing 5-7, but there are several new components that are worthy of note. First, the application now requests three new permissions: android.permission.MANAGE_ ACCOUNTS, android.permission.GET_ACCOUNTS, and android.permission.USE_CREDENTIALS. The first of these was added to support the menu item introduced in the previous section. The remaining two permissions support the sync adapter.

Next, note the declaration of the content provider. Its implementation was copied, very nearly verbatim, from the RESTContacts application and will not be explored here. The declaration, though, is important because it defines the provider's authority. That authority will be used again, shortly.

A sync adapter declaration is, like an account manager declaration, a service that filters a particular intent and declares a special metadata resource. The android:name attribute for both filtered intent and the metadata declaration are the same: android.content.SyncAdapter. When the application is installed, the Android system will discover this declaration and, in addition to making it available as a bindable service, will record it as the service that supports the account type mentioned in the metadata resource.

A minimal sync adapter's metadata resource looks like this (Listing 15-14):

LISTING 5-14: A sync adapter metadata resource

RES/XML/SYNC.XML

```
<?xml version="1.0" encoding="utf-8"?>
<sync-adapter xmlns:android="http://schemas.android.com/apk/res/android"
    android:accountType="@string/account_type"
    android:contentAuthority="@string/contacts_authority" />
```

RES/VALUES/STRINGS.XML

```
<?xml version="1.0" encoding="utf-8"?>
<resources>

<!-- ... string declarations omitted -->

    <!-- Sync -->
    <string
        name="contacts_authority"
            >com.enterpriseandroid.syncadaptercontacts.CONTACTS</string>
    <string
        name="account_type"
            >com.enterpriseandroid.syncadaptercontacts.ACCOUNT</string>

</resources>
```

This declaration links the account type from the previous section with the authority for the content provider. The references to string resources used here reduce the possibility of problems caused by typos.

There are several other attributes that can be added to the `sync-adapter` element. For instance, although synchronizers are, by default, listed on the Sync Settings page (Figure 5-8), the `android:userVisible` attribute makes it possible to hide them. Setting the `android:isAlwaysSyncable` attribute to true — the default is false — has the same effect as that achieved in Listing 5-11 by calling `ContentResolver.setIsSyncable`. Although current documentation describes the attribute, `android:syncAdapterSettingsAction`, that specifies an intent that will start an activity to configure the sync adapter, the resource compiler will not compile it.

Again, like the account authenticator, the implementation of the sync adapter service is very simple. It is just a factory whose `onBind` method returns an `IBinder` object that supports the inter-process communications channel through which the Android framework's `SyncManager` sends requests.

Listing 5-15 shows it in its entirety.

LISTING 5-15: A sync adapter service

```java
public class SyncService extends Service {
    private volatile SyncAdapter synchronizer;

    @Override
    public void onCreate() {
        super.onCreate();
        synchronizer = new SyncAdapter(getApplicationContext(), true);
    }

    @Override
    public IBinder onBind(Intent intent) {
        return synchronizer.getSyncAdapterBinder();
    }
}
```

As with the account manager, the inter-process communication interface used by the `SyncManager` to communicate with clients, `ISyncAdapter`, is not published as part of the Android API. You must subclass the framework class `AbstractThreadedSyncAdapter`, which wraps that interface, to implement a sync adapter. Its `getSyncAdapterBinder` method returns the IPC channel.

Perhaps a surprise — and unlike the account manager — the sync manager itself is also hidden from the API. It is used only by the framework to implement behavior accessible through other objects, mostly the `ContentResolver`.

`AbstractThreadedSyncAdapter` is an abstract class. Extending it requires you to implement only one method, `onPerformSync`. Listing 5-16 gives an implementation of that method. Finally! The implementation of a sync adapter!

LISTING 5-16: Implementing a sync adapter

```java
@Override
public void onPerformSync(
        Account account,
```

```
            Bundle extras,
            String authority,
            ContentProviderClient provider,
            SyncResult syncResult)
    {
        AccountManager mgr = AccountManager.get(ctxt);
        String tt = ctxt.getString(R.string.token_type);

        Exception e = null;
        String token = null;
        try { token = mgr.blockingGetAuthToken(account, tt, false); }
        catch (OperationCanceledException oce) { e = oce; }
        catch (AuthenticatorException ae) { e = ae; }
        catch (IOException ioe) { e = ioe; }

        if (null == token) {
            Log.e(TAG, "auth failed: " + AccountMgr.acctStr(account) + "#" + tt, e);
            return;
        }

        new RESTService(ctxt).sync(account, token);

        // force re-validation
        mgr.invalidateAuthToken(account.type, token);
    }
```

There are many possibilities for the implementation of a sync adapter. This particular implementation is based on an architecture in which the authentication process results in a token, which is then used by the client to demonstrate to the remote service for a limited period of time that the requesting account has been authenticated. Calls to blockingGetAuthToken return a cached copy of that token.

In the example, the only failure mode occurs if the attempt to retrieve the token fails. If that happens, the service simply returns without attempting synchronization.

Real enterprise applications will encounter another, much more interesting failure mode. Once the Android framework gets an authentication token, it will cache it for a very long time. At some point, though, the token will by definition expire. When that happens, the upstream server will refuse to honor it any longer. In order to proceed, it is necessary to get a new token.

To do this, an application must, first, remove the existing token from the cache. It does this by marking the token invalid, with the account manager method invalidateAuthToken.

The code in Listing 5-16 illustrated the use of this method by implementing a one-time token. It invalidates the existing token after every successful server transaction. While an interesting demonstration, this is almost certainly not a good idea for production code. Instead, a real enterprise application will invalidate the token in response to an HTTP 401 status (Unauthorized) from the server.

When the new token is requested, the Android framework forwards the request to the authenticator built in the previous section. When you left that section, there was only one method implemented in the authenticator class, addAccount. It is now necessary to implement a second, as shown in Listing 5-17.

LISTING 5-17: Obtaining authentication tokens

```
@Override
public Bundle getAuthToken(
        AccountAuthenticatorResponse response,
        Account account,
        String authTokenType,
        Bundle options)
{
    Bundle reply = new Bundle();
    reply.putString(AccountManager.KEY_ACCOUNT_TYPE, account.type);
    reply.putString(AccountManager.KEY_ACCOUNT_NAME, account.name);
    reply.putString(KEY_TOKEN_TYPE, authTokenType);

    String tt = ctxt.getString(R.string.account_type);
    if (!tt.equals(account.type)
        || !ctxt.getString(R.string.app_name).equals(account.name))
    {
        reply.putInt(AccountManager.KEY_ERROR_CODE, -1);
        reply.putString(AccountManager.KEY_ERROR_MESSAGE, "Unrecognized account");
        return reply;
    }

    String token = obtainToken(authTokenType);
    if (null == token) {
        reply.putInt(AccountManager.KEY_ERROR_CODE, -1);
            reply.putString(
                    AccountManager.KEY_ERROR_MESSAGE,
                    "Unrecognized token type");
        return reply;
    }

    reply.putString(AccountManager.KEY_AUTHTOKEN, token);
    return reply;
}
```

This implementation is, as was the implementation of addAccount, very simple. It delegates the actual task of obtaining a token to the obtainToken method. In this example, the implementation of that method (not shown here) simply looks up a per-installation unique id string. A more realistic implementation might, instead, use Google's utility class GoogleAuthUtil.

With this addition to the authentication manager, you can return to the examination of the sync adapter. Notice, in passing, that all of the warnings from the previous section about the length of time required to complete an authenticator method apply in spades here. The getAuthToken method might have to go through the entire authentication process again. It might require a series of activities and several round trips to the remote server to present credentials and, perhaps, to confirm their receipt in order to get a new token. The call to blockingGetAuthToken in the sync adapter might not return for quite a long time.

As the name of the sync adapter base class, AbstractThreadedSyncAdapter, suggests a sync adapter does not run on the UI thread. Long running processes are, while never desirable, at least tolerable.

This completes the essentials of sync adapter construction. At this point, returning to the Settings application and navigating through the process of account creation will result in pages like those shown in Figure 5-9.

FIGURE 5-9

Though the figure is in black and white here, the sync icon in the left window in this figure is green instead of gray and the Sync Settings page now has information about the last synchronization time and a check box checked to indicate that the account is being synchronized.

The implementation of the `RESTService.sync` method — the method called from the sync adapter of this new application to perform the actual synchronization with the remote service — is very similar to other methods built for the RESTfulContacts application in the first half of this chapter. It will use JSON over HTTP to communicate change to the upstream service for incorporation into the remote database.

The architecture for the new application, however, is dramatically simpler. RESTfulContacts used a "CRUD over the wire" design. As a first foray into RESTful design, the content provider in that application is a strict, local, in-line, RESTful cache for calls to the remote service. It proxies the local calls nearly verbatim to the network. While queries are handled locally, inserts, updates, and deletes are all applied to the local cache and then forwarded, literally, to the remote.

SyncContacts, on the other hand, uses the single method, `sync`, to handle any necessary changes. With careful design it is even possible to implement a synchronization protocol that supports multiple sources for changes and handles conflicts in a convergent manner. While the sync method is more complex than any one of the methods it replaces, the overall architecture is much simpler. There is one isolated component that is responsible for synchronizing differences between a client and a server. In order for this to work though, the content provider has to be able to schedule synchronization when the local database is changed.

Scheduling the Sync Adapter

There are several ways to schedule a run of a sync adapter. The Sync now item in the Settings application Sync settings menu, shown in Figure 5-10, will work, for any visible account.

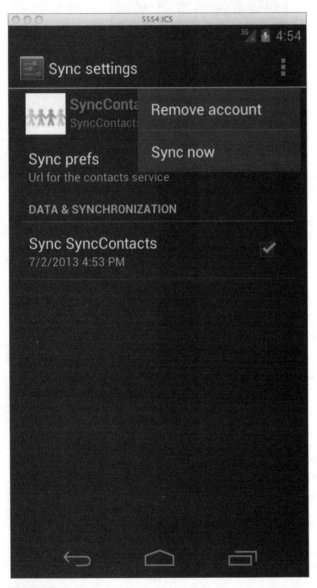

FIGURE 5-10

That's fine, as a last resort. An application must have a way, though, to schedule synchronizations dynamically. There are two ways to do that. The first is brute force and the second is pure Android magic.

Listing 5-18 demonstrates scheduling a synchronization by brute force.

LISTING 5-18: Scheduling a synchronization by force

```
private void requestSync() {
    Account[] accounts = AccountManager.get(this)
        .getAccountsByType(getString(R.string.account_type));
    if ((null == accounts) || (0 >= accounts.length)) {
        Toast.makeText(this, R.string.msg_no_account, Toast.LENGTH_SHORT).show();
        return;
    }

    // Just use the first account of our type.
    // This works because there should be at most one.
    // If there were more, we'd have to choose an account in prefs or something.
    ContentResolver.requestSync(accounts[0],
    ContactsContract.AUTHORITY,
    new Bundle());
}
```

This method, called from a menu item in the SyncContacts application, simply requests a list of accounts of the type it declares. In order to do this, it must use the permission `android.permission.GET_ACCOUNTS`, as shown in Listing 5-13. Once it has the account, it uses a content resolver method to request that a synchronization be run. The method's second argument, the authority for the content provider to be synchronized, is simply the authority from the content provider's contract. If it were necessary to pass parameters to the sync adapter, they would be passed in the bundle supplied as the third argument. Even if there are no parameters for the sync adapter, the third argument cannot be null.

Saving the best for last, the other way to schedule synchronization between a remote service and the local data model employs exactly the same code used back in Chapter 4 to schedule synchronization between the local data model and the local view components: the content resolver method `notifyChange`.

That is nearly all there is to it. Because a sync adapter is tied to a content provider authority, a change notification for that authority will cause the sync adapter to be scheduled. The content provider code from the previous client nearly works without any change.

The one change that is necessary prevents extraneous updates. Consider, for instance, what happens when an application user adds a new contact from the UI. Adding the record to the content provider database generates a change notification. The change notification schedules the sync adapter. The sync adapter run is scheduled a bit in the future, in case, as is likely, the user makes other changes at about the same time. In many versions of Android, this delay is 30 seconds.

When the sync adapter runs, it looks in the database for records that are marked as dirty, bundles them up into a JSON document, and sends them off to the server. When the server replies, the sync adapter marks the records as synced with a call to the content provider's update method. That call generates another change notification, as it must, to update the record state in the UI: the status bar changes from yellow, syncing, to green, synced.

It would be bad, however, if that second notification caused the sync adapter to be scheduled again! In order to prevent that, there are two, overloaded versions of `ContentResolver.notifyChange`.

Recall that the version of this method used in the code in Chapter 4 takes two arguments: a URI and a content observer. It signals a change in the dataset that backs the URI. That version is an abbreviation for the three argument version:

```
notifyChange(Uri uri, ContentObserver observer, boolean syncToNet)
```

The third argument indicates whether or not this notification should be broadcast to sync adapters. Listing 5-19 shows its use in one of the content provider methods from the SyncContacts, updated from the similar method in the RESTfulContacts application shown in Listing 5-5.

LISTING 5-19: Using notifyChange's third argument

SYNCUTIL.JAVA

```
private static final Uri CONTENT_URI = ContactsContract.URI.buildUpon()
        .appendQueryParameter(ContactsProvider.SYNC_UPDATE, "true")
        .build();
```

CONTACTSPROVIDER.JAVA

```
private Uri localInsert(Uri uri, ContentValues vals) {
    long pk = localInsertRow(getDb(), vals);

    if (0 > pk) { uri = null; }
    else {
        uri = uri.buildUpon().appendPath(String.valueOf(pk)).build();
        getContext().getContentResolver()
            .notifyChange(uri, null, !isSyncUpdate(uri));
    }

    return uri;
}

private boolean isSyncUpdate(Uri uri) {
    return null != uri.getQueryParameter(ContactsProvider.SYNC_UPDATE);
}
```

The methods in `SyncUtil`, part of the sync adapter, call content provider methods with a version of the URI that has a query parameter appended to it. Within the content provider, code that must notify observers that changes have taken place simply checks for the query parameter. If the query parameter is not present, the call should schedule a sync. If the query parameter is present, the call is already from the sync adapter and should not schedule additional synchronizations.

SUMMARY

This chapter reviewed the RESTful architectural style and demonstrated its use, both using HTTP as transport and within Android itself. You've read about both the basics of network client implementation and the essentials of Java concurrency and how they apply in the context of an Android application.

From this basis, the chapter turned to a discussion of specific challenges inherent in the Android architecture — the UI-imposed concurrency requirements and their relation to objects with managed lifecycles — and introduced three powerful approaches to solving them.

While differing in the specifics of their implementation, the three approaches all share a few common features. All are based on RESTful architecture and the fact that a content provider can be used as a caching proxy for a remote service. All represent the need to synchronize data with a remote server as persistent data stored locally in a content provider database. Perhaps most important, all three move network communications out of the UI layer and into a separate, independent service component. In none of these approaches is UI code cluttered with the details of initiating or managing network connections.

This chapter also introduced Android's complex, powerful, and poorly documented synchronization framework, sync adapters.

Finally there was in-depth discussion of two different concrete example implementations of a client that demonstrated the use of these concepts. These examples not only establish the efficacy of the approach, they also show, in their simplicity, that the overhead for adopting the RESTful approach is not significant. Instead, the RESTful approach leads to clear, elegant maintainable code.

SPRING FOR ANDROID

The Spring project is well known among Enterprise Android developers. It provides a well-known and widely used Java technology used for developing backend services. You'll use it in the next chapter for exactly that purpose.

SpringSource, the organization that manages Spring, has ported parts of it to the Android platform. The resulting library provides a less well known but excellent networking framework for Android application development. The Android version uses the same metaphors found in the server-side counterpart. Some of its desirable characteristics include:

➤ Code that is automatically up to date with networking changes in Android. As noted previously, recommendations about whether to use the core Java networking APIs or their Apache equivalents have changed over time. A Spring client will always make the best choice.

➤ A rich and convenient API, called RestTemplate.

➤ Parameter-based method invocation.

continues

continued

The following code is a brief example of the use of the Spring RestTemplate. For more information on Spring for Android, visit the project's website:

http://www.springsource.org/spring-android

```
// Add a message converter
restTemplate.getMessageConverters()
    .add(new MappingJacksonHttpMessageConverter());

// Make the HTTP GET request, marshaling the response
// from JSON to an array of Contacts
Contact[] contacts = restTemplate.getForObject(url, Contact[].class);

// Set the Accept header
HttpHeaders requestHeaders = new HttpHeaders();
requestHeaders.setAccept(
    Collections.singletonList(new MediaType("application", "json")));
HttpEntity<?> requestEntity = new HttpEntity<Object>(requestHeaders);

// Create a new RestTemplate instance
RestTemplate restTemplate = new RestTemplate();

// Add the Jackson message converter
restTemplate.getMessageConverters()
    .add(new MappingJacksonHttpMessageConverter());

// Make the HTTP GET request, marshaling the response
// from JSON to an array of Events
ResponseEntity<Contact[]> responseEntity = restTemplate.exchange(
    url,
    HttpMethod.GET,
    requestEntity,
    Contact[].class);
Contact[] contacts = responseEntity.getBody();
```

6

Service Development

WHAT'S IN THIS CHAPTER?

- ➤ Understanding the many choices in service development
- ➤ Learning the three-tier service architecture
- ➤ Understanding Spring and Hibernate: A conservative service stack
- ➤ Building a RESTful web service for contacts
- ➤ Building a synchronization service for contacts
- ➤ Learning best practices for service design

WROX.COM CODE DOWNLOADS FOR THIS CHAPTER

Please note that all the code examples in this chapter are available at `https://github.com/wileyenterpriseandroid/Examples.git` and as a part of the book's code download at `www.wrox.com` on the Download Code tab.

This chapter provides a getting started tutorial that enables developers to write their first backend data service — making sure that the service integrates well with Android. The focus is on web service development that supports mobile applications with code running on a backend service host, not in an Android handset.

The discussion addresses mobile computing issues raised in earlier chapters. The following problems hold particular relevance when thinking about backend services for mobile clients:

- ➤ The network is not always available.
- ➤ Scalability requires efficiency in network use and power consumption.
- ➤ Mobile network connectivity is intermittent, slow, or altogether gone (when users drive into tunnels or otherwise off the grid).

The chapter example implements the RESTful contacts interface introduced in the previous chapter, and also explores the patterns from the previous chapter that will provide the focus for several subsequent chapters. This chapter will discuss implementations of the /Contacts REST methods and the /Contacts/sync POST method showing how a backend service should support these operations.

To elaborate, caching data on mobile devices has many advantages, such as reducing load on backend services, lowering the cost of user data bills, and allowing applications to keep working when the network becomes unavailable. Such benefits incur the cost of increased complexity in the form of synchronization logic that can handle data changes from concurrent hosts. If an app makes changes off the network, it needs to be able to sync with changes made in its absence on return. You can commonly find sophisticated synchronization behavior in enterprise applications like Gmail from Google. The next several chapters will explain how to integrate this type of support into services and applications that you develop. Along the way, you'll pick up lucrative development skills for popular cloud providers.

A CHOICE FOR SERVICE DEVELOPMENT

Developers writing web applications and web services face an overwhelming array of architectural choices. Even selection of a software language or operating system doesn't limit the options much. This chapter builds a simple three-tier RESTful service based on the Java-based software tools Spring, Hibernate, and Java Database Connectivity (JDBC). This is a commonly used technology stack, but there are many other valid alternatives.

This chapter makes getting started easier, and also provides background on more traditional software development tools. This software service stack provides a number of benefits, including wide deployment and a well understood feature set. The chapter notes the benefits of using this particular approach; the next chapter will cover more recent styles of persistence associated with modern cloud platforms.

The Lifecycle of a Request

Previous chapters discussed the widely popular web services protocol called REST from the perspective of client usage. This chapter focuses on implementing a RESTful interface by providing service for each RESTful URI. But what does that mean exactly? Software service implementations revolve around serving requests, like a GET for a contact. When a service receives a request, it's possible that the service itself was not even running prior to receiving the invocation. Each request should run in isolation from other requests and should not make assumptions about the condition of memory (for example, it should not rely on memory in static fields) or about the machine on which they run. Distributed services usually run on a large number of different hosts inside a cloud provider. Well-written request implementations should seek to minimize the use of system resources such as memory, storage, and processing time. Figure 6-1 shows that a service request can run on many hosts in several different geographies. The code itself should not need to "know" about any other requests.

A well designed request should read arguments sent from the client, perform its function in isolation from other requests, store all its state in a persistence layer, return its result to the client, and finish by deleting any intermediate state from memory.

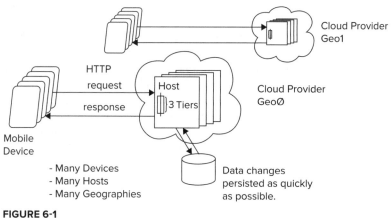

- Many Devices
- Many Hosts
- Many Geographies

FIGURE 6-1

Application Containers

Now that you know what requests are, you'll need to know where they live: Traditional service deployments have relied on a software service known as an *application container*. Application containers are web servers that support an application archive format that contains application logic and supporting libraries. When installed from an archive into a container, a web application will configure for a particular URL namespace. The container then forwards all HTTP requests to the URI space of the registered application, which entirely defines the behavior of the request.

Three-Tier Service Architecture

The most common style of web application and service is the three-tier service architecture. This approach, illustrated in Figure 6-2, separates processing of request data parameters, called the *presentation tier* (or remote interface), from the logic of the application or service, the *logic tier,* and then again relies on a clearly defined data persistence layer known as the *data tier.* In large commercial systems, different layers can reside on different physical hardware. You can find extensive details on this type of service architecture here:

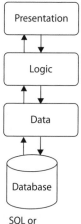

SQL or
NonSQL (Key, Value)

FIGURE 6-2

```
http://en.wikipedia.org/wiki/Three-tier_architecture#Three-tier_architecture
```

Figure 6-2 illustrates a basic three-tier service architecture.

Service Development Background

The array of choices for architecting a web service solution can be mind-boggling, especially for a software developer who has not settled on a useful set of tools. But to start thinking about how to narrow the choices, it's important to be aware of the issues involved. These issues are covered in the following sections.

Language Choice (Type Safety vs. Convenient Syntax)

Choosing a server development environment begins with choosing a software language. Since backend applications do not mandate a language (the way Android requires Java and iOS requires Objective-C), language designers have taken every opportunity to explore this space with popular languages ranging from those on the type safe side, like Java, Dart, and Go, to those with more flexible language design like server JavaScript, Ruby, and Perl. Each popular language supports a plethora of software libraries, and it's possible to build sophisticated applications in all of them. One of the main differentiating features between languages is type safety, and the lack of it. Proponents of type safety advocate the ability to find syntax errors at build time, rather than at run time.

It's hard to overstate the potential benefits of finding errors at compile time instead of run time. Compiler found bugs shorten code ⇨ test ⇨ debug cycles. Also, you find your bugs instead of your customers running into them and disliking your product.

> **NOTE** *The utility of type safety tends to be a highly controversial topic. If you are interested, you can read the following sobering blog post:*
>
> http://www.artima.com/weblogs/viewpost.jsp?thread=36525

Application Container

Java alone supports several commercial and open source application containers, including JBoss, Apache Tomcat, WebLogic, and Glassfish, among others. The language Python supports Zope 1, 2, 3, BlueBream, and Grok. You can start to see that even when you pick a language, it's still difficult to know what software to use to build a given application.

In Java, web applications and services almost exclusively require the support of an "application server," which, as mentioned, is just a web server that can load and serve applications in the form of "web archives," or .war files. Application servers support a programming interface called a "servlet container." A servlet is a low-level Java service and application interface that uses an API tailored specifically to handling raw HTTP requests. Many open source libraries exist to add higher level implementation support on top of servlets, such as for JSON and REST support, or for older applications, SOAP. The file web.xml, part of a war file, provides the main point of configuration for these value-add libraries and enables developers to list the following components of their application — classpath, URL mapping, servlet dispatcher, and the files that are part of the application.

Prolific Software Libraries

Fortunately for application developers it's possible to integrate a plethora of software libraries for all popular languages. The following list of functional areas provides a small taste of the richness and diversity of commercial and open source libraries available for popular languages: multiple web MVC frameworks per language, object relational mapping, JSON mapping, natural language processing, artificial intelligence, API libraries for communicating with Amazon web services, Google App Engine APIs, and so on. You can find library repositories by language in the following locations:

➤ **Ruby** — http://rubygems.org/gems

➤ **Java** — http://mvnrepository.com

➤ **Python** — http://pypi.python.org/pypi

Choice of MVC

The de facto standard tool for building web-based user interfaces is a web MVC framework. Examples of popular frameworks include Ruby on Rails, Play, Groovy and Grails, Spring MVC3, and JSF. These frameworks provide:

➤ View languages composed of different types of markup, including Java Server Pages (jsp), Groovy Server Pages (gsp), and Ruby Server Pages (rsp), which compile to HTML output for browser consumption

➤ Controller bindings that map web events, such as a user clicking on a button or link, to registered language level controller components, and that allow application logic to handle browser events

➤ A data model, a persistence layer such as the standard JPA, or Java Persistence API, that stores data in a SQL or key value datastore

Figure 6-3 illustrates the web MVC architecture.

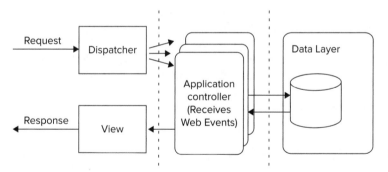

FIGURE 6-3

Unless developers plan to run services on their own hardware, they will need to pick from a growing selection of cloud service providers that provide computing power for a usage fee. Here is a list of some significant cloud providers:

➤ Google App Engine

➤ Amazon Web Services

➤ Joyent

> **NOTE** *Chapter 7 introduces the various differentiating features available in these providers to give you a sense of why you might choose one over another.*

Databases

Like all other areas of service development just discussed, choices of software for application persistence seems to be growing exponentially. Today developers need to think beyond just SQL databases from different vendors, but also about newly popular schema-free databases built on JSON and plain key, value storage. Persistence tools in these categories include:

➤ **SQL** — MySQL, PostgreSQL, and Oracle

➤ **Key, Value** — Cassandra, DynamoDB, Voldemort, and Riak

➤ **JSON** — MongoDB

➤ **Google App Engine** — GQL

➤ Hadoop — HBase

You can find more detailed explanations of these tools in later chapters of this book. Chapter 7 introduces web services from Amazon — specifically examples based on DynamoDB.

> **NOTE** *One important differentiator between SQL databases (such as MySQL) and key, value stores (such as DynamoDB) is the inherent ability of key, value storage to seamlessly distribute data across many hosts. This characteristic can lead to greater scalability than SQL-based systems, but often goes in hand with less flexibility. Chapter 7 delves more deeply into the differences between modern persistence mechanisms.*

BUILDING A RESTFUL SERVICE FOR CONTACTS

Now that you have completed a brief tour of the myriad different kinds of service development technologies, it should be clearer why this chapter uses a simple tried-and-true software stack to introduce you to the backend service development in the context of Android technology. Also, as an Android developer, you have some familiarity with Java.

A Conservative Software Stack

Let's dig into the chapter examples: persistence and synchronization backend support for the contacts remote interface from Chapter 5. The example code is simple, but provides functional client-to-server solutions for Android. The contacts service uses a conservative but still relevant and productive environment based primarily on the Spring service framework and the Hibernate and JDBC persistence APIs. Although newer languages like Ruby and Scala have been gaining traction recently, a significant server-side contingent depends heavily on Java tools for existing and new projects — mainly for the reasons described earlier in this chapter: Java is a stable environment geared toward precluding the possibility of bugs, rather than finding them during runtime tests, or worse, in a production environment.

Let's examine the technologies underlying the examples.

Spring

The power of Spring comes from *dependency injection*. Say you're writing a `Bank` class for a finance program, and the class has a reference to an ATM cash machine object. Without dependency injection, you might write code that constructs a new ATM object and invokes it as needed. This is fine, but in the long run it is harder to maintain and test. In essence, you have hardcoded the dependency between the `Bank` class and the `ATM` class. With Spring, instead of constructing a new `ATM` object, you inject an implementation of the `ATM` interface into the `Bank` class through the constructor or through a public setter method. For testing, you could pass in a dummy `ATM` class that doesn't make any real calls through the bank network. However, in your production servers, you have Spring inject an `ATM` interface, which does actual financial transactions. Through dependency injection, you can inject whichever dependency you want and the `Bank` code remains exactly the same. Not having to change the `Bank` class when you make changes in the `ATM` class makes the overall program easier to maintain and test in the long term.

Figure 6-4 shows an `ATM` implementation loaded into a `Bank` class using dependency injection.

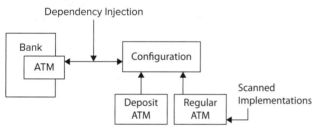

FIGURE 6-4

Spring injection uses a configuration system to track implementation classes for a particular component that should be assigned to a field of an object. The service or application only knows about a Java interface that the component implements, and at run time, the configuration system "injects" the implementation component into the proper field values. The system finds out what implementation object to inject only by reading the Spring configuration.

You may be familiar with using a properties file to avoid hard-coding `String` values into your programs. This is useful for `Strings`, but becomes very cumbersome if you want to define complex objects. Spring allows you to specify an object's data in an XML file (or through Spring Java annotations). Once you have defined your Objects, they can be referred to by a key/name, just like a property in a property file.

Applications do not use the `new` operator to instantiate its dependencies. Additionally, long chains of implementation inheritance constitute one of the more significant anti-patterns in object-oriented programming. Dependency injection encourages object composition over object inheritance to avoid this problem. See `http://en.wikipedia.org/wiki/Composition_over_inheritance`.

> **NOTE** *For more information on Spring, see* `http://www.springsource.org/.`

JDBC

This is the standard library for accessing a SQL database in Java. The major functions of JDBC include:

➤ SQL language support including `select`, `insert`, `update`, and `delete`

➤ Statement and prepared statement support

➤ Query statements return JDBC result sets

> **NOTE** *For more information, see* `http://en.wikipedia.org/wiki/Jdbc.`

Hibernate

Hibernate, the most common Java Object Relational Mapping (ORM) layer, and JDBC, which provides a direct SQL language binding, represent the two most widely deployed Java persistence technologies. You'll need to decide for yourself whether an ORM makes sense for your application. The chapter example supports both technologies using a simple abstraction layer. Both example persistence mappings make use of high-level utilities of the Spring project, thereby increasing the ease of programming with both approaches.

The Hibernate package provides an ORM on top of Java JDBC. Features of Hibernate include:

➤ Ability to transparently map Java POJO objects to and from database rows

➤ An object-oriented query language called HQL

> **NOTE** *For more information, see* `http://www.hibernate.org/` *and* `http://en.wikipedia.org/wiki/Hibernate_(Java).`

METHOD-ORIENTED PERSISTENCE

Another promising framework, `MyBatis`, provides an alternate way of solving the service persistence problem; this system is method-oriented rather than object-based. `MyBatis` uses Java annotations to attach SQL statements to Java methods. The chapter material is not based on this library due to the longer-term use and greater community experience of Hibernate. For now, you can find more information on the `MyBatis` home page at `http://www.mybatis.org/.`

Writing the Examples: Spring Contacts Service and its Synchronization Variant

The following code examples demonstrate basic service development with a specific example of a contacts service with a "three-tier" architecture — a standard way of writing web services. This contacts service supports the remote interface listed in Chapter 5. The example uses Spring for the presentation layer, Java for the logic tier, and a simple custom abstraction layer for the data layer. The data layer also uses Spring to inject the use of either direct JDBC or Hibernate.

> **NOTE** *The* CODE *variable refers to the location of the* wileyenterpriseandroid/ Examples *directory. The reader should interpret* CODE *references as a shorthand for this directory. It's optional for readers to actually set this variable in their shell of choice. For example, with Windows cmd, you might use* %CODE%/Examples, *or in bash you could use* $CODE/Examples — *but only if you set the variable yourself.*

The files for a CRUD oriented REST contact service reside in the examples project called *$CODE/* springServiceContacts. The chapter also describes a second variant of this service that adds synchronization support. You can find the variant of this service with synchronization support added in the project, *$CODE/*springSyncServiceContacts.

> **NOTE** *Please keep in mind that the examples for getting started with service development have significantly more setup overhead than examples in earlier chapters. However, once you complete them, you'll be able to reuse much of this work in Chapters 7, 9, and 10.*
>
> *Additionally, the book project site has information that can ease setup of back- end services discussed in this book. Please see:*
>
> https://github.com/wileyenterpriseandroid/Examples/wiki
>
> *Also, note that the examples have duplicate, and potentially more up-to-date, sets of instructions in the following files:*
>
> *$CODE/*springServiceContacts/README
> *$CODE/*springSyncServiceContacts/README

Prepare: Prerequisites and Getting Ready

Chapter 1 covered the use of Eclipse for Android; this chapter discusses how to use the IDE for service development. You'll need to configure some tools first on the host that will run the service (localhost assumed). You can use any of the three major operating systems for PCs to develop the web backend: Linux, Mac OS, or Windows. The OS is not particularly relevant for backend services. The code is likely to work on a variety of software versions, but was specifically tested on Java (1.7.0_25), MySQL (5.7), Ant (1.9.1), EclipseEE (Kepler), and Tomcat (7.0.12).

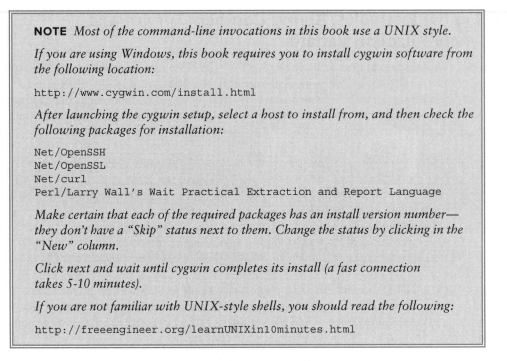

> **NOTE** *Most of the command-line invocations in this book use a UNIX style.*
>
> *If you are using Windows, this book requires you to install cygwin software from the following location:*
>
> `http://www.cygwin.com/install.html`
>
> *After launching the cygwin setup, select a host to install from, and then check the following packages for installation:*
>
> ```
> Net/OpenSSH
> Net/OpenSSL
> Net/curl
> Perl/Larry Wall's Wait Practical Extraction and Report Language
> ```
>
> *Make certain that each of the required packages has an install version number—they don't have a "Skip" status next to them. Change the status by clicking in the "New" column.*
>
> *Click next and wait until cygwin completes its install (a fast connection takes 5-10 minutes).*
>
> *If you are not familiar with UNIX-style shells, you should read the following:*
>
> `http://freeengineer.org/learnUNIXin10minutes.html`

Prepare

1. Install `MySQL` Community Server Edition

   The data tier of this example relies on `mysql` for SQL persistence; consequently, you'll need to download it after creating an Oracle account:

   `http://dev.mysql.com/downloads/mysql/`

   Select your platform in the list at the bottom of the page, and then pick an appropriate download, like .msi for Windows or .dmg for MacOS. If you need more detailed instructions, see the following URL:

   `http://dev.mysql.com/doc/refman/5.7/en/installing.html`

   > **NOTE** *Make sure to set the root password to be "mysql", or edit the file* `$CODE/springContactsService/src/jdbc.properties` *to use a root password of your choosing. You will also need to use the default mysql port 3306, though you should not need to explicitly configure it.*
   >
   > *If you are installing on MacOS, make sure to get the DMG archive and install it using the setup script.*
   >
   > *On Windows, execute the .msi file and complete the wizard.*
   >
   > *If asked during the install, indicate that the service should start on boot.*

2. Install the latest version of the Java from the following location:

`http://www.oracle.com/technetwork/java/javase/downloads/index.html`

3. Install Apache Tomcat.

The code uses Apache Tomcat as its application server, so you'll start by downloading Tomcat from the following location:

`http://tomcat.apache.org/download-70.cgi`

And then follow the installation instructions on the Tomcat site:

`http://tomcat.apache.org/tomcat-7.0-doc/appdev/installation.html`

Basically, just uncompress the download archive where you would like Tomcat to reside. Then set the shell variable, CATALINA_HOME to that directory. There's lots of documentation about Tomcat online:

`http://tomcat.apache.org/tomcat-7.0-doc/index.html`

After you install it, Tomcat is very easy to use. To install an application, you just need to place the application's `war` file into `$CATALINA_HOME/webapps` and then restart Tomcat with:

`$CATALINA_HOME/bin/shutdown.sh`
`$CATALINA_HOME/bin/startup.sh`

On windows, these scripts end with .bat

Set `CATALINA_HOME` to the directory where you unpack Tomcat.

> **NOTE** *Throughout the chapters on server development, the book will say to "restart Tomcat" as a shorthand for restarting the server if it's running or starting it if it's not.*

Of course, if you'll be using Eclipse, it's even easier than that — the IDE will deploy your application and handle the installation for you.

4. Install ant.

The most popular build tool for Java is called ant, and it uses a simple XML format for listing commands that can perform operations required for building a Java project, such as compiling classes, copying files to a directory, or creating a Java archive `.jar` file.

Set the shell variable `ANT_HOME` to the directory where you unpack ant. Place the directory `$ANT_HOME/bin` in your System Path environment variable.

For more information on ant, see:

```
http://ant.apache.org
```

To install ant, see

```
http://ant.apache.org/manual/install.html
```

5. Open a shell prompt; on Windows, use cygwin. Build the project using ant and set up the database (must be done before using Eclipse):

```
cd $CODE/springServiceContacts
ant dist
```

Initialize the service database:

```
ant builddb
```

> **NOTE** *These ant targets need Internet connectivity to download the ivy utility dependencies and build successfully.*

Now that you have set up the required tools, you can move to deploying the projects.

Deploying Using Ant

1. Build the project, whenever you make code changes (if not done already):

```
ant dist
```

2. Copy the war file to Tomcat:

```
$CODE/springServiceContacts/dist/springServiceContacts.war
```

to

```
$CATALINA_HOME/webapps
```

3. Restart Tomcat (discussed previously)

Loading the Project in Eclipse

Perform all steps in the "Prepare" section.

1. If its not already running, start the Eclipse IDE for Java EE Developers from:

```
http://www.eclipse.org/downloads/
```

> **WARNING** *Make sure you are using Eclipse Enterprise Edition (standard edition is not sufficient for service development). Also make sure that the build of Java, 32- or 64-bit, matches that of Eclipse.*

2. Run the following commands in a shell:

```
cd $CODE\springservicecontacts
ant eclipse
```

Like other chapters, this command copies the Eclipse project files from the tools directory to the root directory. Note that if you do not run this step, Eclipse will not see the project folder as an Eclipse project, and you will not be able to open the project in Eclipse.

3. Add Ivy support to Eclipse:

    a. Select Help ⇨ Install new software

        Work with the url:

        `http://www.apache.org/dist/ant/ivyde/updatesite`

        Check the following for install:

```
Apache Ivy Library
Apache IvyDE Eclipse plugins
```

    b. Click Next.

    c. Accept the terms, finish, and restart Eclipse.

4. Import the Eclipse project.

    a. Import the project with File ⇨ General ⇨ Import Existing Project.

    b. Click the Browse button, and choose the `$CODE/springServiceContacts` directory; then check the checkbox to select the `springServiceContacts`. Click the Finish button.

    c. Click Next.

Example Dependencies with Ivy

With Ivy, developers just need to specify top-level dependencies and their version, and then Ivy will download and install any dependency libraries. Listing 6-1 shows a list of Ivy dependencies for the contacts service, contained in the file:

    `$CODE/springServiceContacts/ivy.xml`

LISTING 6-1: ivy.xml

```
<dependencies>
    <dependency org="org.hibernate" name="hibernate-entitymanager"
        rev="3.6.10.Final"/>
    <dependency org="org.hibernate" name="hibernate-tools" rev="3.2.4.GA"/>
    <dependency org="org.codehaus.jackson" name="jackson-core-asl" rev="1.9.5" />
    <dependency org="org.codehaus.jackson" name="jackson-mapper-lgpl" rev="1.9.5"/>
    <dependency org="org.springframework" name="spring-core" rev="3.1.1.RELEASE" />
    <dependency org="org.springframework" name="spring-webmvc"
        rev="3.1.1.RELEASE" />
    <dependency org="org.springframework" name="spring-oxm" rev="3.1.1.RELEASE"/>
    <dependency org="org.springframework" name="spring-orm" rev="3.1.1.RELEASE"/>
    <dependency org="org.springframework" name="spring-aop" rev="3.1.1.RELEASE"/>
    <dependency org="org.aspectj" name="aspectjweaver" rev="1.6.12"/>
    <dependency org="cglib" name="cglib-full" rev="2.0.2"/>
```

continues

LISTING 6-1 *(continued)*

```
        <dependency org="log4j" name="log4j" rev="1.2.16"/>
        <dependency org="commons-dbcp" name="commons-dbcp" rev="1.4"/>
        <dependency org="junit" name="junit" rev="4.10"/>
        <dependency org="org.springframework" name="spring-test" rev="3.1.1.RELEASE"/>
        <dependency org="mysql" name="mysql-connector-java" rev="5.1.18"/>
        <dependency org="commons-httpclient" name="commons-httpclient" rev="3.1"/>
    </dependencies>
```

> **NOTE** *You can learn more about the Ivy project on its home page at* http://
> ant.apache.org/ivy.

Tools and Software Stack

It's worth spending a minute to discuss Listing 6-1 to talk about other software that has not yet been highlighted, but is involved in the chapter example and in future chapters. As mentioned, these examples rely heavily on Spring and Hibernate, versions 3.1.1 and 3.6.10.Final, respectively. The following libraries are also included:

➤ **Jackson** — Supports JSON Java object serialization and JSON Schema, which is needed for serializing and deserializing service parameters and return values:

http://jackson.codehaus.org/

➤ **Spring WebMVC** — The Spring answer to MVC web architecture; enables the use of Spring controllers:

http://static.springsource.org/spring/docs/2.0.x/reference/mvc.html

➤ **MySQL** — The open source and most popular SQL database on the Internet. Provides underlying persistence support for Hibernate:

http://www.mysql.com/

➤ **Commons httpclient** — Apache Java libraries for HTTP communication; superior to core Java networking libraries for backend development.

Configuring Spring

When you create your own new application, you will need to take the following steps to configure Spring. Of course, the springServiceContacts code example has already completed these tasks.

As noted, with Java web applications, the common practice is to use servlets as hooks for layering value add frameworks. The code in web.xml for inserting Spring is shown as the main servlet dispatcher:

```
    <servlet>
        <servlet-name>DispatcherServlet</servlet-name>
        <servlet-class>org.springframework.web.servlet.DispatcherServlet
            </servlet-class>
        <init-param>
```

```
        <param-name>contextConfigLocation</param-name>
        <param-value>classpath:spring/application*.xml</param-value>
    </init-param>
</servlet>
<servlet-mapping>
    <servlet-name>DispatcherServlet</servlet-name>
<url-pattern>/</url-pattern>
</servlet-mapping>
```

This code indicates to the Spring framework the location of the example Spring configuration files. The example has three configurations for rest, storage, and test. Let's take a look inside the rest configuration file:

```
$CODE/springServiceContacts/src/spring/applicationContext-rest.xml
```

The most significant part of the file is a command for scanning class files, the effect of which is to search all classes in the named base package annotated with Spring annotations, like @Controller. This search is an automatic component-registering process. You only need to annotate your controllers and Spring will integrate them for you:

```
<!-- Enable annotation scanning. -->
<context:component-scan base-package="com.enterpriseandroid.springServiceContacts" />
```

When the application container runs the Spring servlet, org.springframework.web.servlet .DispatcherServlet, Spring will load the components of the contact service. This servlet will forward all requests to scanned controllers.

The previous discussion defines the Spring dispatcher servlet in the web application. The contextConfigLocation defines the location for the Spring configuration files. In this case, you set it to the spring directory of the classpath. You also want the Spring dispatcher servlet to handle all the client requests that are sent to the / path of your service servlet, so you need to add the servlet mapping to the following:

```
<!-- mapping all request to "/" to the Dispatcher Servlet -->
 <servlet-mapping>
    <servlet-name>DispatcherServlet</servlet-name>
    <url-pattern>/</url-pattern>
 </servlet-mapping>
```

Example Code

At this point it's time to jump into the example code itself. We start with the overall architecture diagram of the contact service, showing the significant dependent libraries and layers of this simple three-tier architecture. (Figure 6-5 shows the three-tier architecture and its component dependencies.) The rest of the chapter explains the service and its code in detail.

Contacts Data Model

We start by looking at what the service does — often called the service domain. The example service provides persistent access to contact information. The code uses the following data model class, Contact, shown in Listing 6-2, to manipulate contacts in memory, transmit them to the network, and store them in MySQL. This class is central to the role of the contact service and is known as a model object.

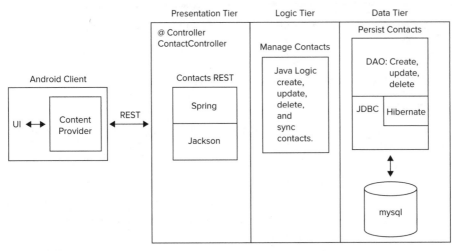

FIGURE 6-5

LISTING 6-2: The contacts data model

```
public class Contact implements Serializable {
    private static final long serialVersionUID = 5322847412825669350L;
    private Long id;
    private String firstName;
    private String lastName;
    private String phone;
    private String email;
    private Long version;
    private long updateTime;
}
```

At this point, you should pause a moment to consider the similarity of this class to the schema defined model from Chapter 5. The listing here is the backend service equivalent of it.

Example Spring Controller

Next, we look at the events that drive the operation of contacts service requests — the heart of our three tier web service. Spring controllers receive the action of web UI remote requests as controller actions. When a Spring-based service receives a remote request, it delegates the request service to a scanned Spring controller, specifically to the class `ContactsController`, which will implement the backend service version of the RESTful contacts API from Chapter 5, listed for review as follows:

1. Access a contact:

   `GET /Contacts/{id}`

2. Access all contacts:

   `GET /Contacts`

3. Create or modify a contact:

```
POST /Contacts
PUT /Contacts/{id}
```

4. Delete a contact:

```
DELETE /Contacts/{id}
```

Contact Service Controller

Now you'll see how to use the Spring framework to implement these requests. You start by defining the class, ContactController, in Listing 6-3.

LISTING 6-3: Annotations for a controller

```
@Controller
@RequestMapping("/Contacts")
public class ContactController {
```

ContactController gets marked as a Spring controller, which means that it can receive the action of the contact service REST methods (as mentioned, this means Spring will find it during the configuration scan).

The code requests a mapping for the namespace, "/Contacts". This will cause the application container and the Spring framework to direct contact requests that start with "/Contacts" to the implementation methods in the ContactController class. The following section explains these implementation methods as well as the RequestMapping annotation.

Presentation Tier: Spring Annotations

Now that you have a controller to contain it, it's time to define the presentation layer for the contacts service. Recall that the presentation layer for a RESTful service encapsulates the processing of service parameters. The annotations provided next do this for the contact operations. We'll start with the first RESTful operation listed previously. Listing 6-4 shows the Spring-based presentation layer implementation for a contact GET operation.

LISTING 6-4: Annotations for getting a contact

```
@RequestMapping(value = "/{id}", method = RequestMethod.GET)
@ResponseBody public Contact getContact(@PathVariable Long id,
    HttpServletResponse resp)
```

This segment of the presentation layer consists of the associated annotations, RequestMapping and ResponseBody. The RequestMapping annotation causes the contact service to use the getContact method to respond to any HTTP GET request for a specific given id, as indicated by the value and method annotation parameters. The ResponseBody annotation indicates that the method return value will be returned directly as an HTTP response. Spring passes the contact id to the method as a PathVariable, which is an elegant way of referring to variables embedded in RESTful URLS, such as:

```
http://host:port/Contacts/1
```

where the `1` is the URL embedded `id` of the desired contact, or path parameter. You can use `PathParam` to refer to any variable embedded in a URL path.

The logic in the method itself and the persistence abstraction used in the method form the other two layers in the three-tier architecture — which you'll read about shortly.

Next, you can find the Spring mappings for the remaining service operations. They work in roughly the same way as the one you just saw. Listing 6-5 shows the Spring-based presentation layer implementation for getting all contacts.

LISTING 6-5: Annotations for getting all contacts

```
@RequestMapping(value = "", method = RequestMethod.GET)
@ResponseBody public List<Contact> getAllContacts(@RequestParam(value="start",
    required=false)
```

The `getAllContacts` method uses a blank value to indicate that all contacts should be returned for a `GET` request on the `"/Contacts"` URL.

Listing 6-6 shows the implementation for creating a contact.

LISTING 6-6: Annotations for creating a contact

```
@RequestMapping(value = "", method = RequestMethod.POST)
@ResponseBody public Map<String, String> createObject(
@RequestBody Contact contact, HttpServletRequest req)
```

The value is blank here since the namespace is `"/Contacts"`. The `createObject` creates the object and the contact ID does not yet exist. The `@RequestBody` annotation indicates that the `POST` payload should be deserialized to a `Contact` Java object. The Spring annotation framework delegates the deserialization process to a registered Jackson deserialization handler — more about that in a minute.

Listing 6-7 shows the implementation for updating a contact.

LISTING 6-7: Annotations for updating a contact

```
@RequestMapping(value = "", method = RequestMethod.PUT)
@ResponseBody public Map<String, String> updateObject(@PathVariable Long id,
@RequestBody Contact contact, HttpServletRequest req)
```

Again, the namespace is `"/Contacts"`, although an `id` is passed to this method in the form of a `PathVariable`, where the code passes the `id` to the utility method `createOrUpdate`, which will update the indicated and already existing `contact`. The `contact` must exist, because it has an `id`. The request body `contact` is again deserialized from the request input, and becomes the information to update.

Finally, Listing 6-8 shows the implementation for deleting a contact.

LISTING 6-8: Annotations for deleting a contact

```
@RequestMapping(value = "/{id}", method = RequestMethod.DELETE)
@ResponseBody public String delete(@PathVariable Long id) throws IOException {
```

The ID value here refers to a pre-existing contact ID just like the getContact method. The URL for deletion is "/Contacts/{id}".

Data Marshaling

To wrap up the presentation layer, take a look at how input parameters and response values get marshaled back and forth between the client and server over the network: Jackson, a JSON serialization library, provides the answer. The following lines in the Spring configuration file (Listing 6-9) set up the use of a Jackson class as the system that maps Java objects into a wire transfer format.

LISTING 6-9: Spring configuration for setting the marshalling converter

```
<bean id="marshallingHttpMessageConverter"
    class="org.springframework.http.converter.json.MappingJacksonHttpMessageConverter">
</bean>
```

Next, Listing 6-10 shows an example of using Jackson to convert objects to JSON.

LISTING 6-10: A method that depends on Jackson for data marshalling

```
@RequestMapping(value = "/{id}", method = RequestMethod.GET)
@ResponseBody public Contact getContact(@PathVariable Long id,
    HttpServletResponse resp)
        throws IOException
{
    Contact c = service.getContact(id);
    if (c == null) {
       resp.setStatus(HttpStatus.NOT_FOUND.value());
    }
    return c;
}
```

You can see that all the code has to do to get objects on and off the wire is use them as parameters and as standard return values — no manual coding required.

Logic Tier: Java Code

As mentioned, the logic tier of a three-tier service is where service domain operations take place. They usually consist of manually written code in the service language of choice. Example operations for the logic tier of a contact service could involve finding the geographic distance between the handsets of two contacts, comparing the "Facebook likes" of one set of contacts against another set, or obtaining a list of bookmarks for a contact.

The logic tier of the chapter example contacts service is not particularly demonstrative of what you might expect to see in a "real-world" service because it's part of the design of the example service to be simple.

This section focuses on a Java method, getAllContacts, from the logic tier of the chapter example contacts service interacting with the values from the Spring "presentation layer."

Getting All Contacts

The getAllContacts method shown in Listing 6-11 does not have much of a logic layer, but it should serve to show that more complex domain operations could take place in a Spring controller method.

LISTING 6-11: Method for getting all contacts

```
@RequestMapping(value = "", method = RequestMethod.GET)
@ResponseBody public List<Contact> getAllContacts(
    @RequestParam(value="start", required=false) String startStr,
    @RequestParam(value="num", required=false) String numStr)
        throws IOException
{
    int start = 0;
    int num = 100;

    if (startStr != null) {
        start = Integer.parseInt(startStr);
    }

    if (numStr != null) {
        num = Integer.parseInt(numStr);
    }

    return service.getAll(start, num);
}
```

Take note of the following in the preceding code:

➤ An empty mapping value to "/Contacts" means get all contacts.

➤ The code includes the parameter bounds of the resulting contacts window.

➤ The code queries the contacts persistence service to return the requested window of contacts.

Data Tier: Persistence Layer

As illustrated in Figure 6-6, the contacts service persistence service layer has two layers of its own for service abstraction and data access.

The Service Interface

The service interface provides a layer of abstraction that can hide information about the initialization of the data access layer from the logic layer and other parts of the persistence layer. The service interface shown in Listing 6-12 provides operations for storing and finding contacts. The operations support the contact controller, as discussed previously.

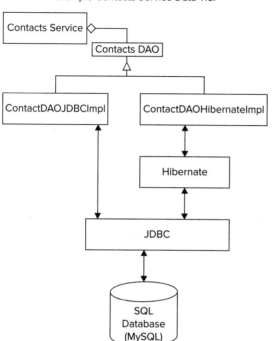

Example Contacts Service Data Tier

FIGURE 6-6

LISTING 6-12: The contacts data service interface

```
import java.io.IOException;
import java.util.List;

import com.wiley.demo.android.dataModel.Contact;

public interface ContactService {
    Long storeOrUpdateContact(Contact c) throws IOException;

    List<Contact> findContactByFirstName(String firstName,
    int start, int numOfmatches) throws IOException;
    List<Contact> getAll( int start, int numOfmatches) throws IOException;
    Contact getContact(long id) throws IOException ;
    void deleteContact(long id) throws IOException;
}
```

The DAO Interface

The contacts example service provides support to its data service interface using a well-established metaphor — that of the data access object, or DAO. A DAO maps object persistence operations to a persistence layer. The example contacts DAO provides methods for finding, deleting, and saving contacts. Later you'll see the implementations for mapping this DAO interface to JDBC and Hibernate. The DAO interface is shown in Listing 6-13.

LISTING 6-13: The contacts DAO interface

```
import java.io.IOException;
import java.util.List;
import com.wiley.demo.android.dataModel.Contact;

public interface ContactDao {
    Contact getContact(Long id) throws IOException;
    Long storeOrUpdateContact(Contact contact) throws IOException;
    List<Contact> findContactFirstName(String firstName, int start,
        int numOfmatches);
    List<Contact> findChanged(long timestamp, int start, int numOfmatches);
    void delete(Long id) throws IOException ;
    List<Contact> getAll(int start, int numOfmatches) throws IOException;
}
```

This interface supports methods to create a new contact or update an existing one; the other methods do what their self-documenting names describe.

Also, take note of the following in Listing 6-13:

➤ The methods getContact and delete both take an identifier that refers to a unique contact object. When supported with a SQL implementation, this identifier will most likely be a SQL primary key.

➤ Several of the DAO operations support the ability to select a window from possible database results, allowing a client to access sections of queries with a large number of results into small chunks or pages that do not overwhelm client resources.

Implementing the DAO Interface

In keeping with the example, the ContactDao interface is quite simple, and provides only the operations needed to support the contacts REST interface. This chapter provides two implementations of it for these reasons:

➤ To give you an idea of what it's like to work with two commonly used Java technologies

➤ To help demonstrate why some groups of developers advocate using an ORM and why others feel that this class of technology can introduce hard-to-debug problems that do not arise with direct use of JDBC

➤ To demonstrate the flexibility of the three-tier service architecture and how it can support different storage solutions, like those found in different cloud vendors

Using Hibernate

After browsing the Hibernate code shown in Listing 6-14, one of the first takeaways you may notice is that it is short. Each method consists only of accessing a Spring Hibernate template — an API object that contains a slew of methods for accessing and modifying data — and then calling the right template operation to achieve the appropriate effect of a given DAO method. Proponents of Hibernate argue that this brevity is one of the main advantages of using the ORM. You just need to work with objects, and the Hibernate mapping will take care of all the details of getting your data into the underlying database. See the following link for more information on Hibernate mapping:

```
http://docs.jboss.org/hibernate/orm/3.3/reference/en-US/html/mapping.html
```

LISTING 6-14: The Hibernate contacts DAO implementation

```
package com.wiley.demo.android.dao.impl;

import java.io.IOException;
import java.util.List;

import org.hibernate.Query;
import org.springframework.orm.hibernate3.HibernateTemplate;
import org.springframework.orm.hibernate3.support.HibernateDaoSupport;

import com.wiley.demo.android.dao.ContactDao;
import com.wiley.demo.android.dataModel.Contact;

public class ContactDaoHibernateImpl extends HibernateDaoSupport implements
    ContactDao {
  @Override
  public Contact getContact(Long id) throws IOException {
      return getHibernateTemplate().get(Contact.class, id);
  }

   @Override
   public Long storeOrUpdateContact(Contact contact) throws IOException {
      contact.setUpdateTime(System.currentTimeMillis());
      getHibernateTemplate().saveOrUpdate(contact);
      return contact.getId();
   }

  @SuppressWarnings("unchecked")
  @Override
  public List<Contact> findContactFirstName(String firstName, int start, int
      numOfmatches) {
  String hql="from Contact where firstName = ?";
  return (List<Contact>) getHibernateTemplate().find(hql,
      new Object[] {firstName});
  }

  @Override
  public List<Contact> findChanged(long timestamp, int start, int numOfmatches) {
      String hql="from Contact where updateTime > " + timestamp ;
      Query q = getSession().createQuery(hql);
      q.setFirstResult(start);
      q.setMaxResults(numOfmatches);

      @SuppressWarnings("unchecked")
      List<Contact> list =  q.list();
      return list;
  }

  @Override
  public void delete(Long id) throws IOException {
      getHibernateTemplate().delete(getContact(id));
```

continues

LISTING 6-14 *(continued)*

```
    }

    @Override
    public List<Contact> getAll(int start, int numOfmatches)
        throws IOException
    {
        String hql = "from Contact";
        Query q = getSession().createQuery(hql);
        q.setFirstResult(start);
        q.setMaxResults(numOfmatches);
        @SuppressWarnings("unchecked")
        List<Contact> list =  q.list();
        return list;
    }
}
```

Take note of the following:

➤ The single line `getContact` method gets a Hibernate template and then calls the `get` operation to access an object of type `Contact.class`. The method returns a `Contact` object.

➤ This code sets the update time for use in sync operations.

➤ The Hibernate template `storeOrUpdate` method stores the updated object. Note that the code also updates the contact with the service timestamp, enabling the application to know the last time a contact object changed.

➤ This code shows the use of a data language called HQL (Hibernate Query Language), which is a fully object-oriented version of SQL. In this case, the code just shows a simple query to select a contact by name. With the query in hand, the `findContactFirstName` method uses the Hibernate template to find contacts with the given parameter name `firstName`.

> **NOTE** *The Hibernate website has excellent resources on HQL:*
> `http://docs.jboss.org/hibernate/orm/3.3/reference/en/html/queryhql.html`

➤ The `findChanged` method enables finding users changed after a given timestamp, thus taking advantage of the information left behind by `storeOrUpdateContact`.

➤ The query for the method to get all contacts, no arguments acts like a wild card.

Using JDBC

In Listing 6-15, you'll find an implementation of the contact DAO interface based on JDBC. Your first reaction on reading this code might be that this version is quite a bit longer, coming in at well over twice the number of lines of code as the Hibernate equivalent. Of course, the main differences are that the JDBC code does not have the benefit of either the object-oriented nature of the Hibernate template class, nor the Hibernate object mapping. All contact insertions must consist of invocations on the contact POJO class, concatenated into strings to make SQL commands, much as is the case when using the raw SQL interface to SQLite on Android.

Although the code is not as terse as the Hibernate side, it allows you to quickly see exactly how it uses JDBC. The number of lines of code taken to write the Hibernate implementation, *including* the Hibernate libraries, would be significantly greater than the code shown here. Hibernate is a reliable ORM implementation, but it does have significant complexity in its session and object mapping support. Developers do need to understand Hibernate well enough to use it correctly.

Listing 6-15 does not use a Hibernate template, but instead relies on a Spring JDBC template. This template provides a large number of convenience methods for using JDBC directly without an ORM. The code uses SQL statements to pass DAO parameters to the underlying database connection. Two of the more interesting pieces of code include the use of a prepared statement to insert a contact object into a database row and a Spring row mapper that enables a binding from a row of a JDBC result set to a contact POJO.

LISTING 6-15: The JDBC contacts DAO implementation

```
1   package com.wiley.demo.android.dao.impl;
2
3   import java.io.IOException;
4   import java.sql.Connection;
5   import java.sql.PreparedStatement;
6   import java.sql.ResultSet;
7   import java.sql.SQLException;
8   import java.util.List;
9   import java.util.Map;
10
11  import javax.sql.DataSource;

12  import org.springframework.dao.EmptyResultDataAccessException;
13  import org.springframework.jdbc.core.JdbcTemplate;
14  import org.springframework.jdbc.core.PreparedStatementCreator;
15  import org.springframework.jdbc.core.RowMapper;
16  import org.springframework.jdbc.support.GeneratedKeyHolder;
17  import org.springframework.jdbc.support.KeyHolder;
18
19  import com.wiley.demo.android.dao.ContactDao;
20  import com.wiley.demo.android.dataModel.Contact;
21
22  public class ContactDaoJdbcImpl implements ContactDao {
23      private static final String FIND_FIRSTNAME_SQL =
24          "select * from contact where firstName = ?";
25      private static final String FIND_UPDATETIME_SQL =
26          "select * from contact where updateTime > ?";
27      private static final String GET_SQL =
28          "select * from contact where id = ?";
29      private static final String GET_ALL_SQL = "select * from contact ";
30      private static final String INSERT_SQL =
31          "Insert into contact( firstName, lastName, phone, email, updateTime,
               version)" +
32          VALUES(?,?,?,?,?,?);";
33      private static final String UPDATE_SQL = "update contact set firstname = ?, " +
34          lastname=?, phone=?, email=?, updateTime=?, version=? where id = ? and " +
```

continues

LISTING 6-15 *(continued)*

```
35            "version=?";
36      private static final String DELETE_SQL = "delete from contact where id =?";
37
38      private DataSource dataSource;
39      private JdbcTemplate jdbcTemplate;
40
41      public void setDataSource(DataSource ds) {
42          dataSource = ds;
43          jdbcTemplate = new JdbcTemplate(dataSource);
44      }
45
46      @Override
47      public Long storeOrUpdateContact(Contact contact) throws IOException {
48          contact.setUpdateTime(System.currentTimeMillis());
49          if ( contact.getId() != null) {
50              update(contact);
51          } else {
52              create(contact);
53          }
54          return contact.getId();
55      }
56
57      @Override
58      public List<Contact> findContactFirstName(String firstName, int start,
59          int numOfmatches)
60      {
61          String query = FIND_FIRSTNAME_SQL + " limit " + new Long(start).toString()
                + " , " +
62              new Long(numOfmatches).toString();
63          return jdbcTemplate.query(query, getRowMapper(), new Object[] {firstName});
64      }
65
66      @Override
67      public List<Contact> getAll(int start, int numOfmatches) throws IOException {
68          String query = GET_ALL_SQL + " limit " + new Long(start).toString()
                + " , " +
69              new Long(numOfmatches).toString();
70          return jdbcTemplate.query(query, getRowMapper());
71      }
72
73      private void create(final Contact contact) {
74          if (contact.getVersion() != null) {
75              throw new IllegalArgumentException("version has to be 0 for create");
76          }
77
78          KeyHolder keyHolder = new GeneratedKeyHolder();
79          jdbcTemplate.update(new PreparedStatementCreator() {
80          public PreparedStatement createPreparedStatement(
81              Connection connection) throws SQLException
82          {
83              PreparedStatement ps = connection.prepareStatement(INSERT_SQL,
84                      new String[] { "id" });
```

```
85                ps.setString(1, contact.getFirstName());
86                ps.setString(2, contact.getLastName());
87                ps.setString(3, contact.getPhone());
88                ps.setString(4, contact.getEmail());
89                ps.setLong(5, contact.getUpdateTime());
90                ps.setLong(6, new Long(1));
91                return ps;
92            }
93        }, keyHolder);
94        contact.setId(keyHolder.getKey().longValue());
95        contact.setVersion(new Long(1));
96    }
97
98    private void update(Contact contact)  throws IOException {
99        Long version = contact.getVersion();
100       contact.setVersion(version +1);
101       int rowupdated = jdbcTemplate.update(UPDATE_SQL, getUpdateSqlArgs(contact,
              version));
102
103       if (rowupdated != 1)  {
104           throw new IllegalArgumentException("Verson mismatch. row updated : " +
105               rowupdated);
106       }
107    }
108
109    private Object[] getInsertSqlArgs(Contact contact) {
110        return new Object[] {
111        contact.getFirstName(), contact.getLastName(),
112        contact.getPhone(), contact.getEmail(), contact.getUpdateTime(),
              new Long(1L)};
113    }
114
115    private Object[] getUpdateSqlArgs(Contact contact, Long version) {
116        return new Object[] { contact.getFirstName(), contact.getLastName(),
117            contact.getPhone(), contact.getEmail(), contact.getUpdateTime(),
118            contact.getVersion(), contact.getId(), version };
119    }
120
121    @Override
122    public Contact getContact(Long id) {
123     try {
124         return jdbcTemplate.queryForObject(GET_SQL, getRowMapper(), id);
125     } catch( EmptyResultDataAccessException e) {
126         return null;
127     }
128 }
129
130 @Override
131 public void delete(Long id)  throws IOException {
132     jdbcTemplate.update(DELETE_SQL, new Object[] {id});
133 }
134
135 private RowMapper<Contact> getRowMapper() {
136     RowMapper<Contact> mapper = new RowMapper<Contact>() {
```

continues

LISTING 6-15 *(continued)*

```
137         public Contact mapRow(ResultSet rs, int rowNum) throws SQLException {
138             Contact obj = new Contact();
139             obj.setId(rs.getLong("id"));
140             obj.setFirstName(rs.getString("firstName"));
141             obj.setLastName(rs.getString("lastName"));
142             obj.setPhone(rs.getString("phone"));
143             obj.setEmail((rs.getString("email")));
144             obj.setUpdateTime(rs.getLong("updateTime"));
145             obj.setVersion(rs.getLong("version"));
146             return obj;
147         }
148     };
149
150     return mapper;
151 }
152
153 @Override
154 public List<Contact> findChanged(long timestamp, int start, int numOfmatches) {
155     String query = FIND_UPDATETIME_SQL + " limit " + new Long(start).toString()
        + " , " +
156         new Long(numOfmatches).toString();
157     return jdbcTemplate.query(query, getRowMapper(), new Object[] {new
        Long(timestamp)});
158 }
159 }
```

Take note of the following lines in Listing 6-15:

➤ **Lines 23-36** — Contain SQL convenience strings used later in the implementation of the DAO methods.

➤ **Lines 38 and 39** — Represent the connection to the JDBC database and a Spring JDBC template, respectively. The DAO code uses the template to persist the contact state, and the template uses the database connection to write the information to the database.

➤ **Line 47** — This time, the `storeOrUpdateContact` method uses two private implementation methods, `update` and `create`, on lines 50 and 52, respectively, depending on whether the contact object has an existing ID (also the primary key in the contacts database). On line 101, you can see the invocation of a template query method, passing in the SQL convenience string, `UPDATE_SQL` template.

➤ **Lines 58-62** — Shows the implementation of `findContactFirstName` using `FIND_FIRSTNAME_SQL` and the JDBC Spring template. Allows one to query for contacts that have the first name as supplied by the `firstName` method parameter.

➤ **Lines 78-93** — Use a prepared statement as mentioned earlier to insert a new contact row into the database. The prepared statement uses the `INSERT_SQL` string and the fields of a contact object as the parameters to the prepared statement.

➤ **Lines 137-147** — Demonstrate the use of a Spring framework JDBC row mapper to map a JDBC result set row to a contact POJO object. The Spring row mapper nicely adds some object-oriented behavior to direct JDBC. With Spring, you can attain some significant benefits of Hibernate, but still work much closer to JDBC.

➤ **Lines 154-156** — The findChanged implementation and the query it uses, FIND_ UPDATETIME_SQL, enable finding contacts changed since a given timestamp.

➤ **Lines 63, 70, 124, and 157** — All make use of the row mapper to convert result set rows into a Contact object that then is returned as a Java type from the relevant method.

To conclude the discussion of the springContactsService, you can switch DAO implementations by moving the x character between the following lines:

```
<!-- use jdbc dao -->
<bean id="contactServicex" class=← - The x disables this DAO
  "com.enterpriseandroid.springServiceContacts.service.impl.ContactServiceImpl"
  p:contactDao-ref="contactDaoJdbc" />


<bean id="contactService" ← - Move x to here to switch impls
class="com.enterpriseandroid.springServiceContacts.service.impl.ContactServiceImpl"
p:contactDao-ref="contactDaoHibernate" />
```

in the file:

> $CODE/springServiceContacts/src/spring/applicationContext-storage.xml

and load it into Eclipse

Code Example: Spring Sync Contacts Service

The chapter began with a discussion of the benefits of synchronization in enterprise Android applications. Now that you have seen a CRUD-only version of the contacts RESTful service, the next example adds a simple but powerful synchronization system that works well with the sync adapter ⟳ content provider pattern developed in the last chapter. This service resides in the project:

> $CODE/springSyncServiceContacts

And you can build it and load it into Eclipse with the same instructions you used in the previous example.

The following sections look at the relevant components of the contacts synchronization example.

Presentation Tier: Spring Controllers

The synchronization contact controller is identical to the CRUD version, except for two significant differences:

1. The synchronization service adds a fifth spring contact controller operation, sync:

```
POST /Contacts/sync
```
The Spring controller declaration appears as follows:

```
@RequestMapping(value = "/sync", method = RequestMethod.POST)
@ResponseBody
public SyncResult sync(@REQUESTBODY SyncRequest syncR) throws IOException
```

2. The controller operations take a UUID string ID instead of a `long` ID. Many RESTful web services refer to specific objects using a simple numeric `long` — a natural choice for SQL databases with an autoincrement feature. UUIDs represent another common referencing scheme in an era of SQL alternatives (see Chapter 7). A UUID is typically a 128-bit value described as follows:

`http://docs.oracle.com/javase/6/docs/api/java/util/UUID.html`

> **NOTE** *An interesting feature of a randomly created UUID is that collisions (that is, equivalent UUIDs) with other random UUIDs are incredibly unlikely to occur due to the size of the UUID number—128 bits. This characteristic enables clients to make up their own UUIDs without having to rely on the server to create them.*

The Spring controller definition that follows takes a UUID string, instead of a long ID as in the previous example:

```
@RequestMapping(value = "/{id}", method = RequestMethod.GET)
@ResponseBody
public Contact getContact(@PathVariable String id,
    HttpServletResponse resp)
```

Clients for all services, except for `springServiceContacts`, will use RESTful URLs that look like the following:

```
http://localhost:8080/Contacts/ab619fb-4331-4826-b2e9-9516efd4d953
```

which seems more complex, but is actually used the same way as a URL like the following:

```
http://localhost:8080/Contacts/1
```

Logic Tier: Java Synchronization Logic

You can find the simplified contact synchronization example in Listing 6-16. In production, it would be necessary to improve its robustness, but the code should give you an idea of how backend service side synchronization with a mobile client can work, with a brief introduction as follows:

The synchronization example contact service contains an internal Spring contacts persistence service. Mobile clients have their own contact storage, likely in a SQLite table. When a sync operation kicks off after being initiated by the client or the service, the client will send its outstanding changes to the service, along with a timestamp, recorded on the service but stored in the client, of the last time the client synced with the service.

The service will first query for changes to its own persistent contacts made since the timestamp from the client. The service then merges with changes from the client. Finally, the service sends its own changes, from before any client merges, back to the client, where the client can ask users to resolve any conflicts between their own data and the data from the service. When the user finishes resolving the changes, the client should then perform another sync. This will ensure that conflict resolutions also make it back into service persistence. Figure 6-7 shows the example synchronization operation.

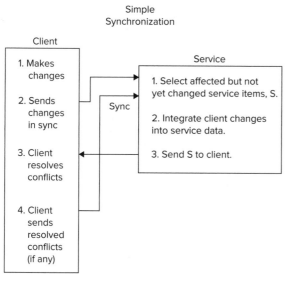

FIGURE 6-7

Listing 6-16 shows a simplified implementation of a synchronization routine for the synchronization controller.

LISTING 6-16: A method for synchronizing contacts

```
@RequestMapping(value = "sync", method = RequestMethod.POST)
@ResponseBody
public SynchResult sync(@RequestBody SynchRequest clientData),
    throws IOException, ParseException
{
    List<Contact> dataList = clientData.getContactList();
    Long now = clientData.getSyncTime();
    List<Contact> changedData = service.findChanged(syncTime, 0, 1000);
    SynchResult ret = new SynchResult(changedData, now);
    for (Contact c : dataList) {
        if (c.isDeleted()) {
            service.deleteContact( c.getId());
        } else {
            service.storeOrUpdateContact(c);
        }
    }
    return ret;
}
```

Take note of the following in the preceding code:

➤ The client passes in a SyncResult object, which contains a list modified contacts and a sync time.

➤ The code gets the current time. This time gets passed back to the client, and the client will pass it back during the next sync operation – the time allows the service to know its modifications since the last sync with a given client.

➤ If the client has deleted the object, it must be deleted on the server.

➤ The code updates the contact on the server.

➤ The server responds with the list of items it has changed since last sync.

Sync Client Implementation

You can find the corresponding client implementation of this synchronization protocol in the project `syncAdapterContacts`. This project implements the Sync Adapter+Content provider pattern discussed at length in Chapter 5. You've seen some details of how the synchronization algorithm works on the service side. It's now time to take a look at the operation of the client at a high level:

1. The contacts `SyncAdapter.onPerformSync` method delegates to `RESTService.sync`, which then performs a synchronization operation for a given user account.

2. As mentioned, the client needs to send the server's last sync time back to the server for each new sync; this client stores that time as metadata with the Android account manager:

   ```
   String ts = mgr.getUserData(account, KEY_SYNC_MARKER);
   ```

3. `RESTService.sync` then calls `RESTService.syncContacts`, which begins by creating a transaction ID to track this sync operation with:

   ```
   String xactId = UUID.randomUUID().toString();
   ```

   And then follows by collecting all modified objects (that is, dirty) for the current transaction using:

   ```
   List<Map<String, Object>> localUpdates = syncUtil.getLocalUpdates(cr, xactId);
   ```

4. The code then converts those updates into a JSON marshaled format:

   ```
   String payload = gson.toJson(syncUtil.createSyncRequest(
       localUpdates, account.name, auth, clientId, lastUpdate));
   ```

5. This is then sent to the backend contacts sync operation for integration with service contacts:

   ```
   String resp = sendRequest(HttpMethod.POST, uri, payload).getBody();
   ```

6. The code then unpacks the results of the processing:

   ```
   Map<String, Object> syncResultMap = gson.fromJson(resp, SyncUtil.MAP_TYPE);
   ```

7. Then it merges the results into the local SQLite database:

   ```
   t = syncUtil.processUpdates(cr, syncResultMap);
   ```

   which requires processing server modifications and resolving conflicts:

   ```
   processServerUpdates(cr, (List<Map<String, Object>>)

   resolveConflicts(cr, (List<Map<String, Object>>)
   ```

8. The code stores the service's time of last sync back into the account manager:

   ```
   mgr.setUserData(account, KEY_SYNC_MARKER, String.valueOf(lastUpdate));
   ```

9. Finally, the code marks local objects complete by:

   a. Removing the dirty flag

   b. Removing the transaction ID (sync)

   c. Incrementing versions where appropriate

Due to the detailed nature of the protocol implementation, it's recommended that you look at the code in the following classes to gain a greater understanding of the sync protocol.

```
$CODE/syncAdaperContacts/src/com/enterpriseandroid/syncadaptercontacts
.svcsyncAdapterContacts/SyncUtil.java
$CODE/syncAdaperContacts/src/com/enterpriseandroid/syncadaptercontacts/svc
/RESTService.java
```

Running the Services

At this point, all the coding is done, and you are ready to run `springServiceContacts`, and its `springSyncServiceContacts` variant, with the following steps, which you'll run independently for each service.

Using Eclipse

1. Configure Eclipse to use Tomcat:

   Use Window ⇨ Preferences ⇨ Server (on the left) ⇨ Runtime Environments ⇨ Server ⇨ Runtime Environments.

   Select Add ⇨ Apache Tomcat v7.0. Click Next.

   Select the Tomcat Installation directory (`CATALINA_HOME`).

   Browse to the directory where you previously unpacked Tomcat and select it.

   Select a JRE: Make sure to use the previously installed "JDK" Java installation—a JRE is not sufficient. If you don't see a JDK choice in the JRE drop-down, click the installed JRE's button.

   a. Click the Add button.

   b. Select Standard VM ⇨ Click Next.

   c. Click Directory to edit the JRE home.

   d. Browse and select the directory where you previously installed the Java JDK

   e. Click Finish.

   If a JRE is selected, unselect it, and select the JDK instead.

   Click OK.

   Back in the Tomcat Server window under the JRE drop-down, if the JDK is not selected, make sure you select it now.

   Click Finish again to complete server configuration.

   Click OK again to leave preferences.

2. Show the server's view: Window ⇨ Show view ⇨ (Other) ⇨ Server ⇨ Servers ⇨ OK.

3. Click the link in the server view to create a new server.

Select the server type (your previously configured Tomcat7)

Leave the variables unchanged.

Click Next ⇨ Select (`springServiceContacts` or `springSyncServiceContacts`).

Click Add.

Click Finish.

4. Create a new configuration and run:

    a. Right-click (springServiceContacts or springSyncServiceContacts) in the package explorer.

    b. Select Run as ⇨ Run Configurations.

        Select Apache Tomcat on the left.

        Click the New icon on the upper left.

    c. Enter the server name, `contact_configuration`; replace `New_configuration`.

Then click Apply.

Then click Run.

> **NOTE** *Windows firewall will/may block the server, so hit "Allow Access" when dialog opens.*

Watch the log file for errors, and keep in mind that it will take a few minutes for ivy to download dependencies the first time the service runs. To see that each service is running correctly, load the URL `http://localhost:8080/springServiceContacts/Contacts` in a browser. If you see an empty array symbol (that is, "[ ]") then it's working.

Using Ant

1. Start a shell for your platform (for example, on windows use cygwin). Then build the project:

```
$CODE/springServiceContacts
ant dist
```

2. Copy the war file to tomcat, copy:

```
$CODE/springServiceContacts/dist/springServiceContacts.war
```

to

```
$CATALINA_HOME/webapps
```

3. Restart Tomcat.

Invoking Requests

Since you've just written a simple web service, it's possible to drive its operation using only a web browser using the endpoint URL:

```
http://localhost:8080/springServiceContacts/Contacts
```

If the servers are running correctly, when you load this URL, the browser will simply show "[]" for an empty array - indicating an empty contacts database.

Another convenient way to drive the operation of the browser is to use a command like `curl`:

```
http://en.wikipedia.org/wiki/cURL
```

You can also install the Advanced Rest Client Chrome extension — a third convenient way to run REST requests.

Figure 6-8 shows the output of a request to list contacts in a web-based REST invocation tool. This service contains two contacts, "John Smith", and "Mark Jackson".

You can install this particular tool in the Chrome browser from Google using:

```
https://chrome.google.com/webstore/detail/advanced-rest-client/
hgmloofddffdnphfgcellkdfbfbjeloo/related?hl=en-US
```

Once you have installed the extension, you can run it using the following URL:

```
chrome-extension://hgmloofddffdnphfgcellkdfbfbjeloo/RestClient.html
```

FIGURE 6-8

Sample Requests

Here you can find a list of CURL operations you can type into your shell of choice to try out contact service operations.

Create an initial contact:

```
curl -H "Content-Type: application/json" -X POST -d '{"firstName":"John",
"lastName":"Smith", "phone":2345678901, "email":"jsmith@nosuchhost.com" }'
http://localhost:8080/springServiceContacts/Contacts
```

Get back the contact that you just sent:

```
curl -X GET http://localhost/Contacts/1
```

The following command should return a 404 error code response:

```
curl -X GET http://localhost:8080/Contacts/2
```

Since no contact exists for the ID 2.

> **NOTE** *Numeric IDs will only work for* springServiceContacts; *you'll need to use UUIDs for the other services in the book.*

It's now possible to run the Chapter 5 Android clients as standard APKs in Eclipse using the configuration from Chapter 1 — you can edit contacts and see them modified in the backend services that you just learned to run.

To see the client and service operate, start restfulCachingProviderContacts, and then start springServiceContacts. Add a contact in the Android client. Enter the URL listed in the previous section; now instead of any empty array, you should see the contact you added. You can also run syncAdapterContacts with springSyncServiceContacts and use the browser to verify changes to contacts.

The project restfulCachingProviderContacts works with all services discussed in this book; the example syncAdapterContacts works with all services except springServiceContacts (because that service does not support synchronization). Set endpoint URLs as described in project README files after starting up the services.

You can try out a mix of interactions between the Chapter 5 clients and the previously listed curl commands. As before, refer to the README files contained in the repos for the most up-to-date versions of chapter instructions.

SUMMARY

This chapter provided an introduction to service development using Spring, Hibernate, and JDBC. Along the way, the discussion noted some common pain points in service development, as follows:

➤ The contacts service required an explicit definition of a RESTful protocol for transferring objects over the wire. Although the protocol for the contacts service was simple, real-world services often require more involved RESTful operations.

➤ The code showed a simple way to track changes to objects over time. Adding synchronization support to enable contact versioning from changes to multiple sources would add significant complexity as well.

➤ Both DAO implementations made use of a static SQL schema, thereby making the addition and deletions of fields difficult after initial schema creation.

The chapter produced two working backend service implementations to support the clients written in the previous chapter. You now have a complete mobile application and supporting web services that can use a RESTful CRUD protocol or can use Android sync adapters to perform a simple but powerful synchronization algorithm. The service code used a flexible three-tier architecture to enable its portability to other styles of persistence, as the next chapter on cloud-based backend services will demonstrate. When you work through the examples in Chapter 7, you'll have ported the contacts service to the Amazon and Google clouds, thus allowing your Android applications to take advantage of the formidable resources offered by those platforms.

7

Mobile and the Cloud

WHAT'S IN THIS CHAPTER?

➤ Understanding cloud performance and scalability

➤ Considering mobile scalability, push, and synchronization

➤ Understanding cloud persistence: SQL and NoSQL

➤ Considering design issues when building scalable services

➤ Looking at some popular cloud providers

➤ Exploring the code examples: RESTful contacts using Amazon DynamoDB and Google App Engine

WROX.COM CODE DOWNLOADS FOR THIS CHAPTER

Please note that all the code examples in this chapter are available at https://github.com/wileyenterpriseandroid/Examples.git and as a part of the book's code download at www.wrox.com on the Download Code tab.

Chapter 6 introduced a simple but functional backend RESTful contacts service based on SQL persistence. But now that you have a backend service, how will you deploy it? Will your chosen software technologies scale to meet demand as your traffic grows? If you don't want to use your own service hardware, how do you pick from the many available cloud service platforms?

Most Android developers know that cloud providers will save them the hassle of building and maintaining their own massive banks of application servers, but persistence support and pricing arrangements vary widely. As you learned in Chapter 6 selecting a cloud provider and service software requires deep knowledge of several vendors and many different types of databases. This chapter digs into the design and capabilities of cloud-based software, and walks through the pros and cons of choosing one provider over another.

The chapter begins with a discussion of why performance and scalability are so crucial to web and mobile applications. Then it delves into the pro and cons of SQL and NoSQL databases and covers the differences among basic APIs from Amazon, Google, and other cloud vendors. The chapter then provides a broad overview of several popular platforms and solutions, instead of diving deep into any specific technology.

After walking through the chapter code examples, you'll understand the basics of Amazon's most popular cloud service platform AWS (Amazon Web Services) and DynamoDB, and Google's App Engine and GQL (Google Query Language). You'll have enough information to make high-level decisions about the backend solutions for your mobile applications.

CLOUD PERFORMANCE AND SCALABILITY

Fulfilling user requests as quickly as possible is the bread and butter of backend services, and maintaining performance during spikes in application usage presents a significant challenge to service developers. By far the most successful way to increase server availability is to run cloud-based applications on large arrays of identical hosts. Application requests usually run entirely independent of each other, and as long as the underlying persistence mechanism supports parallel access, it's possible to support large numbers of simultaneous requests simply by throwing large numbers of commodity servers at an application. Each user sees that the application performs well for them and does not need to know that perhaps thousands of other machines performed the exact same operation for other users at the same time. Figure 7-1 illustrates the cloud. It's called the cloud because you don't know where or how many hosts run your application; they are just available on demand, as from an amorphous "cloud" of resources.

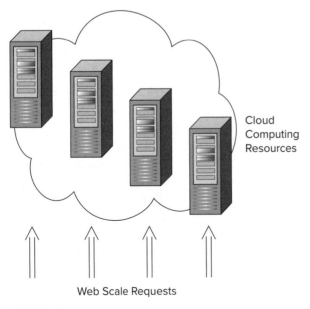

Cloud Computing Resources

Web Scale Requests

FIGURE 7-1

The Scale of Mobile

As this book describes, supporting native Android clients involves a significant set of challenges for service developers. However, when you consider the domain logic of applications, you'll find that there are more similarities than differences between mobile and desktop service development. Both clients require REST support and use similar domain objects. The most drastic difference, besides a smaller screen, is the sheer scale of clients that can make a request on a mobile service. In the United States, not everyone in a household has his or her own laptop or desktop, but almost everyone has at least one device. In developing nations, extremely cheap Android tablets are bringing the Internet to billions of people who have never used a computer.

Using Push Messages

Given the sheer volume of traffic possible with mobile computing, it's critical to consider strategies that reduce redundant client communication. Client-based polling represents a glaring form of unnecessary communication; push-based protocols allow the service to inform clients about relevant changes, rather than clients constantly asking if "they are there yet." Chapter 6 introduced a lightweight synchronization protocol that can work well with a push-based model, where the push message itself can either directly include synchronization state, or simply indicate that a client should initiate synchronization itself. When you think about hundreds of millions of devices all simultaneously initiating wasteful poll requests, a push-based approach becomes highly desirable.

It's relatively simple for a given device to initiate contact with a service, but it's not nearly as straightforward for a service to contact a device. Devices run on intermittently connected networks where it's not even guaranteed that a service will physically be able to contact a device — if there is even a consistent way of contacting devices. Devices run on WiFi and a wide variety of 3G and 4G carrier networks. Sometimes devices have IP addresses and sometimes they do not. Most of the time applications do not have permission to listen on ports to create a service. Traditionally, the simplest and perhaps the most reliable and cross-platform way of sending a message to a device is to use an SMS message. As primitive as it sounds, SMS works pretty well. Another common means to implement push capabilities is by having a client just leave open a persistent HTTP connection through which a service can push messages to the client for the duration of the connection.

> **NOTE** *Google and Apple both support platform-centric push technologies. Google's approach is called Google Cloud Messaging (GCM). Apple's solution is called Apple Push Notification service. Many cross-platform solutions exist, such as technology from a company called Urban Airship. The following link provides instructions to get started with GCM:*
>
> ```
> http://developer.android.com/google/gcm/gs.html
> ```

Synchronization

Chapter 6 introduced synchronization from the perspective of backend development, but with no particular emphasis on scaling or implementation. In this section, you'll consider how the combination of push and synchronization technology can pair to create a drastic reduction in traffic and polling. Picture the following scenario:

➤ Clients can make changes locally without needing to poll the service, since they can rely on push messages (the server can notify on change) to stay up to date.

➤ The client does not need to create a new request for every change it makes; a synchronization request can batch client changes.

➤ The service is free to accept changes from and sync with other devices.

➤ Clients can lose network connectivity and remain functional, since the client has local state it can edit and display.

➤ The developer has flexibility in configuring synchronization times — periodically or as needed depending on system resources.

As you can see, a push and synchronization-based system has significant advantages over polling CRUD protocols. Consequently, this book spends a significant amount of time getting you to think about specific sync-based approaches.

Persistence in the Cloud: From SQL to NoSQL

Of the many challenging aspects of designing an app to have a flexible and scalable architecture, persistence represents one of the thorniest problems. Recent trends in data-driven applications have involved the use of traditional SQL as well as newer scalable architectures that rely on a persistence technology called *NoSQL*. The next sections address important strengths and weaknesses of SQL and discuss why NoSQL was created to maximize scalability for modern applications. Keep in mind that the following discussions are a matter of some debate.

SQL Databases

Many proponents of NoSQL systems argue that the nature of SQL itself tends toward the creation of static schema that have limited capability to evolve as underlying changes in schema become necessary. By contrast, NoSQL approaches can handle such changes intrinsically. Although it's true that schema changes can be difficult to implement in a typical SQL model, it's actually straightforward to create a SQL schema that can accommodate changes over time. Consider the schemas shown in Listings 7-1 and 7-2.

LISTING 7-1: Static schema

```
CREATE TABLE contacts (
    id INT NOT NULL AUTO_INCREMENT PRIMARY KEY,
    firstName VARCHAR(50),
    middleName VARCHAR(50),
    lastName VARCHAR(100)
);
```

LISTING 7-2: Dynamic schema

```
CREATE TABLE KeyValue (
    id INT NOT NULL AUTO_INCREMENT PRIMARY KEY,
    objectId INT,
    key VARCHAR(100),
    value VARCHAR(100)
);
```

Suppose your application inserted thousands of records into the table for Listing 7-1, and you needed to add a new field for a second middle name, due to a few users having non-standard names. SQL supports schema modification using the `alter table` command. However, changing the table structure would require all contacts to have a second middle name field, which would likely be overkill and would waste resources.

Consider the alternative schema in Listing 7-2. This schema is similar to the `KeyValueContentProvider` content provider from Chapter 4. With only a minimal amount of extra overhead, you can store objects with arbitrary fields all in the same table. To retrieve a complete object, you just select for a given `objectID`, and you will get a result set with rows (instead of columns) that are the fields of the object. "Schema changes" in this scenario become simply a matter of adding and deleting `KeyValue` rows and maintaining an object ID.

You might be thinking, okay, it's possible to create flexible schema in SQL, but is it convenient? The answer is a matter of opinion, but as you'll soon learn, newer schema-less or NoSQL systems can handle such behavior with less up-front design. For example, with MongoDB, a popular NoSQL database, all database rows in a table are JavaScript objects; you don't need to define flexible schema, you just insert objects that have different fields into the same table, and MongoDB, supports their storage by default.

SQL Indexes

SQL has supported indexes out of the box for most of its multi-decade history. When a developer needs to speed up searching on a particular column, it's as easy as declaring an index on the relevant table and column, as is shown with the line that follows using the table from the previous chapter:

```
create index updateTimeIndex on contact (updateTime);
```

This declaration is all an application needs to create and maintain an index as data is inserted and deleted over time. SQL indexes have made it very easy to enable efficient lookup times for a highly significant number of web applications. Although this is a straightforward observation, please keep it in mind for the upcoming discussion on NoSQL databases.

SQL Transactions

SQL supports a wide array of powerful programming functions, the most significant of which is *transactional support*. Transactions ensure that a set of database operations has atomic or "all or none" behavior, guaranteeing that errors do not leave the database in an inconsistent state if only part of the set operations were to succeed (for example, a bank account transaction whereby a debit succeeds, but an intended subsequent credit fails). SQL databases have rich transaction support that guarantees so-called ACID properties (Atomicity, Consistency, Isolation, and Durability) for all transactions on a database.

Transactions also have a standardized locking level scheme, whereby applications specify the level of concurrency allowed for each transaction. The level of most isolation is SERIALIZABLE or no concurrent access at all. Clearly higher isolation levels reduce parallel scalability, when a single user can have exclusive access to data.

> **NOTE** *Databases have taken novel approaches to implementing ACID. For example, the PostgreSQL database uses something called MVCC, or multi-version concurrency control, whereby every transaction actually gets its own copy of the relevant persistent state to increase concurrent access.*

Single Host Database

In previous chapters, you saw how SQL, and SQLite in particular, provides fine-grained query capabilities and high-level features like transaction support and the ability to apply indexes to column data.

When considering scalability requirements for web scale solutions, such expressiveness does not come without cost. To start, the most widely used SQL databases — such as MySQL and PostgreSQL — represent a single point of failure where a single machine stores a database for what might be a cluster of application containers serving parts of a single application in parallel (see Figure 7-2).

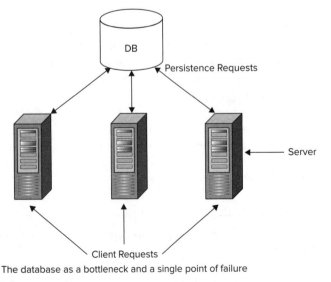

The database as a bottleneck and a single point of failure

FIGURE 7-2

> **NOTE** *More advanced database systems such as Oracle RAC do support data replication techniques where components of tables and database schema transparently copy between systems. However, such feature sets are not standard with SQL database deployments, and they don't necessarily scale up as well as fully distributed databases — for example, you may have to pay a license fee for each added CPU.*

Scaling Relationships

Providing a significant basis for relationships between entries, the SQL join feature is among the most useful of traditional database operations. Unfortunately it's hard to distribute joins across parallel data hosts, due to the inherent expense of accessing join data that resides on more than one machine. To understand the problem a little better, consider that in a scalable persistence solution, an element of data will reside on roughly a single machine (data redundancy for robustness aside). Assembling data in multiple tables and columns needed for a join is likely to require many round trips to different hosts. The communication and data marshaling make joins expensive. Additionally, you'll see how hard drive seek time plays a significant role.

Database File Format

The file format that a database uses to persist information to disk has significant implications for the performance of the database. For years, SQL databases have innovated in various ways with their file format (like PostgreSQL and its versioning system), but the high-level layout of data has been the same, as discussed in the following sections.

Row-Oriented

The SQL `create table` command enables the declaration of two-dimensional data structures. To support this function, traditional SQL databases use a two-dimensional row-oriented format. So a very simple row oriented table could look like Listing 7-3, where a row contains `id`, `firstName`, `lastName`, and `age` columns.

LISTING 7-3: An example two-dimensional row-oriented table

```
id, firstName, lastName, age
0, jon, smith, 12
1, kate, hughes, 32
2, joan, molan, 29
```

As concerns database implementers, seeking to a particular location in a file is as expensive as seeking and loading a moderate amount of data (such as 1MB) from that file. Seeks take a long time due to the need to physically orient a hard drive to the location of relevant data — once in position it's ideal if the data nearby is useful. For a given SQL query, if you were to search on an indexed `firstName`, you would incur as many seeks as there are rows with the name selected in the query. A query with no index (the default) would need a seek for every row in the table.

As you can see, traditional SQL database designs have some issues that could limit their use in massively scalable deployments.

> **NOTE** *Recent novel SQL database solutions from vendors, such as VoltDB, state that it's entirely possible to achieve web scale with SQL, and that the features just listed are critical to successful application deployment. See:*
>
> `https://voltdb.com/`

Column-Oriented

So take a step back for a minute. Is there a way to structure data to turn hard disk seek limitations to the advantage of the database designer? In contrast to the row-oriented format used in SQL databases, consider a column-oriented approach. The layout shown in Listing 7-4 reformats the row-based data from the earlier section to use columns instead.

LISTING 7-4: An example two-dimensional column-oriented table

```
id: 0, 1, 2
firstName: jon, kate, joan
lastName: smith, hughes, molan
age: 12, 32, 29
```

Recall that multiple seek operations take more time than one seek plus reading up to about 1MB of data. Suppose you wanted to compute the average age of all people in the table in Listing 7-4. With one seek, you could read out an entire column and then compute the average in a single pass. In contrast, a row-oriented format would require many seeks and reads to load the rows for all people into memory and then select each age to compute the average. For certain types of operations, called *aggregate functions,* columnar organization has enabled vast performance improvement.

Due to its heavy use in data intensive applications, it's worth pointing out that sorting is effectively an aggregate function as well. If it's quick to read out values of a column into memory, you can subsequently sort those values in memory. So for example, if you have a query that sorts by first name, it's much faster to have all first names in one file, rather than spread across a set of rows, each of which would need its own seek to read a single first name.

For more information on this topic, see Wikipedia:

`http://en.wikipedia.org/wiki/Column-oriented_DBMS`

Record Size

Because of the way the SQL language defines schema, a `create table` is effectively a declaration of the sizes of the data types in a row, and the size of the two-dimensional structure that holds them. The `create table` statement does not allow for varying element sizes. Of course, dropping the SQL language would mean you could support that capability.

NoSQL Persistence

As discussed, the demands of web and mobile scalability have driven the design of large-scale storage systems. As you might have guessed, distributing request load and avoiding unnecessary seek operations held critical importance in meeting scalability requirements. All of the major so-called "NoSQL" databases — like Amazon DynamoDB, Google App Engine Datastore, Cassandra, and MongoDB — use a column-oriented format for the reasons just discussed, and the presence of an ID or key is the only requirement they place on the number of fields for a given element. In these systems it does not make sense to think of a "column" as similar to a column in a SQL table. This NoSQL key is a lot more like a key/value pair in a persistent map data structure. As their name suggests, none of these databases support the SQL language, and they do not require that records contain the same number of fields or have a static size.

Searching NoSQL

So far, NoSQL databases sound like a pretty solid way of meeting web scale requirements. They minimize hard disk overhead and allow specific column flexibility not found in SQL. But do they have any drawbacks? The answer seems to be a clear yes. For example, searching with Amazon DynamoDB is entirely unlike querying a SQL database and in many ways is much more primitive. You don't get a nice `index` keyword, and the database does not automatically update indexes on your behalf. Your application must include code that creates and updates its own index whenever you insert or delete new data. Perhaps not surprisingly, the reason for such "retro" coding techniques is a result of aggressive optimization on the part of the database providers. Using a primitive API enables database developers to increase the performance of their service platform as a whole, as you'll see in the next section.

> **NOTE** *You can expect rapid feature improvements in the data systems of all major cloud vendors. For example, DynamoDB has recently added support for a "secondary index" capability.*

NoSQL Scan Queries

Querying a NoSQL database depends significantly on intelligent sorting of column-based data. The Google App Engine Datastore (which is built on a NoSQL technology called BigTable) sorts column data using a hierarchical primary key. The basic layout of BigTable consists of a column containing rows with the following layout:

```
Row Name: Column Set
```

It looks somewhat like a traditional database table, but the column is the row name and its column set — only the row name is directly searchable. The row name or key is "known" to the implementation of the database and all data in the database is sorted on it. The result of this simple structure is that database queries simply scan the database for row names or, alternatively, for a range of row names. In the case of BigTable, you can search based on a prefix. You can return all row names that start with a given prefix (such as all the names that begin with the letters "ca") or return a range of row names starting with one prefix and ending with another. To understand a little better how this works for BigTable, consider Figure 7-3, which shows the parent-child relationships of rows in BigTable.

```
↓ /Grandparent:Jane
↓ /Grandparent:Jane/Parent:Bill
↓ /Grandparent:Jane/Parent:Bill/Child:John
```

FIGURE 7-3

What you see in Figure 7-3 illustrates the hierarchical key structure used with BigTable. Keys are sorted according to name in hierarchical order. This clever arrangement allows not only fast scanning lookup, but fast scanning of an element and its descendants. Such organization greatly benefits any data with a hierarchical relationship, such as geodata (for example, cities in a state), players on a team, and so on. The keys in Figure 7-3 are built from a construct known as an *entity* that this chapter will explore further in the App Engine code example later.

> **NOTE** *Google's BigTable carries out scan queries with an impressive constant number of disk seeks. A scan query uses one seek, and then maximizes disk bandwidth to optimally read out the results of a given query. For their raw performance speed, scan queries are considered the bread and butter of a NoSQL database.*

Significant operations like search are extremely fast with NoSQL databases, but the downside of less structure is the significant complexity pushed out of the persistence layer into the application space. Done right, NoSQL applications may scale better and run faster, but developers must address tricky synchronization and performance issues that the database solves with SQL-based approaches.

> **NOTE** *Google's BigTable database is fully distributed and designed to handle petabytes of data across thousands of inexpensive servers. BigTable uses a shared nothing database partitioning scheme, also referred to as sharding. Sharding breaks up data into smaller sections and distributes it across a large number of hosts. You can think of sharding as pieces of a broken window; if you have all the pieces, they will make the whole pane of glass.*
>
> ```
> http://en.wikipedia.org/wiki/Big_table
> ```
>
> *Additionally, Google has made the following highly informative video, which introduces the Datastore design:*
>
> ```
> http://www.youtube.com/watch?v=tx5gdoNpcZM
> ```

Key Distribution

Column-oriented databases that "shard" their data based on row keys rely on applications to evenly distribute data across different hosts. When applications fail to achieve this distribution, scalability will degrade when the system becomes less than fully distributed — data will reside on fewer hosts than possible thus increasing load on specific servers. Such overload points are known as "hot spots" or "hot keys" and developers can avoid them by using a sufficiently distributed hash key. Figure 7-4 shows key distribution and scalability hot spots.

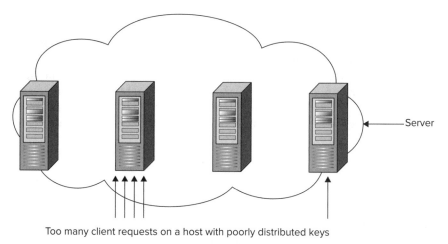

Too many client requests on a host with poorly distributed keys

FIGURE 7-4

DESIGN CONSIDERATIONS FOR SCALABLE PERSISTENCE

Now that you understand the basics of scalable cloud persistence and some pros and cons of using SQL, the next few sections take the discussion into practical design matters like what to consider when selecting a database style and when to update indexes, among others.

To SQL or Not to SQL?

Application developers making a decision about whether to use SQL should consider a number of variables:

➤ Does your application handle vast amounts of data, on the order of serving millions of users?

➤ Will the structure of your data benefit from using a flexible column set? Will you need to add or remove columns on the fly?

➤ Does your application require sophisticated query support?

➤ Do you have the resources to host your own server farm?

➤ Can your engineering team handle the added development complexity of NoSQL?

If your application will use only moderate amounts of web traffic (such as what most web applications encounter), the limited querying capabilities of NoSQL could prove to be a significant hurdle, and without much benefit. In many cases, starting with or using SQL will deliver the flexibility you need and will help you to develop safer applications. On the other hand, large datasets work well with NoSQL due to its fast scanning capabilities.

Using Schema

Even with NoSQL datastores, developers will find it useful to employ a schema-like definition for their application data model. Although NoSQL does not require similar columns between elements, it's useful if elements at least share a subset of fields. For example, a business contact could support all the same fields as a contact, but also add a business phone number and business e-mail. Often the form of such schema will bind to objects in the developer language of choice (such as a class in Python or Java). You'll see how this works later in the chapter in the Google code example with queries on the `contact` class.

Handling NoSQL Indexes

SQL or NoSQL, data indexes — or precomputed answers to queries — are the primary method of improving the performance of persistence queries. As mentioned, implementing your own indexes with NoSQL databases adds significant complexity to your application. It's possible to avoid some of this complexity by integrating an existing search solution, such as Apache Lucene or Solr, into your product. So, instead of building your own indexes, you can integrate a search engine into your application and use it to implement queries.

Updating Indexes Asynchronously

Indexes must reflect the current state of the database in order to return accurate results, which means indexes must be updated when data changes. The work of managing the database while satisfying user requests has the potential to degrade request performance. A common method of dealing with this overhead is to handle it asynchronously from the requests themselves. It's convenient to use a persistent task queue. Amazon released a tool called Amazon SQS, which is covered shortly.

Stateless Design

Continuing to hit on the main theme of the chapter, a successful cloud data model will seek to maximize scalability of requests. A stateless service stores all persistence information in its data tier and does not seek to reuse state across requests. A stateless request relies only on the content of the request and persistent state in the database.

A typical example of shared state is a session-oriented protocol where session information must be part of every request. Shared state requires blocking while different hosts access the shared information where it happens to live in the database, and is generally the enemy of parallel execution.

Eventual Consistency

NoSQL systems generally do not strive to maintain ACID-level consistency due to the noted trade-off between exclusive access to data and optimal scalability. Indeed the formal CAP theorem remarks on the extreme difficulty of building a system that is strongly consistent, highly available, and fault tolerant:

```
http://en.wikipedia.org/wiki/CAP_theorem
```

Most NoSQL systems, like DynamoDB, do not support complex transactions. Google Datastore is a notable exception and does support them. On systems that do not support transactions, how do NoSQL applications guarantee consistent state? Most modern cloud services rely on the principle of *eventual consistency*. This principle states that if the users were to all of a sudden stop making requests on a given service, the data for the service would be brought to a consistent state. The database would have time to edit its internal state to make the effects of each request consistent.

Optimistic Concurrency Control

Massive simultaneous request execution provides the mechanism by which web scale applications achieve high levels of scalability. With so many clients hitting the data simultaneously on different machines, and only eventual consistency to hold the system together, it might seem that preventing an inconsistent state would be impossible.

As it turns out, an extremely simple rule called *optimistic concurrency control* provides a solution. Imagine that when a client attempted to submit changes to the database, the database detected whether any changes from the client were in conflict with changes already in the service. Detecting changes in the service is application-specific but can be as simple as checking modification times or version numbers on data. If the service does find a conflict, the client aborts its change and gets the latest state from the service. When the client is ready to resubmit, the process repeats, until the service accepts the client's changes, and the client's data gets written to the service datastore (see Figure 7-5). The rule is called "optimistic" because the client always makes its best attempt to commit data. Typical usage patterns suggest that in the majority of cases, it will succeed.

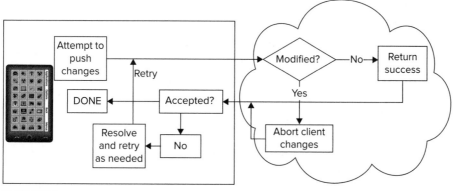

FIGURE 7-5

Load Balancing

To take advantage of simultaneous data requests, an application needs to direct requests across a large number of hosts. Developers call this distribution process *load balancing*. Most cloud providers support load-balancing functions to make it easier to scale service traffic. For example, Google App Engine provides a built-in load balancer that automatically distributes the requests among your servers, whereas AWS provides a technology called elastic-load-balancing. Making your server stateless is critical to effective load balancing.

Optimizing Costs

One of the most important advantages of using a cloud service is the flexibility to scale up *and down* as needed, which means you can add more servers during peak times and reduce service use during down times. Your application only uses resources when it needs them. If you own your own bank of servers capable of handling a massive peak, those servers are likely to sit idle and cost you money during slow periods of traffic.

> **NOTE** *AWS and most cloud providers provide traffic-monitoring tools that allow you to add or remove virtual server support as appropriate for your traffic load.*

LOOKING AT POPULAR CLOUD PROVIDERS

Cloud-based hosting has grown to encompass a vast technology industry. Most major technology corporations host cloud platforms, but a few clear winners have emerged. The next section highlights a few of them.

Amazon AWS

Amazon hosts a wide array of cloud products to support web applications and backend services, and generally could be regarded as a 900-pound gorilla in cloud hosting services. Amazon provides a large family of complementary technologies, and the following are relevant to the chapter examples:

➤ **DynamoDB** — Foremost among these services is DynamoDB, with which you are now well familiar. It's a scalable column-oriented database for storing structured data.

➤ **Amazon S3** — Amazon Simple Storage Service, designed for storing large data blobs ranging from up to 5 terabytes of data. The service could be used to store any large file, including videos or sensor data, but generally does not hold structured data.

➤ **Amazon SQS** — A distributed queue-based messaging service that supports guarantees on message delivery. Amazon SQS supports "at most once" message delivery semantics, meaning an app can resend a message without fear of redundant application. Many readers will be familiar with the Java Message Service (JMS); the SQS fulfills the same role. Amazon SQS might be used to deliver periodic Android sensor data to a scientific monitoring service.

> **NOTE** *The chapter's example code suggests a use for SQS in conjunction with transaction support for DynamoDB. The AWS code walkthrough discusses how it would work.*

➤ **AWS Management Console** — In addition to supporting cutting edge cloud services, Amazon also supports easy-to-use online management tools for creating, modifying, and monitoring running services.

➤ **AWS Free Usage Tier** — Most Amazon services have some sort of free introductory usage. As of the time of writing of this book, DynamoDB supports 100MB of storage, five units of write capacity (5 writes/second), and 10 units of read capacity (10 reads/second), available to new and existing customers. With Amazon, each service has its own free plan:

```
http://aws.amazon.com/free/faqs/
```

Amazon AWS online:

```
http://aws.amazon.com/
```

Google App Engine

Clearly Google itself is a highly significant player in the cloud hosting space. Like Amazon, Google also supports a large suite of mature, complementary services for running third-party applications on Google's formidable cloud infrastructure. Here are a few to get started:

➤ **Datastore** — This is Google's persistence service based on the structured data, column-organized BigTable, as discussed in this chapter.

➤ **Blob store** — Large object data storage, for objects that will not fit in Google's structured datastore. Blob files are submitted using HTTP operations, often with a simple form.

➤ **Memcache API** — A high-performance distributed in-memory cache that applications access in front of persistent storage, like Datastore. Memcache uses the JCache API, a standard caching interface. Redundant queries accessing the same data should make use of the memcache API. The memcache API is designed to work in a highly scalable load-balanced environment.

For App Engine pricing:

```
https://cloud.google.com/pricing/
```

Joyent: Hosted MongoDB+node.js

The Joyent cloud-hosting platform optimizes the performance of several widely popular cloud-computing technologies not presented in this version of Enterprise Android. Joyent is notable as having hosted Twitter for a time — certainly a web scale application. These components include:

➤ **MongoDB** — A horizontally scaled, completely JSON-oriented columnar style database. MongoDB is a "document-centric" database in which developers can directly insert or delete JSON objects with no requirement to pre-define schema for storage.

➤ **node.js** — An event-driven service development platform that leverages client-side web development mindshare by using JavaScript as a server-side development technology. Developers write services completely in JavaScript. Node.js strongly defines methods of interaction, so all services running on a node.js installation integrate with each other by default.

➤ **Hadoop** — A platform that supports data-intensive applications, supporting petabytes of data. Hadoop supports a computational paradigm known as MapReduce that enables processing of large datasets. MapReduce breaks up large computing problems into small pieces so that they can be processed on parallel hardware:

```
http://en.wikipedia.org/wiki/Hadoop
```

Red Hat OpenShift

Red Hat has created an open source cloud-computing platform called OpenShift. OpenShift is notable because it takes a different approach than some of the other providers. Where Amazon or Google create an explicit API for their services that they intend developers to consume directly, OpenShift allows developers to select a pre-configured, usually open source API for development. Developers also have the option to define their own new "cartridge" or set of OpenShift APIs. The result is that developers end up using the API of their choice while still getting the benefit of cloud hosting. For those concerned about "vendor lock-in," becoming too directly dependent on the APIs of any particular vendor, OpenShift can potentially help developers avoid this pitfall.

OpenShift supports the following set of default cartridges, which provide support for environments from JBoss (a popular Java server technology) to Ruby (a popular open source programming language):

```
https://openshift.redhat.com/community/developers/technologies
```

Now with enough background on cloud computing and service development technologies, you're ready to jump into the chapter code examples.

EXPLORING THE CODE EXAMPLES

This chapter provides contact service implementations for the two most popular cloud service platforms discussed in this chapter: Amazon Web Services (AWS) and Google App Engine. The examples build on the work done in Chapter 6 with the Spring-based contacts services — you'll build two new contact service variants for both of these service platforms. The examples will walk through specific code that demonstrates topics this chapter has covered so far, such as building NoSQL indexes and using range queries. Each service reuses much of the code from Chapter 6, taking advantage of its three-tier architecture. With some configuration aside, these services only need to provide their own new implementation of the contact DAO interface. In a production deployment this architecture would mean that you could easily switch between cloud providers and databases. This is a nice advantage given competing prices and designs prevalent in today's cloud services market.

Note that the idea behind these examples is to give you a taste of what it's like to develop in each environment and to get you thinking about how to solve common mobile data problems with these technologies. The examples are not intended to provide a comprehensive introduction to the relevant platforms. Authors have filled volumes on both of them.

The Contacts DAO Interface (Again)

Recall the contacts DAO interface introduced in the previous chapter. The DAO interface for this chapter includes methods for finding and manipulating contacts, as shown in Listing 7-5.

LISTING 7-5: Contact DAO review

```
package com.wiley.demo.android.dao;

import java.io.IOException;
import java.util.List;

import com.wiley.demo.android.dataModel.Contact;

public interface ContactDao {
    Contact getContact(String userId, String id) throws IOException;
    String storeOrUpdateContact(String userId, Contact contact) throws IOException;
    List<Contact> findContactFirstName(String userId, String firstName,
        int start, int numOfmatches);
    List<Contact> findChanged(String userId, long timestamp, int start, int
        numOfmatches);
    void delete(String userId, String id) throws IOException;
    List<Contact> getAll(String userId, int start, int numOfmatches) throws
        IOException;
}
```

The remaining sections of the chapter will cover example code for implementations of this interface using Amazon DynamoDB and Google App Engine.

Writing the Code: Amazon Contacts Service

This example focuses on how to integrate with Amazon Web Services and how the tiers of the contact service have changed to make use of DynamoDB, thus enabling the contacts service on the highly available Amazon cloud. This section of the chapter investigates the contact DAO implementation as implemented on Amazon's DynamoDB. You can find a complete working example in the following directory:

```
$CODE/awsServiceContacts
```

Prepare: Prerequisites and Getting Started

Chapter 6 covered all the requirements for developing a Java web application based on Spring, Jackson, and the application container, Tomcat. The Amazon Web Services DynamoDB service example leverages many of these same tools, but also requires the presence of the Amazon Web Services SDK, an AWS account, and credentials.

Step 1: Create an Amazon Account

Create an Amazon AWS account if you do not have one. To create the account, go to http://aws .amazon.com/ and click the Sign Up button. You should be able to follow the instructions from that point to create the account. You will need a credit card to complete sign-up.

Step 2: Configure DynamoDB with Application Schema

Once you have created an account, you can visit the AWS management console at:

```
https://console.aws.amazon.com
```

From there, click the DynamoDB link under the Database category. This takes you to the UI for managing the DynamoDB. Follow the instructions there to create application tables in DynamoDB — the table wizard may pop up by default.

Working with AWS is different than working with traditional SQL databases — schema management takes place in an online editing tool, rather than with a source code-based SQL language. At the top of the page in the Dynamo DB section, you should see a row of buttons. Find the one labeled Create Table and repeat the table creation process for the next tables. You need to create the following three tables: `Contact`, `ContactFNameIndex`, and `ContactUpdateTimeIndex`.

➤ The `Contact` table stores contact data. When creating each table, you will need to decide whether the table will use a hash key and range key, or a hash key only. This table needs only a hash key, which the UI will prompt you to add as a hash attribute name. Click the appropriate radio button. The name should be `id`.

Next, continue through the optional add indexes screen — nothing to add right now, none of the tables use a secondary index — then use Step 3 for each table to specify read/write throughputs.

➤ `ContactFNameIndex` stores the index for searching on the first name. This table needs both a hash key and a range key, and you should define the type of the keys as `String`. The hash attribute name is `userId`, and the range attribute name is `firstName`.

Hit continue to skip adding indexes.

Use Step 3 to specify the read and write throughputs.

➤ `ContactUpdateTimeIndex` stores the index for searching on update time. This table needs both hash and range keys, and the range and hash attribute names are `userId` and `updateTime`, respectively. Again, the types of the keys are `String`.

You may see a message regarding throughput warnings being sent to the designated e-mail recipient. Click continue if you haven't responded to the confirmation e-mail yet.

Hit continue to skip adding secondary indexes.

Use Step 3 to specify the read and write throughputs.

Figure 7-6 shows the Amazon AWS online schema-editing tool showing the schema you'll need to create to use the contacts service.

> **WARNING** *One interesting characteristic of Amazon's pricing policy is that if you create a schema under a pricing plan, the existence of the schema itself, rather than actual traffic, can drive service charges! In other words, it's possible to define a schema, have no traffic, but still get a bill.*

Amazon has provided DynamoDB documentation on its developer site as well:

```
http://aws.amazon.com/dynamodb/
```

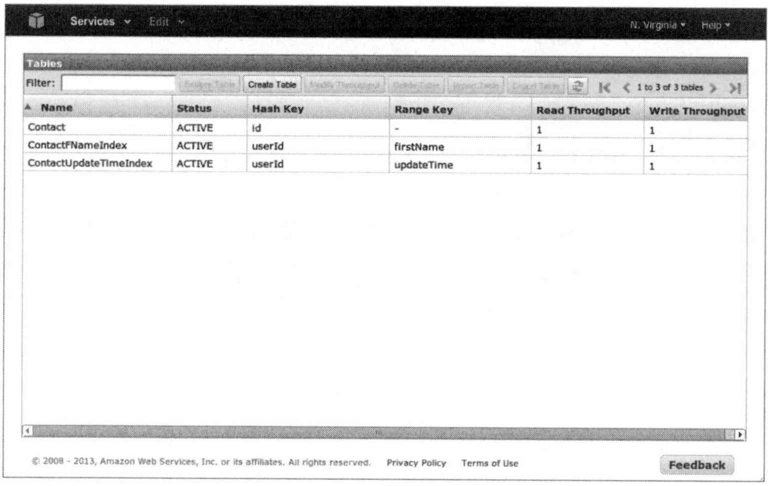

FIGURE 7-6

Step 3: Specify the Read/Write Throughputs

For each table you define, you need to specify the Read Throughput and the Write Throughput. If you are using the AWS free tier account, set both Read Throughput and Write Throughput capacity units to 2 to avoid being charged. The higher you go, the more you will pay. You can find specific AWS pricing details on their site:

```
http://aws.amazon.com/dynamodb/pricing/
```

Click Continue. The next screen optionally allows you to monitor your request rates and set throughput alarms. We won't be doing that for our example, so just enter an e-mail address for notification and click Continue to finish table creation.

The final page provides a summary for your review. Click Create, and you'll be taken to the Services page, providing both editing capabilities and detailed information about the table(s) you just created.

Step 4: Create Access Credentials

Before your client can communicate with AWS, you need to create an access key, as follows: AWS Management Console ⇨ Your Name menu ⇨ My Account ⇨ Security Credentials (on the left).

> **NOTE** *You will need permission to modify the AWS account to edit Security Credentials.*

This brings you to the AWS security credentials page where you can create an *access key* with: (Preferred) `https://console.aws.amazon.com/iam/home?#security_credential` ⇨ Access Keys ⇨ Create New Root Key

Create the key and download its corresponding csv file—it contains the access and secret keys.

Or use: (Deprecated) Access Credentials ⇨ create new access key

Your key will be displayed; use the UI to show the secret key.

Step 5: Install Amazon Web Services SDK (Optional)

To work with Amazon Web Services, you'll need to download the SDK from Amazon's development center from the following location:

```
http://aws.amazon.com/sdkforjava/
```

> **NOTE** *Strictly speaking, you only need the SDK for its* `.jar` *file, which can be resolved in the project's* `ivy.xml` *file. Thus, it's optional for you to download the Amazon SDK.*

Step 6: Add Security Credentials

Add the access key and secret access key to the file:

```
$CODE/awsServiceContacts/src/main/resources/com/enterpriseandroid/awsContacts
/dao/impl/AwsCredentials.properties
```

By entering the keys as follows:

```
1 secretKey=<Insert your secret key here>
2 accessKey=<Insert your access key here>
```

Finally, change the following field:

```
$CODE/awsServiceContacts/src/main/java/com/enterpriseandroid/awsContacts
/rest/ContactController.USER_ID
```

to be your Amazon account user name.

> **NOTE** *While it's possible to run the contacts service with DynamoDB remotely, performance will improve significantly by running the tomcat instance on an EC2 instance. See the AWS console for more information on EC2. It's fine to run the examples on your local machine; contacts will save to DynamoDB remotely.*

Step 7: Tools and Software Stack

This chapter has fewer libraries to cover in its software stack than in the previous chapter, given how much code is the same for the presentation and logic tiers. The Amazon SDK is the only new tool in the software stack, and its APIs are only used in the Data tier DAO. All the other software dependencies from Chapter 6 apply here as well. For your convenience, the project `ivy.xml` contains a dependency on the App Engine SDK, as follows:

```
<dependency org="com.amazonaws" name="aws-java-sdk" rev="1.3.26" />
```

Example Code: Replacement Contact DAO

As mentioned, the Amazon sample code demonstrates how to port the RESTful contacts service to the Amazon cloud. The class, `ContactDaoDynamoDBImpl`, provides the relevant implementation code for the contact's DAO, which contains significant differences from the SQL or Hibernate versions of the previous chapter.

Instead, the Dynamo API client class, `AmazonDynamoDBClient`, supports all persistence operations, which in turn uses the Amazon API for persistence as follows:

➤ The example uses a less sophisticated version of object serialization for persistence due to the way that Dynamo structures return values. The Dynamo client returns objects in the form of Java maps. Consequently, the example accesses object field values using simple constant access, as follows:

```
item.get(FIRST_NAME).getS();
```

➤ As discussed earlier in the chapter, DynamoDB uses scan queries. To find contacts, the DAO implementation uses the composite string key `userId:contactID`.

➤ The code uses two contact fields to find contacts to support the contacts sync algorithm: contact first name and contact update time.

➤ As mentioned earlier, DynamoDB does not support SQL style indexes. As a result, the code also contains two methods for updating indexes for its two search fields.

Listing 7-6 shows the documentation for the AWS DAO class.

LISTING 7-6: DAO implementation for DynamoDB

```java
package com.wiley.demo.android.dao.impl;

import com.amazonaws.ClientConfiguration;
import com.amazonaws.auth.AWSCredentials;
import com.amazonaws.auth.PropertiesCredentials;
import com.amazonaws.services.dynamodb.AmazonDynamoDBClient;
import com.amazonaws.services.dynamodb.model.*;
import com.wiley.demo.android.dao.ContactDao;
import com.wiley.demo.android.dataModel.Contact;

import java.io.IOException;
import java.util.ArrayList;
import java.util.HashMap;
import java.util.List;
import java.util.Map;
import java.util.UUID;

/**
 * Enterprise Android contacts RESTful service implementation that uses the
 * Amazon Dynamo DB API for scalable, hosted persistence.
 */
public class ContactDaoDynamoDBImpl implements ContactDao {
    private final String ID = "id";
```

Key names for the contacts search fields, first name, and last name are as follows:

```java
    private final String FIRST_NAME = "firstName";
    private final String LAST_NAME = "lastName";
    private final String EMAIL = "email";
```

```
private final String UPDATE_TIME = "updateTime";
private final String VERSION = "version";
private final String HASH_KEY = "userId";
```

These are the names of the search field indexes. The relevant indexes get updated in the methods `updateUpdateTimeIndex` and `updateFnameIndex`.

```
private final String FIRST_NAME_INDEX_TABLE = "ContactFNameIndex";
private final String UPDATE_TIME_INDEX = "ContactUpdateTimeIndex";
private final String CONTACT_TABLE = "Contact";

private AmazonDynamoDBClient client;

public ContactDaoDynamoDBImpl() throws IOException {
```

This code initializes the Amazon DynamoDB client with credentials obtained from the properties file, `AwsCredentials.properties`.

```
AWSCredentials credentials = new PropertiesCredentials(
        ContactDaoDynamoDBImpl.class
            .getResourceAsStream("AwsCredentials.properties"));

ClientConfiguration config = new ClientConfiguration();
client = new AmazonDynamoDBClient(credentials, config);
}

@Override
```

The method for getting a contact takes a `userId` and a contact `id`. It uses the Amazon request class, `GetItemRequest`, to build a request consisting of a table name and a composite key, which has the aforementioned format: `userId:contactId`. DynamoDB will service the request with a fast scanning search.

```
public Contact getContact(String userId, String id) throws IOException {

//      List<String> attributesToGet = new ArrayList<String>(
//          Arrays.asList(ID, FIRST_NAME, LAST_NAME, EMAIL,
//              UPDATE_TIME, VERSION));

    // Get a contact with the composed string key, userId:id to identify
    // the row for the contact. We're not explicitly specifying the
    // columns to get, since we want all of the columns. But you could
    // specify columns using the code commented out above and below.
    GetItemRequest getItemRequest = new GetItemRequest()
            .withTableName(CONTACT_TABLE)
            .withKey(new Key().withHashKeyElement(new AttributeValue()
                .withS(this.composeKeys(userId, id))))
//          .withAttributesToGet(attributesToGet)
            .withConsistentRead(true);

    awsQuotaDelay();
```

The DAO implementation delegates to the Dynamo client to get the results of the request.

```
GetItemResult result = client.getItem(getItemRequest);
Map<String, AttributeValue> item = result.getItem();
if (item == null) {
    return null;
}
```

When the results return as maps, a utility method converts them into contact objects.

```
    return item2Contact(item);
}
```

The method `storeOrUpdateContact` adds a contact under the given `userId`. The contact gets updated if it already exists.

```
@Override
public String storeOrUpdateContact(String userId, Contact contact)
        throws IOException
{
    Map<String, ExpectedAttributeValue> expectedValues =
            new HashMap<String, ExpectedAttributeValue>();
    Contact oldContact;

    String oldFirstName = null;
    long oldUpdateTime = -1;

    if (contact.getVersion() != 0) {
        expectedValues.put(VERSION,
                new ExpectedAttributeValue()
                        .withValue(new AttributeValue()
                                .withN(Long
                                        .toString(contact.getVersion()))));
        oldContact = getContact(userId, contact.getId());
        if ( oldContact != null) {
            oldUpdateTime = oldContact.getUpdateTime();
            oldFirstName = oldContact.getFirstName();
        }
    }

    contact.setUpdateTime(System.currentTimeMillis());
```

Create the values for the contact object, making sure to increment the version, and set the update time to the current time. The scan key is the same as before, `userId:contactID`.

```
    Map<String, AttributeValue> item = contactToItem(contact);
    item.put(VERSION, new AttributeValue()
            .withN(Long.toString(contact.getVersion() + 1)));
    item.put(ID, new AttributeValue().
            withS(composeKeys(userId, contact.getId())));

    /***
     * AWS does not provide transaction support, and cannot guarantee that
```

```
 * all the writes to DynamoDB are successful. To avoid this problem, we
 * recommend using AWS SQS service. The idea is to wrap both update
 * operations into a task, and then put the task into SQS. If and only
 * if both operations succeed, would we remove the task from the SQS.
 */
putItem(CONTACT_TABLE, item, expectedValues);
```

Insert the given contacts object into the contact table, making sure to update the update time index and the first name index. Take note that this is where the code needs to manually update its own index. With SQL you would not need to remember to add this type of code — it's critical to performance that you maintain indexes correctly.

```
updateUpdateTimeIndex(userId, oldUpdateTime, contact);
updateFnameIndex(userId, contact.g etFirstName(),
        oldFirstName, contact.getId());

return contact.getId();
}

private void updateUpdateTimeIndex(String userId,
                            long oldUpdatTime, Contact contact)
{
    if (oldUpdatTime == contact.getUpdateTime() ) {
        return;
    }
```

Updating the update time index consists of putting an item into the update time index table, with the hash key of `userId` and a composite update time key of `updateTime:contactID`.

> **NOTE** *Remember, the index is just another custom created table with normal object fields; there is no special support for indexes.*

The newly inserted object enables lookup by `userId` of the `lastUpdate` time of a contact with the given `contactID`.

```
Map<String, AttributeValue> item =
        new HashMap<String, AttributeValue>();
item.put(HASH_KEY, new AttributeValue().withS(userId));
item.put(UPDATE_TIME, new AttributeValue().
        withS(composeKeys(Long.toString(contact.getUpdateTime()),
            contact.getId()))));
putItem(UPDATE_TIME_INDEX, item, null);
if ( oldUpdatTime > 0  ) {
    // delete the old index
    deleteDo(userId,
            composeKeys(Long.toString(oldUpdatTime), contact.getId()),
            UPDATE_TIME_INDEX);
    }
}
```

```
private void updateFnameIndex(String hashKey,
                      String fname, String oldFirstName, String id)
{
    if (oldFirstName !=null && oldFirstName.equals(fname)) {
        return;
    }

    Map<String, AttributeValue> item =
            new HashMap<String, AttributeValue>();
    item.put(HASH_KEY, new AttributeValue().withS(hashKey));
    item.put(FIRST_NAME, new AttributeValue()
            .withS(composeKeys(fname, id)));
    putItem(FIRST_NAME_INDEX_TABLE, item, null);
```

Here, the code updates the first name index. Recall that the hash key in this case is the contact first name. So in this case, the HASH_KEY = userId, and a first name attribute consists of a composed key, firstName:contactID. This code sets the two fields that are the hash key and the range key used to locate contact data in the example DynamoDB.

Not pretty compared to a SQL index, but still an index of sorts — and you don't have to host your own machines. And at least in this simplified example, it was not too difficult to set up the data model and indexes for contacts.

```
    if( oldFirstName != null) {
        deleteDo(hashKey, composeKeys(oldFirstName, id),
            FIRST_NAME_INDEX_TABLE);
    }
}
```

Here's a simple utility method for putting items into a Dynamo table:

```
private void putItem(String indexName, Map<String, AttributeValue> item,
                    Map<String, ExpectedAttributeValue> expectedValues)
{
    PutItemRequest putItemRequest = new PutItemRequest()
            .withTableName(indexName)
            .withItem(item);

    if(expectedValues != null) {
        putItemRequest.withExpected(expectedValues);
    }
```

This call prevents clients from accessing the service too quickly and incurring usage charges.

```
        awsQuotaDelay();
        client.putItem(putItemRequest);
}
```

This is a search method to find a contact by the first name. The method finds contacts based on a Dynamo condition that matches a scan when a hash key starts with the first name of a given contact. With the query condition established, the method then delegates to the utility query method.

```
@Override
public List<Contact> findContactFirstName(String userId, String firstName,
                                          int start, int numOfmatches)
{

    Condition rangeKeyCondition = new Condition().withComparisonOperator(
            ComparisonOperator.BEGINS_WITH.toString())
            .withAttributeValueList(
            new AttributeValue().withS(firstName));

    return query(userId, rangeKeyCondition, start, numOfmatches,
            FIRST_NAME, FIRST_NAME_INDEX_TABLE);
}

@Override
```

The findChanged method also sets up a range key condition to use with a scan query, and then delegates the find request to the query utility.

```
public List<Contact> findChanged(String userId, long timestamp, int start,
                                 int numOfmatches)
{

    Condition rangeKeyCondition = new Condition().withComparisonOperator(
            ComparisonOperator.GE.toString()).withAttributeValueList(
            new AttributeValue().withS(Long.toString(timestamp)));

    return query(userId, rangeKeyCondition, start, numOfmatches,
            UPDATE_TIME, this.UPDATE_TIME_INDEX);
}
```

The query utility method supports Dynamo queries for all RESTful contact operations. The method begins and sets up its main query. It sets the relevant table, hash, and range keys, as well the number of desired matches.

The loop converts maps into contact objects to hold the content results.

```
private List<Contact> query(String userId, Condition rangeKeyCondition,
                            int start,
                            int numOfmatches, String rangeKeyName,
                            String table)
{
    Key lastKeyEvaluated = null;
    List<Contact> ret = new ArrayList<Contact>();

    QueryRequest queryRequest = new QueryRequest()
            .withTableName(table)
            .withHashKeyValue(new AttributeValue().withS(userId))
            .withRangeKeyCondition(rangeKeyCondition)
            .withLimit(numOfmatches)
            .withExclusiveStartKey(lastKeyEvaluated)
            .withScanIndexForward(true);

    QueryResult result = client.query(queryRequest);
```

```
            int pos = 0;
            for (Map<String, AttributeValue> indexItem : result.getItems()) {
                pos++;
                if (pos > start ) {
                    String[] ids = fromComposedKeys(indexItem
                            .get(rangeKeyName).getS());
                    Contact contact;
                    try {
                        contact = getContact(userId, ids[1]);
                        if (contact != null) {
                            ret.add(contact);
                        } else {
                            // delete the index if the data does not exists
                            deleteDo(userId, composeKeys(ids[0], ids[1]), table);
                        }

                        // awsQuotaDelay();
                    } catch (Exception e) {
                        // if we cannot load the contact, we just continue
                    }
                    if (ret.size() == numOfmatches) {
                        break;
                    }
                }
            }

            return ret;
        }

        @Override
```

Since this DAO class needs to maintain its own indexes, the `delete` method must delete the contact object as well as its associated indexes. Deletion happens by calling the `deleteDo` query method:

```
        public void delete(String userId, String id) throws IOException {
            Contact contact = getContact(userId, id);
            deleteDo(composeKeys(userId, id), null, CONTACT_TABLE);
            deleteDo(userId, composeKeys(contact.getFirstName(), id),
                    FIRST_NAME_INDEX_TABLE);
            deleteDo(userId, composeKeys(
                    Long.toString(contact.getUpdateTime()), id),
                    UPDATE_TIME_INDEX);
        }
```

The `deleteDo` method deletes a data object with the given `hashKey` and optional `rangeKey`. The data object is deleted using the DynamoDB client.

```
        private void deleteDo(String hashKey, String rangeKey, String table) {
            Key key = new Key()
                    .withHashKeyElement(new AttributeValue().withS(hashKey));

            if ( rangeKey != null) {
                key = key.withRangeKeyElement(new AttributeValue().withS(rangeKey));
            }
```

```
        DeleteItemRequest deleteItemRequest = new DeleteItemRequest()
                .withTableName(table)
                .withKey(key);
        DeleteItemResult result = client.deleteItem(deleteItemRequest);
    }

    @Override
    public List<Contact> getAll(String userId, int start, int numOfmatches)
            throws IOException
    {
        return findChanged(userId, 0, start, numOfmatches );
    }
```

Next is a utility method that converts a map-based Amazon return value into an internally used contact object. Constant values access enables you to set contact fields.

```
        private Contact item2Contact(Map<String, AttributeValue>item ) {
            Contact contact = new Contact();
            String ids[] = fromComposedKeys(item.get(ID).getS());
            contact.setId(ids[1]);
            contact.setFirstName(item.get(FIRST_NAME).getS());
            contact.setLastName(item.get(LAST_NAME).getS());
            contact.setEmail(item.get(EMAIL).getS());
            contact.setUpdateTime(getLong(item.get(UPDATE_TIME)));
            contact.setVersion(getLong(item.get(VERSION)));
            return contact;
        }
```

Here is the reverse: A utility method that converts a contact into a map-based Amazon item that can be sent to the Amazon API. Constant value access enables you to set map fields from the contact object.

```
        private Map<String, AttributeValue> contactToItem(Contact contact) {
            String id = contact.getId();
            Map<String, AttributeValue> item =
                    new HashMap<String, AttributeValue>();
            if ( id == null) {
                id = UUID.randomUUID().toString();
                contact.setId(id);
            }
            item.put(ID, new AttributeValue().withS(id));
            item.put(FIRST_NAME, new AttributeValue()
                    .withS(contact.getFirstName()));
            item.put(LAST_NAME, new AttributeValue().withS(contact.getLastName()));
            item.put(EMAIL, new AttributeValue().withS(contact.getEmail()));
            item.put(UPDATE_TIME, new AttributeValue()
                    .withN(Long.toString(contact.getUpdateTime())));
            item.put(VERSION, new AttributeValue()
                    .withN(contact.getVersion().toString()));
            return item;

        }
        private Long getLong(AttributeValue attr) {
            return Long.parseLong(attr.getN());
        }
```

The following two methods enable you to split and compose a composite key. A composite key contains a hash key and a range key, and you can use it as an argument in a scan query.

```java
private String composeKeys(String k1, String k2) {
    return k1 + ":" + k2;
}

private String[] fromComposedKeys(String k) {
    return k.split(":");
}

/**
 * The free AWS account only allows 5 read/write per second, so insert a
 * delay to stay under that quota.
 */
private void awsQuotaDelay() {
    try {
        Thread.sleep(250);
    } catch (InterruptedException e) {
        e.printStackTrace();
    }
}
}
```

Deploy the Service

> **NOTE** *Late in the development of this book, Amazon added support for secondary indexes to remove the need for developers to have to write their own, as discussed in this chapter. We have provided code for an alternate DAO implementation that uses them but don't include a detailed writeup in the first release of this book:*
>
> `$CODE/awsServiceContacts/com/enterpriseandroid/awsContacts/dao/impl/`
> `ContactDaoDynamoDBV2Impl.java`
>
> *For more information see:*
>
> `http://aws.amazon.com/about-aws/whats-new/2013/04/18/amazon-dynamodb-`
> `announces-local-secondary-indexes/`

Now that you've developed a Dynamo-based contact service, you'll need to deploy the code to a Tomcat instance. Since the AWS SDK knows how to talk to the Dynamo backend, you can use a local Tomcat instance, like the one from the last chapter, and as assumed in the instructions that follow, or you can set one up in an Amazon VM. To do this, select My Account ⇨ AWS Management Console ⇨ EC2 ⇨ Launch Instance.

The instructions here describe how to build and deploy the code using Ant or using Eclipse.

Deploying the Code with Ant

1. Build the code with:

```
cd $CODE/awsServiceContacts
ant dist
```

2. Deploy the code to Tomcat:

```
cp dist/awsServiceContacts.war $CATALINA_HOME/webapps
```

3. Restart Tomcat.

Deploying the Code with Eclipse:

1. Run ant to initialize Eclipse

As with other chapters, you'll need to use ant to initialize Eclipse:

```
cd $CODE/awsServiceContacts
ant eclipse
```

2. Import the AWS project directory in Eclipse, as was done in Chapter 6 for `springServiceContacts`:

```
$CODE/awsServiceContacts
```

Use File ⇨ Import ⇨ General ⇨ Existing Projects into workspace

3. Add a run configuration

Right-click awsServiceContacts in the Package Explorer.

Select Run As ⇨ Run on server ⇨ and select the previously added Tomcat Configuration.

Wait for ivy to resolve dependencies.

The AWS service should now be running with persistence in DynamoDB, assuming that the Amazon SDK can connect to AWS services.

> **NOTE** *If you need to add a Tomcat configuration, please see the instructions for doing so in Chapter 6.*

Congratulations, you've now ported the contacts example to AWS using DynamoDB. You can use both of the Chapter 5 clients with this service simply by changing the client endpoint URL to point to your AWS instance. As in Chapter 6, edit the variable SERVICE in either of the `ContactsApplication.java` classes in the `restfulCachingProviderContacts` or `syncAdapterContacts` projects, or set the system preference `RESTfulContact.URI`. You now have a working mobile app that can harness the power of the Amazon cloud. Since it's a good idea to avoid vendor lock-in, next you'll see how to build an example for another large cloud provider, Google.

Run the Chapter 5 clients and curl against the following local endpoint:

```
http://localhost:8080/awsServiceContacts/Contacts
```

Test Your New DynamoDB Service

Test your service using the following commands.

Create contacts:

```
curl -H "Content-Type: application/json" -X POST -d '{"firstName":"John",
"lastName":"Smith", "phone":2345678901, "email":"jsmith@nosuchhost.com" }'
http://localhost:8080/awsServiceContacts/Contacts
```

Get contacts:

```
curl -X GET
http://localhost:8080/awsServiceContacts/Contacts
```

Writing the Code: Google App Engine Contacts

The next code walkthrough focuses on how to integrate with Google App Engine and its BigTable-based Datastore. The Google example shares the three-tier architecture with the two previous contacts examples, and the relevant DAO class, the focus of the code walkthrough, is `ContactDaoGoogleAppEngineImpl`.

Prepare: Prerequisites and Getting Started

The App Engine example also relies on Spring and Tomcat, and of course, requires a Google account for App Engine use, so create one if needed. Log in to your Google account and then go to:

```
https://appengine.google.com/
```

Step 1: Create a Google App Engine Service

Click the Create Application button, and then follow the subsequent instructions to create a Google App Engine application. Start by creating a Google "application identifier," which is a unique string you pick between 6 and 30 lowercase characters; be forewarned, many strings are already taken, we used `wileyenterpriseandroidae`. Pick a title, select an access level, and sign the terms of use. Your application should now be registered. Save the values that you enter. You'll use them in subsequent steps.

Step 2: Install the App Engine SDK

To work with App Engine, you'll need to download the SDK for Java from Google's developer site at the following location:

```
https://developers.google.com/appengine/downloads#Google_App_Engine_SDK_for_Java
```

> **NOTE** *Make sure that you download the App Engine SDK for Java, not for Python or another language. It's easy to pick the wrong one on the download page. Also choose a version that matches your OS and Java binary version, 32- or 64-bit.*

Of course, Google has significant documentation online:

```
https://developers.google.com/appengine/
```

Step 3: Import the Project into Eclipse

Just like you have done for the other service projects in the book so far, import the project into Eclipse:

```
cd $CODE/googleAppEngineContacts/
ant eclipse
```

Then import the project folder into Eclipse.

Step 4: Install the Google Plugin for Eclipse

Follow the instructions below to install the Google plugin for Eclipse:

```
https://developers.google.com/appengine/docs/java/tools/eclipse
```

Edit the build properties file:

```
$CODE/googleAppEngineContacts/build.properties
```

to enter the path where you installed the App Engine SDK.

Step 5: Configure an Application Identifier

You need to put the application identifier you created in Step 1 into the `$CODE/war/WEB-INF/appengine-web.xml`, as follows:

```
<?xml version="1.0" encoding="utf-8"?>
<appengine-web-app xmlns="http://appengine.google.com/ns/1.0">
  <application>Add_your_application_id_here</application>
<version>1</version>
```

Step 6: Create an Application-Specific Password

You won't be able to deploy updates to your app engine service using your normal account password; instead you must create an application-specific password from the following location:

```
https://accounts.google.com/IssuedAuthSubTokens?hide_authsub=1#acccess_codes
```

Application-specific passwords require you to have two-step verification in place, so if you don't have it on your Google account, you'll have to turn it on and authorize your computer before completing the process. Be sure to have a phone or a device on which you can receive text messages available. The included link provides a YouTube tutorial on this process.

When invoking update requests from ant or in eclipse, use the following credentials:

➤ **E-mail address**—Your account e-mail address

➤ **Password**—An application-specific password

Example Code: Replacement Contact DAO

The Google App Engine Datastore sample code illustrates how to port the RESTful contacts service into the Google's BigTable for structured data. When you examine the App Engine code, it'll be clear that the App Engine API is in many ways significantly more user friendly than DynamoDB. Google's Query Language (GQL), loosely based on SQL, has many convenience features that help developers write App Engine services. Such services are not necessarily always beneficial, given that they may interfere with developers' abilities to optimize performance and scalability in their applications.

The class, `ContactDaoAppEngineImpl`, provides the relevant implementation code for the contacts DAO. The App Engine contact DAO uses the Datastore Entity API, which revolves around the entity construct, and also Google's Query Language, which enables SQL-like operations on entities.

Entities Table

The Datastore API stores persistent objects in the form of entities. All entities have a write-once key that uniquely identifies them in the entities table, and a collection of typed properties that contain the data associated with the entity. The entity key contains the following pieces of information:

➤ **Application ID** — Uniquely identifies the application in App Engine.

➤ **Kind** — Categorizes the entity for queries.

➤ **Entity ID** — An ID unique to the application. The application can define the ID, or the Datastore can automatically generate it. Entity names are also called key names.

> **NOTE** *The entity table stores all entities for all App Engine applications. This should give you an idea of the scalability that the Datastore can support. The uniqueness of the application ID guarantees that other applications cannot access your application's data, and vice versa.*

Recall that because the App Engine Datastore is a NoSQL database, the property set of two entities of the same kind do not need to be the same — developers can add or remove properties at will.

Google Query Language

Recall that BigTable is a column-oriented database. The design of the GQL language reflects this underlying structure. Likely, developers familiar with SQL are better off thinking about GQL in terms of what it does not do, rather than about the features it does support. GQL enables "SQL-like" queries on cloud data, with the following restrictions:

➤ `JOIN` is not supported.

➤ Applications can `SELECT` from at most one table at a time.

➤ You can name only one column in a query `WHERE` clause.

As stated in the earlier discussion regarding the limitations of implementing a multi-host JOIN operation with a column-oriented database, it's not hard to see where the limitations regarding GQL versus SQL arise. Although developers may find these limitations frustrating, Google has still provided a useful data language that will be familiar to SQL developers in an environment (such as a scalable cloud development) where less friendly programming techniques are not uncommon.

This chapter provides only a brief explanation of tools related to BigTable and App Engine. The Google GQL documentation is a great way to get started with the language:

```
http://code.google.com/appengine/docs/datastore/gqlreference.html
```

For the purposes of the App Engine RESTful contacts example, consider the following queries, which find a contact by name and by modified time:

```
SELECT c FROM Contact c where c.updateTime > ?1
```

This query returns all contact entities changed after the specified update time. The following query yields contacts with a requested first name:

```
SELECT c FROM Contact c where c.firstName = ?1
```

The Java Persistence API

The App Engine API borrows significantly from a Java community standard called the Java Persistence API (JPA), which has a long evolutionary history from Enterprise Java Beans (EJB). JPA supports an API-based data querying capability and defines persistence support from a Java perspective. The most important API from the perspective of the DAO object is `javax.persistence.EntityManager`, which becomes the main interface into the App Engine Datastore and the entities it contains. JPA defines a large and rich API, most of which is outside the scope of this example. You can learn more about JPA online:

```
http://en.wikipedia.org/wiki/Java_Persistence_API
```

All most Datastore developers need to know is that Google has solid support for JPA, and the implementation of the API works its magic to translate JPA requests into Datastore requests. For example, QGL queries are automatically converted into a range key search when appropriate.

The Code: Contacts DAO Implementation

At this point, having gained an overview of all the concepts used in the Google App Engine example, you're ready to jump into the code. Listing 7-7 shows a documented version of the App Engine DAO class.

LISTING 7-7: DAO implementation for Google App Engine ("BigTable").

```
package com.enterpriseandroid.googleappengineContacts.dao.impl;

import java.io.IOException;
import java.util.List;
import java.util.UUID;
import java.util.logging.Logger;
```

```
import javax.persistence.EntityManager;
import javax.persistence.PersistenceContext;
import javax.persistence.TypedQuery;

import org.springframework.stereotype.Repository;
import org.springframework.transaction.annotation.Transactional;

import com.enterpriseandroid.googleappengineContacts.dao.ContactDao;
import com.enterpriseandroid.googleappengineContacts.dataModel.Contact;
```

The following annotations indicate that this class is a Spring repository or DAO — this is the contact DAO.

```
@Repository
@Transactional
public class ContactDaoGoogleAppEngineImpl implements ContactDao {
    private static final Logger log = Logger
            .getLogger(ContactDaoGoogleAppEngineImpl.class.getName());
    @PersistenceContext
    private EntityManager entityManager;
```

Finding a contact is a simple matter of delegating to the entity manager for an object of type `Contact.class`, and then passing in the ID of the contact.

```
@Override
public Contact getContact(String id) throws IOException {
    return entityManager.find(Contact.class, id);
}
```

To store or update a contact, you just need to ask the entity manager to persist the contact if it already has an ID (update), or first create an ID, and then persist the object.

```
@Override
public String storeOrUpdateContact(Contact contact)
        throws IOException {
    contact.setUpdateTime(System.currentTimeMillis());
    if( contact.getId() != null) {
        entityManager.persist(contact);
    } else {
```

Using a random UUID is a simple and effective way of ensuring an even distribution of contacts in the Datastore. It's a good way to avoid "hot keys" that can limit application scalability.

```
contact.setId(UUID.randomUUID().toString());
```

To store a contact, just ask the entity manager to persist it.

```
entityManager.persist(contact);
}
```

```
        return contact.getId();
   }

   @Override
```

You can find a contact by first name by using a simple GQL query. The query selects a contact from the contact table with a first name matching the firstName parameter. As you can see, the code looks a lot like many standard SQL-based programs:

```
   public List<Contact> findContactFirstName(String firstName,
                                      int start, int numOfmatches)
   {
       TypedQuery<Contact> query = entityManager.createQuery(
           "SELECT c FROM Contact c where c.firstName = ?1",
           Contact.class);
        query.setParameter(1, firstName);
        query.setFirstResult(start);
        query.setMaxResults(numOfmatches);
        List<Contact> list = query.getResultList();
       return list;
   }
```

Another query supports finding all contacts changed after a given timestamp, thus helping to implement the example sync algorithm:

```
   @Override
   public List<Contact> findChanged(long timestamp, int start,
                                int numOfmatches) {
       TypedQuery<Contact> query = entityManager.createQuery(
             "SELECT c FROM Contact c where c.updateTime > ?1",
             Contact.class);
       query.setParameter(1, timestamp);
       query.setFirstResult(start);
       query.setMaxResults(numOfmatches);
       List<Contact> list = query.getResultList();
       return list;
   }
```

Delegate to the entity manager to remove the contact:

```
   @Override
   public void delete(String id) throws IOException {
       log.info( "delete: "+ id);
       try {
           Contact c = getContact(id);
           entityManager.remove(c);
       } catch (Exception e ) {
           e.printStackTrace();
       }
   }
```

Another GQL request selects all relevant contacts and returns them to the client:

```
@Override
public List<Contact> getAll(int start, int numOfmatches)
        throws IOException
{
    TypedQuery<Contact> query =
            entityManager.createQuery("SELECT c FROM Contact c",
                    Contact.class);
    System.out.println(" size :"  + query.getResultList().size());
    return query.getResultList();
}
}
```

Deploy the Code

As with other projects, you can run the code from the command line or in Eclipse.

Deploying the Code with ant

1. Deploy the project:

   ```
   cd $CODE/googleAppEngineContacts
   ant
   ```

2. To run the code locally on port 8080:

   ```
   ant runserver
   ```

   The local endpoint is:

   ```
   http://localhost:8080/Contacts
   ```

3. To deploy to the Google cloud, run the command:

   ```
   ant deploy-app
   ```

   Enter credentials as specified previously for your application-specific password.

Testing the Local Service

To test the service, run the following commands in a shell (cygwin for Windows).

Create contacts:

```
curl -H "Content-Type: application/json" -X POST -d '{"firstName":"John",
"lastName":"Smith", "phone":2345678901, "email":"jsmith@nosuchhost.com" }'
http://localhost:8080/Contacts
```

Get contacts:

```
curl -H "Content-Type: application/json" -X GET
http://localhost:8080/Contacts
```

Deploying with Eclipse

1. Set up the Eclipse build files:

   ```
   cd $CODE/googleAppEngineContacts
   ant eclipse
   ```

   > **NOTE** *In this project, this command also resolves ivy dependencies.*

2. As shown in springServiceContacts, import the project directory in Eclipse:

   ```
   $CODE/googleAppEngineContacts
   ```

3. Add the AppEngine SDK to the classpath.

   a. Right-click the googleAppEngineContacts project.

   b. Go to Project menu and select properties.

   c. Click the Java Build Path on the left. When the dialog opens, click the Library tab.

   d. Click the Add Library button.

   e. Select Google App Engine, and then click the Next button.

   f. Select the App Engine SDK, choose Use default if you've just installed a single copy, and then click Finish.

   Click OK and Eclipse will build the project.

4. To run the sample code locally, right-click the googleAppEngineContacts and select the Run As ⇨ Web Application menu.

5. To deploy the app to Google:

   a. Right-click googleAppEngineContacts.

   b. Select Google ⇨ Deploy to App Engine.

   > **NOTE** *You can view log messages or check the status of your app by selecting your_app_id from the list of apps listed from* http://appengine.google.com/. *Google provides a large array of service statistics here as well.*

Testing the Deployed Service

Run commands from a shell as follows.

Create contacts:

```
curl -H "Content-Type: application/json" -X POST -d '{"firstName":"John",
"lastName":"Smith", "phone":2345678901, "email":"jsmith@nosuchhost.com" }'
http://<your_ae_id>.appspot.com>/Contacts
```

Get contacts:

```
curl -i -H "Content-Type: application/json" -X GET
http://<your_ae_id>.appspot.com/Contacts
```

Replace `<your_ae_id>` with your application ID.

Congratulations! You can now change the Chapter 5 endpoint again to point to your new service URL on Google. If the contacts service was a product, you would now, thanks to its flexible architecture, be able to deploy it on your own hardware, the AWS cloud, or Google's App Engine cloud.

> **NOTE** *Please keep in mind that as with Chapter 6, you can find up-to-date instructions for building and running the chapter examples in the following locations:*
>
> `$CODE/awsServiceContacts/README`
>
> `$CODE/googleAppEngineContacts/README`

SUMMARY

This chapter discussed implementing scalable cloud-based services to support mobile clients. The two example service implementations ported the three-tier architecture from Chapter 6 onto Amazon's DynamoDB and Google App Engine BigTable, which are two of the more scalable and popular cloud services available today.

The chapter discussed the idea of cloud computing, the major scalability problems cloud services face, and how different database designs solve them. The chapter showed how NoSQL databases achieve high scalability and in some ways allow flexibility that can be harder to achieve with SQL. However, you learned that SQL has significantly safer and higher level APIs than column-oriented databases like DynamoDB.

The chapter showed how to write a cloud-based RESTful service, while emphasizing the importance of using an architecture that can port easily between various cloud products. Such practices allow developers to focus on the issues that will really matter to their business goals.

Developers typically choose cloud platforms for systemic reasons, rather than functional ones. For example, they don't want to run their own server hardware, they need to leverage cloud scalability, and they want to use the cheapest service platform to run their traffic. Even though it's more difficult to implement your own indexes with DynamoDB, an investment in code is likely small compared to what you might save in the long run by being able to pick the cheapest cloud provider. The databases discussed in this chapter have architectural differences for demanding applications, but for most enterprise scale applications, performance of all platforms discussed is likely excellent.

8

Complex Device-Based Data: Android Contacts

WHAT'S IN THIS CHAPTER?

➤   Using the Android Contacts database

➤   Using the ContactsContract API

➤   Learning how the Contacts database illustrates content provider concepts

WROX.COM CODE DOWNLOADS FOR THIS CHAPTER

Please note that all the code examples in this chapter are available at `https://github.com/wileyenterpriseandroid/Examples.git` and as a part of the book's code download at www.wrox.com on the Download Code tab.

Most of this book is about innovative techniques that simplify your use of databases in Android and in network services backing Android applications. However, this chapter looks at a complex multi-table database with a complex content provider API that has a conventional design in the context of the database APIs in the Android system. That is, this chapter shows an example of how to create a big, complex SQL database and provider interface as a contrast to using the kinds of techniques covered in the rest of this book.

> **NOTE** *To get the most out of this chapter, you should have read Chapter 2, on relational database concepts and SQL, and Chapter 4, on the* ContentProvider *class and related classes.*

PIM DATABASES: FOSSILS FROM SMARTPHONE PRE-HISTORY

The Contacts database was influenced by earlier smartphone architectures. The first smartphones were devices that combined mobile phones with personal information managers (PIMs). These pre-iPhone smartphones dated back to an era when there was no wide-area data connectivity, cloud services didn't exist, and syncing meant syncing to data on your PC. These smartphones enabled you to carry your PIM data in your phone.

Android's designers might have done most of this "in the cloud," but that would have made Android less open, and more closely tied to Google's cloud services. And there are still places where your contacts and other PIM data are useful without data connectivity. If the goal is to provide flexible, unified contact information using the capabilities available on a mobile device, the Android Contacts provider is a good example.

ANDROID'S CONTACTS PROVIDER

The Contacts database API, called *ContactsContract*, isn't a "normal" Java API. It isn't a set of methods contained in a `ContentProvider` subclass. Instead, it consists mostly of constants — strings, values, and static objects — that help you access information using the URL-based API style of a content provider.

When you get contact information, you get `Cursor` objects, and you get them through a loader or, more directly, through a content resolver. There is no object-relational mapping (ORM) in the ContactsContract API, and there are no objects that model individual contacts. The API and the `Cursor` objects put as little as possible between you, the contacts data, and the UI widgets. If you look at the example code listed later in this chapter, you can see where the program gets a Cursor object where the data from a table will be loaded into a view.

When databases get more complex in Android, the APIs to access them provide access to the tables in the database, of course, but they also provide access to "abstract" tables, which are the results of SQL queries that select and combine information across the tables in the database. This is how an Android content provider-style API abstracts queries from users of the API. You will explore this provider in two ways and will see which tables are "real" and which are created on the fly.

THE CONTACTSCONTRACT API

The ContactsContract API consists mainly of constants. For example, the constant `AUTHORITY` has the value `com.android.contacts`, which is the string you need to form a URL to access the Contacts provider. To take another example, the tables in the Contacts provider are represented by embedded subclasses, and you access those tables using the `CONTENT_URI` static object. Commonality in constants is created using interfaces. By implementing interfaces with no methods, the ContactsContract classes achieve a kind of multiple inheritance of constants and static objects.

You can find the documentation you need to understand this API in two places. First, you need to understand the Contacts provider, which is the part of the Android system that implements the API you'll use. Documentation on the Contacts provider is found here:

```
http://developer.android.com/guide/topics/providers/contacts-provider.html
```

You also need the ContactsContract API documentation, which you can find here:

> http://developer.android.com/reference/android/provider/ContactsContract.html

Not only is the Contacts provider a complex database, the API to access it is an example of a complex hierarchy of classes and interfaces. If you are still puzzled about the difference between the Contacts provider and the ContactsContract API, take a look at the documentation on designing and creating content providers:

> http://developer.android.com/guide/topics/providers/
> content-provider-creating.html

What you are looking at in the Contacts provider is a particularly complex and evolved provider.

The API style used in the ContactsContract API is common and idiomatic in Android, but unusual in Java practice, in general. We have been using the term API, but that usually means a collection of classes and methods. Here, you have constants and static objects organized into classes and interfaces. It's an unusual style of API: It combines Java classes and interfaces with a REST-style system of URI objects to access the information in the provider.

There are benefits and drawbacks to this unusual API style: The benefits come, chiefly, from the way the API style mirrors REST stylistically. Among the drawbacks is the fact that the API style invites probing through reflection, and, if that probing uncovers undocumented parts of the API, the API can be accused of failing to abstract its implementation.

To illustrate these points, we want you to take a look at an app in the next section that explores the Contacts provider via the ContactsContract API.

A CONTACTS PROVIDER EXPLORER

The example application for this chapter explores the data contained in the Contacts provider. It does so by enumerating the classes that represent tables in the API, and by enumerating the columns in each table — that is, it queries the Contacts provider for all the rows in all the tables named in the API and displays all the columns in each row. As noted earlier in the chapter, you can get the source code for this application at https://github.com/wileyenterpriseandroid/Examples.git and as a part of the book's code download at www.wrox.com.

To follow along with this chapter, you should import the example source code into a project in your Eclipse workspace.

Running the application results in displays like the one shown in Figure 8-1. Be aware that if you have no contacts in the database, there will be no contacts to display.

The Option menu, shown open and on the right in Figure 8-1, enables you to select a table to peruse. The list on the left side of the screen in Figure 8-1 shows a column from the table (in this figure the table selected is an empty one), enabling you to select a row based on the data from that column.

When you select a row, the row information is shown in the Item tab (see Figure 8-2).

The table information is shown in the Table tab (see Figure 8-3).

FIGURE 8-1

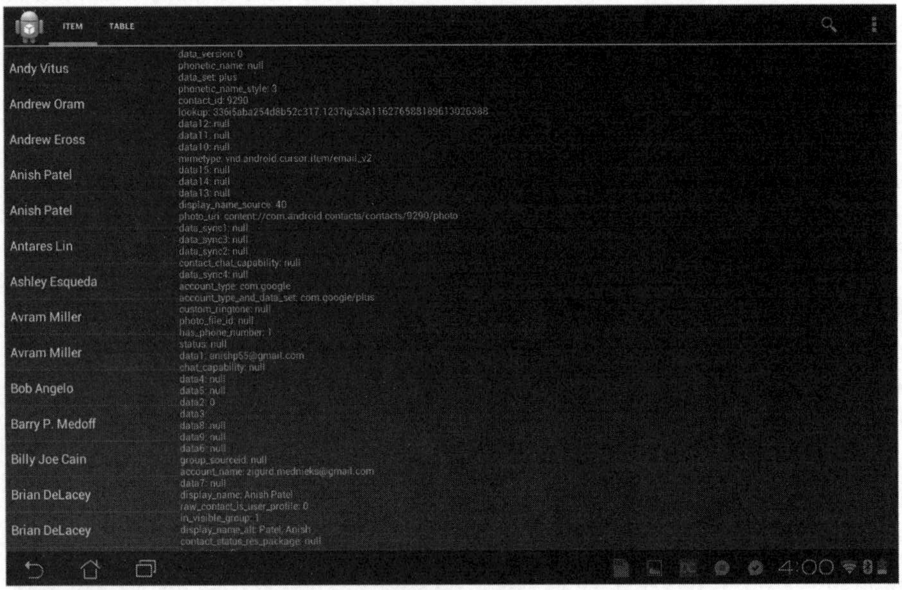

FIGURE 8-2

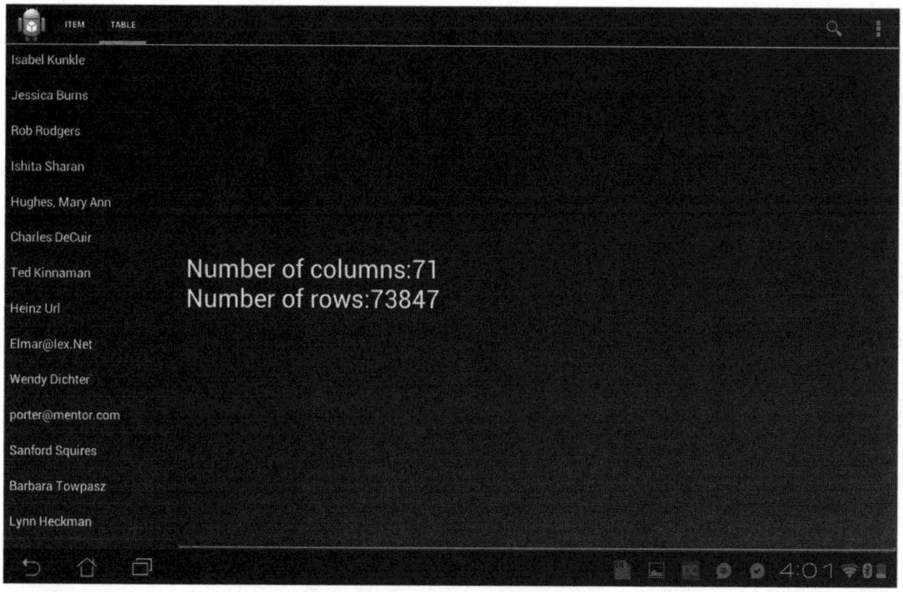

FIGURE 8-3

Code for Exploring a Database

Rather than just run down a list of constants and explain what they mean, it's better to show how they are used. Using these constants in the context of Android's content provider and related APIs illustrates more clearly what is inside the Contacts provider.

The goals for this example program are as follows:

➤ Enabling you to find every table corresponding to every class that contains a static object named CONTENT_URI, which is to say every table accessible through the ContactsContract API

➤ Enabling you to see the structure of the table, including the names of every column and the number of rows in a large, real-world address book

➤ Enabling you to see the data in a real address book

In order to see what's in your address book, compile and run the example, and make sure you see something similar to the figures shown previously in this chapter. Select different tables from the Option menu. Select the Table and the Data tabs to view the information about the table and about the row in the table you selected from the list on the left side of the screen.

Source Code for a Contacts Provider Explorer

The listings that follow are really all part of one long program listing.

Only the `PickFragment.java` class is included here, because all the important code for exploring the Contacts provider via the ContactsContract API is in this class.

Exploring the Menu of Tables

This application (starting with Listing 8-1) explores an API with unusual characteristics. It consists mostly of constants that have to do with tables that can be queried in a content provider.

LISTING 8-1: Your first look at PickFragment.java

```java
package com.enterpriseandroidbook.contactscontractexample;

import java.util.ArrayList;
import java.util.Arrays;
import java.util.ListIterator;

import android.app.Activity;
import android.app.Fragment;
import android.app.ListFragment;
import android.app.LoaderManager;
import android.content.CursorLoader;
import android.content.Loader;
import android.content.res.Configuration;
import android.database.Cursor;
import android.net.Uri;
import android.os.Bundle;
import android.provider.BaseColumns;
import android.provider.ContactsContract;
import android.util.Log;
import android.view.LayoutInflater;
import android.view.Menu;
import android.view.MenuInflater;
import android.view.MenuItem;
import android.view.MenuItem.OnMenuItemClickListener;
import android.view.View;
import android.view.ViewGroup;
import android.widget.CursorAdapter;
import android.widget.LinearLayout;
import android.widget.ListView;
import android.widget.SimpleCursorAdapter;


/**
 * @author default-name
 *
 */
/**
 * @author default-name
 *
 */
public class PickFragment extends ListFragment implements
```

```
        LoaderManager.LoaderCallbacks<Cursor>, OnMenuItemClickListener {

        // Turn logging on or off
        private static final boolean L = true;

        // String for logging the class name
        private final String CLASSNAME = getClass().getSimpleName();

        // Tag my loader with this ID
        public static final int LOADER_ID = 42;

        // Labels for members saved as state
        private final String STATE_LABEL_NAME = "tablename";

        //The current table's class name
        private String tableName;


        public void onAttach(Activity activity) {
            super.onAttach(activity);

            // Notification that the fragment is associated with an Activity
            if (L)
                Log.i(CLASSNAME, "onAttach " + activity.getClass().getSimpleName());
        }

        public void onCreate(Bundle savedInstanceState) {
            super.onCreate(savedInstanceState);

            // Tell the system we have an options menu
            setHasOptionsMenu(true);

            doLoaderCreation(savedInstanceState);

            // Notification that
            if (L)
                Log.i(CLASSNAME, "onCreate");
        }

        @Override
        public View onCreateView(LayoutInflater inflater, ViewGroup container,
                Bundle savedInstanceState) {

            final LinearLayout listLayout = (LinearLayout) inflater.inflate(
                    R.layout.list_frag_list, container, false);
            if (L)
                Log.i(CLASSNAME, "onCreateView");

            return listLayout;
        }

        @Override
        public void onSaveInstanceState(Bundle outState) {
            super.onSaveInstanceState(outState);
```

continues

LISTING 8-1 *(continued)*

```java
            outState.putString(STATE_LABEL_NAME, tableName);
    }

    public void onStart() {
        super.onStart();
        if (L)
            Log.i(CLASSNAME, "onStart");
    }

    public void onresume() {
        super.onResume();
        if (L)
            Log.i(CLASSNAME, "onResume");
    }

    public void onPause() {
        super.onPause();
        if (L)
            Log.i(CLASSNAME, "onPause");
    }

    public void onStop() {
        super.onStop();
        if (L)
            Log.i(CLASSNAME, "onStop");
    }

    public void onDestroyView() {
        super.onDestroyView();
        if (L)
            Log.i(CLASSNAME, "onDestroyView");
    }

    public void onDestroy() {
        super.onDestroy();
        if (L)
            Log.i(CLASSNAME, "onDestroy");
    }

    public void onDetach() {
        super.onDetach();
        if (L)
            Log.i(CLASSNAME, "onDetach");
    }

// ////////////////////////////////////////////////////////////////////////
// Minor lifecycle methods
// ////////////////////////////////////////////////////////////////////////

    public void onActivityCreated() {
        // Notification that the containing activiy and its View hierarchy exist
        if (L)
            Log.i(CLASSNAME, "onActivityCreated");
```

```
    }

// ////////////////////////////////////////////////////////////////////////
// Overrides of the implementations of ComponentCallbacks methods in Fragment
// ////////////////////////////////////////////////////////////////////////

    @Override
    public void onConfigurationChanged(Configuration newConfiguration) {
        super.onConfigurationChanged(newConfiguration);

        // This won't happen unless we declare changes we handle in the manifest
        if (L)
            Log.i(CLASSNAME, "onConfigurationChanged");
    }

    @Override
    public void onLowMemory() {
        // No guarantee this is called before or after other callbacks
        if (L)
            Log.i(CLASSNAME, "onLowMemory");
    }

// ////////////////////////////////////////////////////////////////////////
// ListFragment click handling
// ////////////////////////////////////////////////////////////////////////
```

Handling Clicks in the List View

The onListItemClick method (in Listing 8-2) implements the callback for the way a list fragment handles clicks in the list view contained in the fragment.

In the case of this application, data about the database and data about the row selected are prepared and displayed in the tabs. The data is placed in a Bundle object in case the tabs are in a separate activity, in order to support the way that this application approaches the problem of scaling across small- and large-screen devices.

> **NOTE** *Chapter 1 explains this approach in detail.*

LISTING 8-2: Handling clicks

```
public void onListItemClick(ListView l, View v, int position, long id) {
    Cursor c = ((CursorAdapter) getListView().getAdapter()).getCursor();
    String item = buildItemInfo(c, position);
    String tableInfo = buildDatabaseInfo(c);
    Bundle data = ((MainActivity) getActivity()).buildDataBundle(item,
            tableInfo);
    ((TabbedActivity) getActivity()).loadTabFragments(data);
```

continues

LISTING 8-2 *(continued)*

```
    }

// /////////////////////////////////////////////////////////////////////////////
// Implementation of LoaderCallbacks
// /////////////////////////////////////////////////////////////////////////////
```

Implementing the Loader Callbacks Interface

This application uses a `Loader` and `LoaderManager` to handle long-running code — in this case the code for accessing a content provider. If you have a large number of contacts, you can readily see that querying a content provider would result in hanging the UI for the duration it takes the query to run. The `CursorLoader` used here prevents the UI from locking up by performing query operations on a separate thread.

In Listing 8-3 you can see implementations for all three Loader callback methods.

➤ `OnCreateLoader` creates and returns the `CusorLoader` object initialized by a query from the specified table, taken from the member `tableName`.

➤ The `onLoadFinished` method gets a reference to the `Adapter` object, which puts data into the list's views and sets the new cursor for the list.

➤ The `onLoaderReset` call sets the cursor to null.

LISTING 8-3: Implementing Loader callbacks

```
// Create the loader, passing in the query
public Loader<Cursor> onCreateLoader(int id, Bundle args) {
    return new CursorLoader(this.getActivity(), uriForTable(tableName),
            null, null, null, null);
}

// Get results
public void onLoadFinished(Loader<Cursor> loader, Cursor cursor) {
    ((SimpleCursorAdapter) getListAdapter()).swapCursor(cursor);
}

// Reset
public void onLoaderReset(Loader<Cursor> loader) {
    ((SimpleCursorAdapter) getListAdapter()).swapCursor(null);

}

// /////////////////////////////////////////////////////////////////////////////
// App-specific code
// /////////////////////////////////////////////////////////////////////////////
```

```
private final static String NL = System.getProperty("line.separator");


/**
 * Called from onCreate. restore state if available
 *
 * @param savedInstanceState
 */
private void doLoaderCreation(Bundle savedInstanceState) {
    super.onCreate(savedInstanceState);

    // If no saved state, start fresh with the Data table
    if (null == savedInstanceState) {
        openNewTableByName("android.provider.ContactsContract$Data");
    } else {
        // See if we can recreate the query from saved state
        tableName = savedInstanceState.getString(STATE_LABEL_NAME);
        if (null == tableName) {
            doLoaderCreation(null); // Nope
        } else {
            openNewTableByName(tableName);
        }
    }


}
```

Opening a New Table

In Listing 8-4, the method openNewTableByName calls some other methods that turn a class name into a URI, and result in a query based on that URI. The uriForTable method goes from class name to URI object. The newTableQuery method starts the query operation.

LISTING 8-4: Opening a new table

```
/**
 * Open a new table, based on the name of the class
 * from the API.
 *
 * @param tableClassName
 */
private void openNewTableByName(String tableClassName) {

    Uri table = uriForTable(tableClassName);
    if (null == table) {return;} // Fail silently
    tableName = tableClassName;
    newTableQuery(table, ListColumnMap.get(table));
}
```

From a Name to a Query

In Listing 8-5, you can see the methods that go from the name of a class to a query for the contents of a table corresponding to the CONTENT_URI URI object in that class. The name of the class comes from a menu selection, built from the content provider's own information, so error checking here is minimal.

The uriForTable method takes the information the app gets when a user makes a menu selection — which is the name of a class — and returns the CONTENT_URI object, which is a static object in that class.

First, the forName method of the class Class is used to turn the name of a class into a reference to the class object. Then a reference to the CONTENT_URI static object is returned.

Even though you should be confident that your class names and field names are valid, a lot can go wrong during the process of going from the string that names a class, to the class object itself, and then to a field, which is also retrieved by name. This method therefore catches all the exceptions that could result from an incorrect class or field name and fails silently. If a table selected by class name does not exist or cannot be accessed by the means used in this app, the app does nothing.

LISTING 8-5: Going from the name of a class to a query for the contents of a table

```java
/**
 * Get the content uri, given the corresponding
 * class name
 *
 * @param name The name of the class in ContactsContract
 * @return The content uri for the corresponding class
 */
private Uri uriForTable(String name) {
    Class<?> tableClass;
    Uri table;

    // Get the table's class
    try {
        tableClass = Class.forName(name);
    } catch (ClassNotFoundException e) {
        return null;
    }

    // Get the content Uri, which should be static, hence no instance for get
    try {
        table = (Uri)(tableClass.getDeclaredField("CONTENT_URI").get(null));
    } catch (IllegalArgumentException e) {
        return null;
    } catch (IllegalAccessException e) {
        return null;
    } catch (NoSuchFieldException e) {
        return null;
    }
    return table;
}
```

From a URI to a Query

When you choose a table to explore in this app, two things happen. A `Cursor` object is created with all the data in the table, and the list on the left side of the screen is loaded with values that help you pick rows in that table. For example, contact names help you pick rows that correspond to information about the people with those names.

In Listing 8-6, the `NewTableQuery` method sets this process in motion. First, it determines whether the column name that is supposed to go in the list is null, in which case the `_ID` field of the `BaseColumns` interface is used. If that happens, the list will contain record ID numbers.

Next, arrays that specify the mapping of the named column to a view ID are created. Because there is only one column and one view being used, these arrays have one member each.

Then an `Adapter` instance is created. The subclass `SimpleCursorAdapter` is used, and it is provided with the arrays specifying the mapping of columns to views. The new adapter is set to be the adapter for the list view in this fragment.

Now that the `ListView` object is ready to display new data, a loader is created and started with the help of the `LoaderManager` object associated with this fragment. That new loader is assigned an ID, and any existing loader is destroyed.

LISTING 8-6: Going from a URI to a query for the contents of a table

```java
private void newTableQuery(Uri table, String column) {

    if (null == column || column.isEmpty()) {
        column = BaseColumns._ID;
    }

    String[] fromColumns = { column };
    int[] toViews = { android.R.id.text1 };

    // Create an adapter without a cursor
    SimpleCursorAdapter adapter = new SimpleCursorAdapter(this.getActivity(),
            android.R.layout.simple_list_item_1, null,
            fromColumns, toViews, 0);
    setListAdapter(adapter);

    // Make a new loader
    LoaderManager m = getLoaderManager();
    if (null != m.getLoader(LOADER_ID)) {
        m.destroyLoader(LOADER_ID);
    }
    m.initLoader(LOADER_ID, null, this);
}
```

Formatting Data for Display

In Listing 8-7, two methods for formatting data are defined: `buildItemInfo` returns a string that contains all the data from a row in a database, and `buildDatabaseInfo` returns a string containing the number of rows and columns in a database. In both these methods, as with other code in this application, you want to avoid entering a lot of strings for the purpose of labeling, and you want to avoid table-specific UI constructs. So each column in the table gets one line of output in the Item fragment, and is labeled with the name of the column.

You can see you get the names of the columns from the Cursor object. Then you iterate over the columns, get the data for the specified row and column, and concatenate this to a string that's returned.

LISTING 8-7: Formatting data for display

```
/**
 * Extracts, labels, and formats all the information in
 * all the columns in a row.
 *
 * @param c The cursor
 * @param position The position in the cursor
 * @return The formatted data from the row
 */
private String buildItemInfo(Cursor c, int position) {

    int i;
    int columns = c.getColumnCount();
    String info = "";

    c.moveToPosition(position);
    String names[] = c.getColumnNames();

    for (i = 0; i < columns; i++) {
        info += names[i] + ": ";
        try {
            info += c.getString(i);
        } catch (Exception e) {
            // Fail silently
        }
        info += NL;
    }

    return info;
}

private String buildDatabaseInfo (Cursor c) {
    String info = "";

    info += getString(R.string.column_count_label) + c.getColumnCount() + NL;
    info += getString(R.string.row_count_label) + c.getCount() + NL;

    return info;

}
```

```
///////////////////////////////////////////////////////////////////////////
// Methods for transferring data between Fragments
///////////////////////////////////////////////////////////////////////////
```

Packaging Data for Tabs

In Listing 8-8, the method `buildDataBundle` packages the data in a way that one or two fragments can appear on the screen at one time. If the screen is small and only one fragment is displayed, and the user clicks on a list item, a new activity is started to display the Item and Table tabs. A single string contains all the data for each tab. These strings are placed in two places in the `Bundle` object, each with names specified in the XML file that specifies the layout for each tab.

LISTING 8-8: Packaging data for tabs

```java
/**
 * Build a Bundle that holds the database and item information
 *
 * @param item Information about the selected row
 * @param dbInfo Information about the database
 * @return the Bundle containing the above information
 */
public Bundle buildDataBundle(String item, String dbInfo) {
    Bundle data = new Bundle();

    data.putString(getDataLabel(R.id.item_frag), item);
    data.putString(getDataLabel(R.id.detail_frag), dbInfo);
    return data;

}

public String getDataLabel(int id) {
    Fragment frag = getFragmentManager().findFragmentById(id);
    String label = ((TabbedActivity.SetData)frag).getDataLabel();
    return label;
}
```

```
// ///////////////////////////////////////////////////////////////////////////
// Menu handling code, including implementation of onMenuItemClickListener
// ///////////////////////////////////////////////////////////////////////////
```

Creating the Menu

The menu for selecting a table is created in the `onCreateOptionsMenu` method in Listing 8-9. You could type in all the table and column names from the documentation, but that defeats the purpose of exploring this large and unusual API by writing an app.

LISTING 8-9: Creating the menu

```
public void onCreateOptionsMenu(Menu menu, MenuInflater inflater) {
    buildTableMenu(menu);
    super.onCreateOptionsMenu(menu, inflater);
}
```

Selecting a Table from the Option Menu

In Listing 8-10 the `onMenuItemClickListener` method handles the selection of a table name from the menu and calls the `openNewTableByName` method. In the previous listing, you could see when the menu is created, and shortly you will see the code for building the menu.

LISTING 8-10: Selecting a table

```
@Override
public boolean onMenuItemClick(MenuItem item) {
    openNewTableByName((String) item.getTitle());
    return true;
}



// /////////////////////////////////////////////////////////////////////////
// App-specific code to create a menu of tables
// /////////////////////////////////////////////////////////////////////////
```

Finding Possible Tables

Instead of hard-coding table names and copying them from the API documentation, all the tables are enumerated in a general-purpose way, with a method called `buildTableMenu` (see Listing 8-11). This will also enable you to see if there are undocumented tables in this database.

First, an array of all the classes in `ContactsContract` is created by using the `getClasses` method of the `ContactsContract` class object. This array might contain classes that don't correspond to any table. An array isn't the best way to filter out everything that isn't a table, so on the next line an array list is created using the array of classes.

Building an Option Menu for Tables

Now that the list of tables has been built and scrubbed in Listing 8-11, the `buildTableMenu` method uses the `add` method of the `Menu` class to add each table name to the option menu and the `setOnMenuItemClickListener` method to set this fragment as the click listener for the menu item.

LISTING 8-11: Finding tables and building an Option menu

```
/**
 * Add a MenuItem to the specified menu for each table in the
      ContactsContract
 * class
 *
 * @param menu
 */
private void buildTableMenu(Menu menu) {
    Class<?>[] tablesArray = ContactsContract.class.getClasses();
    ArrayList<Class<?>> tablesList = new ArrayList<Class<?>>
            (Arrays.asList(tablesArray));
    deleteNonTables(tablesList);
    for (Class<?> c : tablesList) {
        menu.add(c.getName()).setOnMenuItemClickListener(this);
        }
}
```

Scrubbing the Menu of Tables

Previously, the `deleteNonTables` method was called from `buildTableMenu`. In Listing 8-12, this method scrubs the list of possible tables and eliminates those that can't be tables. Interfaces can't represent tables. The `isInterface` method of the `Class` object determines whether a class is an interface and, if so, drops it from the list.

LISTING 8-12: Scrubbing the menu list of tables

```
/**
 * Delete the embedded classes of ContactsContract that are not tables
 * i.e. not the interfaces, and not the classes that do not implement
 * BaseColumns.
 *
 * This might miss tables that do not, in fact, implement BaseColumns
 * but are still tables (but not ones that follow ContactsContract API
 * conventions)
 *
 * @param tablesList The raw list of embedded classes
 */
private void deleteNonTables(ArrayList<Class<?>> tablesList) {
    ListIterator<Class<?>> l = tablesList.listIterator();
    while (l.hasNext()) {
        Class<?> c = l.next();

        // Might be belt-and-suspenders
        if (true == c.isInterface()) {
            l.remove();
        }
        else if (false == implementer(c, BaseColumns.class)) {
            l.remove();
```

continues

LISTING 8-12 *(continued)*

```
            }
        }
    }
```

The `implementer` method (Listing 8-13) is called to test if the specified class implements the specified interface. The `implementer` method gets an array of interfaces for the specified class. Iterating over the array determines whether the class includes the interface. But it does not determine whether a parent class includes the interface, so this method recurses to walk the inheritance hierarchy for the specified class.

LISTING 8-13: The implementer method

```
/**
 * Does the specified class implement the specified interface?
 *
 * @param c The class
 * @param interf The interface
 * @return True if the interface is implemented by the class
 */
private boolean implementer(Class<?> c, Class<?> interf) {
    for (Class<?> ci : c.getInterfaces()) {
        if (ci.equals(interf)) {
            return true;
        } else {
            // Recurse, getInterfaces only gets one level (?!)
            if (true == implementer(ci, interf)) {
                return true;
            }
        }
    }
    return false;
}

}
```

SUMMARY

In this chapter you learned how to automatically find out about the tables in and explore one of the most complex SQLite databases you are likely to encounter in Android programming. Though complex, it is also a notably small database — usually no more than a few thousand rows in any table.

The setting for this kind of database is also unusual: It exists in a mobile handset, managed by the SQLite library. Rarely is a SQL database so intensively designed when it holds a relatively small amount of data. You can consider it the pinnacle of an unusual breed: the PIM database.

However, that is not to say it is just a curiosity. You may want to use it in your applications, and knowing it thoroughly will help in both scoping the possibilities when using the Contacts provider and in designing apps that use it.

And, not least of all, it serves as a contrast to the approach in the rest of this book, which emphasizes JSON over multiple tables for flexibility and simplicity of design.

9

Generic Data Synchronization: Project Migrate and the WebData API

WHAT'S IN THIS CHAPTER?

➤ Understanding the common problems that Android developers encounter when interacting with network data

➤ Solving common mobile data problems in a generic way with project Migrate and the WebData API

➤ Looking at the WebData protocol in detail

➤ Noting advantages of a WebData API–based system

WROX.COM CODE DOWNLOADS FOR THIS CHAPTER

Please note that all the code examples in this chapter are available at `https://github.com/wileyenterpriseandroid/Examples.git` and as a part of the book's code download at www.wrox.com on the Download Code tab.

As you've read in this book, mobile developers face similar problems on many platforms when writing applications that use network services to store data. Developers getting started with Android face problems associated with network data loading right off the bat. A typical first application for many developers will include a list of items loaded from a network service. The items will use thumbnails that require lazy loading. Developers with a bit more experience will start to use more sophisticated techniques like paging schemes that avoid the need to load all the results of a query over the network — large queries are loaded in pieces. Developers will also need a RESTful protocol for communicating with a backend service, and that protocol is likely to need synchronization support to deal with multiple hosts changing the same state. Developers often want offline data editing that allows an app to remain useful if the network becomes unavailable. Ideally, developers won't have to reinvent the wheel to address concerns such as these, but Android out of the box could do more to help developers solve these problems correctly.

As noted in earlier chapters, when implementing these functions, developers are likely to create similar bugs such as long-running UI events, hanging UI threads, or inflexible code that requires frequent application updates. Developers often write inefficient network protocols that rely on polling to update application data.

Why not create a system that solves all of these problems in a generic way that can be reused for many applications?

Of all the expressive web services and built-in content providers available on mobile platforms today, we see a gap in the available features — a *generic* data service explicitly designed to plug into a mobile MVC client in a way that extracts the redundantly implemented chores of handling data from the user interface of a mobile application.

This chapter introduces a new and simple RESTful network API that leverages the Android content provider system to facilitate seamless custom data integration into the Android platform. It covers a service implementation of that API and a mobile client for the API that communicates directly with user interface components. The chapter ends by summarizing advantages of deploying applications around an architecture that uses this technology. The next chapter digs into writing some real applications using this system.

INTRODUCING WEBDATA AND PROJECT MIGRATE

The *WebData API* and an open source implementation of it called, project *Migrate* provide a solution in this space. These technologies relieve Android developers from the need to write their own SQL tables, create their own synchronized and RESTful protocol, and integrate with the Android view components in a way that is resilient to all of the problems described in this and previous chapters. At the time of writing of this book, Migrate and WebData represent a fledgling open source effort. Consequently, you should expect to see significant changes in the project in the coming months. The Migrate feature set currently just puts "meat on the bones" of a compelling set of ideas and in terms of features that can make this system convenient for developers, the project has room to grow. For this reason, this chapter delves into both the existing Migrate implementation and important future enhancements for the project.

> **NOTE** *You can find more information about the Migrate project, including future architectural directions, on the following github wiki:*
>
> ```
> https://github.com/wileyenterpriseandroid/migrate/wiki
> ```

How Project Migrate Works

We've focused on the third pattern from Chapter 5, content providers used with sync adapters, and created a specific RESTful protocol that supports robust Android network communication for custom data with synchronization support. The Migrate project provides a generic data binding framework that links standard Android UIs to backend service persistence on a remote host. The API is geared toward a persistent key/value interface like that of `android.content.Cursor` that enables WebData service implementations to easily leverage web-scale databases like DataStore, MongoDb, DynamoDb, etc.

With WebData, developers use a schema format to define custom data in a backend service. The Migrate client, an Android-based content provider and sync adapter, can synchronize this data to a device and bind it into UI components. An Android application UI only needs to communicate with an Android-based API to store and access data (for example, a provider contract). Project Migrate handles the REST (pun intended). The Migrate provider API shares characteristics of built-in Android content providers, like the calendar and contacts providers, but also enables applications to define their own types of data and reuse a generic framework to create data that can serve a diverse range of applications.

The WebData API enables developers to define and synchronize persistent "objects" or map oriented key/value pairs (like JavaScript objects). The Migrate system takes care of persisting and synchronizing changes in these objects between a backend service with scalable storage, and mobile clients using SQLite over time. The API is event oriented, so it fits seamlessly into the network-oriented MVC pattern discussed in Chapter 5.

Figure 9-1 provides an illustration of the Migrate and WebData architecture with an Android client.

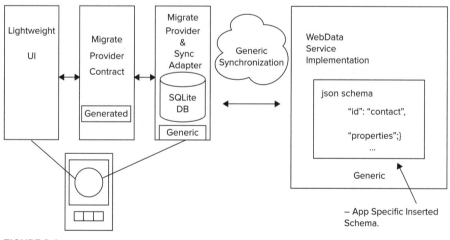

FIGURE 9-1

How Project Migrate Streamlines the Mobile Connection to the Enterprise

The following characteristics of the WebData API and project Migrate drastically reduce the amount of overhead required to create robust Android network applications:

➤ The WebData protocol replaces many transactions that would normally require the development of a custom RESTful web protocol.

➤ Migrate provides a seamless connection from a backend service to the Android UI using Android content providers and cursors.

➤ Migrate also provides streamlined synchronization built into the central Android provider sync adapter framework.

➤ The WebData API provides an event-oriented, reusable, and scalable synchronization protocol.

➤ The Migrate client creates and manages SQL tables on behalf of client applications.

➤ The Migrate service maintains a managed data connection that supports service managed data evolution.

➤ Developers do not need to "know" the correct way to program the handset and service — the Migrate framework enforces correct programming techniques (for example, correct synchronization, proper use of the UI event thread, and efficient network programming).

➤ Migrate supports a transparent and flexible data paging scheme for efficient use of system resources.

➤ Migrate enables support for UI component validation that leverages the same schema that defines data.

The WebData API in Detail

The WebData API reuses standard web services concepts wherever possible in order to permit as wide a range for integration as possible (we currently support an Android client, foresee an iPhone client, and may eventually provide HTML5 integration). The API stipulates a serialization format based on JSON, which is both widely deployed and efficient, and on JSON schema, a simple object schema format. The API also requires RESTful URL-based protocol requests. Here's a complete list of the components of the WebData API specification:

➤ Schema-based definition of objects to define the structure of objects (for creation of SQLite tables)

➤ A RESTful request protocol for modifying and transmitting objects

➤ An object serialization format based on JSON; see:

```
http://en.wikipedia.org/wiki/Json
http://en.wikipedia.org/wiki/Json#Schema
```

➤ Paging parameters that enable client- and server-side specification of the size of data "windows" that clients will use to transmit collections of data

➤ An integrated synchronization scheme

➤ A notification system that enables event-based interaction between a WebData instance and mobile clients to support MVC-style client architectures

➤ Application of schema data for user interface component validation

The next sections provide detailed descriptions of relevant aspects of the WebData API protocol. As you read, keep in mind that the Migrate WebData client API relies on the standard content provider API CRUD operations and sync adapter synchronization to access and update WebData objects.

The following explanations of protocol operations only serve as an overview for developers who want to understand the details of the Migrate client and synchronization protocol. In explicit terms, the Migrate client directly uses these operations; UI developers do not. Note also that we have structured the design of protocol operations to preserve the standard sequence of the built-in providers — the CRUD operations operate on local SQLite state, and the synchronization operation is the only time that the provider communicates with the backend service.

The WebData API RESTful Protocol

The WebData API specifies a REST-based synchronization protocol. The API revolves around schema that define data, REST operations that modify persistent objects, and a synchronization system that uses those operations to keep data consistent between a service and multiple clients.

Using Schema to Define Data

Before a client can use a WebData service to store domain objects, the service must have schema information that defines those objects. WebData uses JSON schema, http://json-schema.org/, as an object schema format, and a WebData JSON envelope to support synchronization. JSON schema is an extremely simple object definition language that supports the declaration of an array of domain objects with corresponding <key, type> properties that define fields of those objects.

Applications that need to define new schema, simply POST JSON schema to WebData service instances. The POSTing entity will typically be a backend service itself, rather than a mobile client. Using a third party program to define schema allows the schema to change in backward-compatible ways (for example, fields used by clients are not removed, and so forth) after an application is deployed.

> **NOTE** *It's a general architectural theme of Migrate to enable post-deployment configuration of handset applications.*

The schema in Listing 9-1 defines a domain object for a contact usable in a hypothetical contacts application. To define this contact type, you'll need a utility that POSTs the schema and Sync envelope into the following WebData service URL:

```
http://host:port/contacts/scheme/com.enterpriseandroid.webDataContacts.dataModel
.Contact
```

Figure 9-2 shows a web application posting a schema into a WebData service implementation. After the web app POSTs this schema, clients can read and write objects with fields that conform to the schema.

The schema payload includes the synchronization envelope and the schema itself. Listing 9-1 shows the contact POST.

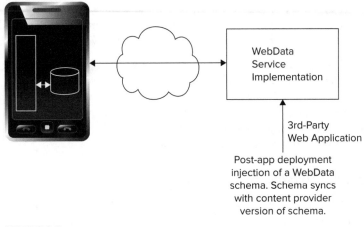

WebData
Service
Implementation

3rd-Party
Web Application

Post-app deployment
injection of a WebData
schema. Schema syncs
with content provider
version of schema.

FIGURE 9-2

LISTING 9-1: A WebData schema creation POST payload

```
1 POST\
    http://host:port/context/schema/com.enterpriseandroid.webDataContacts.Contact
2 {
3      "wd_version":1,
4      "wd_id":"com.enterpriseandroid.webDataContacts.Contact",
5      "wd_classname":"com.migrate.webData.model.PersistentSchema",
6      "wd_namespace":"__schema",
7      "wd_deleted":false,
8      "wd_status":0
9      "jsonSchema":{
10         "properties":{
11             "status":{
12                 "type":"string"
13             },
14             "lastname":{
15                 "type":"string"
16             },
17             "email":{
18                 "type":"string"
19             },
20             "age":{
21                 "type":"integer"
22             },
23             "birthDate":{
24                 "type":"integer"
25             },
26             "phoneNumber":{
27                 "type":"string"
28             },
29             "wd_id":{
30                 "required":true,
31                 "type":"string"
32             },
33             "firstname":{
```

```
34                    "type":"string"
35                },
36                "wd_namespace":{
37                    "type":"string"
38                },
39                "wd_classname":{
40                    "type":"string"
41                },
42                "wd_updateTime":{
43                    "required":true,
44                    "type":"long"
45                },
46                "wd_version":{
47                    "required":true,
48                    "type":"integer"
49                },
50                "wd_deleted":{
51                    "required":true,
52                    "type":"integer"
53                },
54            },
55        "type":"object"
56        },
57 }
```

We want to take a minute to point out some interesting details about this code:

➤ **Lines 3-8** — Specify envelope information that enables synchronization of the schema itself whenever the POSTing application needs to modify the schema to support new versions of the application. The fields work as follows:

  ➤ wd_id — Defines the JSON schema ID that the Migrate project uses as the name of the domain object in reverse domain name format. This name can be used to create names of tables for client or service SQL storage.

  ➤ This is the first version of the schema, so the value of wd_version: is 1; the version will increment on subsequent POSTs to this URL.

  ➤ The wd_namespace field specifies that this payload pertains to " __schema" and not to " __data".

  ➤ The wd_deleted field indicates that this schema has not been deleted.

➤ **Line 9** — Starts the listing of JSON that conforms to the JSON schema specification. The JSON schema is the largest part of the schema payload — it defines the typed fields of each WebData object.

➤ **Lines 29-53** — Show the definition of fields that Migrate requires in the domain object itself to enable synchronization in instances of the type — the WebData fields will be part of the data object itself. Migrate won't directly show these fields to UI code; they assist with internal bookkeeping.

➤ **Lines 20-22** — A declaration of a domain field, age. The declaration has a type of integer, and note that type is contained in a map of its own — thus allowing the possibility of other metadata associated with the age field, such as UI validation information (for example, the format of the field, if the field is required, etc.).

Referencing Data

WebData supports both CRUD and Sync based access to schema and domain data. For example, the following URI format provides access to contact objects with fields defined by the schema in the previous section:

```
http://host:port/contacts/classes/com.enterpriseandroid.webDataContacts.api.
Contact/{id}
```

The general form of WebData data URIs follows:

```
http://host:port/context/classes/{class}/{id}
```

where `class` denotes the schema id of the requested object, and `id` indicates the UUID of the object. GET, PUT, POST, and DELETE operations on URIs like the one shown here have the standard RESTful effect — POST creates an object, PUT updates it, GET returns it, and DELETE removes the object. Requests select specific object instances using the UUID. The next few code listings show significant example protocol requests, to give you a sense of how WebData works.

Listing 9-2 shows an example POST payload that creates a new contact instance.

LISTING 9-2: An example domain object POST request

```
1 POST\
  http://host:port/context/classes/com.enterpriseandroid.webdataContacts.Contact/\
  b83296c4-2bdb-438e-a789-57536431026c
2
3 {
4       "wd_version":1,
5       "wd_namespace":"__data",
6       "wd_deleted":0,
7       "firstname":"John",
8       "lastname":"Smith",
9       "birthDate":136194847583,
10      "email":"johnSmith4321@yahoo.com",
11      "age":23,
12      "phoneNumber":"978-123-4567",
13      "status":"some status",
14 }
```

This POST creates a new WebData object with data and envelope fields described as follows:

➤ **Line 1** — Specifies the complete RESTful URL for the object, including a client created UUID that allows the WebData service to create new data, or correlate the POST with pre-existing persistent storage. The class, or type of the object is `com.enterpriseandroid.webdataContacts.Contact`.

➤ **Line 4-6** — WebData synchronization support fields:

   ➤ On creation, the WebData object version is 1.

   ➤ The `wd_namespace` is "`__data`", since this is object information, not schema related.

   ➤ The object is new and not deleted, `wd_deleted` is 0.

➤ **Line 7-12** — Actual data field values for the POSTed object.

Listing 9-3 shows a WebData GET request for the object posted in Listing 9-2. Such a request would return a JSON-formatted WebData object, as listed.

LISTING 9-3: An example WebData GET response

```
1  GET
http://host:port/context/classes/com.enterpriseandroid.webDataContacts.Contact/\
    b83296c4-2bdb-438e-a789-57536431026c
2  {
3       "wd_id":"b83296c4-2bdb-438e-a789-57536431026c",
4       "wd_version":1,
5       "wd_classname":"com.enterpriseandroid.webDataContacts.Contact",
6       "wd_namespace":"__data",
7       "wd_updateTime":1369022907831,
8       "wd_deleted":0
9       "firstname":"John",
10      "lastname":"Smith",
11      "birthDate":136194847583,
12      "email":"johnSmith4321@yahoo.com",
13      "age":23,
14      "phoneNumber":"978-123-4567",
15      "status":"some status",
16 }
```

The response retrieves the formerly POSTed contact object. The following highlights the lines that should catch your interest:

➤ **Line 1** — The URI is the same as that in Listing 9-2, but the operation is GET.

➤ **Lines 3-8** — Contain the WebData envelope information.

➤ **Lines 9-14** — Show the same contact data as that from Listing 9-2.

Searching

The WebData API supports CRUD-based queries; however, the typical usage pattern for Migrate at the time of writing of this book is to rely on synchronization and local content provider operations. A future edition of this book may cover more detail on Migrate CRUD operations, such as remote search. For now, Migrate relies on the ContentProvider.query method to enable searching for data in content provider managed SQLite tables.

Notifications

WebData specifies support for push messaging notification to prevent clients from needing to poll a WebData implementation service for data changes. The WebData payload for push messages merely contains a list of schema identifiers that indicate the data that has changed since the last client update. Once the client has received this list from the push notification, it should engage in the synchronization protocol outlined in the next section for each modified schema identifier. Listing 9-4 shows an example WebData schema modification notification, where lines 4 and 5 list the schema ids for which data has changed.

LISTING 9-4: An example WebData schema modification notification

```
1 {
2     "modified":
3         [
4             "com.enterpriseandroid.webDataContacts.Contact",
5             "com.enterpriseandroid.webDataAutomobile.Automobile"
6         ]
7 }
```

Synchronization

Data travels or "migrates" between a WebData client and a WebData service instance during a synchronization operation. Such operations are central to the concept of the WebData API. These exchanges of data allow clients to merge local changes with remote changes in a service host, and also represent the mode of transport of the objects between the client and the service. The WebData API specifies synchronization support according to the following protocol:

1. WebData clients persistently maintain a timestamp of the last synchronization operation with a particular service host. The synchronization time is recorded on the service host, and then passed to clients at synchronization time.

2. During any synchronization operation between a WebData client and a service, the client will first send changes it has made locally since it last updated with the service, to the service host. The client should maintain a "dirty" flag to know which elements it has changed. The service host will attempt to resolve the client's changes against any changes that may have taken place in the service since the last update.

3. When the service is ready, it will send back to the client all changes that took place since the client's last update. The client updates its timestamp from the service accordingly to reflect that the synchronization operation has completed successfully.

4. Synchronization operations can originate from the client (a "pull" or "poll") or from the service host (a "push"). The WebData content provider makes use of local Android network APIs to poll the service. Push operations will use one of several commercially available mobile push services such as Google Cloud Message for Android, Apple Push Technology, or a commercially available push technology aggregator.

5. If a client application knows that it needs new data, it can request a sync operation to take place. Application developers should use such requests judiciously given that polling-based applications can place a great strain on network resources.

Conflict Resolution

Because the WebData API permits concurrent changes on multiple devices, it's possible for conflicts to arise between data modifications from different sources. The WebData API specifies the transmission of version information to enable the resolution of versioning conflicts when data is modified between the backend service and multiple clients. WebData objects must always contain a version field that is incremented every time the client or service succeeds in changing a given object. When a client updates an object, the server checks the version against the one stored on the server. The update operation succeeds only when the version numbers match.

WebData implementations should resolve conflicts as follows:

➤ The service first attempts to resolve changes sent from clients.

➤ The service sends conflicts it cannot resolve to the client for resolution.

➤ A client can request all conflicts since the last synchronization.

➤ The Migrate client attempts to resolve the conflicts. If the Migrate client cannot resolve a change automatically, the client delegates to the end user to resolve it.

➤ If a client is unable to resolve the conflict, the server keeps its own version of the data and ignores the version of the data sent by the client.

These operations should look similar to the ones outlined in Chapter 6, which intentionally built a foundation for WebData synchronization as discussed earlier in this chapter.

An Example Synchronization and Conflict Resolution Scenario

To help you understand how synchronization and conflict resolution works in practice, we've created a simple scenario in which:

1. A client makes changes to a contact object.

2. The server has a change to the same contact, creating a conflict for id `a7329678-4bdc-536a-b234-78236431026a`.

3. A different client has also added a new contact to the service (not in conflict).

The client will need to sync the server contact that is not in conflict (that is, make its own copy locally) and will need to resolve differences between its own version of the conflicted contact and the server's version. Listings 9-5, 9-6, and 9-7 show these changes and Figure 9-3 illustrates the interaction. Changes are flowing in and out of the local SQLite cache on the client. Changes from the client and service are selected based on timestamp, similar to what you saw in Chapter 6.

The scenario begins with Listing 9-5, when a client initiates a sync request.

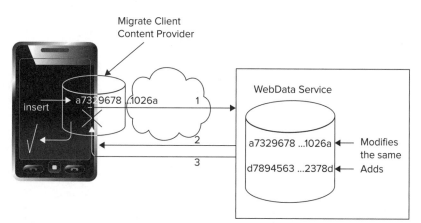

Changes in steps 1 and 2 conflict. The server sends its own non-conflicting change, and then asks the client to resolve the conflict.

FIGURE 9-3

> **LISTING 9-5: A client initiates sync with objects changed since last sync time**

```
1  POST http://host:port/migrate/context/classes/\
   com.enterpriseAndroid.webDataContacts.dataModel.Contact?syncTime=13423220558251
2
3  {
4      "modified":[
5          {
6              "firstname":"Mark",
7              "lastname":"Johnson",
8              "birthDate":135579679583,
9              "email":"mj234@yahoo.com",
10             "age":43,
11             "phoneNumber":"781-201-4567",
12             "status":"some status",
13             "wd_id":"a7329678-4bdc-536a-b234-78236431026a",
14             "wd_version":1,
15             "wd_classname":"com.enterpriseandroid.webDataContacts.Contact",
16             "wd_namespace":"__data",
17             "wd_updateTime":1369010208846,
18             "wd_deleted":0
19         }
20     ],
21     "resolved" : []
22  }
```

The sync request shows the client has changed a contact "Mark Johnson". The following points explain the payload:

➤ **Line 1** — Shows a POST from a Migrate client to sync changes it has made since the last time it sync'ed, syncTime. The client has made one change provided in the modified list, and has no conflict resolutions to send; the resolved list is empty.

➤ **Lines 6, 7** — The modified contact name is "Mark Johnson."

➤ **Line 13** — Shows the unique identifier for this contact object.

➤ **Line 14** — This is still version 1 of the contact object. It will be up to the server to increment the version if it accepts the change.

The service responds to the sync request with the payload in Listing 9-6.

> **LISTING 9-6: The service response — the service has changed two contacts and one modification has resulted in a conflict**

```
1  {
2      "syncTime":13690102023423,
3      "modified":[
4          {
5              "firstname":"Andrew",
6              "lastname":"Smith",
7              "birthDate":135579679583,
8              "email":"asmith@gmail.com",
```

```
 9                  "age":12,
10                  "phoneNumber":"781-201-4567",
11                  "status":"some status",
12                  "wd_id":"d7894563-9edf-378w-u907-94675342378d",
13                  "wd_version":1,
14                  "wd_classname":"com.enterpriseandroid.webDataContacts.Contact",
15                  "wd_namespace":"__data",
16                  "wd_updateTime":1369010208846,
17                  "wd_deleted":0
18              }
19      ],
20      "conflict":[
21          {
22                  "firstname":"Mark",
23                  "lastname":"Johnson",
24                  "birthDate":135579679583,
25                  "email":"mj234@gmail.com",
26                  "age":43,
27                  "phoneNumber":"781-223-1234",
28                  "status":"some status",
29                  "wd_id":"a7329678-4bdc-536a-b234-78236431026a",
30                  "wd_version":2,
31                  "wd_classname":"com.enterpriseandroid.webDataContacts.Contact",
32                  "wd_namespace":"__data",
33                  "wd_updateTime":1369010208846,
34                  "wd_deleted":0
35          }
36      ]
37 }
```

The server response contains a new contact for "Andrew Smith" that the client can simply add locally. However, the contact with an id "a7329678-4bdc-536a-b234-78236431026a" for "Mark Johnson" is in conflict. The version of this contact from Listing 9-5 has a phone number of 781-201-4567, and the server has a version of the contact with phone number 781-223-1234. The Migrate client will call back to the relevant Android UI to ask the application user to pick the right phone number. Points to note in the payload include:

➤ **Line 2** — The server sends the time of sync, that the client will store persistently. The client will send this sync time the next time it syncs, so the server can send back any changes the client has missed in the interim.

➤ **Lines 10, 27** — As noted, the phone number for "Mark Johnson" is changed to different values by both the client and backend.

➤ **Line 30** — Since the server already accepted a change for "Mark Johnson" the value of wd_version is now 2.

To resolve the conflict in the service, the client needs to POST the resolved object back with the new version in another sync request as follows (Listing 9-7).

LISTING 9-7: The client resolves the conflicting phone number

```
1 POST \
    http://host:port/migrate/contact/classes/\
    com.enterpriseAndroid.webDataContacts.Contact?syncTime=1342322066851
2 {
3       "modified":[],
4       "resolved":[
5           {
6               "firstname":"Mark",
7               "lastname":"Johnson",
8               "birthDate":135579679583,
9               "email":"mj234@gmail.com",
10              "age":43,
11              "phoneNumber":"781-223-1234",
12              "status":"some status",
13              "wd_id":"a7329678-4bdc-536a-b234-78236431026a",
14              "wd_version":2,
15              "wd_classname":"com.enterpriseandroid.webDataContacts.Contact",
16              "wd_namespace":"__data",
17              "wd_updateTime":1369010208846,
18              "wd_deleted":0
19          }
20      ]
21}
```

With the sync request in Listing 9-7, the client has selected the desired phone number on line 11, and used the same version as was sent to it as a conflict from the service, on line 14. The service will see that this is a resolution request, from line 4, and apply the change from the client to increment the object to version 3, assuming no other conflicting changes happen in the interim — which demonstrates optimistic concurrency control as applied to WebData.

Now that you understand WebData synchronization, it's time to take a look at some other features.

Polling

Polling for changes in data goes somewhat against the grain of the design of the WebData API. In the absence of a push notification system, a WebData client should periodically invoke synchronization to ensure data stays current for a particular schema identifier. In Android, polling should be invoked using the Android sync adapter API `ContentResolver.requestSync`.

Paging

The WebData API provides parameters for paging that enable a client to download subsets of results when a query would return a large number of objects. The client can use these paging controls to conserve memory and storage space as needed. The following URL query parameters provide paging controls to a WebData client:

➤ `maxSize` — Specifies the maximum number of results that should be present in the response to a given query

➤ `startPosition` — Specifies the start position in a given query

The following GET request shows an example query with paging parameters:

```
GET http://host:port/context/classes/{classname}?startPosition=30&maxSize=10
```

The WebData Specification

Now that you've learned a bit about the components of the WebData API, it's a good time to look at the complete WebData specification, which is available at the following location:

```
https://github.com/wileyenterpriseandroid/migrate/wiki/WebData
```

PROJECT MIGRATE IN DETAIL

The project Migrate client currently provides a complete implementation of the WebData API and supports an API for UI integration on the Android platform. Future versions of Migrate may provide iPhone and Objective C support, and potentially support for JavaScript. However, this book focuses on Migrate support for Android. As of the time of writing of this book, the Migrate open source project supports a working Android client implementation.

The Migrate Project Android WebData Client

The Migrate project supports an Android client that leverages the Android content provider framework. Although the WebData API may be useful on IOS and on other platforms, it's not an exaggeration to say that the API was designed to take advantage of the Android content provider infrastructure. Recall that with project Migrate, developers can create their own synchronized data services that offer the convenience of the built-in Android content providers, but allow application-defined data types. The project Migrate Android client uses the service schema definition to create local SQLite tables as needed to store synchronization data. The client also uses the WebData versioning protocol to update data and schema information as directed by the WebData service host.

Project Migrate Android Features

The bulk of the Migrate WebData client on Android resides inside a custom Android content provider. This provider supports the following features that help developers manage data for Android mobile applications:

➤ **Semantics similar to the built-in providers** — The Migrate project maintains the goal of keeping the semantics of its provider as similar to the built-in Android content providers as possible. In most cases, developers use the Migrate content provider just as they use the built-in content providers, using URIs, Cursors, and ContentObservers to track data.

➤ **Integrated synchronization** — When an application modifies local Migrate content provider data, the Migrate client leverages the Android synchronization system to upload the changes to the Migrate backend service. Specifically, the Migrate client uses a custom synchronization adapter, as described in Chapter 5, to initiate synchronization. Developers can use the standard android.content.SyncStatusObserver to check on synchronization operations in progress.

As mentioned, there are a couple of ways in which the Migrate content provider differs from the built-in providers, specifically:

➤ **Access to WebData schema** — The Migrate content provider API provides access to the data schema using a simple content provider URI.

➤ **Service-side configurability** — It's possible to use Migrate schema to evolve a client SQLite database schema in a deployed Migrate-based application. By invoking versioned PUTs of a Migrate schema, it's possible for a web app to drive schema evolution on a Migrate service, and consequently when synchronization happens, also on Migrate clients. When the Migrate client updates schema from the service, it will automatically update SQL tables to reflect the changed schema.

Synchronization

The project Migrate Android client uses the WebData synchronization protocol to maintain a local persistent SQLite-based data cache that tracks changes from the client and service, updating and replacing elements that change in the service host. The Migrate WebData Android client implements the WebData synchronization protocol using a sync adapter implementation, using the standard `onPerformSync` method, as shown in the pseudo-code in Listing 9-8:

LISTING 9-8: Illustrating sync from onPerformSync

```
1 onPerformSync(Account account, Bundle extras, String authority,
2      ContentProviderClient provider, SyncResult syncResult)
3 {
4   // The Migrate client synchronizes with its service host
5   Map serverData =
6       WebDataClient.syncData(className, values, lastUpdateTime);
7   . . .
8 }
```

Searching

A client that needs to query Migrate data should just use the standard `ContentProvider.query` method.

Notification

The Migrate client implementation can use Google Cloud messaging for Android to avoid polling the Migrate service. In the absence of push notification support, the Migrate client can use a polling system that operates out of band of the normal WebData synchronization protocol. The implementation can periodically invoke a WebData synchronization operation.

Google has made documentation available on its website:

```
http://developer.android.com/google/gcm/index.html
```

THE WEBDATA CONTENT PROVIDER ANDROID API

Now that you have seen the features offered in the Migrate client and its content provider, this section explains how to access Migrate data in an Android UI. Currently, the Migrate project supports a slightly modified version of the API style used by the built-in Android content providers.

Android Built-In Provider APIs

The APIs of built-in Android content providers each revolve around a contract class, like the one for the contacts provider, ContactsContract:

> http://developer.android.com/reference/android/provider/ContactsContract.html

The central purpose of the Android built-in content provider APIs is to host constant fields in classes like ContactsContract.Email.DATA, which can be used to index the Cursor results of invoking a query method as follows:

```
Cursor email = ContentResolver.query();
final Cursor email = … // use of LoaderManager to access an email query cursor
final int contactEmailColumnIndex = email.getColumnIndex(Email.DATA);
String emailData = email.getString(contactEmailColumnIndex);
```

The last two lines show the indexing of a cursor to obtain its e-mail data.

These fields — in combination with content provider URIs as discussed in Chapter 4 — compose the APIs that developers use to access the Android contacts data and that of other built-in providers. These column classes (ContactsContract.Email, ContactsContract.Settings, ContactsContract.StatusUpdates, and so on) map to SQLite database tables that provide content provider persistence. This API approach relies on a set of hard-coded constants to access the central Android key/value-oriented data structure, Cursor. These constants must be "well known" to the application developer in order to load cursor data.

The Migrate Provider API

The Migrate provider API uses the same style of contract API as discussed in the previous section; however, the usage model has a significant difference: Migrate provides a utility in its SDK that *generates* the code for a contract class given a service POJO with Migrate annotations as input. The same tool also creates a WebData schema for POSTing to a WebData service instance. The next chapter demonstrates how this works in a detailed example.

SUMMARY

This chapter has covered the WebData protocol and its application in the Migrate Android open source project. Migrate has significant potential for Enterprise Android application development. Much of this book has built a foundation in technical understanding that enables you to appreciate the benefits of using Migrate to bridge the gap between enterprise Android applications and scalable cloud infrastructure.

Now that you have learned about the operation of the WebData API, the Migrate backend service, and the Migrate Android client, the chapter concludes with a discussion of the benefits of deploying a mobile infrastructure based on a WebData style architecture.

Service-Side Advantages

The WebData API encourages efficient network communication that reduces service load and enhances application protocols in the following ways:

➤ WebData includes a push-oriented lightweight synchronization protocol out of the box. Pushing data reduces the need to poll to detect service-side data changes, thus reducing service load.

➤ WebData and Migrate enforces a data transmission format based on JSON and JSON schema. This required structure enables you to create service management tools that can interpret, manage, and create analytics for applications that use the WebData API.

➤ The WebData protocol can stand as a generic replacement for many custom-developed RESTful protocols.

➤ Clients maintain an intelligent cache that precludes the need for redundant requests to retrieve data, again reducing service load. Clients request new data only when notified that their current set is out of date.

➤ Clients use paging size and have the opportunity to select only the data that they need to see, rather than having to preconfigure a one-size-fits-all data window. Clients only request data they need, which also reduces service load.

➤ It's easy to implement the key/value-oriented WebData API on highly scalable columnar style databases, like DynamoDB or App Engine.

Client Advantages

Properties of WebData and the Migrate client that benefit handset applications include the following:

➤ The Migrate framework has the potential to move applications from the mode of static configuration, which can be changed only at deployment time, to a flexible deployment environment in which a backend service can change the behavior and configuration of a client on the fly. Such flexibility arises from supporting schema that can be pushed and synchronized to clients.

➤ The Migrate client can function as a secure proxy for applications that do not have to request Internet permission.

➤ You will see a decrease in the size and development cost of applications that do not need to reinvent the wheel to access and synchronize network data with local SQLite tables.

Now that you've looked at the WebData and Migrate Android APIs in detail, you'll jump into building an actual application with project Migrate in the next chapter.

WebData Applications

WROX.COM CODE DOWNLOADS FOR THIS CHAPTER

Please note that all the code examples in this chapter are available at https://github.com/
wileyenterpriseandroid/Examples.git and as a part of the book's code download
at www.wrox.com on the Download Code tab.

In this chapter you learn about an implementation of the WebData protocol called *Migrate*. The
discussion walks through a single application — the simple Contacts application introduced in
Chapter 5. It then implements the Contacts application on top of the Migrate framework.

Chapter 9 introduced the concept of the WebData API and described Migrate, a generic
content provider that can be used as a backend for a wide variety of applications.
This chapter looks at what an application that uses such a generic provider might look like.
You'll be writing an application similar to the restfulCachingProviderContacts project
from Chapter 5 that uses Migrate instead of its own, private data-synchronization code.

This chapter demonstrates:

➤ Creating a new project using the Migrate tools

➤ Converting an existing project to use the Migrate framework

➤ Installing the Migrate generic content provider on a device and creating an
automatically synchronized account to support it

➤ Running a Migrate-based application

➤ The future of the Migrate platform

> **NOTE** *We are actively engaged in developing Migrate. Although the concepts and structures described in this chapter will endure, the specifics of their implementation may change as the framework grows and matures. Please be sure to use the latest versions of these projects, found in the code repository at the project's website,* `https://github.com/wileyenterpriseandroid`, *or at the* `www.wrox.com` *website at this book's web page. We strongly encourage you to check out and explore the Enterprise Android and Migrate open source repositories provided at this github location.*

THE MIGRATE CLIENT

Chapter 5 described how the adoption of REST changed the architectural focus for distributed APIs from the content that they carry (in APIs like CORBA, RMI, and SOAP) to the medium over which their content is transported: an unreliable network. Chapter 5 also pointed out that Android's internal architecture brings similar concerns into the application. An Android application is subject to interruptions in connectivity, access to the CPU, and even power. Although these interruptions may be of some concern in an application designed for a stationary device (a rack mounted server or even a laptop), they are much less likely to occur. With mobile applications, they are an unavoidable part of life.

Given these constraints, it makes a great deal of sense to pull REST-style access up one level. Instead of using REST at the device boundary — only as a means of accessing remote data — what if, as proposed in Chapter 9, you use REST right on the device? What if you pull the REST proxy — made possible by adopting a REST-style architecture — off the network and put it right into the phone?

In such an architecture, the UI — instead of expecting reliable access to a content-specific network library — simply performs RESTful requests against a local proxy for the network. The UI makes its request to a local service and cannot tell that the service is a proxy for an endpoint that is sometimes unreachable. Whether a given record in the cache is out of date with respect to some external, upstream instance of the same data, is simply a piece of local state information.

There is an additional motivation for this approach that has not yet been discussed. Developers who have built several content providers will have noticed that there are substantial internal similarities among them. The code shown in Chapter 5 is very nearly generic already. Most of the specifics that customize the implementation of the Contacts provider shown in that chapter — the things that specialize it to apply to a database of contacts — have been abstracted out into statically defined constants: column names and Java constants that hold them. At some point, a developer who wants to get some work done will begin to look for ways — perhaps along the lines of Ruby on Rails — to avoid writing these hundreds of lines of boilerplate code for each new application.

These two insights together make a framework that provides REST access to application-specific data through a generic, local, device-wide proxy a very appealing idea, to say the least. The ability to create applications by focusing on powerful acquisition, manipulation, and presentation of data, while leaving the details of robust, enterprise-wide synchronization of that data to automation, could save hundreds of developer hours and avoid hundreds of unpleasant bugs.

Chapter 4 assumed the existence of a content provider and built code that revealed its behavior. This chapter takes the same approach. It assumes the presence of the Migrate SDK — a toolkit that supports building Migrate clients — and, by building code, reveals the contents of the toolkit and the architecture of the Migrate itself.

CREATING A MIGRATE PROJECT

This section begins the exploration of the Migrate WebData framework by converting the simplified Contacts program built in Chapter 5 for use in this context. Because that project is familiar, it is a logical starting point. Because it is very simple, the size and complexity of the converted result will be very instructive in evaluating the basic concepts.

Much of the code will, of course, stay the same. The whole point of the WebData API is to provide a foundation to implement arbitrary UIs.

> **NOTE** *The "zeroth" step to creating a Migrate-based application, of course, is to download the Migrate SDK, which contains a backend Migrate service deployment* (migrate.war), *the Migrate provider proxy* (migrate-client.apk), *and tools for managing Migrate provider contract APIs. The SDK is available as a zip file from the migrate wiki,* https://github.com/wileyenterpriseandroid/migrate/wiki

Step 1: Importing the Project

Start by importing the project $CODE/MigrateContacts into Eclipse (see Figure 10-1), as you did for the clients in Chapter 5. Remember to set up the project for Eclipse first as described in Chapter 5 and in $CODE/MigrateContacts/README. Please keep in mind that the project will not immediately compile — it needs a contract class that you will generate shortly.

Step 2: Enabling the Project as a Migrate Client

To enable this project as a Migrate client you need to add the Migrate client library, migrate-api .jar, from the Migrate SDK, by dragging and dropping it on the libs directory, as shown in Figure 10-2.

> **NOTE** *Note that the window on the left, in Figure 10-2, is a file browser window (an OS X Finder window, to be specific) and that it is on top of an Eclipse window. Dragging files from the file browser and dropping them on Eclipse will copy them from the source (the SDK in this case) into the Eclipse project.*

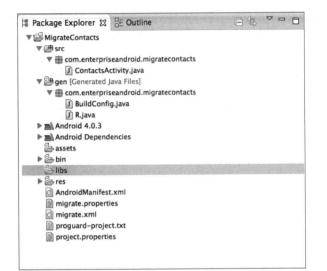

FIGURE 10-1

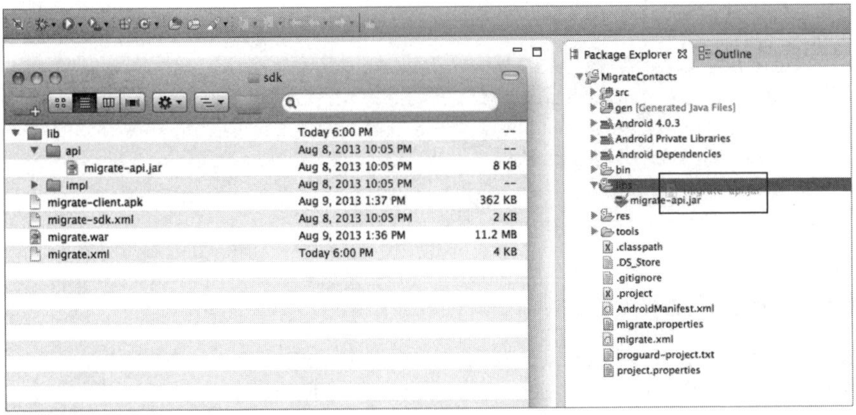

FIGURE 10-2

Step 3: Defining the Information to Be Managed by Migrate

You'll need to define the information that will be managed by Migrate and synchronized with a network backend. Because this data description will be used in multiple places — the UI code in an Android client; the contract and SQLite tables in the Migrate cache; the JSON messages exchanged between the Migrate cache and a Migrate enterprise backend service; and, perhaps, even the SQL DDL for tables in a database supporting that service — it is desirable that it be automatically generated from a single source. The current implementation of the Migrate framework does this by using Java annotations and introspection on a Java class definition — of course, there's no reason not to support different language bindings, or web-based definition systems in the future.

This form of definition makes a great deal of sense in applications that represent data internally as POJOs (plain old Java objects, which are objects that do little but represent data). It was made popular by Java frameworks like XDoclet and Hibernate, and its use continues in App Engine. As you saw in Chapter 6, the ability to generate both network and database representations automatically for a data object from the single definition makes sense as a way of saving time and preventing errors. The obvious choice for that single definition, in a Java application is the representation actually used throughout that application and verified by the Java complier. As you've read, that's the class that represents the data — the POJO.

In an Android program, on the other hand, this particular data-definition object will not likely be used. Throughout this book the discussion has advocated the use of a REST-like style all the way up to the UI. In that style, an Android program is likely to use either `Cursor` or `ContentValues` objects, instead of POJOs, to represent data for the short period of time that it is in flight between a datastore and the screen.

In either of those representations the application code uses, as demonstrated in Chapter 5, a special file, the data contract, to identify a content provider, its virtual tables, and the columns in those tables. As it is currently implemented, Migrate generates that contract automatically by analyzing a data-definition POJO.

The POJO for the MigrateContacts project resides in the following location:

```
$CODE/MigrateContacts/src-schema/com/enterpriseandroid/migratecontacts/
Contact.java
```

You need to build this source file using:

```
cd $CODE/MigrateContacts
ant -f build-schema.xml
```

Note: Once you have built this file, you won't use its output class directly in any Android application; instead, you'll use the Android contract that you generate from it.

Listing 10-1 shows the definition for the Contact data-definition POJO.

LISTING 10-1: The MigrateContacts Contact object

```java
package com.enterpriseandroid.migratecontacts;
import net.migrate.api.annotations.WebDataSchema;

@WebDataSchema(version="1")
public interface Contact {
    public String getFirstname();
    public String getLastname();
    public String getEmail();
    public String getPhoneNumber();
}
```

The `@WebDataSchema` annotation on the interface allows the Migrate contract definition tool to identify it as the target for analysis. Data member names and types are inferred from getter methods and their return types.

Step 4: Generating the Contacts Contract

Now you'll generate the contacts contract. The Migrate contract definition tool is part of the Migrate SDK. At this time it is an ant script named `migrate.xml`. To use it, copy it from the SDK distribution into the root of your project, as shown in Figure 10-3.

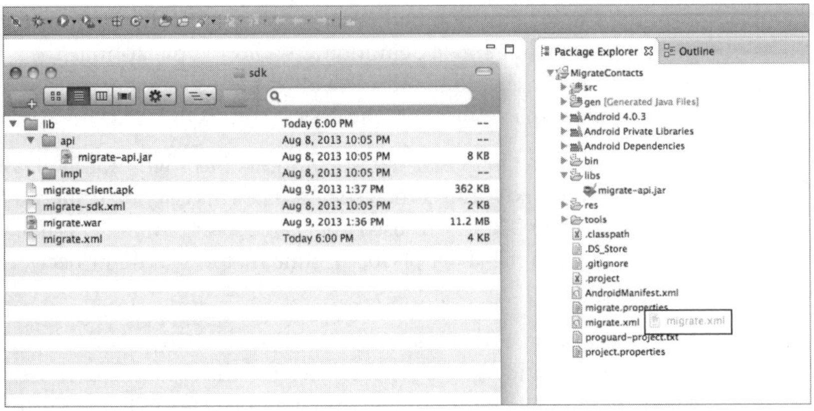

FIGURE 10-3

In order to use the contract definition tool, you must configure it by creating an ant properties file. This properties file will supply the parameters specific to the particular project. The configuration file for this project resides in `$CODE/MigrateContacts/tools/migrate.properties` and is shown in Listing 10-2. Copy this file into place:

```
cp $CODE/MigrateContacts/tools/migrate.properties $CODE/MigrateContacts/
```

LISTING 10-2: Migrate contract definition tool configuration

```
migrate.sdk.root=../../migrate-sdk-beta/
migrate.object=com.enterpriseandroid.migratecontacts.Contact
migrate.class.root=build/classes-schema
migrate.gen.root=gen
migrate.endpoint=http://localhost:8080/migrate
```

The configuration file specifies several things:

➤ `migrate.sdk.root` — The directory containing the Migrate SDK.

➤ `migrate.object` — This is the fully qualified name of the object that will be used as a template for creating the data description. This is the Java interface definition shown in Listing 10-1.

➤ `migrate.class.root` — This is the directory containing a compiled version of the class named in the `migrate.object` property. Recall the earlier instructions regarding building the migrate schema classes — the ant script places the compiled classes here. Be sure that this property points at the root of the directory containing the class file, not the actual directory containing the file. In this case, for instance, the property's value is `build/classes-schema`, not `build/classes-schema/com/enterpriseandroid/migratecontacts`.

➤ `migrate.gen.root` — This is the root of the file tree into which the Migrate tool will put the generated contract file. This example uses the `gen` directory, the same directory that the Android toolkit uses for its generated files. Although this has a certain elegance, remember that cleaning the project from Eclipse will delete the file. Unlike the files that are automatically generated by the ADK, files generated by the Migrate tool will not be recreated until the tool runs again. Again, the full path to the resulting generated file, as is standard for Java source files, will mirror the fully qualified name of the class it contains. In this case, for instance, the complete pathname for the contract class generated by the Migrate tool is .../ `gen/com/enterpriseandroid/migratecontacts/ContactContract.java`.

➤ `migrate.endpoint` — This is the URL for the Migrate service with which the client will synchronize data. Subsequent sections will demonstrate using the Migrate tool to send a copy of the data descriptor it generates to this endpoint.

Developers who are familiar with ant will realize that it is possible to specify or override any of these definitions from the command line. As intrinsic properties of the project, however, it makes a lot of sense to put them in a file, where they can be managed with a version control system.

Once you have specified the tool parameters, run the tool to generate the contract file. From Eclipse, select the ant build file, `migrate.xml`, and run it as an external tool, as shown in Figure 10-4, making sure to select the first target.

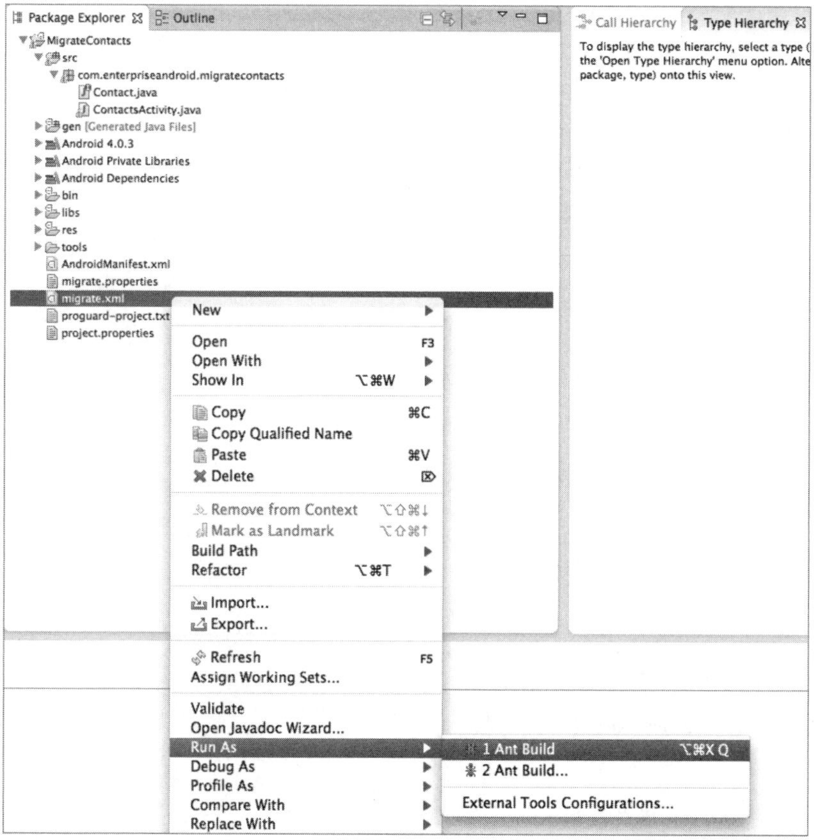

FIGURE 10-4

The tool should complete successfully, producing the `ContactContract` class in the `gen` directory. You may have to refresh the project to see it; it's shown in Figure 10-5. The MigrateContacts project code should now compile sucessfully, and the errors should go away in Eclipse. Note though, you should not try to run the project yet.

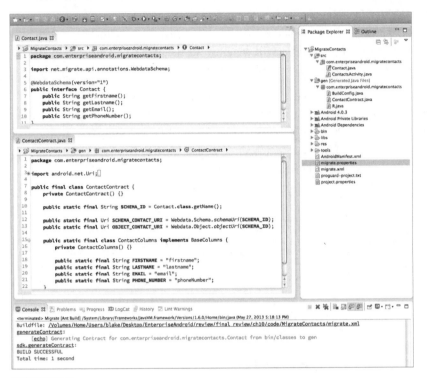

FIGURE 10-5

Listing 10-3 examines the newly generated contract.

LISTING 10-3: The SDK-generated contract

```
/* Generated Source Code - Do not Edit! */
package com.enterpriseandroid.migratecontacts;

import android.net.Uri;
import android.provider.BaseColumns;
import net.migrate.api.WebData;

public final class ContactContract {
    private ContactContract() {}

    public static final String SCHEMA_ID = com.enterpriseandroid.migratecontacts.Contact

    public static final Uri SCHEMA_CONTACT_URI = WebData.Schema.schemaUri(SCHEMA_ID);
    public static final Uri OBJECT_CONTACT_URI = WebData.Object.objectUri(SCHEMA_ID);

    public static final class ContactColumns implements BaseColumns {
```

```
        private Columns() {}

        public static final String FIRSTNAME = "firstname";
        public static final String LASTNAME = "lastname";
        public static final String EMAIL = "email";
        public static final String PHONE_NUMBER = "phoneNumber";
    }
}
```

There are a couple of things to consider here. Certainly there are definitions for column names, exactly as expected. However, in addition, note the definition, early in the file, of a schema ID. This ID identifies to Migrate which of the many datastores Migrate manages that the given application wishes to use.

Finally — and perhaps this is a surprise — notice that there are two URIs in the contract. The first, the schema URI, is the URI for the metatable. The metatable holds data about the datasets that Migrate manages. An application must be able to discover the state of the dataset it intends to use. It will use the row in the metatable identified by the schema ID to find that state. This process is discussed in the next section.

The second URI — the object URI — is for the actual contact data. Like the schema URI, this URI's authority section also belongs to Migrate. The virtual table it identifies, however, will contain the contact data.

At this point, the Migrate framework has been fully integrated into the MigrateContacts project. All that remains is to write the code that uses it.

INTERFACING WITH THE MIGRATE REST PROXY

Nearly all of the code that comprises the MigrateContacts project is taken directly from its Chapter 5 predecessor, restfulCachingProviderContacts. Notice, on the other hand, that half of the classes and more than half of the code have not been copied to the new project: They've been replaced by the Migrate framework and left behind. Only the UI components of the, admittedly simple, application are still needed. So far, so good!

There is one new class that you can find in the migrate-client source repository, SchemaManager. This class replaces the entire data and service sections from the Chapter 5 version of the application. It is instructive to walk through it in order to understand how it works.

The main problem that the client application must solve is very similar to that addressed by SQLiteOpenHelper: the initialization problem. Recall from Chapter 3 that an application newly installed on a device must initialize any SQLite databases that it needs before they are used for the first time. It accomplishes this by requesting instances of the open database exclusively from a subclass of SQLiteOpenHelper. The helper instance determines if the database exists. If getWritableDatabase is called ten million times during the installed life of an application, SQLiteOpenHelper simply returns the cached, open database for all but one of those calls. That single first time it is called, though, it finds that the database does not exist (or needs an update). Since the helper contains the initialization code for the database, it can create or update it before it returns. The calling code is none the wiser.

In a similar manner, the Migrate content provider must initialize its copy of any given schema the first time it encounters it, before it can provide data from that schema to its clients. This initialization is not a request for data from the schema. Instead it is a meta request, asking Migrate to initialize the schema.

Recall from Chapter 3 the oblique process of obtaining a cursor by using the loader manager. When the code needs a cursor, instead of simply asking for it, it undertakes a three-step process. First it initializes the loader manager. Next, it responds to a callback from the manager to `onCreateLoader` by creating an instance of a loader. Finally, when the loader manager runs the loader, it receives the resulting cursor in a callback to `onLoadFinished`.

When using the Migrate framework these two processes are combined: First, the Migrate framework must be initialized — using a loader, incidentally. Then once it is initialized, you can query it — using another loader — for the needed data. You'll explore this in the context of the sample project. `ContactsActivity` needs to display a list of all contacts. It will ask Migrate, a generic content provider, for a cursor, just as the previous version made the same request of an internal content provider in the original, pre-Migrate implementation. In that original implementation, though, `SQLiteOpenHelper` invisibly managed initialization when the application was newly installed and the database did not yet exist.

The new Migrate-based version of the program, however, must handle the analogous case, the case in which the Migrate framework has not yet created a table for the contacts data. Listing 10-4 contains the code for the `SchemaManager` class.

LISTING 10-4: The schema manager

```
 1 public class SchemaManager extends ContentObserver
 2     implements LoaderManager.LoaderCallbacks<Cursor>
 3 {
 4     public static interface SchemaLoaderListener { void onSchemaLoaded(); }
 5
 6     private static boolean ready;
 7
 8
 9     private final int loaderId = new Random().nextInt();
10     private final Uri uri;
11     private final String user;
12     private final String schema;
13
14     final Activity ctxt;
15     final SchemaLoaderListener listener;
16
17     public SchemaManager(
18         Activity ctxt,
19         String schema,
20         Uri uri,
21         String user,
22         SchemaLoaderListener listener)
23     {
24         super(new Handler());
25         this.ctxt = ctxt;
```

```
26          this.schema = schema;
27          this.uri = uri;
28          this.user = user;
29          this.listener = listener;
30      }
31
32      public void initSchema() {
33          if (ready) { listener.onSchemaLoaded(); }
34          else { ctxt.getLoaderManager().initLoader(loaderId, null, this); }
35      }
36
37      @Override
38      public boolean deliverSelfNotifications() { return true; }
39
40      @Override
41      public void onChange(boolean selfChange) {
42          ctxt.getLoaderManager().restartLoader(loaderId, null, this);
43      }
44
45      @Override
46      public Loader<Cursor> onCreateLoader(int id, Bundle args) {
47          return new CursorLoader(
48              ctxt,
49              uri,
50              new String[] { WebData.Schema.STATUS },
51              WebData.Schema.SCHEMA_ID + "=?",
52              new String[] { schema },
53              null);
54      }
55
56      @Override
57      public void onLoadFinished(Loader<Cursor> loader, Cursor data) {
58          if (schemaReady(data)) { listener.onSchemaLoaded(); }
59          else {
60              data.registerContentObserver(this);
61              startSync();
62          }
63      }
64
65      @Override
66      public void onLoaderReset(Loader<Cursor> arg0) { }
67
68      private boolean schemaReady(Cursor data) {
69          ready = data.moveToFirst()
70              && (WebData.Schema.STATUS_ACTIVE
71                  == data.getInt(data.getColumnIndex(WebData.Schema.STATUS)));
72          return ready;
73      }
74
75      private void startSync() {
76          ContentResolver.requestSync(
77              new Account(user, WebData.ACCOUNT_TYPE),
78              WebData.AUTHORITY,
79              new Bundle());
80      }
81 }
```

Examine this code by walking the path of execution. In order to ensure that Migrate has loaded the necessary schema — and then obtained a cursor to data in that schema — the client must do the following:

1. (Lines 32-35) Verify that Migrate has initialized the needed schema. The client code does this by creating a new instance of the SchemaManager class and calling its initSchema method. If the manager has already discovered that the necessary dataset is present and ready, it can skip to Step 9.

2. (Line 34) If the manager must determine whether the requested schema is present, it must do so by obtaining the metatable from Migrate. The metatable was mentioned earlier. It is not the table that contains the list of contacts. Instead, it is a list of schemas that Migrate knows about along with descriptions of their states. In order to get the metatable, the schema manager initializes a loader requesting a cursor for it.

3. (Lines 45-63) There is nothing special about the request; it is just a standard cursor loader query against the metatable, one of Migrate's virtual tables. It is the metatable that is a little bit special. In typical three-phase loader fashion, the schema manager initializes the loader manager to load a cursor from the metatable. That causes the loader manager to request a loader using the onCreateLoader method. When that loader completes, onLoadFinished is called with the cursor it returns.

4. (Lines 68-74) When the loader manager returns a cursor to the metatable to the schema manager's onLoadFinished method, there are two possibilities. If there is a row in the metatable recording the state of the contacts schema (identified by the schema ID from the contract), and if that state indicates that the table is ready, then the schema is initialized, and processing can skip to Step 9.

5. (Lines 59-62) In any other case — the row does not exist or the schema is not ready — the application cannot proceed. Before it can display the list of contacts, it must wait for the Contacts dataset to be created and pre-populated from the network. So that it can receive notifications of any changes in state of the metatable, it registers as a content observer for the cursor obtained in the query in Step 4.

6. (Lines 75-80) Once it has been registered to receive notifications, the schema manager must do something to induce Migrate to fetch the necessary schema. It does this by placing a request for an update with the SyncManager. Of course, in order for this request to succeed — for the SyncManager to successfully download the new schema — the device user must have created a WebData account that can connect to an appropriate backend service. You'll see how this is accomplished in the next section of this chapter. The name associated with the account is one of the parameters to the manager.

7. When the SyncManager successfully downloads the data for the new schema, it will push the new data into the Migrate metatable. Migrate will, in turn, notify all observers of the metatable update. Since the schema manager registered as an observer in Step 5, it will receive the notification.

8. (Lines 41-43) In response to the notification, the schema manager will reload the metatable, essentially returning to Step 3. This loop repeats until the manager finds the requested schema as "ready" in the metatable.

> **NOTE** *Although all of this is happening asynchronously with respect to the UI, it may take a significant amount of time. The delay may well be visible to a user. In order to provide an acceptable user experience, applications will have to be designed to accommodate this one time delay.*

9. (Line 58) At this point, the metatable indicates that the Migrate content provider has created and populated the requested schema. At last, there is data available and the application can use it! The schema manager has completed its work. It uses the callback method `onSchemaLoaded` to notify its listener that the data is ready.

10. The client can now begin the standard three-step download process. In its `onSchemaLoaded` method, it initializes a new loader manager instance to get the contact data from Migrate. The loader manager obtains a loader, runs it, and, finally, calls the activity `onLoadFinished` method with data from the requested table.

Although this process looks convoluted, remember that nearly all of it happens only once. As with the `SQLiteOpenHelper` — which may, on some occasions, have to copy an entire database — the worst case looks pretty bad. Most of the time, though, most of these steps won't happen at all. Even when initialization is necessary, it usually completes very quickly and with delays no greater than those imposed by the network.

The rest of the code in the ported version of the simple Contacts application is nearly unchanged. Other than the changes in symbol names due to the automatically generated contract, only three other changes are necessary. They are shown in Listing 10-5.

LISTING 10-5: Porting a client activity

```java
public class ContactsActivity extends BaseActivity
    implements LoaderManager.LoaderCallbacks<Cursor>,
    SchemaManager.SchemaLoaderListener
{
    // … code elided
    @Override
    public void onSchemaLoaded() {
        getLoaderManager().initLoader(CONTACTS_LOADER_ID, null, this);
    }

    @Override
    protected void onCreate(Bundle savedInstanceState) {
    // … code elided
        new SchemaManager(
            this,
            ContactContract.SCHEMA_ID,
            ContactContract.SCHEMA_CONTACT_URI,
            ((ContactsApplication) getApplication()).getUser(),
            this)
        .initSchema();
    }
}
```

Note that in its `onCreate` method, the activity initializes the schema manager. This is entirely analogous to initializing a loader manager: It kicks off the process of getting the data that the activity will display, as described previously. The name of the user account, used by the `SynchManager` to log into the remote service, comes from the application object. You'll see how that works in a moment.

Next, notice that the activity extends `SchemaManager.SchemaLoaderListener`. This allows it to receive the callback indicating that the dataset it requires has loaded. Its implementation of the method required by the interface `onSchemaLoaded` initializes a loader manager instance to get the data cursor. This is the call to `initLoader` that would have been in `onCreate`. It has simply been delayed by one layer of indirection.

Just as all requests for databases must be made of the `SQLiteOpenHelper`, in order for it to be effective, all requests for data from the Migrate service must be made through a schema manager. Both of the application's activities have been modified to add this new layer of indirection.

Careful observers will notice that there is one additional change in the ported version of the simple Contacts application. In the original version, there were colored bars that provided feedback to the user about the state of a record: synched, synching, failed. Although the information that makes that feature possible is not available in the current implementation of Migrate, it is regarded as essential by the developers, and is scheduled for addition in the near future.

As noted, a Migrate client application must be able to identify the account to use, in order to log in to and synchronize with a remote service. Android's `SyncManager` is a powerful and secure tool for managing remote accounts. It safely manages credentials and optimizes the process of synchronizing data. It is, however, completely external to the client application. An installation of Migrate may have to communicate with several different backend services and may do so using accounts that exist only on your private device. An application must be able to discover the account to use in order to synchronize the data. The sample application does that using a standard preferences activity and a specialized Application class so that the information is available application-wide. That is demonstrated in the next section.

Step 5: Starting a Local Migrate Service

This task should be pretty easy if you have run through the examples in Chapter 6. If you have not, we suggest that you do so now. After you have installed the required tools for Chapter 6, simply copy the `$MIGRATE_SDK/migrate.war` binary to `$CATALINA_HOME/webapps` directory and restart Tomcat.

> **NOTE** *Make sure that your Migrate service is running and that a MySQL instance is available on port 3306, with credentials available for the root user as: username: root, password: mysql. You can check the status by visiting* `http://localhost:8080/migrate` *in a browser. If you are having trouble with this step, see the README file for information about troubleshooting MySQL.*

Step 6: Publishing Your Application's Schema

The last step of creating a Migrate-enabled application is publishing its schema into your new local service instance. You do this, once again, using the ant tool. Select the tool, migrate.xml, in Eclipse but instead of running it directly, choose Run As ➪ External Tools ➪ Configurations, as shown in Figure 10-6.

This will bring up a dialog box shown in Figure 10-7. Choose the Targets tab.

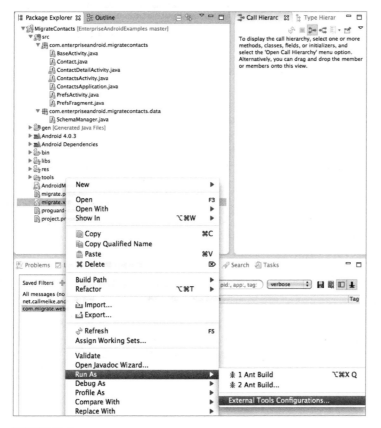

FIGURE 10-6

FIGURE 10-7

In the Targets tab, select the second target, `postSchema`. Click Run to run the tool. The console should confirm that your schema has been posted to the site you named with the `migrate.endpoint` property, in the `migrate.properties` file.

Once you have posted the Migrate schema, you can check the presence of the new metadata by loading the following URL in a browser: `http://localhost:8080/migrate/schema/com.enterpriseandroid.migratecontacts.Contact`. The response should be JSON that contains recognizable contact fields.

SETTING UP A DEVICE

The first step to running a Migrate client on a device or an emulator, of course, is installing the Migrate generic content provider itself. There are several ways to do this. If you have cloned the open-source project and have it open as an Eclipse project, you can run it as you would any other Android project. It should also soon be possible to download Migrate directly to your emulator from several Android storefronts. For now, you should install the version found in the Migrate SDK.

In this command-line session (for example, in `Bash` on `Linux`, `MacOS`, or `cygwin`) the shell variables `$MIGRATE_SDK` and `$ADK_HOME` point to the root of the installation of the Migrate SDK and the Android Developers Toolkit, respectively.

> **NOTE** *If you are not familiar with* `adb`, *you can learn about it here:*
>
> `http://developer.android.com/tools/help/adb.html`
>
> *It is a tremendously useful tool for understanding an Android system. It is part of the ADK that you installed, when you started doing Android development, and can be found in the* `$ANDROID_HOME/platform-tools` *directory.*

Before you begin, be sure that the emulator you intend to use is up and running:

```
$ adb devices
List of devices attached
emulator-5554   device
```

Or you can just look in the DDMS perspective in Eclipse, and you can find available devices on the left side.

Step 1: Installing the Migrate Client

Start the AVD manager, launch an AVD, and before you continue, ensure the emulator is running. Then install the Migrate client, located in `<migrate_sdk>/migrate-client.apk`, as follows:

```
$ cd $MIGRATE_SDK
```

The `adb` command that installs an application is `adb install`. If the Migrate client has already been installed on the emulator, `adb` will refuse to install it again unless you specify the `-r` flag, which indicates that you want to reinstall the apk.

```
$ adb install /migrate-client.apk
2660 KB/s (356476 bytes in 0.130s)
        pkg: /data/local/tmp/migrate-client.apk
Success
```

Verify that Migrate has been installed and start it (see Figure 10-8). If you're successful, you'll get a Toast message indicating that Migrate is up, as shown in Figure 10-8.

Step 2: Adding a WebData Account

Next, recall that Migrate depends on the sync manager. In order to work correctly, the manager must be configured with an account. To create this account, use the Settings application shown in Figure 10-9.

From the Settings application (leftmost pane) choose "Add account." This will bring up a new page showing the types of accounts known to the Account manager (the center pane). Among the choices you should see "webdata SyncAdapter" (at the bottom of the list, in this case), the type of account used by the Migrate framework. Selecting the account type will bring up a dialog (the rightmost pane) that allows you to log into the Migrate service. If this were a real Enterprise application, you would have to provide real credentials here. If you are using the

FIGURE 10-8

demonstration service, described in Chapter 9, any username and password will work, and you should not change the endpoint URI. The default will work with the local service instance if you are running in the emulator.

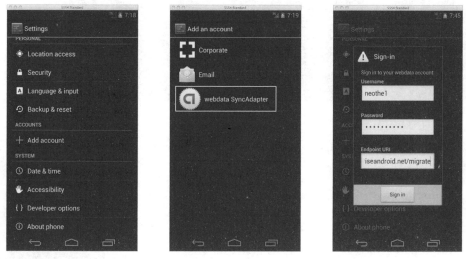

FIGURE 10-9

Step 3: Turning on Synchronization

Before you can start the Migrate contacts application, you now just need to activate synchronization for your new Migrate account. Do so using Settings ⇨ Accounts ⇨ webdata SyncAdapter ⇨ Migrate. Then check the sync checkbox.

Step 4: Running the Application

Run the MigrateContacts application using Run As Android application, as you've done for other Android projects in this book.

Step 5: Configuring an Account in Migrate Contacts (Optional)

Recall that in order to use the Migrate service, the application must know which account to use. In order for it to get data from the Migrate service, it must be configured to use the correct account. You configure this account using the Settings activity, which appears as a wrench in the action bar. Configure the application to use the same account used previously, as shown in Figure 10-10.The application will not work until this account has been configured correctly.

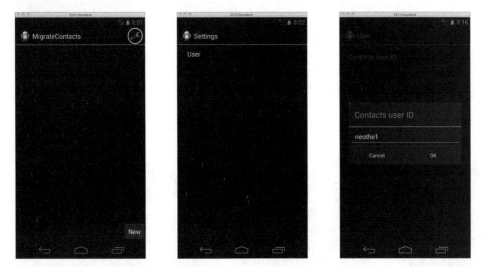

FIGURE 10-10

Select the "Preferences" item in the application's Action Bar. It's represented by the standard wrench icon (the leftmost pane in Figure 10-10). Since this is a very simple demonstration application, there is only one item in the preferences: the user configuration (the center pane). Selecting the single item brings up a standard preferences edit text dialog that allows you to enter the name of the account configured in the previous section.

Congratulations, you have successfully set up MigrateContacts! Return to the main activity to manage the contacts (see Figure 10-11).

FUTURE DIRECTIONS: MIGRATECLINIC

While `MigrateContacts` is appealing, it is certainly not ready for prime time yet. In order to be ready for use in real enterprise environments, future implementations of Migrate will have to support things like large

FIGURE 10-11

data objects, joins between virtual tables, schema versioning, and security (security issues in general are discussed in Chapter 12).

The example code for this chapter includes a second application, MigrateClinic, that hints at the how the Migrate framework might address some of these things.

> **NOTE** *MigrateClinic is not working code. It suggests one of several possible directions that the Migrate framework might take in implementing some of the features above.*

In order to manage large objects, the Migrate tool will support a new datatype. In the prototype code in Listing 10-6, this type is InputStream.

LISTING 10-6: Proposed Migrate InputStream type

```
@WebdataSchema(version="1")
public interface XRay {
    public String getSsn();
    public String getDescription();
    public String getNotes();
    public Long getTimestamp();
    public InputStream getXRay();
}
```

When the Migrate framework encounters a field with this special datatype, it populates it not with the actual data, but instead with a URL. That URL can be used, as demonstrated in Chapter 4, to get an input stream from the Migrate content provider. Listing 10-7 shows the implementation of a Loader that reads the input stream into a bitmap and then displays the result in an ImageView.

There are two classes (XRayLoader, XRayLoaderCallbacks) and one method (populateXRay) in this listing. They are not discussed here in detail because they are nearly identical to their analogs in Chapter 4.

LISTING 10-7: Using the proposed type extension

```
private static class XRayLoader extends AsyncTaskLoader<Bitmap> {
    private volatile boolean loaded;
    private final Uri uri;

    public XRayLoader(Context context, Uri uri) {
        super(context);
        this.uri = uri;
    }

    @Override
    public Bitmap loadInBackground() {
        Bitmap xray = null;
```

continues

LISTING 10-7 *(continued)*

```
            InputStream in = null;
            try {
                in = getContext().getContentResolver().openInputStream(uri);
                xray = BitmapFactory.decodeStream(in);
            }
            catch (FileNotFoundException e) { }
            finally {
                if (null != in) { try { in.close(); } catch (IOException e) { } }
            }

            return xray;
        }

        // see bug: http://code.google.com/p/android/issues/detail?id=14944
        @Override
        protected void onStartLoading() {
            if (!loaded) { forceLoad(); }
        }
    }
}

// code omitted...

class XRayLoaderCallbacks implements LoaderManager.LoaderCallbacks<Bitmap> {

    @Override
    public Loader<Bitmap> onCreateLoader(int id, Bundle args) {
        Uri uri = null;
        if (null != args) {
            String s = args.getString(PARAM_XRAY);
            if (null != s) { uri = Uri.parse(s); }
        }
        return (null == uri) ? null : new XRayLoader(XRayActivity.this, uri);
    }

    @Override
    public void onLoadFinished(Loader<Bitmap> loader, Bitmap bm) {
        populateXRay(bm);
    }

    @Override
    public void onLoaderReset(Loader<Bitmap> loader) {
        populateXRay(null);
    }
}

// code omitted...

void populateXRay(Bitmap xray) { xrayView.setImageBitmap(xray); }
```

The ability to do table joins is also a critical feature for Migrate. As the code in this chapter has shown, Migrate maintains a virtual metatable describing the schemas it supports, at any given time. One possible implementation of table joins simply inserts descriptions for a new view into this metatable. The code to do that might look something like Listing 10-8.

LISTING 10-8: Proposed Migrate view feature

```
ContentValues view = new ContentValues();
view.put("name", SCHEMA_ID);
view.put("tables", TABLES);
view.put("projection", PROJECTION);
view.put("selection", SELECTION);
Uri schemaUri = resolver.insert(XRayContract.SCHEMA_XRAY_URI, view);
```

The URI returned by the insert statement is the object URI for the new table. As shown in Listing 10-9, if the insert completes successfully, the new URI could be used as the object URI in any other Migrate contract. The contract is simply created dynamically instead of statically.

LISTING 10-9: Using the proposed Migrate dynamic contract

```
new SchemaManager(
        activity,
        SCHEMA_ID,
        schemaUri,
        getUser(),
        listener)
    .initSchema();
```

Dynamic contracts introduce a small additional constraint: The URI for the data is no longer static. It will be null until the new view is created. If the new view cannot be created, perhaps because some parent table cannot be downloaded, it will stay null. The fact that code uses a dynamically created view and must protect itself from a null valued content URI is, actually, not that significant. As demonstrated earlier in this chapter, the application may already have to wait for the data to which the URI refers, to become "ready." This new constraint simply means that the URI may not be ready either.

The Migrate framework is an attempt to prove a concept. It is useful to engage in speculation of the sort pursued in this section to understand whether or not it is up the task. Certainly, the system has promise.

SUMMARY

The MigrateContacts application is intended as an interesting proof of concept. The process of creating it should reveal some of the details of the WebData architecture and give you substantial insight into its viability as a real tool.

This chapter began by offering several potential strategic advantages for the WebData approach:

➤   It is an implementation of enterprise-wide data sharing that doesn't attempt to sweep the challenges of mobile synchronization under the rug.

➤ It makes good use of the Android components designed for the job: content providers, synchronization manager, service-based threading, and the best networking packages.

➤ Because it is a single implementation used by multiple clients, it is likely that serious bugs will occur less often in production and be fixed more quickly if they do occur.

➤ It completely removes the issue of implementing one somewhat complex piece of code from an application.

The list is obviously appealing but so is faster than light travel. What did the exercise of building an actual application demonstrate?

There are some real high points. The ported application started simple and, for the most part, got much simpler. The `restfulCachingProviderContacts` project is something like 1,700 lines of Java and XML code. `MigrateContacts` is something like 500 lines, which is almost entirely hooking the provider contract to the application view. At least in this constrained context, the approach is a win. Even the final bit of speculation in the "Future Directions: MigrateClinic" section suggests that Migrate can be extended into a practical and useful platform.

11

Building Human Interfaces for Data

WHAT'S IN THIS CHAPTER?

- ➤ UI conventions for data-oriented apps
- ➤ Scaling the display
- ➤ Combining Tab and Fragment
- ➤ Using the ActionBar
- ➤ Touch and direct manipulation

WROX.COM CODE DOWNLOADS FOR THIS CHAPTER

Please note that all the code examples in this chapter are available at https://github.com/ wileyenterpriseandroid/Examples.git and as a part of the book's code download at www.wrox.com on the Download Code tab.

Chapter 1 introduced the basics of an application framework. The example code in Chapter 1 showed how to handle an application lifecycle correctly and illustrated good practices in scaling applications to fit many screen sizes.

That basic framework introduced the use of the Fragment class, which enabled the application to spread out across the screen of a tablet and "fold up" to fit on a handset. The framework integrated the use of fragments with tabs in the Action Bar.

Now that you have an application that meets those basic requirements and actually does something, it's time to upgrade the ease and facility of interaction with that application and to implement a more complete range of Android conventions in the UI.

The users should find the UI obvious, and where it isn't obvious at first glance, it should be explorable. Users should be able to guess at outcomes with reasonable success. That is, the application should encourage experimentation. It should avoid disappointing the users by having them find that a touch or a gesture that could do something useful does nothing.

MODULARITY AND FLEXIBILITY COMPARED WITH A "COOKBOOK" APPROACH

The "recipe" you find in this chapter shows you how to combine the scaling and `Fragment`-based modularity described earlier in this book with the direct manipulation and animation needed to create a UI that has a more satisfying touch experience than simply selecting list items and tabs.

You may wonder why in Google's Android reference material there isn't a model Android app that illustrates all the conventions covered in this chapter. In part this is due to the generality of each part of the Android user interface APIs. Each can be used separately, and in a near-infinite number of combinations. It's also easier to make examples that focus on one feature or capability at a time. The example in this chapter shows some of the places where the API design hasn't perfectly dovetailed, even when features should work well together.

Overview of Modules

Before you start looking at code, take a look at the modules, which have been added to achieve this boost in user interface sophistication:

```
ItemDetailFragment.java

ItemFragment.java

ListColumnMap.java

MainActivity.java

PickFragment.java

TabActivity.java

TabbedActivity.java

TabbedPagedFragment.java
```

So compared to what was discussed in Chapter 1, the number of modules in this program has increased.

The `TabbedPagedFragment` class is a class that `ItemFragment` and `ItemDetailFragment` both inherit from in order to acquire some common capabilities and behaviors.

We have also added a subclass of `FragmentPagerAdapter` called `TabbedFragmentPagerAdapter`, which works with the `ViewPager` to enable direct manipulation of the fragments. This is implemented in a private class within `TabbedActivity` in order to share information with that class.

Sideways swiping to "page" among items has become a popular Android UI convention, and the `ViewPager` class was created to make implementation of this convention convenient.

Layout Changes

Some of the layouts have changed, too. The following code shows the layout file called data_only.xml, where we have replaced the Fragment subclasses specified in XML with a ViewPager. The Fragment subclasses are instantiated by the TabbedFragmentPagerAdapter constructor, an implementation strategy that's explained in depth later in this chapter.

Listing 11-1 is the layout for an activity containing just one ViewPager nested inside a LinearLayout.

LISTING 11-1: data_only.xml

```xml
<?xml version="1.0" encoding="utf-8"?>
<LinearLayout xmlns:android="http://schemas.android.com/apk/res/android"
    android:layout_width="match_parent"
    android:layout_height="match_parent"
    android:orientation="vertical" >

        <android.support.v4.view.ViewPager
            android:id="@+id/pager"
            android:layout_width="match_parent"
            android:layout_height="match_parent">
        </android.support.v4.view.ViewPager>

</LinearLayout>
```

Similarly, the layout-large version of main.xml (Listing 11-2) has a pager in place of the Fragment subclasses:

LISTING 11-2: main.xml

```xml
<LinearLayout xmlns:android="http://schemas.android.com/apk/res/android"
    android:layout_width="fill_parent"
    android:layout_height="fill_parent"
    android:id="@+id/content_layout"
    android:orientation="horizontal" >

        <fragment
            android:id="@+id/list_frag"
            android:name=
            "com.enterpriseandroidbook.contactscontractexample.PickFragment"
        android:layout_width="250dp"
        android:layout_height="match_parent"
        class="com.enterpriseandroidbook.contactscontractexample.PickFragment"/>

        <LinearLayout
            android:layout_width="match_parent"
            android:layout_height="match_parent"
            android:orientation="vertical" >

        <android.support.v4.view.ViewPager
```

continues

LISTING 11-2 *(continued)*

```
            android:id="@+id/pager"
            android:layout_width="match_parent"
            android:layout_height="match_parent">
    </android.support.v4.view.ViewPager>

    </LinearLayout>
```

These layouts are the way this app differentiates between running on a small screen and a large screen. This approach has the benefit of leaving the decision of whether to put multiple fragments on a screen to the Android system, and we want to maintain this benefit as we integrate paging with tabs.

DIRECT MANIPULATION

In Figure 11-1 we demonstrate the ability to page, using one's finger, between fragments that otherwise require selecting a tab to navigate to. Drag a fragment left or right, and watch the other fragment come into view. Drag far enough and let go, and you switch between fragments.

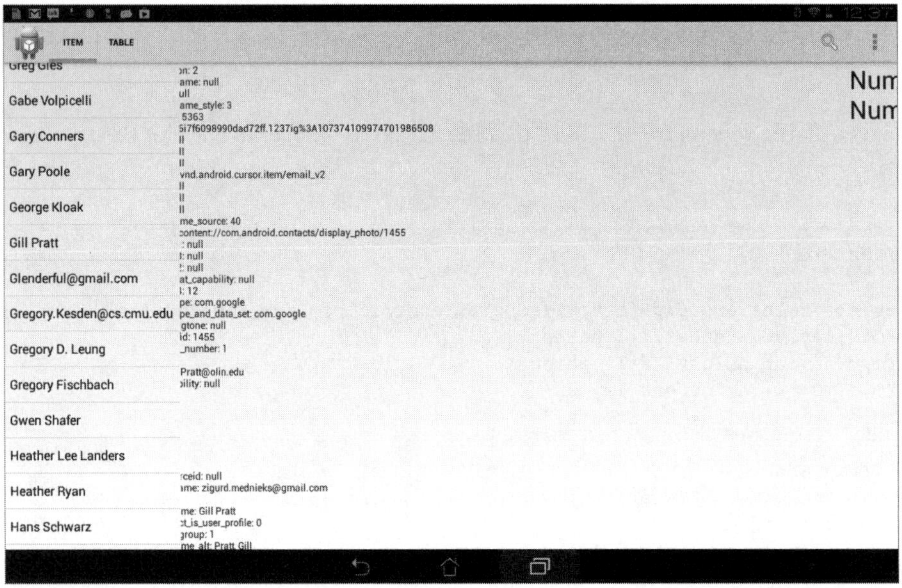

FIGURE 11-1

Both dragging and flinging gestures are supported. You can drag a page almost fully into view and then drag it back to the side of the screen from which you dragged it. Or you can fling a page into view, something like the way you might leaf through a book or magazine.

The TabbedActivity Class

The `TabbedActivity` class incorporates both the code for initializing tabbing and all of the code for page-swiping functionality because it must be aware of changes in the display commanded by switching among fragments using tabs. This is where most of the interesting modifications to support swiping were made. The next sections look at the details of how and why.

The Support Library

To implement this family of gestures and related UI behaviors, you use a `ViewPager`, which also requires use of the Support Library. In Listing 11-3, you see some imports related to the `ViewPager` class. Please note that you can find the code for Listings 11-3 through 11-12 in `TabbedActivity.java` in the code download for the chapter.

LISTING 11-3: Declaring use of the Support Library

```
package com.enterpriseandroidbook.contactscontractexample;

import android.app.ActionBar;
import android.app.ActionBar.Tab;
import android.app.ActionBar.TabListener;
import android.app.Activity;
import android.app.Fragment;
import android.app.FragmentTransaction;
import android.content.Intent;
import android.os.Bundle;
import android.support.v4.view.ViewPager;
import android.support.v4.view.ViewPager.OnPageChangeListener;
```

The first thing to notice is that we use the Support Library. The Support Library is installed by the SDK Manager. Once the Support Library is installed, you copy the `jar` file from the SDK file hierarchy to your project's `libs` folder and add the `jar` to the libraries listed in your project properties. In this case we are using the v13 library.

Once you have the `jar` file copied into your `libs` folder, add it to the build path of your project. Figure 11-2 shows a properly configured build path.

Why do we have the `import` statements for support.v4 in the list of imports in Listing 11-3? Because, even though we are using the v13 version of the Support Library, the package names for the imports use "v4" in the current version of the online documentation, and we chose to be consistent with the documentation. The v13 library supports import statements using v4 or v13. There are a few places, which will be pointed out, where you do need to specify a v13 package, however. The following shows the heading of the class definition for `TabbedActivity`. It implements `OnPageChangeListener`. A discussion about why the `OnPageChangeListener` is implemented here occurs later in this chapter:

```
public abstract class TabbedActivity extends Activity implements
        ViewPager.OnPageChangeListener {
```

As before, `TabbedActivity` inherits from `Activity`. That's because you're not using the Support Library to implement compatibility with earlier versions of Android that don't directly support `Fragment`. Essentially, there are two main use cases for the Support Library:

1. Implementing support for `Fragment` and other newer APIs that were not part of Android's APIs prior to Android 3.1

2. Making use of new APIs that have not yet officially "made the team"

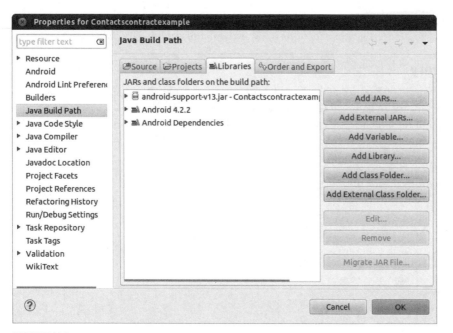

FIGURE 11-2

This application is an example of the latter case. Using the Support Library for back-compatibility with early versions of Android introduces more complexity than we want to present here.

> **NOTE** *This book is about enterprise software, and we are making the assumption that since that is a nascent topic, it implies new deployments of new mobile devices. If we were making mass-market software for the Google Play store, we might draw different conclusions about how to use the Support Library.*

Initializing Tabs and the ViewPager

The `initializeTabs` method (Listing 11-4) has the same signature as before, but most of the initialization has been moved from this method into the constructor for the private nested class `TabbedFragmentPagerAdapter`. As you'll see, the reason for moving that code and the reason its new class is private and nested are intertwined.

LISTING 11-4: Initializing tabs

```
private NerfTabListener nerfTabListener = new NerfTabListener();

/**
 * Initialize tabs in an activity that uses tabs to switch among fragments
```

```
 *
 * @param defaultIndex
 *             The index of the Fragment shown first
 * @param nameIDs
 *             an array of ID for tab names
 * @param fragmentClasses
 *             an array of Class objects enabling instantiation of Fragments
 *             to be tabbed/paged
 */
public void initializeTabs(int defaultIndex, int[] nameIDs,
            Class<?>[] fragmentClasses) {

    // Find the pager
    ViewPager pager = (ViewPager) findViewById(R.id.pager);

    // If there is no pager, there are no tabs
    if (null == pager) {
                return;
    }

    // Set the action bar to use tabs
    getActionBar().setNavigationMode(ActionBar.NAVIGATION_MODE_TABS);

    /*
     * Create an adapter that knows our Fragment classes and Activity. This
     * constructor does most of the heavy lifting because it knows about
     * both the tabs and the pager.
     */
    TabbedFragmentPagerAdapter adapter = new TabbedFragmentPagerAdapter(
                pager, nameIDs, fragmentClasses);

    // Tell the adapter it has new items to display
    adapter.notifyDataSetChanged();

    // Select the tab designated as default
    getActionBar().getTabAt(0).select();
    }
```

Moving Data between Fragments

The code for loading data into the fragments to display it is much the same as it was in previous versions of this code. That's on purpose. We didn't want to disrupt the strategy for scaling this app over small and large screen sizes, and we didn't want to give up the modularity of pushing the tab listener code out into the Fragment classes. After all, Fragment prevents you from having to place all your interaction code into Activity subclasses.

The method shown in Listing 11-5 is key to implementing that scaling. Notice that this is where a decision is made about layout. Not screen size. Not density. If the layout includes certain Fragment objects and their corresponding tabs, you can show the data for the item you selected.

LISTING 11-5: Bundle for moving data between components

```
/**
 * If we have tabs and fragments in this activity, pass the bundle data to
 * the fragments. Otherwise start an activity that should contain the
 * fragments.
 *
 * @param data
 */
public void loadTabFragments(Bundle data) {
        int n = getActionBar().getTabCount();
        if (0 != n) {
            doLoad(n, data);
            } else {
            startActivity(new Intent(this, TabActivity.class).putExtras(data));
            }
}
```

You can show the item list and data in one of two ways. Either the screen is big enough for both the item list and the data for each item, or you must start a new activity to show the data. Since this is an abstract parent class of the `Activity` classes that can be in either role, the same code works in either case.

The code lets the system decide and follows the layout decision made by the system. That way you don't have to take into account whether the users have changed font size and other often-overlooked factors in how much information can be displayed.

Abstract Methods and Nested Interfaces

To build the interface, you need a list of `Fragment` classes that should be represented by tabs in the Action Bar and the `ViewPager` needs to know about these classes. The `abstract` method here ensures that the child classes provide that information:

```
/**
 *
 * @return The array of Classes to be instantiated and tabbed/paged
 */
// public abstract Class<?>[] getTabFragmentClasses();
```

You could have put the following interface definition into a separate file, but it is so intimately tied to what this class does that it might as well remain here. And it serves as a useful contrast to the `abstract` method you just added. Why use an `abstract` method in one case and an interface in another? The `SetData` interface consists of more than one method, and its implementer isn't going to be a child class of this class. In contrast, the `getTabFragmentClasses` `abstract` method doesn't need to be grouped with other methods and is implemented only by its child classes.

```
/**
 * An interface to pass data to a Fragment
 */
    public interface SetData {
    public void setData(Bundle data);

    public String getDataLabel();

    void setDataLabel(String label);
    }
```

Connecting Tabs and Fragments

A key element in the architecture of this UI framework example is the use of the `Tab` object's tag fields as references to the `Fragment` objects the tabs are related to. In Listing 11-6, you can see that the `doLoad` method uses this aspect of the implementation to find and call the `setData` method of the `SetData` interface implemented by each fragment. This is what happens when the user selects an item from the list: Related data is serialized into a bundle object, which is used to convey the data to the fragment objects that display it.

LISTING 11-6: Delivering the data

```java
/**
 * Iterate over the tabs, get their tags, and use these as Fragment
 * references to pass the bundle data to the fragments
 *
 * @param n
 * @param data
 */
private void doLoad(int n, Bundle data) {

        // Null check - harmless if no data
        if (null == data)
            return;

        int i;
        ActionBar actionBar = getActionBar();

        for (i = 0; i < n; i++) {
            SetData f = (SetData) actionBar.getTabAt(i).getTag();
            f.setData(data);
        }
}
```

Mixing in the ViewPager

Although the previous code did not change from the example used in Chapter 8, the following code is new. Mixing tabs, the `Fragment` class, and `ViewPager` requires mixing two different APIs that, in some places, don't mix that well. As you have seen in the XML for the layouts, the `Fragment` instances you can page among are not created by inflating the XML any longer. That is because the `ViewPager` uses an `Adapter` class that behaves something like a `ListView`'s adapter.

Unlike tabs, where each tab can have its own listener and where an instance of a fragment can implement that listener interface, a pager wants one adapter and one listener and has no provision in the API design to call each fragment being paged. In part this is a consequence of working like the adapter of a `ListView`, which may be used to create and destroy items in the `ViewPager` container dynamically. So, though here we don't use the adapter in the way that adapters are used to put arrays of data into `ListViews`, some of the same architectural constraints apply.

The question is, "Can you deal with these constraints while meeting the key architecture and implementation goals?" Consider these questions:

➤ Can you avoid having the TabListener pulled out of the Fragment class and having one place where all these interfaces converge?

➤ Can you avoid holding references to Android components, especially instances of this activity, in multiple other objects?

➤ Can you coordinate swiping a page with tapping a tab and be able to use both interaction gestures?

A Nested Subclass of FragmentPagerAdapter

A ViewPager is generic: It will page anything you give it. In this case, you are giving it Fragment objects and their view hierarchies. What makes this ViewPager page Fragment objects is its adapter class. The adapter class is a subclass of FragmentPagerAdapter, whose name is a dead giveaway to what it does.

As we mentioned earlier, the trick here is getting Fragment objects, Tab objects, the ActionBar object in its enclosing activity, and a ViewPager and its FragmentPagerAdapter object to all coordinate. That way, when the users use a tab or a swipe gesture, they get the expected result. The Tab objects should be highlighted correctly and the correct fragment should be displayed. This should happen no matter how the users choose to interact.

As it turns out, by embedding the FragmentPagerAdapter subclass (see Listing 11-7), and at the cost of a fairly complex constructor, you can retain the way your scaling decision is made, and you can retain the implementation of TabListener in the Fragment classes controlled by the tabs. You can also coordinate between the tabs in the Action Bar and the Fragment objects being paged by the ViewPager.

LISTING 11-7: The pager's adapter

```
/**
 * This class is private because we only access it from here and it is
 * intimately tied to instances of this class. That is, unless it was nested
 * it would be holding a reference to instances of this component
 */
private class TabbedFragmentPagerAdapter extends
        android.support.v13.app.FragmentPagerAdapter {

private Class<?> fragmentClasses[];
private int[] nameIDs;
```

The TabbedFragmentPagerAdapter Constructor

The code in Listing 11-8 illustrates why nested classes are sometimes useful and sometimes confusing. For example, the keyword this refers to two different instances of two different classes in this method. When used this way, it is qualified with the class name.

`FragmentPagerAdapter` is nested to give it access to the members of the `TabbedActivity` class, especially to the instances of its subclasses, which are accessed through the keyword `this`. The `TabbedActivity` class name qualifies the use of the `this` keyword. `TabbedActivity.this` refers to the instance of `TabbedActivity` that called the constructor, whereas the `this` keyword without any qualifier refers to the instance of `TabbedFragmentPagerAdapter` being initialized by this constructor.

Only the abstract `Activity` subclass needs to refer to instances of `TabbedFragmentPagerAdapter`, which means you can make the class private and prevent the concrete subclasses from having to be aware of what happens at this layer. Among the benefits of this approach is that references to instances of this component don't leak out of this component, while the code of this constructor has access to the `Activity` instance and its members. Also, you know that the only user of this class is the enclosing abstract `Activity` class.

Most of the following code (Listing 11-8) appeared in the `initializeTabs` method in the example code for Chapter 8. The reason it is now here is that tab initialization and pager initialization need to happen alongside each other. They both use information common to the pager subclass and the fragments to be paged.

LISTING 11-8: Creating tabs

```
/**
 * Create an instance of TabbedFragmentPagerAdapter. This constructor
 * sets up later instantiation of fragments, and tab creation
 *
 * @param tabbedActivity
 *              - the activity with tabs and a pager
 * @param pager
 *              - the pages that pages the fragments
 * @param nameIDs
 *              - the names identifying the fragments
 * @param fragmentClasses
 *              - the Fragment subclasses to instantiate
 */
TabbedFragmentPagerAdapter(ViewPager pager, int[] nameIDs,
            Class<?>[] fragmentClasses) {
            super(TabbedActivity.this.getFragmentManager());

            /*
             * The activity implements PageChangeListener, we
             * set it here, though
             */

    pager.setOnPageChangeListener((OnPageChangeListener) TabbedActivity.this);
```

A Placebo Tab Listener

Here (Listing 11-9) is where you set up the tabs. But wait! You don't have the real `Fragment` objects yet, and the `Fragment` classes implement `TabListener`. The `Fragment` objects are created in a `FragmentPagerAdapater` callback and passed to the `ViewPager`. You need to use a placebo called nerfTabListener in case the TabListener is called before it is set. Because of the way the Tab API works, it is more convenient to use a placeholder tab listener than it is to check the validity of the TabListener every time you do something that might invoke it.

LISTING 11-9: Adding tabs to the Action Bar

```
// Check if there are any Fragments to instantiate
if (null != fragmentClasses && fragmentClasses.length != 0) {

    /*
     * Stash a reference to the fragment classes and names for
     * later use in the callbacks
     */
    this.fragmentClasses = fragmentClasses;
    this.nameIDs = nameIDs;

    // Get the action bar and remove existing tabs
    ActionBar bar = TabbedActivity.this.getActionBar();
    bar.removeAllTabs();

    // Make new tabs
    int i = 0;
    for (; i < fragmentClasses.length; i++) {

    // Create the tab
    Tab t = bar.newTab().setText(nameIDs[i]);

    // Give it a placebo to chew on
    t.setTabListener(nerfTabListener);

    // Add the tab to the bar
    bar.addTab(t);
    }
}

    // Set the pager's adapter to this
    pager.setAdapter(this);

    notifyDataSetChanged();
}
```

FragmentPagerAdapter Callbacks

Here you override some methods of the FragmentPagerAdapter class. The way that tabs and the pager are woven together is such that when a fragment is instantiated, the instance is stored with the tab that is used to select it. When the pager asks its adapter for a fragment at a position, you use the fact that fragment and tab positions are always the same. The position in the Action Bar's tabs returns a tab with a fragment instance stored in the tag. This results in using the Action Bar tabs as the "data model" for the pager and its adapter.

The following methods (Listing 11-10) override the getItem and getCount methods. You can see how the tabs of the Action Bar are accessed to retrieve Fragment instances. The index or position parameter identifies which tab holds the requested fragment instance.

Note that the fragments are instantiated in the getItem method. This is due to the way that a ViewPager uses the FragmentPagerAdapter. The ViewPager is enabled to think that it never needs to instantiate the fragments.

LISTING 11-10: Accessing the fragments being paged

```
@Override
public Fragment getItem(int index) {

    ActionBar bar = TabbedActivity.this.getActionBar();
    TabbedPagedFragment f = (TabbedPagedFragment) bar.getTabAt(index)
      .getTag();

    if (null == f) {

        /*
         * Instantiate the Fragment here. Otherwise it is never
         * added to the pager.
         */
        f = (TabbedPagedFragment) Fragment.instantiate(
            TabbedActivity.this, fragmentClasses[index].getName());

        // Set the data label to the name of the corresponding tab
        f.setDataLabel(TabbedActivity.this.getString(nameIDs[index]));

        // Set the tab's tag and the TabListener
        bar.getTabAt(index).setTag(f).setTabListener((TabListener) f);
        }

    return f;
    }

@Override
public int getCount() {
    return TabbedActivity.this.getActionBar().getTabCount();
}

/**
 * Find a fragment by position
 *
 * @param position
 *                The position of the fragment in both the ViewPager and as the
 *                tag of tab
 * @return
 */
public Fragment getFragmentByPosition(int position) {
    return (Fragment) getActionBar().getTabAt(position).getTag();
}
```

OnPageChangeListener and Tabs

The following code (Listing 11-11) implements the OnPageChangeListener interface. The onPageSelected callback connects the ViewPager to the tabs. When a page is selected, the Action Bar is told to set the selected navigation item using the same position. When you are notified of a new selection via tabs, the obverse is implemented in the tab listener.

Recall from earlier that, when initializing the `Fragment`, `Tab`, `ViewPager`, and other objects, you used a temporary tab listener. That's because the `TabListener` and `OnPageChangeListener` don't simply call each other. The link between them runs through the Action Bar in one direction and the `ViewPager` in the other direction.

LISTING 11-11: OnPageChangeListener implementation

```
//////////////////////////////////////////////////////////////////////////
// Implementation of OnPageChangeListener
//////////////////////////////////////////////////////////////////////////

@Override
public void onPageScrollStateChanged(int arg0) {
    // Do nothing

}

@Override
public void onPageScrolled(int arg0, float arg1, int arg2) {
    // Do nothing

}

@Override
public void onPageSelected(int position) {
    getActionBar().setSelectedNavigationItem(position);

}
```

The Placebo

This class (Listing 11-12) enables you to decouple the way `Fragment` objects get instantiated from the `Tab` objects that are created, without subclassing `Tab` or implementing null checks in all the code that uses the `Tab` API.

LISTING 11-12: A convenient placeholder

```
private class NerfTabListener implements TabListener {

    @Override
    public void onTabReselected(Tab tab, FragmentTransaction ft) {
      // Do nothing

    }

    @Override
    public void onTabSelected(Tab tab, FragmentTransaction ft) {
      // Do nothing

    }

    @Override
```

```
        public void onTabUnselected(Tab tab, FragmentTransaction ft) {
          // Do nothing

        }

      }

    }
```

The TabbedPagedFragment Class

We need to make some additional changes from the previous version of this example from Chapter 8. One is that the implementation of the TabListener interface has been pulled into a new abstract class called TabbedPagedFragment, so it can be easily shared among tabbed fragments as you can see in Listing 11-13.

LISTING 11-13: TabbedPagedFragment.java

```
package com.enterpriseandroidbook.contactscontractexample;

import android.app.ActionBar.Tab;
import android.app.ActionBar.TabListener;
import android.app.Fragment;
import android.app.FragmentTransaction;
import android.support.v4.view.ViewPager;


public abstract class TabbedPagedFragment extends Fragment implements TabListener {

@Override
public void onTabReselected(Tab tab, FragmentTransaction ft) {
      // Do nothing

}
```

Completing the Circuit

This (Listing 11-14) is where you tell the ViewPager, if necessary, to change which Fragment object is in view. You must check to see that a change is necessary; otherwise, you might ping pong back and forth between the TabListener here and the OnPageChangeListener.

LISTING 11-14: Coupling tabs to the pager

```
@Override
public void onTabSelected(Tab tab, FragmentTransaction ft) {

    if (true == attached) {

        // The ViewPager is used to show the specified Fragment
        ViewPager pager = (ViewPager) getActivity()
                .findViewById(R.id.pager);

        // Check that we need to change current fragments
```

continues

LISTING 11-14 *(continued)*

```
                if (pager.getCurrentItem() != tab.getPosition()) {
                    pager.setCurrentItem(tab.getPosition());
                }
            }
        }

        @Override
        public void onTabUnselected(Tab tab, FragmentTransaction ft) {
            // Do nothing

        }

    }
```

At this point, you have taken three separate parts that can be used in any combination with other ways of building Android user interfaces and combined them into a UI that fits many common use cases. You have multiple fragments that can be brought into view as needed. These fragments are controlled by tabs and through direct manipulation using a pager.

NAVIGATION

Navigation and flow from one activity to another is a fundamental aspect of the architecture of Android applications, and it goes hand in hand with lifecycle. In a mobile device with a small screen, having an intuitive flow among multiple screens is the key to maximizing the visual information the user can access and use.

When applications are correctly implemented and seamlessly cooperative, users can navigate among several activities, each implemented in a separate application, and think they have used only one application.

Multitasking in a Small-Screen Environment

Keeping track of multiple tasks on a PC — multiple programs, documents, and so forth — is so commonplace that you might not think much about how it is accomplished. Multiple documents, overlapping windows, and a mouse pointer are all ingredients of a user interface paradigm called the "desktop metaphor." Your personal computer screen is a metaphor for a real desk, with overlapping documents on it. Move a document to the top by selecting it with the pointer, and it becomes the active document.

On a small screen, the entire screen is devoted to a single task, and the concept of a task, and task switching, is inherently less visual, since other tasks are not visible in other windows. In mobile interfaces, a *back-stack* — the stack of activities you can go back to — is often a central concept. In Android, the back-stack is called the "activity stack."

The Android Task Model

If an activity is the basic unit of Android user interaction, a "task" is the next grouping. In Android, the word *task* does not denote an executable object such as a process or application; instead, it refers to a single activity stack with, potentially, multiple activities from multiple applications in it.

As the user interacts with the system, sometimes one activity will — by way of an `Intent` object — ask the system to find an activity that matches the intent's specifications. If that activity is in another application, it usually becomes part of the task the users began when they launched an application from the launcher or home screen shortcut. When users launch what they think of as an application, they also start the "root activity" of a task.

Concepts like a "root activity" become concrete to the users through Android's methods of task switching. If users touch an application icon in the Home activity or use the Recent Tasks switcher after an application has been launched, in most cases the system goes back to an already started task.

Tasks and the Conventional Process Model

Tasks are not always processes. Even when the process containing the current activity of a task has been killed, it will be restarted when users switch to the task where that activity is in the foreground. A new instance of the `Activity` object is created in a new process. Every other component in that process is re-created and their states are restored as needed.

Android provides developers with rich control over the behavior of interactive components in tasks. Used correctly, your control over task behavior will reinforce the Android concept of tasks and make the users feel as though the Back button always does what they expect. If it's used incorrectly or inconsistently, the users might be wondering, "How did I get here?"

Modifying Task Behavior

Some task behavior is determined by the argument to the `launchMode` attribute in the activity tag of the manifest.

If you think of activities as cards in a stack, think of these `launchMode` variants as ways of stacking new cards or re-ordering the stack.

➤ The `standard` launch mode is the default. Default back-stack behavior when launching a new activity is to create a new instance of the `Activity` object and put it on top of the stack. This is the correct behavior in most cases.

➤ The `singleTop` launch mode diverges from the default behavior by checking if an instance of the specified `Activity` already exists in the stack, and bringing it to the top. Let's say you have an activity for setting global parameters and it has an "OK" button for committing changes. You would want only one such `Activity` instance, with one set of state, in your back-stack.

Two other launch modes are seldom used and not recommended.

➤ `LaunchMode` variants are a way to specify behavior that differs from the default when you declare an activity in the manifest. But there are a surprisingly large number of ways to modify task behavior in `intent` flags.

➤ `Intent` flags are usually used in the code that builds an `Intent` object for the purpose of launching an activity, so these are more dynamic.

Some are obviously useful, but others are just perplexing (in an area of functionality that is perplexing enough as it is):

➤ FLAG_ACTIVITY_BROUGHT_TO_FRONT — Used by the system to implement the behavior to be used when an activity has the singleTask or singleInstance launch mode attribute specified.

➤ FLAG_ACTIVITY_CLEAR_TASK — Indicates the tasks to be cleared before the new activity starts. This means the new activity is the new root activity of the task, and no other activities are stacked on it or under it.

➤ FLAG_ACTIVITY_CLEAR_TOP — Puts the matching activity on top of the activity stack, if it is in the activity stack of the current task, by finishing all activities on top of the one the Intent object matches. If the specified activity is at the top of the activity stack, it is finished and re-created, unless it is capable of receiving a new intent via the onNewIntent() method. This is a complex combination of effects, especially since the default behavior without using onNewIntent is to both chop off the top of the activity stack and replace the existing matching activity with a new instance. Be sure your use-case supports using this flag.

➤ FLAG_ACTIVITY_CLEAR_WHEN_TASK_RESET — Indicates that the activity being launched should be on top of the activity stack if the task is reset.

➤ FLAG_ACTIVITY_EXCLUDE_FROM_RECENTS — Normally the recent applications list displays to the top of each task's stack of activities. If you use this flag, the activity started with this Intent (and hence the task that would be represented by this activity) is not presented among the recent applications.

➤ FLAG_ACTIVITY_FORWARD_RESULT — The new activity can provide a result to the activity that launched the current activity. This enables substituting for an activity started with the startActivityForResult method. In other words, "Here, you answer this."

➤ FLAG_ACTIVITY_LAUNCHED_FROM_HISTORY — The new activity was, in effect, launched from the "Recent Applications" list.

➤ FLAG_ACTIVITY_MULTIPLE_TASK — The new activity can be the root of multiple tasks. This is used to launch a launcher so that it can be the bottom or the back-stack for all the activities it launches.

➤ FLAG_ACTIVITY_NEW_TASK — The new activity is the root of a new task.

➤ FLAG_ACTIVITY_NO_ANIMATION — Suppresses transition animation.

➤ FLAG_ACTIVITY_NO_HISTORY — The new activity is not on the back-stack. It is the same as the noHistory attribute.

➤ FLAG_ACTIVITY_NO_USER_ACTION — Suppresses the onUserLeaveHint callback for the current activity. Assuming this callback is used to clear alerts, the alerts will stay up. This is useful for activity transitions the users did not initiate, such as displaying an incoming call or message.

➤ FLAG_ACTIVITY_PREVIOUS_IS_TOP — The new activity will not be treated as the top of the activity stack, and the previous top activity will be treated as the top for the purposes of deciding whether an Intent should be delivered to the top activity, or whether a new activity should be created.

➤ FLAG_ACTIVITY_REORDER_TO_FRONT — If the activity is already running, it will be raised to the top of the activity stack and made visible.

➤ FLAG_ACTIVITY_RESET_TASK_IF_NEEDED — This activity becomes the task root, even if it is pre-existing activity in a pre-existing task and is not the task root.

➤ FLAG_ACTIVITY_SINGLE_TOP — Equivalent to the singleTop launch mode: If the activity is already the top of the back-stack of the task, a new Activity is not created.

➤ FLAG_ACTIVITY_TASK_ON_HOME — Puts that new activity just above Home in the task. This has the effect of making back-navigation from that activity go to Home, rather than to the activity that launched it.

Together, launch modes specified in the manifest and flags set in the Intent objects that cause activities to be launched enable manipulation of navigation by arranging the back-stack, and, in turn, affecting the behavior of the Back button in the Android user experience. While the examples here are simple, with one or two Activity components on the back-stack, your applications will likely need to consider how they arrange the back-stack as they contain more activities.

Navigation in Tablets

Critics have said that the Back button should really be called "Shuffle" because you never know where you will end up. More recently, Google has promulgated some conventions that make navigation less of an adventure for the user.

The original navigation conventions in Android were so simple, app developers had hardly any work to do to implement them. As Android scaled up to tablet size and acquired new features for creating richer user interfaces, the burden on developers grew. Developers now need to be aware of more conventions and to embody those conventions in their code.

You might ask why isn't there an application or activity class that embodies these conventions and makes life easier for the developers. It's hard to pick a set of conventions to enshrine in a framework. Android enables a variety of styles and infinite variations on those styles, for better or worse. We can show you one "slice" or path through those choices, but you are free to make your application as distinctive as you like, and branch off from Android's framework at a variety of levels.

CHOOSING TO USE THE SUPPORT PACKAGE

The Android SDK includes a library commonly referred to as the Support Package or Support Library. It used to be called the Android Compatibility Package. When it was first released, it was used mainly for providing back-compatibility for applications. Recently, it incorporated a utility library that can be used with both "green-field" applications targeted at recent API levels and back-compatible applications.

In creating enterprise applications, you can set reasonable standards for using current versions of Android, even in bring your own device (BYOD) environments. Therefore, we encourage you to develop for and use recent APIs and test for API availability to achieve some back-compatibility. You will save significant effort if you can avoid back-porting, since, among other complications, not all recent APIs are supported by the Support Package. That is how the Support Package has been used in this book.

If you need more back-compatibility than you can reasonably achieve by testing for API availability, use the Support Package's `Activity` subclass and `Fragment` back-port and other classes to create a branch of your code-base for the purpose of back-porting your application. You will also need to find a substitute for the `ActionBar` class, which is not included in the Support Package. That is one of the reasons back-compatibility is outside the scope of this book, and of this UI framework, which depends on `ActionBar` for a lot of functionality.

For some mass-market apps that need to hit the market targeting every possible user, back-compatibility dominates decision making about which APIs can be used. In general, however, back-compatibility strategies are outside the scope of this book and need to be tailored to the requirements of specific apps, developers, and user communities.

Here, you use the Support Package only for utility classes, especially for swiping between `Fragment` objects.

SUMMARY

In this chapter, we combined two previous examples and expanded on them to show how a user interface framework can be created for data-oriented applications. While we used local data to keep our dependencies manageable for the purposes of an example, this framework is applicable to applications that use web APIs as well.

This chapter tied together the classes that form a common user interface idiom in Android: the Action Bar, tabs, fragments, swipe gestures, the option menu, a list of items; and we combined these elements with the declarative layout-driven strategy for scaling from small to large screens. Together these elements form a solid foundation for implementations that do not force an artificial decision to go handset-first or tablet-first and that make use of up-to-date APIs and idioms.

Security

Mobile devices present one of the most profitable hacking targets in the average person's digital world. They contain copious amounts of personal information, often include access to bank and retirement accounts, contain all your contacts, and can access your e-mail. They can also fall, without a sound, out of your pocket. They know where you are, can see your face, and can eavesdrop on your conversations while they sit in your backpack. They might also randomly load malicious code from the phones of other people as they walk nearby in the street. Clearly, the stakes in securing mobile applications are high.

Hacking for profit or espionage has become big business worldwide. Keeping user data safe and developer assets secure requires vigilance on the part of mobile developers and handset owners. This chapter covers Android techniques for enhancing security for both handset users and application developers regarding the following topics:

➤ Android platform security

➤ User techniques for keeping phones secure

➤ Writing secure applications that protect privacy and prevent theft

➤ Protecting applications from piracy

PLATFORM SECURITY

The previous paragraphs painted a potentially bleak picture of mobile security, but of course those scenarios depend on circumventing Android platform security controls. Mobile device features are generally safe as long as malware does not subvert formidable operating system and application protections.

When confronting long-standing security problems, recent mobile operating systems employ defenses that are leaps and bounds better than security techniques used in traditional desktop platforms like Windows and Mac OS. One of the most common ways to get a desktop virus is to unwittingly open a malicious e-mail attachment. Another pitfall is to allow insecure plugins to run in your web browser — desktop Java Technology from Oracle has recently encountered a string of serious and high-profile security flaws related to Java running in web pages. For years, Windows would run all programs downloaded from the Internet or even from floppy disks with administrative privileges. Once activated a virus could access sensitive system resources at will. Windows XP corrected this problem with user and file system permissions, but many users still ran all programs as an administrative user, thus nullifying the security enhancements. Linux and Mac OSX have always run user-level processes with a vastly reduced level of access — without admin access.

Android takes OS-level protection a step further, by extending the security model already found on Linux and Mac OS to drastically increase the level of isolation between individual applications. Each application runs as an entirely different UNIX user. This simple but effective step uses the base operating system to prevent applications from tampering with each other's data in the file system, from accessing shared pipes, and a range of Linux resources.

Android also supports application permissions that provide another level of security not found on a platform level in traditional operating systems. Users don't need to fully trust application code; instead, they can rely on OS-imposed limitations to prevent apps from performing sensitive operations, such as covertly slurping a user's contacts list out of a device.

In spite of these improvements, modern mobile attacks take many forms. For example, there was a recent spate of hijacked, Trojan applications posing as popular Android applications, such as "Angry Birds", which caused phones to participate in a spam botnet. The hijacked phones sent out prolific messages at the expense of the end user. Despite enhanced platform security, downloading malicious code onto a device is still a primary concern.

> **NOTE** *For reference, the Google Open Source project provides a comprehensive overview of the Android platform and its security model:*
>
> `http://source.android.com/devices/tech/security/index.html`

KEEPING HANDSETS SAFE

Before you begin writing secure code for Android applications, it's important to be aware of the tools that end users can use to keep their handsets safe and to know which of these tools help developers write secure applications. Before walking through a set of Android security examples, the chapter covers techniques for safe usage of Android by end users. This involves a discussion of several security tools from Google and other vendors, all of which impact the security of the Android ecosystem.

Avoiding Malicious Applications

For several years, the iPhone was king of the mobile application space. As of the time of writing of this book, Android had caught up significantly and was closing in on 800,000 applications listed in the Google Play store. With that many applications, simple probability gives hackers many chances to sneak code onto user's phones.

Attacks on Android systems have several common sources:

➤ Android applications

➤ Browser-based JavaScript

➤ Messaging

➤ NFC and Bluetooth

➤ Kernel root exploits

Secure usage is currently the first defense against these types of attacks. We want to take a look at platform and ecosystem tools that can help handset users keep their phones safe.

Use a Safe Browser Like Google Chrome

If your Android device does not have the Chrome browser pre-installed, you should install it. It's available in the Google Play store. Many attacks against applications involve cooperation on the part of the browser — like an app that directs the browser to malicious websites. Chrome helps to close holes of this nature with built-in malware and phishing protection and — of critical importance — process-level sandboxing support. Chrome is widely regarded to be one of the most, if not *the* most, secure browser.

Understand Google Bouncer

To protect users from application threats, Google created the Bouncer program, which is an application that emulates applications to look for malware patterns. The program prevents malicious applicants from gaining entrance to the Google Play application store. Users and developers don't need to do anything specific to take advantage of Bouncer's protection — apps are rejected on store submission if they don't pass security tests when running on the Bouncer emulator.

Beware Installing from Unknown Locations

Although the Google Play store and the Amazon app store provide the "front door" for application installation on Android devices, Android also supports application installation through SD card side loading, as well as the ability to install applications from unknown locations. As many Android developers know, you can get to this location using the following:

```
Settings -> Applications -> Check Allow "Unknown Sources"
```

On Android 4.0 or greater use:

```
Settings -> Security -> Check "Unknown Sources"
```

Of course, users should keep in mind that although there may be good reasons to download Android applications from unknown sources, careless downloading of applications not fully known to the user is a great way to compromise phone security. For example, one spam botnet attack, that Lookout Security gave the moniker *SpamSoldier*, spread itself by sending SMS messages with a link for unsuspecting users to download — not particularly sophisticated, but successful against teenagers and other newbies using phones.

Use the Application Verifier Service

Although you might think you know an application from an "unknown source" well enough to install it outside of the store, it's smart to check it for viruses just in case. As of Android 4.1/4.2, Jellybean, on Google Nexus, Google has provided users with an additional security check that blocks malicious apps from installation, called the *application verifier service*. The feature is active by default, but users can turn it off, at their own risk, with:

```
Settings -> Security -> Verify Apps
```

When you install a new app — from any app store, or "unknown sources", not just Google Play — the verifier service will collect information about the application. If the Google cloud has information that the application is malicious, it will take one of two actions. If the app is dangerous, Android will not install it. If the app is potentially dangerous, it will warn the user and provide the option of not installing it. You can find instructions for turning on the verifier service for the Google Nexus below:

```
https://support.google.com/nexus/galaxy/answer/2812853?hl=en-CA
```

Consider the Success of Security Measures

Now that you have some awareness of major security measures that Google has put in place for Android, it's time to take a look at publicly available security reviews of them:

Bouncer

Security researchers initially investigated Google Bouncer and found that it was possible to "fingerprint" the service, which meant that it was possible, at one point in time, for applications under review to investigate the Bouncer environment and report back this useful information about it to potentially malicious authors. You can find more information about the review here:

```
http://blog.trendmicro.com/trendlabs-security-intelligence/
a-look-at-google-bouncer/
```

Such transparency might open the door to security attacks.

Nexus Application Verifier Service

As of November 2012, another security researcher investigated the Nexus Application Verifier Service and presented his results online, along with a description of the App Verifier tool:

```
http://www.cs.ncsu.edu/faculty/jiang/appverify/
```

This researcher, a founder of the Android Malware Genome project, attempted to install a large number of known malicious Android applications. Alarmingly, the researcher found a low detection rate of < 20 percent. The results of this research indicate that even with Google's security measures, users should approach the installation of Android applications with a strong sense of caution. Still, keep in mind that this work was very early in the life of the verifier service, and Google is likely to improve it.

Although Google and other vendors have made considerable progress in protecting user security, these results indicate that device users should know enough about the applications and their corresponding developers to self-curate the apps that they install on their phones. According to sources online, detection rates for malicious apps are well below 100 percent — users should not operate under the assumption that all applications in Android app stores are safe.

Use Google Apps Device Management

Users who have Google Apps for Business accounts can take advantage of additional Android Security features, such as requiring a screen lock and pin or password for users, and remote wipe for lost or stolen phones. Users also get the ability to remotely:

➤ Reset pins

➤ Ring devices

➤ Lock devices

➤ Locate devices

After you have a Google Apps for Business account, you also need to download the Device Policy application. You can get this application, like any other, from the Google Play store. Once you have installed it, if you are not signed into your Google Apps account, you will need to add the account to the Device Policy application. Google has provided instructions for installing the Device Policy app:

```
http://support.google.com/a/users/bin/answer.py?hl=en&answer=2364439
```

Once the Device Policy is installed, you can set up the device management features:

```
http://support.google.com/a/users/bin/
answer.py?hl=en&answer=1235372&topic=2365092&ctx=topic
```

Know Alternative Security Products

Beyond tools from Google, the rising need for Android security has bred an industry in advanced mobile application security protection. Some of the more successful companies in this space include Lookout, Appthority, and Bit9. The main features of many of these applications include:

➤ Real-time scanning for malware

➤ Locating lost devices

➤ Remote locking or wiping of handsets to protect security

➤ Securely backing up user data such as contacts and password management

Pay Attention to Your Phone Bill

According to Lookout Security, the most prevalent form of Android malware takes the form of *toll fraud,* which is a covert and particularly common way of sneaking charges into a subscriber's cell phone bill — 72 percent of Lookout-detected malware involved toll fraud. Typically, toll fraud involves billable SMS messages, which is a common way of paying for mobile transactions. Cell phones have supported text-based billing for many years to enable users to buy ring tones, images, and so on.

An example of toll fraud involves the installation of a malicious app that can hide and respond to billable SMS messages. Such an application will work with a cooperating backend that can receive malicious SMS messages sent from the app. The carrier ends up allowing a charge from the malicious service, since the malicious app is able to receive SMS confirmation messages. The carrier interprets access to a device as confirmation of a user's identity. With an insidious twist, the toll fraud application will hide the confirmation SMS message so that the handset user never even sees it. The only way that users will ever know that theft has occurred is by paying careful attention to their cell phone bills. For more information, check out the following:

```
http://bits.blogs.nytimes.com/2012/12/13/lookout-toll-fraud/
```

Understand Malware Mechanics: The Malware Genome

Another promising Android security investigation called the "malware genome" analyzed known Android exploits to discover their modes of operation and the security flaws in Android and applications that they exploit. A brief summary of the findings concerning malware includes:

➤ 86 percent are repackaged legitimate applications.

➤ 40 percent used root-level exploits.

➤ 90 percent turn phones into botnets — device networks that serve a malicious purpose. A typical botnet might recruit hacked devices to send out SMS spam.

➤ 45 percent have built-in support for sending SMS messages, premium rate calls, or making calls without the user knowing.

➤ 51 percent are harvesting user information, including user accounts and short messages stored on phones.

To give you an idea of what's involved in detecting malicious apps, here's a list of the prominent types of attacks:

➤ **Repacking** — Downloading a legitimate application, unpacking the contents, inserting malicious code, and repacking the app to appear as the original app.

➤ **Drive by downloads** — Downloading malicious content, as by an e-mail attachment, where the user either does not know the payload is downloaded, or is unaware that the download could infect their systems.

➤ **Update attacks** — Initial applications have no malicious code, but an application update includes one. This strategy avoids virus scan detection on first download.

➤ **Root exploits** — Involve memory overruns that give malicious code complete system access. After execution, the main defense against this type of attack is application-based encryption. Unfortunately, Android root exploits often persist in devices because the kernel vulnerabilities they use go unpatched as carriers take time to push OS updates to devices.

> **NOTE** *You can learn more about the malware genome here:*
>
> `http://www.malgenomeproject.org/`
>
> *You find the comprehensive review of malware applications in the following document:*
>
> `http://www.csc.ncsu.edu/faculty/jiang/pubs/OAKLAND12.pdf`

WRITING SECURE APPLICATIONS

Compared to traditional desktop systems, Android certainly has improved OS-level protection, but mobile software supports complex and detailed data about its users and faces increasingly sophisticated attacks trying to access that lucrative information. Developers writing applications for Android need to consider security upfront and be sure that they write secure code from the first deployment of their application. It's time to shift focus from keeping malicious code off Android to defending your own application in an environment where malicious code might be present.

> **NOTE** *As you learn about writing secure applications, you will encounter several chapter examples that you can invoke from the user interface of the AndroidSecurity project. Import each project into Eclipse, as in previous chapters, run the main apk, and then invoke each one as you read its section in the chapter. Keep in mind that you will have to modify some of the code as you go, and refer to* `$CODE/AndroidSecurity/README` *for the most up to date instructions.*

Hacking Targets

When it makes its way onto a device, malware seeks access to the system as a whole or to individually installed applications, including the ones you develop. To defend your application, consider these high-value targets that hackers are likely to attack:

➤ **Security keys** — Provide access to encrypted files, which would normally protect even a "rooted" or jail-broken device.

➤ **Passwords:** Passwords provide access to remote web service data, and should not be stored directly on a device.

➤ **Insecure APIs** — Applications that implement Android APIs by creating content providers, using Android Interface Definition Language (AIDL), services, or handling intents should take care to filter out malicious invocations by detecting attack parameters.

➤ **Permission-based privileges** — Unauthorized and transitive use of permissions, also known as "privilege escalation."

➤ **Communication channels** — AIDL, intents, and services all have the potential to leak sensitive information across process boundaries. Effectively sandboxed applications will leverage modes of communication to access privileges available to your application.

➤ **Root-level access** — If an attacker physically holds a device, it's fairly easy for them to unlock it and obtain admin access. More often, inadvertently installed malware will take advantage of vulnerabilities in the base of the operating system itself to gain full system access.

➤ **Billable events** — Most malicious app developers are in the business of making money, which means they seek monetary targets like in-app billing or premium SMS messages.

Before getting too paranoid about the number of possible security holes, keep in mind that most Android settings — including file permissions — have secure default values. Android also protects applications using the Linux file system, process model, and a strong security sandbox. Android employs the following technologies to avoid traditional penetrations due to memory: SLR, NX, ProPolice, safe_iop, OpenBSD dlmalloc, OpenBSD calloc, and Linux mmap_min_addr. Android also has interesting security tricks up its sleeve, like the ability to encrypt an entire file system volume and more described in the following location:

```
http://developer.android.com/training/articles/security-tips.html
```

Ingredients of a Secure Application

The first step in designing any secure application is to consider the principle of least privilege, which means that applications request only the minimum access to sensitive resources and privileges required for an app to perform its functions. For example, if you've written a content provider that needs to be used only in its declaring apk, don't export the provider to other processes. Instead use `android:exported="false"`. If external applications do need to read from the content provider, allow only read access, instead of requiring read/write access by default. If you are writing a location-aware application that does not need incredibly precise location information, request `ACCESS_COARSE_LOCATION` instead of `ACCESS_FINE_LOCATION`. And so on...

Android app developers have important reasons for writing applications that request only the permissions they need:

➤ If a hacker compromises your application's security, either through a published API like a received intent, or any other security backdoor, the privileges granted to your application can become accessible to the attacker. When your app asks only for privileges it needs, it closes unnecessary security risks even in the event of a successful attack. If you "over-privilege" your app, you might leak privileges you did not even need.

➤ Users who read the list of permissions your app declares in its manifest are more likely to install apps with smaller sets of less sensitive permissions.

> **NOTE** *In Android 2.2, Google released a transitive security bug when its power control widget enabled unauthorized modification of system settings:*
>
> ```
> https://code.google.com/p/android/issues/detail?id=7890
> ```

Keep the principle of least privilege in mind, as you read the rest of the chapter, which covers the "ingredients" of a secure application that successfully defend against security attacks. These ingredients include:

➤ Secure use of permissions

➤ Protecting and encrypting data

➤ Protecting communication

➤ Preventing piracy

Secure Use of Permissions

As you discovered when writing your first Android application, you must declare permissions for features, such as Internet access, used in a given application. Applications use these declarations to request the use of permissions from the user installing an application. Explicitly asking end users to grant all permissions used in an app has some associated controversy. On one hand, a careful user has the opportunity to pick up on strange access requests (such as a to-do list application that asks permission to send SMS messages and to manage Android accounts). On the other hand, perhaps the majority of handset users will not have the technical savvy to know why some permissions might be sensitive, and might get tired of trying to review information they do not understand. On the whole, requiring apps to be open with the capabilities they require will almost certainly lead to informed scrutiny from some portion of each application's user base.

When writing Android applications that handle sensitive data, it's important to understand the power of the Android permission system: It's a fine-grained and powerful capability-granting framework. The Android permission system provides another strong example of how the Android platform has improved security over traditional operating systems — applications for the same user don't automatically get access to each other's resources or capabilities. Android enforces strong separation between all running processes.

> **NOTE** *As an aside, it's important not to confuse the Android permission system with the Linux Security model and permissions. In Android, file system permissions are Linux permissions.*

Permissions are likely the most prominent of Android security features that app developers need to consider when developing applications. Developers should keep a vigilant eye on which privileges they request, and how they make them available to other applications. This section provides an overview of how permissions work and includes interesting details of important permissions, including a sense of their comparative danger. This section also shows you when and how to create your own custom permissions.

Permission Basics

To review, a *permission* on Android protects calls that can perform security sensitive operations like sending an SMS message. Permissions can also protect calls that application developers deem sensitive. If a caller invokes a method but does not have the requisite permission, an instance of `java.lang.SecurityException` will be thrown, preventing the call from taking place. Applications request use of permissions in their `AndroidManifest`, as follows:

```
<uses-permission android:name="android.permission.INTERNET" />
```

Upon installation, end users review the list of permissions an app has requested and can reject the app if they deem the list suspicious.

Android Permissions

The base Android operating system provides a wide array of permissions that protect the functions available on Android devices. You can find them all listed in the class `android.Manifest` `.permission`, as follows:

```
http://developer.android.com/reference/android/Manifest.permission.html
```

Every Android permission, including custom application permissions, has an associated protection level that gives users and developers a sense of how concerned they should be about granting and asking to use the permission. For example, the permission `android.permission.BRICK` clearly poses a lot of danger to a device, and is considered a "Dangerous" permission. A declaration of a permission in an `AndroidManifest` file includes specification of a protection level, as follows:

```
android:protectionLevel =
    "normal" | "dangerous" | "signature" | "signatureOrSystem"
```

The following table explains protection levels in detail:

PROTECTION LEVEL	DESCRIPTION
Normal	Minimal level threat that does not pose significant danger to the user or the system. Automatically granted on app installation.
Dangerous	Poses significant threat to the system and to user data. Dangerous permissions require user approval and are generally subject to a large community of users who will spot suspicious permission requests.
Signature	A permission that Android grants only to applications that have the same signature as the app that defined the permission. Automatically granted on signature match.
SignatureOrSystem	Reserved for system use; your application should not use this level.

But what practical knowledge do these levels provide? As you can see, Android end users must manually approve all dangerous permissions in your applications, and you should be aware of the ones that will raise eyebrows so you can work to avoid them. Of critical importance are the permissions users don't want to see when they install your application; you need to convince users that it is okay to download your application.

> **NOTE** *This chapter contains more "real-world" knowledge than readers might expect. The intent of the discussion is to show how exploits subvert Android permissions and how users and developers can understand security attacks to avoid becoming malware victims.*

High Risk Permissions (Users Might Not Want to Grant)

Many of the permissions that should set off red flags for savvy Android users relate to the hacking targets that we have outlined in this chapter. Access to billable events, private data, sensitive user information, and security keys all have significant potential for exploitation. Here are some comments from the malware genome to give you a sense of the priorities of malware applications:

➤ `INTERNET`, `READ_PHONE_STATE`, `ACCESS_NETWORK_STATE`, and `WRITE_EXTERNAL_STORAGE` permissions are widely requested in both malicious and benign apps.

➤ Malicious apps are 10 times more likely to request `CHANGE_WIFI_STATE` than benign applications, likely because the permission enables hot plug events that are needed for root exploits.

➤ Malicious apps clearly tend to request SMS-related permissions — `READ_SMS`, `WRITE_SMS`, `RECEIVE_SMS`, and `SEND_SMS` — more frequently than benign applications.

Users should install only well known apps, like Google Voice, from trusted vendors like Google that seem to have a very good reason for accessing particularly lucrative target permissions like `CALL_PHONE` and `CALL_PRIVILEGED` or the ability access text messages. If a puzzle game requires access to send text messages, it may not be a good idea to download and install it.

The following table lists the top Android permissions requested in malware applications (as provided by the Malware Genome Project) and notes vulnerabilities of each of them.

PERMISSION NAME	ACCESS NOTES
`INTERNET`	`INTERNET` permission is useful to attackers in myriad different ways; here are a few popular ones: 1. Allows an application to open Internet sockets to any outgoing host; contrast to web-based JavaScript which can read responses from connections to its host of origin, excluding HTML5 Cross-Origin Resource Sharing (CORS), which can be as permissive as Android `INTERNET` permission. 2. Enables a botnet to communicate with its command and control (C&C) server. 3. A common hack directs browser and apps that have `INTERNET` permission to load malicious website URLs — more on this in the section, "Checking the Caller's Permissions" later in the chapter. 4. Surprisingly, Android does not require permission to access a user's photos. Any app that has `INTERNET` permission can upload user photos to the site of their choice on the Internet: http://bits.blogs.nytimes.com/2012/03/01/android-photos/
`READ_PHONE_STATE`	Provides read-only access to phone state.

continues

(continued)

PERMISSION NAME	ACCESS NOTES
`ACCESS_NETWORK_STATE`	Allows applications to access information about networks.
`WRITE_EXTERNAL_STORAGE`	Provides the ability to write to the SD card. Example use: to hide the location of a C&C server.
`ACCESS_WIFI_STATE`	Allows access to information about WiFi networks. Potentially related to root-level exploits.
`READ_SMS`	Allows applications to read existing SMS messages that are for other applications; a nice way to get at text sensitive information.
`RECEIVE_BOOT_COMPLETED`	Requested five times more frequently by malware than legitimate applications.
`WRITE_SMS`	Allows an application to write SMS messages.
`SEND_SMS`	Allows an application to send an outgoing SMS, as would have been required by SpamSoldier. Receiving an SMS is a chargeable event, which makes it an attractive target to thieves. Sending SMS messages is especially attractive given the prevalence of toll fraud schemes based on carrier premium SMS messages.
`RECEIVE_SMS`	Allows applications to receive SMS messages as required for an SMS based push notification system. Receiving an SMS is a chargeable event, which makes the action attractive to thieves.
`VIBRATE`	Allows an application to turn on the phone's vibrator.
`ACCESS_COARSE_LOCATION`	Provides access to the phone's coarse or network location — the location value that does not come from the GPS radio.
`READ_CONTACTS`	Provides access to a user's contacts; clearly valuable information for a hacker.
`ACCESS_FINE_LOCATION`	Provides access to fine-grained GPS information; higher resolution than coarse network location.
`WAKE_LOCK`	Prevents the phone from sleeping or the screen from dimming. This plays into the strategy of malicious applications using the phone for botnets that need the ability to run in the background without the user's knowledge.
`CALL_PHONE`	Enables outbound calls potentially to premium phone services, likely outside the United States, which can be associated with significant per instance charges.

PERMISSION NAME	ACCESS NOTES
CHANGE_WIFI_STATE	The ability to change WiFi state is related to system events that enable a malicious application to execute root-level exploits.
WRITE_CONTACTS	The ability to add contacts is useful for malicious apps in a number of ways — for example, to write a contact that looks like someone they recognize, but perhaps representing a malicious phone number.
WRITE_APN_SETTINGS	Allows applications to write the GSM Access Point Name (APN) settings.
RESTART_PACKAGES	The permission is deprecated, and applications should not use it.

Using Application-Defined Permissions

Protecting sensitive resources in your own applications, specifically to protect IPC access to your Android components such as content providers or services, may require the use of application-defined permissions. The manifest declaration in Listing 12-1 creates a permission for reading contacts from the contacts' content provider.

LISTING 12-1: Create a custom permission for accessing contacts

```
<permission
    android:name="com.enterpriseandroid.permission.READ_CONTACTS"
    android:label="Read contact information."
    android:description=
        "Enables reading contacts from the contacts content provider."
    android:protectionLevel="dangerous"
    android:permissionGroup="android.permission-group.PERSONAL_INFO"
/>
```

➤ `name` — The name of the permission that apps will declare in their manifest.

➤ `label` — The label of the permission.

➤ `description` — A description of the permission shown to end users.

➤ `protectionLevel` — The protection level of the permission, as discussed previously. This permission is dangerous, so the user will have to approve it.

➤ `permissionGroup` — The string that defines the group in which the permission will be placed when presented to the end user for permission approval. In this case, the permission relates to personal information.

Enacting the newly defined permission requires checking the required permission when sensitive code is called, as in Listing 12-2.

LISTING 12-2: Checking an application-defined permission

```
PackageManager manager = getPackageManager();
int hasPermission =
    manager.checkPermission(
        "com.enterpriseandroid.permission.READ_CONTACTS",
        "com.enterpriseandroid.androidSecurity");

if (hasPermission != PackageManager.PERMISSION_GRANTED) {
    throw new SecurityException("Permission Denied: Reading Contacts.");
}
```

This snippet of code resides in an application method that needs to read `enterpriseandroid` contacts. To be secure, the method should verify that a caller also has permission to read this sensitive information by comparing the return value of `checkPermission` to `PERMISSION_GRANTED`. If either the calling code or the method code do not have permission, then the method should fail by throwing the security exception.

Protecting Data

As this book has discussed, typical places to store data include files in the file system (both internal flash storage and external SD card devices), SQLite databases, and content providers. Different Android components and files systems require different handling to maintain security. The next several sections cover securing Android file systems and application components.

Securing Data in Files

Android extends the Linux security system and protects files using the base Linux file system. In Linux, file permissions follow a standard format based on binary settings, where individual bits represent whether a given file is readable, writeable, or executable by the file owner, the file group, or by all users. As an example, a file with permissions, (7, 5, 5) or (111, 110, 110) would be readable, writeable, and executable by the owner, and readable and executable by everyone else.

Android relies on the core Java API, specifically `java.io.File`, to enable programmatic control over file system permissions. The following methods on `File` change underlying Linux file permissions:

```
setReadable(boolean readable, boolean ownerOnly)
setWriteable(boolean writeable, boolean ownerOnly)
```

The following sequence of invocations:

```
File myFile = new File(...);
myFile.setReadable(true, false);
myFile.setWriteable(true, false);
```

results in a Linux permission setting of (110,000,000) or (600), which is a secure access setting that allows only the application to read and write a file stored in an application's internal storage.

Internal Storage

Android internal storage supports Linux file system permissions. Applications writing files to their data directory, located at `/data/data/<manifest_package_name>`, can make use of Linux file permissions as described in the previous section. Trolling for inadvertently accessible files is a popular technique for malware to gain access to sensitive data. In almost all cases, applications should create files that are readable and writeable only by the application itself. Keep the following in mind when setting file permissions:

➤ World accessible files should be carefully reviewed for sensitive data.

➤ World writeable files can be filled up with junk to overwrite system memory for denial attacks.

Data on Upgrade

As you learned when deploying your first Android application, all applications that deploy to the Google Play store must have a digital signature. These signatures fulfill several roles for Android applications and the Android platform. In many cases, they prevent malicious applications from pretending to be better known and legitimate applications. They also prevent masquerading applications from "upgrading" in place over the presence of existing applications that may have already written data. For example, if a banking application wrote data into files on Android internal storage, Android does not permit a malicious application claiming to be an upgrade for the legitimate application to access the files.

External Storage

External storage devices on Android, such as removable SD cards, don't support Linux file system permissions for the simple reason that the file system format of most SD cards is a legacy format initially created for DOS, called FAT, which does not support permissions on individual files. Storing sensitive information in files on external storage is usually not a good idea since they can only have world readable permissions and will persist even after the writing application is uninstalled from the device. If you do need to store information on the SD card, it's a good idea to protect it using encryption.

Encrypting Data

Even if a file resides in internal storage with proper file system permissions, it's still a good idea to encrypt its data. File system permissions will not protect bank accounts, passwords, and other information when thieves steal and jail-break phones. It's fairly straightforward to encrypt data using the Android API, but it definitely helps to have basic knowledge of encryption to decide which algorithms you should use to secure data in files, and in RESTful calls (covered a bit later in this chapter).

The field of computer cryptography has a long and diverse history, going as far back as ciphers used by the Roman military and code breaking machines used during World War II. Encryption is the process of applying a mathematical algorithm to data to yield output data that is unintelligible to anyone who does not have a valid decrypting key. If you have this key, you can produce the original data by applying a decrypting algorithm to the encrypted data.

Symmetric and Asymmetric Cryptography

Modern encryption algorithms typically take symmetric or asymmetric forms:

➤ A **symmetric encryption** algorithm means that you use the same key to encrypt and decrypt data.

➤ **Asymmetric encryption**, also known as public key cryptography, involves the use of two different keys — the public key (the encrypting key) and a private key (the decrypting key). Usually, the public, private key pair is created by an entity known as a *certificate authority* (CA). See Figure 12-1.

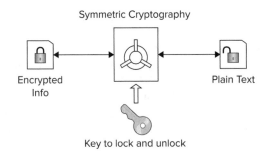

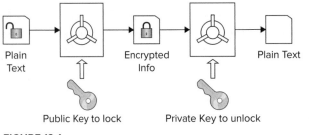

FIGURE 12-1

You can find symmetric and asymmetric encryption applied in modern secure software. Public key cryptography has the significant advantage that two parties can securely exchange data without having to transfer the private key over the Internet. It's possible to send encrypted data using a widely published public key, to a host that has access to the unpublished private key. Clients encrypt data using the public key, and only the receiving host that has the private key can decrypt the data. Public key cryptography in the form of Rivest, Shamir, Adleman (RSA) key exchange is the core of the more commonly recognized SSL/TLS and HTTPS protocols.

The main use of asymmetric encryption is for sending data over the Internet. The advantage of symmetric key encryption is its speed; it's significantly faster than asymmetric encryption. If you need to encrypt data for local file system storage, you would likely use a symmetric algorithm.

Modern encryption algorithms rely on the computational difficulty of guessing unencrypted data from its encrypted counterpart. The data from computationally complex encryption algorithms become exponentially more difficult to decrypt by brute force means as the size of the encrypting key grows. Over the years, the size of keys has grown from 56 bits to the now commonplace 256 bits.

Secure Hashing

The need to determine the identity of arbitrary binary information arises for some important tasks in mobile and service development, such as verifying files are not modified during download and determining uniqueness of files in large file sets. Using a secure hashing function provides an answer for this type of problem. A secure hash, or digest, converts data into a single fixed length value, much smaller than the data itself. A good hash function makes it unlikely that digests for various files collide — have the same binary digest value.

Storing Passwords

Another and perhaps more important use for hashing is for the secure storage of passwords. Android applications often need to use passwords to access symmetrically encrypted files and to provide credentials for accessing RESTful web services. As noted, hackers often seek to acquire these passwords to gain the same access as legitimate application code. Consequently, you should not store user credentials for a RESTful service or an encrypted file on a device. Google recommends performing an initial authentication using credentials your app collects from the user, and then using a short-lived, service-specific authorization token (using OAuth or the account manager).

If an application finds it needs to roll its own password storage, it should hash passwords and store their hashed digest — the output of the hash function. When users give their passwords to an application, the application will hash them, and then compare them against already stored digests. If it finds a match, the application accepts the user's credentials. Modern password storage approaches should include random values, called *salt*, along with the password and hash both together repeatedly.

Practical Encryption for Android

A few encryption techniques stand out as particularly relevant for writing enterprise Android applications:

➤ **Advanced Encryption System (AES)** is the commonly used symmetric encryption used by applications. It's fast, modern, and strong. The current AES standard key size is 256; AES(256).

➤ **HTTPS** is the standard secure mode of Internet transport for most web and mobile applications.

➤ **Secure Hash Algorithm (SHA)** provides cryptographically strong hashing with desirable characteristics, such as uniqueness for datasets and low probability of hash collisions. It's difficult to craft binary data that would contain subtle differences from the data being hashed but still end up with both attack data and original data having the same hash digest. With hashing algorithms, the size of the message digest can be 224, 256, 384, or 512 bits.

Example Code: Symmetric Encryption

It's time to get started with the first of the chapter examples. This code demonstrates the use of symmetric encryption based on the AES algorithm. You can run the AESEncryption Activity in the sample code to show a string, "This is a demo message from Java!" encrypted and then decrypted. If you need to secure data, you should encrypt data as needed and then write the encrypted text into files as appropriate for your application.

The class AESEncryptionHelper has methods to encrypt and decrypt an array of bytes, as shown in Listing 12-3:

LISTING 12-3: Symmetric encryption on Android (AES-256)

```
package com.enterpriseandroid.androidSecurity;

import java.io.ByteArrayInputStream;
import java.io.ByteArrayOutputStream;
import java.io.IOException;
import java.security.InvalidAlgorithmParameterException;
import java.security.InvalidKeyException;
import java.security.NoSuchAlgorithmException;

import javax.crypto.Cipher;
import javax.crypto.CipherInputStream;
import javax.crypto.CipherOutputStream;
import javax.crypto.NoSuchPaddingException;
import javax.crypto.spec.IvParameterSpec;
import javax.crypto.spec.SecretKeySpec;

/**
 * Demonstrates the use of symmetric encryption on Android (AES-256)
 */
public class AESEncryptionHelper {

private String padding =
        "ISO10126Padding"; //"ISO10126Padding", "PKCS5Padding"

private byte[] iv;
private byte[] key;
private Cipher encryptCipher;
private Cipher decryptCipher;

public AESEncryptionHelper(byte[] key, byte[] iv) throws Exception {
    this.key = key;
    this.iv = iv;

        initEncryptor();
    initDecryptor();
    }

private void initEncryptor() throws NoSuchAlgorithmException,
        NoSuchPaddingException, InvalidKeyException,
```

```
            InvalidAlgorithmParameterException
        {

            SecretKeySpec keySpec = new SecretKeySpec(key, "AES");
            IvParameterSpec ivSpec = new IvParameterSpec(iv);
```

Initialize the encryption cipher used to write encryption bytes:

```
        encryptCipher = Cipher.getInstance("AES/CBC/" + padding);
        encryptCipher.init(Cipher.ENCRYPT_MODE, keySpec, ivSpec);
        }

    private  void initDecryptor() throws Exception{
        SecretKeySpec keySpec = new SecretKeySpec(key, "AES");
        IvParameterSpec ivSpec = new IvParameterSpec(iv);
```

Initialize the decryption cipher used to write encryption bytes:

```
        decryptCipher = Cipher.getInstance("AES/CBC/" + padding);
        decryptCipher.init(Cipher.DECRYPT_MODE, keySpec, ivSpec);
    }
```

This is a generic method for *encrypting* an array of bytes and it works by writing all bytes to a `CipherInputStream` that has been configured for AES. The encrypted bytes collect into a byte array output stream, which is converted into a `byte[]` as a return value.

```
        public byte[] encrypt(byte[] dataBytes) throws IOException{
            ByteArrayInputStream bIn =
                    new ByteArrayInputStream(dataBytes);
            @SuppressWarnings("resource")
            CipherInputStream cIn =
                    new CipherInputStream(bIn, encryptCipher);
            ByteArrayOutputStream bOut =
                    new ByteArrayOutputStream();
            int ch;
            while ((ch = cIn.read()) >= 0) {
              bOut.write(ch);
            }
            return bOut.toByteArray();
        }
```

Here is another generic method, this time for *decrypting* an array of bytes; it works by writing all bytes to a `CipherOutputStream` that has been configured for AES. As before, the encrypted bytes collect into a byte array output stream, which is converted into a `byte[]` as a return value.

```
        public byte[] decrypt(byte[] dataBytes) throws IOException {
            ByteArrayOutputStream bOut = new ByteArrayOutputStream();
            CipherOutputStream cOut =
                    new CipherOutputStream(bOut, decryptCipher);
            cOut.write(dataBytes);
            cOut.close();
```

continues

LISTING 12-3 *(continued)*

```
            return bOut.toByteArray();
        }

    public static void main(String[] args) throws Exception {
```

The message to encrypt:

```
        String demoMessage =
                "This is a demo message from Java!";

        byte[] demoMesageBytes =
                demoMessage.getBytes();


        //shared secret
        byte[] demoKeyBytes = "abcdefghijklmnop".getBytes();

        // Initialization Vector - usually contains random data along
        // with a shared secret or transmitted along with a message.
        // Not all the ciphers require IV - we use IV in this
        // particular sample
        byte[] demoIVBytes =
                new byte[] {
                        0x00, 0x01, 0x02, 0x03,
                        0x04, 0x05, 0x06, 0x07,
                        0x08, 0x09, 0x0a, 0x0b,
                        0x0c, 0x0d, 0x0e, 0x0f};

        AESEncryptionHelper aesHelper =
                new AESEncryptionHelper(demoKeyBytes, demoIVBytes);
```

First encrypt the bytes:

```
        byte[] encryptedMsg =
                aesHelper.encrypt(demoMesageBytes);
        System.out.println("Encrypted Msg: " +
                new String(encryptedMsg));
```

Print the encrypted data:

```
        byte[] decryptedMsg =
                aesHelper.decrypt(encryptedMsg);
```

Print the decrypted data:

```
        System.out.println("Decrypted Msg: " +
                new String(decryptedMsg));
        }
    }
```

Now that you can encrypt and decrypt files using AES, it's time to think about how to handle passwords.

Example Code: Password Hashing

The next code example shows how an application uses a hashed password as a key to a symmetrically encrypted data file, which was created in the previous example. The example hashes the password with salt created from a supplied username. A real-world application of this idea would store the password on a remote service to avoid the security risk of saving the password in the local file system. To decrypt a file with such a key, an application would download the remote password, rehash it, and then decrypt the relevant data. Listing 12-4 generates salt and then performs a shaHex on the password and the salt.

> **NOTE** *Listing 12-4 uses a higher-level API,* org.apache.commons.codec
> .digest.DigestUtils, *than the one found on base Android. You can find this*
> *Apache API at* $(CODE)/AndroidSecurity/libs/org.apache.commons
> .codec-1.3.0.jar.

LISTING 12-4: Password hashing

```
package com.enterpriseandroid.androidSecurity;

import org.apache.commons.codec.digest.DigestUtils;

import android.util.Log;

public class PasswordHelper {
private static final String TAG = "PasswordHelper";

private String passwordHash;

    public PasswordHelper(String username, String password) {
        Log.i(TAG, "*****username:" + username + " password:" + password);
        String salt = generateSalt(username);
        Log.i(TAG, "*****salt:" + salt );
```

Generate the password digest:

```
        this.passwordHash = DigestUtils.shaHex(password + salt);
        Log.i(TAG, " hash:" + passwordHash);
    }
```

Generate salt:

```
    private String generateSalt(String s) {
        StringBuffer buf = new StringBuffer();
        for( int i=0; i< s.length(); i++) {
            if ( i % 2 ==0 ) {
                buf.append(s.charAt(i));
            }
        }
```

continues

LISTING 12-4 *(continued)*

```
            return buf.toString();
    }

    public String getPasswordHash() {
        return passwordHash;
    }
```

Perform a repeat hash as would be required when downloading a password for rehashing to unlock decrypted data:

```
    public boolean validatePassword(String username, String password) {
        Log.i(TAG, "username:" + username + " password:" + password);
        String salt = generateSalt(username);
        Log.i(TAG, " salt:" + salt );
        Log.i(TAG, " hash:" + passwordHash);

        Log.i(TAG, "validate hash:" + DigestUtils.shaHex(password + salt));
        return passwordHash.equals(DigestUtils.shaHex(password + salt));
    }
}
```

Encrypting All File System Data

Enterprise and otherwise security conscious users can attain peace of mind by simply encrypting all user data on their devices. Android supports volume-wide data encryption, based on a required phone pin or password (screen lock is not supported). It's simple to enable file system encryption. Make sure your phone is charged and plugged in, and then select the option with:

```
Settings -> Security -> Encrypt Phone
```

> **WARNING** *Make certain that you maintain power to your phone during the encryption process. If it fails part way through, you will likely lose all data on your device. It's definitely a good idea to back up the information on your phone before you start.*

Protecting Data in a Database: Preventing SQL Injection

SQL injection attacks are likely the most significant risk to data in a database. This type of attack is easy for hackers to mount and has traditionally yielded significant low-hanging fruit. SQL injection applies to backend services implemented with Hibernate in SQL, but also to Android applications that use SQLite. Chapter 3 noted the peril of manually composing strings to create SQL queries. Recall that the simple use of query, ?, parameters avoids such attacks. In backend services based on Hibernate, a similar approach enables prevention of most injection attacks. Recall the discussion from earlier chapters regarding usage of Android data APIs, specifically where usage of the method:

```
SQLiteDatabase.query(String table,
    String[] columns,
    String selection,
    String[] selectionArgs,
    String groupBy,
    String having,
    String orderBy,
    String limit)
```

should *always* make use of the `selectionArgs` parameter to replace embedded query occurrences of `"?"` Developers should never build queries by appending search parameters into a large string. Doing so robs the underlying database engine of the ability to determine the bounds of input parameters, which allows those parameters to include SQL designed to get the database to return results that would otherwise never be part of a response.

Protecting APIs

Android supports a rich interprocess communication model, including Remote Procedure Calls (RPC) based on AIDL, intent-based invocation and broadcasting, and a service model for running tasks in the background. The next sections cover how to build security defenses for these components.

Protecting Intents

The Android Intent system supports generic messaging for Android components. The Intent object carries with it a logical operation to perform (such as, take a picture) and arguments to use (like a URI). When you wrote your first Android application, you declared an intent filter to decide which activity would handle starting your application, as follows:

```
<activity android:name=".YourActivity" android:label="@string/your_app_name">
    <intent-filter>
        <action android:name="android.intent.action.MAIN"/>
        <category android:name="android.intent.category.LAUNCHER"/>
    </intent-filter>
</activity>
```

A declaration of an intent filter means that Android should send intents to the declaring component. This opens the door to potential attacks; malicious apps can send intents as easily as legitimate ones. The easiest, but least functional, way to shut them down is to disallow cross process intents by marking components as not exported in your application's manifest, as follows:

```
<service android:exported="false"></service>
```

However, for components that you do export, if malicious code launches your application with attack arguments, it should not end up doing the hacker's bidding. An intent filter is a good start to adding security. Protect your components by specifying a filter that lists the intents your component can handle, as follows:

```
<intent-filter>
    <action android:name="com.enterpriseandroid.androidSecurity.DEMO_ACTION"/>
</intent-filter>
```

The core Android platform defines a set of actions that start with `android.intent.action`, such as `android.intent.action.MAIN` or `android.intent.action.WEB_SEARCH`. You can also define custom intent actions as follows:

```
<action android:name="com.enterpriseandroid.androidSecurity.DEMO_ACTION"/>
```

Although intent filters are convenient, application developers should not rely on them as a "securely hardened" API. You should also filter on permission access, as explained in the next section, and should sanitize intent arguments per the domain logic of your application.

Checking the Caller's Permissions

Your code needs to detect bad arguments and reject those that compromise user security. You can start by looking at the intent methods that provide data to your application, including the following:

```
getBundleExtra, getCharArrayExtra, getIntExtra
```

Then make sure you properly sanitize information from these calls, especially if you need to pass intent arguments to sensitive system calls that your application has permission to access. Android has provided a convenient but underused method called `Context.checkCallingPermissions` for making sure that the call has sufficient privileges to use your application's privileges.

Listing 12-5 demonstrates how to check the calling permissions for intents that seek to take a picture, access the Internet, and load a URI.

LISTING 12-5: Ensures that calling code has permission to access URI permissions for INTERNET and CAMERA

```
1  @Override
2  protected void onCreate(Bundle savedInstanceState) {
3      Intent activityIntent = getIntent();
4      String uriParameter =
5          activityIntent.getStringExtra(URI_PARAMETER);
6
7      Uri uriParam = Uri.parse(uriParameter);
8      int checkCallingUriPermissions =
9          checkCallingUriPermission(uriParam,
10             Intent.FLAG_GRANT_READ_URI_PERMISSION);
11     checkGranted(checkCallingUriPermissions,
12         "Uri: " + uriParam.toString());
13
14     String cameraPermission = "android.permission.CAMERA";
15     int checkCameraPermission = checkCallingPermission(cameraPermission);
16     checkGranted(checkCameraPermission, cameraPermission);
17
18     String internetPermission = "android.permission.INTERNET";
19     int checkUriPermission = checkCallingPermission(internetPermission);
20     checkGranted(checkUriPermission, internetPermission);
21 }
22
23 private void checkGranted(int checkPermission, String mesg) {
24     if (checkPermission ==
```

```
25              PackageManager.PERMISSION_GRANTED) {
26              Log.d(LOG_TAG, "Permission Granted: " + mesg);
27          }  else if (checkPermission ==
28              PackageManager.PERMISSION_DENIED) {
29              Log.d(LOG_TAG, "Permission Denied: " + mesg);
30          }
31  }
```

The code in listing 12-5, verifies that the code that launched the given activity has:

➤ **Lines 11, 12** — Permission to read the URI argument

➤ **Line 16** — Permission to access the CAMERA

➤ **Line 20** — Permission to access the INTERNET

So what are the consequences of not using these simple checks? A group of researchers at MIT created a rigorous review of a large number of applications and looked at how they leak privileges using intents. The researchers found that most applications did check for malicious input, but a few did not. As we have mentioned, most intent-related attacks try to get the target application to perform a sensitive operation using permissions it has that the calling code does not. The Android INTERNET permission was the most commonly leaked privilege, where a calling app that does not have the INTERNET permission can pass a URL to load as an intent parameter and direct another app to visit a malicious web page. Unfortunately, the researchers also found that relatively few app developers checked caller permissions. You can learn more about this study as follows:

```
http://css.csail.mit.edu/6.858/2012/projects/ocderby-dennisw-kcasteel.pdf
```

Securing Activities

As shown previously, several Android components can receive intents, activities included. However, activities also have a convenient attribute, called android:permission, for ensuring that callers have permission to start a given activity. This attribute obviates some of the need shown previously for writing your own intent checks to ensure the caller has a given permission, but will not perform more detailed inspections of intent parameters, such as URIs. The previous code example shows how to protect intents sent to an activity.

Securing Broadcasts

The Android broadcast API supports delivery of an intent to multiple receivers in different applications. An Android component sending a broadcast does not see a list of all receivers of the intent, nor does a receiver have knowledge of what code might be sending it intents. Consequently, filtering of intents gains significant importance, as does ensuring that receivers have permission to receive and senders have permission to send. Fortunately, Android supports ways of enforcing security for both ends of broadcast intent delivery.

Receiving Broadcasts

Broadcast receivers can receive intents for which they did not register, which means developers should be vigilant in filtering their inputs, and only accept broadcast actions that they are designed to accept, as discussed previously. Like the activity tag, the <receiver> tag also supports the android:permission attribute, but it's still advised that you perform detailed caller permission checking on receiving a broadcast intent.

The following example broadcast receiver requires that all senders have the RECEIVE_BROADCAST permission. Additionally, the receiver only accepts intents with action DEMO_ACTION:

```
<receiver android:name=".AndroidSecurityBroadcastReceiver"
    android:permission=
        "com.enterpriseandroid.androidSecurity.permission.SEND_BROADCAST">
    <intent-filter>
        <action android:name=
            "com.enterpriseandroid.androidSecurity.DEMO_ACTION"/>
    </intent-filter>
</receiver>
```

Sending Broadcasts

It's straightforward to send a broadcast intent and require that a receiver have a particular permission to receive, in this case, RECEIVE_BROADCAST:

```
Intent secureIntent = new Intent("RECEIVE_BROADCAST");
String receivePermission =
    "com.enterpriseandroid.androidSecurity.RECEIVE_BROADCAST";
sendBroadcast(secureIntent, receivePermission);
```

Note that receivers that register for the given action, but do not have the specified permission, will simply not receive the message. Android does not throw a security exception, but instead just blocks the receivers from getting the message.

Services

Android can limit the processes that have the ability to bind or interact with a given service component, by again requiring permission for these operations. The android:permission attribute supports this restriction as follows:

```
<service
    android:name="SecurityDemo"
    android:permission="com.enterpriseandroid.androidSecurity.SERVICE_BIND"
    android:exported="true"
    android:enabled="true"
    >

    <intent-filter>
        ...
    </intent-filter>
</service>
```

where you can simply add the permission required for binding to the service declaration. Service operations for starting and stopping all require the specified permission as well.

Content Provider Security

As you've seen in earlier chapters of this book, content providers should be a central part of the data management strategy for your application.

Securing Custom Content Providers

Android provides read and write permissions to limit content provider access to only privileged clients. As you've seen, it's a good idea to use the principle of least privilege to write applications that request read or write access as they need it (for example, to not request read and write, if they only need read). Application developers should also keep in mind that write access does not imply read access. Consider the sync adapter pattern from earlier chapters that reads data from a backend service and pushes it into a content provider, but does not need to read the data it writes; actually the Migrate sync adapter works along these lines. Listing 12-6 shows a provider declaration that requires read and write permissions.

LISTING 12-6: Content provider declaration that requires read and write permissions

```
<provider
    android:name="com.enterpriseandroid.contacts.ContactsProvider"
    android:authorities="com.enterpriseandroid.contacts"
    android:readPermission="com.enterpriseandroid.contacts.READ_CONTACTS"
    android:writePermission="com.enterpriseandroid.contacts.WRITE_CONTACTS"
    >
</provider>
```

When a user has granted permissions as needed to an app, it can invoke content resolver or content provider methods to query, insert, update, and delete contacts. An application that invokes a query but does not have the READ_CONTACTS permission will cause the platform to throw a SecurityException, and likewise the same will happen for a caller that does not have WRITE_CONTACTS but still calls insert, update, or delete.

Sharing Permissions

Read and write access is the minimum control you need to protect content provider data. URI permissions provide an important fine-grained provider access control. They enable content providers to limit access to data for specified namespaces. Consider that the contacts content provider might have grouped contacts into business and personal categories. The following URIs reflect this organization:

```
content://com.enterpriseandroid.contacts/business
content://com.enterpriseandroid.contacts/personal
```

When applications need to share subsets of data, Android does something clever; it enables a dynamic permission grant from one application that already has permission to read or write to temporarily give a specified subset of these same permissions to another application. Imagine a contacts application that needs to share a contact with a vCard application. Assuming the contacts application has full access to the contacts provider when it launches an intent to be handled by the vCard application, it can specify in the intent that the vCard application should also have permission to read the data it needs to display a virtual card. Listing 12-7 shows a provider declaration that enables this type of dynamic grant for the contacts content provider.

LISTING 12-7: A provider declaration that allows dynamic grants to the business and personal categories

```
<provider
    android:name="com.enterpriseandroid.contacts.ContactsProvider"
    android:authorities="com.enterpriseandroid.contacts"
    android:readPermission="com.enterpriseandroid.contacts.READ_CONTACTS"
    android:writePermission="com.enterpriseandroid.contacts.WRITE_CONTACTS"
    >
        <grant-uri-permission android:pathPrefix="/business/"/>
        <grant-uri-permission android:pathPrefix="/personal/"/>
</provider>
```

The code to launch an intent that grants a dynamic permission consists of creating the intent, setting a data URI, and then setting `Intent.FLAG_GRANT_READ_URI_PERMISSION`, which causes Android to grant the permission to the receiving application. See Listing 12-8.

LISTING 12-8: Code that launches an intent to show a vCard

```
Uri contactUri =
    Uri.parse("content://com.enterpriseandroid.contacts/business/1");

Intent vcardIntent = new Intent(Intent.ACTION_VIEW);
vcardIntent.setFlags(Intent.FLAG_ACTIVITY_NEW_TASK);
vcardIntent.setFlags(Intent.FLAG_GRANT_READ_URI_PERMISSION);
vcardIntent.setDataAndType(contactUri, "image/png");
startActivity(vcardIntent);
```

Figure 12-2 illustrates the sharing of dynamic permission grants:

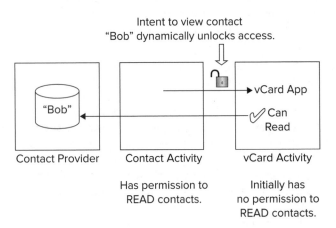

FIGURE 12-2

Note that Android supports wildcarding in provider grant URI declarations. The following example shows an intent that can grant all categories starting with personal, or business followed by a single character:

```
<grant-uri-permission android:pathPrefix="/personal.*/"/>
<grant-uri-permission android:pathPrefix="/business.*/"/>
```

In this case, "." means match any single character and "*" means match one or more occurrences of the preceding character.

Example Code: Protecting RESTful Invocations

As this chapter has shown, most forms of data on a mobile device present lucrative hacking targets, worthy of encryption and careful handling. Sending this information over whatever Internet connection your device happens to be using has serious security implications. Who knows whether or not a hacker is peering at your application traffic using Wireshark on WiFi at the nearest cafe?

Service Authentication

When a client opens a secure connection, a public key handshake takes place that enables an Android client and backend service to communicate over an encrypted communication stream. As you saw in the discussion of public key encryption, the public key enables encryption by all, but decryption only by the holder of the private key. Unfortunately, a guarantee of encrypted communication does not mean a client can be certain of the identity of the service to which it is connected since an unknown public key does not have any distinguishing features by itself.

To enable clients to authenticate the service, all HTTPS sessions make use of digital certificates, which provide a way to ensure that a client can trust a public key for a given service host. As part of the secure handshake, the service will send its certificate to the client. Secure certificates work on a model of transitive trust, whereby a certificate authority (CA) issues certificates that individual websites distribute. Most OS platforms hold a system keystore that contains well known certificate authorities like VeriSign, Google, and so on. When a client downloads a site certificate, it can verify that an already known certificate authority digitally "vouches" for the new certificate.

The hostname of a web service is encoded into each service certificate, which means that the client can extract the name encoded in the certificate, compare it to the DNS name to which it opened its connection, and make sure that they are the same. The combination of hostname and CA validation allows the Android client to trust the identity of the target service.

> **NOTE** *It's a financial advantage for a company to have a root CA pre-installed in Android, in iOS, and in web browsers. Many certificate authorities exist to charge developers a fee for certifying communication of site certificates.*

Code Example: Securing the Chapter 6 Contacts Service Communication

As noted previously, web browsers and Android applications secure Internet traffic using HTTPS, which encrypts data sent between a client and web server and eliminates the risk of a "man in the middle" attack. It's not computationally feasible for an eavesdropper on the network to read the communication. In this code example, you'll invoke a secure request on the Chapter 6 $CODE/ springServiceContacts service. You'll make this request using HTTPS by setting up secure communication on the client and backend service, with the following steps involved:

1. Securing the Chapter 6 contacts web service:

    a. Creating a "Certificate Signing Request"

    b. Creating your own CA (optional)

    c. Obtaining a site certificate for service authentication

    d. Configuring an HTTPS transport for Tomcat: with JSSE or APR

    e. Authenticating the service using basic authentication

2. Invoking a secure connection to the service from Android using HTTP basic authentication

Securing the Chapter 6 Contacts Service

The task of securing a backend web service for an Android application can be quite easy, but securing services with a moderate level of complexity provides significant challenges as hackers find clever ways to get past your defenses. This chapter only covers the straightforward steps involved in securing the RESTful web services from Chapter 6, as follows:

➤ Creating a site certificate and adding it to a keystore for authentication

➤ Modifying the Chapter 6 Spring application context to support basic authentication

➤ Configuring a demonstration user who can log into the Chapter 6 service

The next few sections walk through implementing these tasks using the code in $CODE/ springServiceContacts.

Creating a "Certificate Signing Request"

Before buying or signing your own certificate, you will need to create a "Certificate Signing Request" that you can send to a commercial CA, or sign yourself (with instructions that follow). You can learn more information about this request online:

```
http://en.wikipedia.org/wiki/Certificate_signing_request
```

The following steps for creating this request are based on the OpenSSL tool, which is pre-installed on Linux and Mac OS:

> **NOTE** *When you run the commands that follow, you should answer all of the questions, and answer them consistently (for example, use the same city in all responses).*

1. If you are using Windows, you need to install cygwin software from the following location:

```
http://www.cygwin.com/install.html
```

as described in chapter 6.

2. Start a shell on your particular platform. On Windows, double-click Cygwin-Terminal. The example assumes that the SSL software is located at:

```
/usr/bin/openssl
```

3. Create a CA working directory in `$CA_DIR/AndroidSecurity/cadir` these instructions refer to it as `CA_DIR` — and change directory to it:

```
cd $CA_DIR
```

Run all commands from this directory.

4. Create a private key as follows:

```
/usr/bin/openssl genrsa -out contacts_privkey.pem 1024
```

5. Create a certificate as follows:

```
/usr/bin/openssl req -new -x509 -key contacts_privkey.pem -out
contacts_cert.pem
```

Note that when you generate the certificate, the common name should be the *exact fully qualified hostname, FQDN, of the service site*; it will be accessed from the Android client.

> **NOTE** *Please keep in mind that the FQDN you choose for your site must be an actual resolvable DNS hostname from whatever Android environment you use — the Android emulator or an Android device. It's a good idea to load the site name as a web page in the Android browser to make certain Android can really see it. Note also, that the DNS name must not use a known root domain like amazonaws.com, but must be your own domain. Hover.com is a good place to buy a domain name if you don't already have one.*

6. Create a "request to sign" the certificate, by concatenating the certificate from Step 5 with the private key from Step 4, as follows:

```
cat contacts_cert.pem contacts_privkey.pem |/usr/bin/openssl x509
-x509toreq -signkey contacts_privkey.pem -out contacts_certreq.csr
```

Now that you have a signing request, you can choose to do one of two things with it:

➤ Pay a fee to have a commercial certificate authority, such as VeriSign or StartSSL to sign it. This service varies widely in price, but starts at about $150 for a 2-year certificate.

➤ Create your own certificate authority, recognized by all the applications that you write, and sign the certificate yourself.

Creating Your Own CA

As previously discussed, a service needs a certificate for secure handshakes with clients. It turns out that with mobile applications it's entirely possible to become your own certificate authority and avoid any hassle associated with buying certificates. You can create as many of your own free and valid certificates as you need. If you want to become your own certificate authority, run the following utilities, as per your platform:

1. Create a new CA:

   Linux:

   ```
   /usr/lib/ssl/misc/CA.pl -newca
   ```

   Mac OS:

   ```
   /System/Library/OpenSSL/misc/CA.pl -newca
   ```

   Cygwin:

   ```
   perl /usr/ssl/misc/CA.pl -newca
   ```

2. As you run the `CA.pl` program, answer all questions as follows:

   a. Press Enter when the tool asks for the CA certificate filename.

   b. Enter a PEM passphrase.

   c. Pick values for locality and organization.

   d. The common name is the name of your certificate authority; choose an appropriate name (for example, "my root CA").

   e. Choose passphrases as appropriate.

   f. Enter your e-mail.

   g. Enter a challenge password.

   h. Enter the passphrase from Step b (make certain you enter it correctly).

Don't skip any field, record what you enter, and re-use your answers in future steps.

When the program completes, you should have the files you need to act as your own CA. Your CA certificate should now reside in `demoCA/cacert.pem`, and you can start signing certificates with it. Note that the default expiration period of certificates that you sign with your CA is 365 days, as specified in the `CA.pl` script. If you need to make the time period longer, you'll need to modify `CA.pl` to change the duration.

Obtaining a Site Certificate for Service Authentication

Now sign the certificate request from Step 6 of "Creating a 'Certificate Signing Request'" with the files generated in `demoCA`. Run the following command using the output, `demoCA` directory from "Creating your own CA" (note that the command "knows" the directory name, `demoCA`):

```
/usr/bin/openssl ca -policy policy_anything -in
contacts_certreq.csr -out contactservice.pem
```

1. Enter the passphrase from Step 2, b of the "Creating Your Own CA" section and sign and commit the new certificate.

2. Make sure that the size of `contactservice.pem` is not zero — this file contains your new certificate. Note that you can only sign each cert request once.

3. You can now add `contactservice.pem` to web service backends to communicate using HTTPS with Android applications. You will add `$CA_DIR/demoCA/cacert.pem` to the root store of your Android client, explained shortly.

Configuring an HTTPS Transport for Tomcat: with JSSE or APR

Now that you have a certificate, you can start the process of setting up Tomcat to use it and exporting the contacts service with an HTTPS transport. You can configure Tomcat to use your certificates in two ways:

➤ Using Java Secure Sockets (JSSE), generally used with production deployments

➤ Using a native technology called the Apache Portable Runtime, which is often used in development deployments

Configuring Tomcat Using JSSE

1. Create a service keystore and import the contact private key and service certificate into it.

Tomcat will use the keystore to support HTTPs with the contacts service. Server-side Java supports the keystore file format "JKS" for storing certificates and a utility for editing it called `keytool`.

You'll create the keystore and import the contacts service certificate into it. This is either the commercially signed certificate or your own CA signed certificate called `contactservice.pem`. First, JSSE requires a different certificate format, called DER. Use the following commands to convert your files into the DER format.

Convert the private key:

```
openssl pkcs8 -topk8 -nocrypt -in  contacts_privkey.pem -inform PEM -out
contacts_privkey.der -outform DER
```

Convert the signed certificate:

```
openssl x509 -in contactservice.pem -inform PEM -out contactservice.der
-outform DER
```

It's common to use `keytool` to edit Java keystores, but in this case, you will need to use a Java utility to import the converted certificate files into the keystore. You can download it from the following location:

```
http://www.agentbob.info/agentbob/80/version/default/part/AttachmentData/data/
ImportKey.java
```

Or you can use the version included in:

```
$CODE/AndroidSecurity/ImportKey.java
```

Edit the file to set your keystore password — change the variable, `keypass`. For consistency, use the same passphrase you used in the "Creating Your Own CA" section Step 2, b (if you did that step); otherwise, pick a password.

Compile this utility using the following in the `$CA_DIR`:

> **NOTE** *Commands assume that* `java` *and* `javac` *are in the system classpath.*

```
javac -d . ../ImportKey.java
```

Run `ImportKey` to *create* the keystore and *import* the private key and contacts certificate, as follows:

```
java -Dkeystore=<cadir>/tomcat_keystore.jks ImportKey <cadir>/contacts_
privkey.der <cadir>/contactservice.der
```

You should be able to list the contents of the keystore using Java's keytool:

```
keytool -list -v -keystore tomcat_keystore.jks
```

`keytool` resides in `$JAVA_HOME/bin`, which should be in your system path.

2. Edit the Tomcat server configuration file, called `$CATALINA_HOME/conf/server.xml`, by uncommenting the 8443 ssl connector to make it active. Edit the fields to match the following code:

```
<Connector port="8443" maxThreads="200"
  scheme="https" secure="true" SSLEnabled="true"
  keystoreFile="<ca_dir>/tomcat_keystore.jks" keystorePass="<your_password>"
  clientAuth="false" sslProtocol="TLS"/>
```

3. Enter the password from "Creating Your CA" or the password you used for your commercial certificate. Change `ca_dir` to be the directory where your CA authenticated private key resides.

4. Restart Tomcat.

Configuring Tomcat Using APR

APR is significantly easier to configure than JSSE. You can just use the certificates you have created by directly configuring them into the Tomcat configuration file, `$CATALINA_HOME/conf/server.xml`, as follows:

```
<-- Define a SSL Coyote HTTP/1.1 Connector on port 8443 -->
<!--
<Connector
            port="8443" maxThreads="200"
            scheme="https" secure="true" SSLEnabled="true"
            SSLCertificateFile="<ca_dir>/contactservice.pem"
            SSLCertificateKeyFile="<ca_dir>/contacts_privkey.pem"
            clientAuth="optional" SSLProtocol="TLSv1"/>
-->
```

> **NOTE** *Replace* `ca_dir` *with the directory where the* `contactservice.pem` *resides.* `contactservice.pem` *is the result of either your personal CA or signing with a commercial CA.*

Once you have edited `server.xml`, you'll need to complete one last task: Edit `$CODE/springServiceContacts/applicationContext-rest.xml` and uncomment the following line:

```
<!--<security:http-basic/>-->
```

as documented in the file. Then rebuild `springServiceContacts` and deploy the project war to Tomcat. Now that you have a secure backend, it's time to move on to creating a secure connection to it from Android.

Opening a Secure Connection on Android

As noted in Chapter 5, Android supports a number of ways to open a secure connection. Listing 12-9 demonstrates how to do so using the Apache framework, but you could also use the Spring framework for Android. The example shows that it's a pretty simple operation; you just need to create a connection manager and socket factories for each of the ports you will serve — a secure one for HTTPS and a plain text factory for unencrypted port 80. This example allows you to use the certificates signed using a commercial certificate and your own root CA.

LISTING 12-9: Secure connection using the Apache framework

```java
package com.enterpriseandroid.androidSecurity;

import java.io.IOException;
import java.io.InputStream;
import java.security.KeyManagementException;
import java.security.KeyStore;
import java.security.KeyStoreException;
import java.security.NoSuchAlgorithmException;
import java.security.UnrecoverableKeyException;
import java.security.cert.CertificateException;

import org.apache.http.client.HttpClient;
import org.apache.http.conn.ClientConnectionManager;
import org.apache.http.conn.scheme.PlainSocketFactory;
import org.apache.http.conn.scheme.Scheme;
import org.apache.http.conn.scheme.SchemeRegistry;
import org.apache.http.conn.ssl.SSLSocketFactory;
import org.apache.http.impl.client.DefaultHttpClient;
import org.apache.http.impl.conn.tsccm.ThreadSafeClientConnManager;
import org.apache.http.params.BasicHttpParams;
import org.apache.http.params.HttpParams;
import android.content.res.Resources;

/**
 * Creates an Https client that loads a keystore that can supply an
```

```
     * application defined root certificate authority to validate the client
     * connection.
     *
     * This client can also authenticate using the system keystore which
     * contains standard CAs as well.
     */
    public class HttpsClientHelper {
        public static HttpClient getHttpClient(Resources resources)
                throws KeyManagementException, UnrecoverableKeyException,
                NoSuchAlgorithmException,
                KeyStoreException, CertificateException,
                IOException
        {
```

If you created "your own CA," the following code provides the implementation of the method for avoiding paying for a valid certificate. The code loads your own root CA from a trusted keystore stored in a raw file.

Note though that the format of the keystore must not be "JKS" as used with Tomcat. It needs to be, "BKS" — for Bouncy Castle Keystore, which is the only format that Android supports. To use your own CA certificates, you will need to import the file `<cadir>/demoCA/cacert.pem` into a BKS keystore.

You will need to use a utility to import the converted certificate files into the keystore. Download the following useful graphical tool, called *Portecle*, for this task:

```
http://sourceforge.net/projects/portecle/
```

Unzip the download file and then run Portecle using the following command line from the unzipped directory:

```
java -jar <unzip_dir>/portecle.jar
```

Using the portecle UI, import your CA certificate into a new keystore, which should be of type BKS, and save it into the following directory with the name listed as follows:

```
$CODE/AndroidSecurity/res/raw/your_ownca_keystore.bks
```

Record the password for the keystore. For convenience, you can use the same password you used previously.

When asked, confirm that the certificate is trusted and accept the alias (for example, my root ca); ignore the previous instructions, and comment out the lines to load the BKS keystore.

```
KeyStore localRootStore = KeyStore.getInstance("BKS");
// Contains your application's root CA and allows use of
// certificates that you sign with that CA.
InputStream in = resources.openRawResource(R.raw.your_own_ca_keystore);
localRootStore.load(in, "changeit".toCharArray());
```

A scheme registry will hold the socket factories for port 80 and 443, non-secure and secure.

```
// Use unencrypted factory for http port 80
SchemeRegistry schemeRegistry = new SchemeRegistry();
```

```
        schemeRegistry.register(new Scheme("http",
            PlainSocketFactory.getSocketFactory(), 80));

        // Use a secure socket factory for 443, but this socket
        // factory will consider our "root" trust store when
        // making its connection.
        SSLSocketFactory sslSocketFactory =
            new SSLSocketFactory(localRootStore);
        schemeRegistry.register(new Scheme("https",
            sslSocketFactory, 443));
        HttpParams params = new BasicHttpParams();
        ClientConnectionManager cm =
            new ThreadSafeClientConnManager(params,
            schemeRegistry);

        HttpClient client = new DefaultHttpClient(cm, params);
        return client;
    }
}
```

This code configures an HTTP client that can connect to the Chapter 6 service as follows:

➤ Loads a keystore to use as a root store — the store can contain the root CA created in previous sections.

➤ A schema registry holds socket factories for HTTP and HTTPs.

➤ The SSL socket factory uses the previously loaded keystore as a root store, which enables validation of certificates signed using your own root CA as well as certificates signed by commercial CAs.

Authorizing the Client

Just like the service's site certificate enables the client to trust the host to which it is connecting, the client also needs to authorize its user to the service. Modern mobile and web applications use two standard modes of authentication — HTTP basic authentication and a protocol called OAuth. HTTP basic authentication is by far the most common mechanism for authenticating users to backend services. However, due to greater flexibility, OAuth is quickly replacing HTTP basic as the de facto authorization for accessing service resources.

The various RESTful APIs for Android all directly support HTTP basic. To provide a bit more detail, HTTP basic makes use of a header and a base-64 encoded username:password to transmit credentials in every RESTful invocation of a secure backend service. When using HTTP basic, applications don't so much as log in to a service, as they simply collect user credentials that can be attached to authorize every RESTful request. Readers familiar with JavaScript will recognize the code used to add basic authentication to an AJAX request:

```
import base64
encodedAuth = base64.encodestring('%s:%s' % (username, password))[:-1]
req.add_header("Authorization", "Basic %s" % encodedAuth)
```

The resulting header looks like the following:

```
Authorization: Basic FJkjuekjDFJskjDKlFJSksfspt==
```

Listing 12-10 finishes the secure invocation with an example snippet of how to do basic authentication in Java for Android.

LISTING 12-10: HTTP basic authentication in Java for Android

```
UsernamePasswordCredentials credentials =
    new UsernamePasswordCredentials(user, pass);
```

The code creates a new instance of the HTTPS client utility helper.

```
HttpClient httpClient =
    HttpsClientHelper.getHttpClient(mContext.getResources());
```

It then creates a new `AuthScope` that holds the basic credentials:

```
AuthScope as = new AuthScope(host, 443);
    ((AbstractHttpClient) httpClient).getCredentialsProvider()
        .setCredentials(as, credentials);
```

It then creates a new basic contact and sets the basic auth header:

```
BasicHttpContext localContext = new BasicHttpContext();
BasicScheme basicAuth = new BasicScheme();
    localContext.setAttribute("preemptive-auth", basicAuth);
```

It then creates a new HTTP request and executes the request with attached credentials to authenticate the client:

```
HttpHost httpPost = new HttpHost(host, 443);
HttpResponse response =
    httpClient.execute(httpPost, getRequest);
response.getStatusLine();
```

Running the Example Client

Now that you've seen all relevant concepts, you can run the example:

Launch your securely modified `springServiceContacts` using the configuration changes listed previously.

Make sure to enter the hostname from Step 5 in "Creating a 'Certificate Signing Request'" into the following field:

```
SecureConnectionActivity.SECURE_HOST
```

Additionally, set the password to your BKS keystore in `HttpsClientHelper.CAPASSWORD`.

Then run the `SecureConnectionActivity` in `$CODE/AndroidSecurity` project (choose the secure connection option).

OAuth

Although basic authentication may be common, superior forms of authentication have come into common usage on the Internet. Specifically, OAuth allows clients to access server resources without the liability of using passwords, much like the Android account manager. Clients access user data on behalf of a user, and access a set of resources available under an OAuth ID, which is a one-time temporary identifier that cannot leak the same way as a password. This version of *Enterprise Android* does not provide a code example for OAuth, but you can learn more about it in relation to Android at the following URL:

```
http://developer.android.com/training/id-auth/authenticate.html
```

Android Account Manager

Android APIs greatly simplify the task of managing passwords with the inclusion of the `android` `.accounts.AccountManager` API, which allows an application to list service accounts registered on the system (for Google, Facebook, and MS Exchange, and of course, the Migrate sync account from Chapter 10).

Applications can manage accounts, and most importantly can obtain authorization tokens from them in the style of OAuth. Specifically, the account manager precludes the need for the application to store passwords to remote services.

The URL referenced in the previous section leads to explanations in detail of how the account manager works with OAuth.

Android Account Manager Example

This section contains a simple exploration of how the Android account manager works. The chapter includes code to access the account manager, to list its accounts, and to obtain an auth token from one account.

The code lists Android accounts, looking in particular for the Migrate account, and then acquires an auth token from it for display. In a real usage, the auth token could be used for authorization to access service resources. See Listing 12-11.

LISTING 12-11: A simple demonstration of the Android account manager

```
package com.enterpriseandroid.androidSecurity;

import android.accounts.Account;
import android.accounts.AccountManager;
import android.accounts.AccountManagerCallback;
import android.accounts.AccountManagerFuture;
import android.accounts.AuthenticatorException;
import android.accounts.OperationCanceledException;
import android.app.Activity;
import android.content.Intent;
import android.os.Bundle;
import android.util.Log;
import android.view.View;
import android.view.View.OnClickListener;
import android.widget.Button;
import android.widget.TextView;
```

continues

LISTING 12-11 *(continued)*

```java
/**
 * Use the Android account manger to lists accounts and get
 * an auth token from the Migrate account setup for Chapter 10.
 */
public class AuthTokenActivity extends Activity{
/** The tag used to log to adb console. **/
    private static final String TAG = "AuthTokenActivity";
    private static final String ACCOUNT_TYPE="myAccountType";

    private AccountManager mAccountManager = null;

    @Override
    public void onCreate(Bundle savedInstanceState) {

        super.onCreate(savedInstanceState);
        setContentView(R.layout.auth_token_activity);
        final Bundle bundle = savedInstanceState;
        try {
            mAccountManager = AccountManager.get(this);
```

Access and display the Android accounts:

```java
            Account [] accounts =
                    mAccountManager.getAccounts();
            String accountsList =
                    "Accounts: " + accounts.length + "\n";
            for (Account account : accounts) {
                accountsList += account.toString() + "\n";
            }
            setText(R.id.message, accountsList);

        } catch (Exception e) {
          setText(R.id.message, e.toString());
        }

        Button loginBtn = (Button)
                findViewById(R.id.login);
        loginBtn.setOnClickListener( new OnClickListener() {
            public void onClick(View v) {
                try {
                    Account [] accounts =
                            mAccountManager.getAccounts();
                    if (accounts.length == 0) {
                        setText(R.id.result, "No Accounts");
                        return;
                    }
                    Account account = accounts[0];
```

Obtain the auth token for the Migrate account:

```
                    mAccountManager.getAuthToken(account,
                            "com.migrate.webdata.account", bundle,
                            false, new
                            accountManagerCallback(), null);
                } catch (Exception e) {
                  setText(R.id.result, e.toString());
                }
            }
        });
    }


    private class accountManagerCallback implements
            AccountManagerCallback<Bundle>
    {
        public void run(AccountManagerFuture<Bundle> result) {
            Bundle bundle;
            try {
                    bundle = result.getResult();
                    Intent intent =
                            (Intent) bundle.get(AccountManager.
                                    KEY_INTENT);
                    if(intent != null) {
                        // asked user for input
                        startActivity(intent);
                    } else {
                        setText(R.id.result, "auth token: " +
                        bundle.getString(AccountManager.KEY_AUTHTOKEN));
                    }
            } catch (Exception e) {
                  Log.e("TAG", "accountManagerCallback failed: " + e);
                  setText(R.id.result, e.toString());
            }
        }
    };

    public void setText(int id, String msg) {
        TextView tv = (TextView) this.findViewById(id);
        tv.setText(msg);
    }

}
```

Now that you can secure and authenticate both ends of a secure invocation between an Android client and a backend service you're well on your way to writing secure enterprise Android applications that you can deploy to a variety of major cloud vendors. Now it's time to shift focus to how to protect your Android applications from theft.

Preventing Piracy

Android is designed to be an open platform on which users can install applications from different vendors. Pretty much anyone can create and install an application for Android, with few limitations. It's even possible to download and install entirely new application stores. This flexibility afforded to users does not come without cost to application developers.

Recall the earlier discussion regarding keeping malware off user devices that noted how Android supports several sources from where users can install applications onto Android devices. These sources include the Google Play and Amazon app stores, installing from unknown sources on the Internet, and side loading from SD cards. In contrast, with iOS, Apple allows application installation only from the Apple App store (not counting "jail-broken" devices). Also consider that the Internet has no shortage of industrious hackers eager to break or pirate successful applications so that they can be installed and used free of charge.

The bottom line is Android allows easy installation of pirated applications, as long as users are willing to risk malware infection, assuming they consider the possibility at all. Indeed, many application developers have voiced concerns regarding the ease with which users can install pirated applications. As an example, the first person shooter game "Dead Trigger" dropped its price from $0.99 to free due to extremely widespread piracy:

```
http://www.androidcentral.com/how-high-unbelievably-high-piracy-dead-trigger-devs-
not-saying
```

Some estimates state the revenue for Android applications is as much as 40 percent less than the same or comparable applications on iOS.

The Google Play licensing service is one way to protect revenue from your Android applications from piracy. The Google Play app store provides a license verification service that verifies whether the current user has a valid license. The application can decide to shut the app down or provide appropriate behavior when a user attempts to run an app without a license. You can find out more about the licensing service here:

```
http://developer.android.com/google/play/licensing/index.html
```

SUMMARY

This chapter began by covering the steps that handset users can take to keep malicious applications off their phones. This coverage included a walkthrough of tools from Google and a few other vendors, as well as security reviews of these utilities; it turns out that there is still quite a bit of risk involved when users install applications from unknown vendors. The chapter then moved to present results from the malware genome project and discussed types of security attacks for which application developers should build defenses in their applications. The chapter included an introduction to Android permissions, and promoted an understanding of those permissions as informed by the results of the malware genome project. The chapter directed developers to consider typical application weaknesses and to understand the ingredients of applications that could protect them, which included:

➤ Secure use of permissions

➤ Protecting data

➤ Protecting communication

➤ Preventing piracy

The chapter included practical demonstrations of these security tenants in the form of:

➤ Various code snippets regarding permission use

➤ An example data encryption using symmetric AES256

➤ A demonstration of secure password hashing based on SHA256

➤ An HTTPS version of the RESTful contacts service

➤ An example of how to use the Android account manager

In conclusion, application developers should keep in mind that while Google and other developers are constantly improving malware defenses, malware is also in a race to circumvent safeguards to profit from theft and invasion of user privacy. Developers should consider how users will protect their devices, write their applications to defend against attacks, and beware the significant consequences of lapses in security. To avoid security holes, follow the precautions discussed in this chapter and in the Android developer documentation and stay current with the latest in Android security news.

INDEX